THE GROWTH
OF RELIGION

BY

HENRY NELSON WIEMAN

Professor of Philosophy of Religion
The University of Chicago

WALTER MARSHALL HORTON

Fairchild Professor of Theology
Oberlin College

WILLETT, CLARK & COMPANY

CHICAGO   NEW YORK

1938

CONTENTS

FOREWORD

THERE are certain distinctions which should be carried in the mind as one undertakes the study of the development of religion. Certain great areas of human endeavor are closely allied with the one we are going to explore, hence we need to draw a map, as it were, in order to see how one region is related to the other. There is, for example, the great land of philosophy with its special territory, philosophy of religion. Religion itself is another great expanse and its boundaries must be located in order that we may see how it is related to the total area of philosophy and particularly to that more limited territory called philosophy of religion. Then there is another province which is different from philosophy, from philosophy of religion, and from religion, and yet the lines of demarcation between it and the others are often blurred and invisible. This is theology. We shall not be studying theology, but many of us will be wandering back and forth from one land to the other, not knowing where we are, unless we set up the lines of division so that all can see them.

So our first task will be to survey the country and locate the boundary lines that divide these several regions of human thought and life from one another. To that end we shall seek answers to such questions as the following: How are philosophy, religion, and philosophy of religion related? What is philosophy? What is religion? What is philosophy of religion? How do philosophy of religion and theology differ? After we have made this survey and located these boundary lines we shall be ready to study in Part I the history of the development of religion in human life. After that we shall go on in Part II to an examination of further problems of religion and of religious living which confront the person who lives in the modern world.

How are philosophy, religion, and philosophy of religion related? That there is close connection between philosophy and religion is evidenced by the history of both. Some of the greatest philosophies have grown out of the endeavor to conserve the essential truths and values of some particular religious tradition in an age when that tradition was threatened with sudden overthrow or slow decay. Such were the Vedānta philosophy in India, Platonism and Stoicism in Greece and Rome, and Hegelian idealism in modern Europe. Religious institutions have seldom followed the movements of philosophic thought with great alacrity, but sooner or later they have been profoundly influenced by these movements. "Philosophy," said a witty Frenchman, "is simply religion evolving faster than she's willing to."

This is of course an overstatement. Philosophy has other interests besides the religious interest; it has the scientific interest in truth for truth's sake, in addition to the religious interest in truth for life's sake. Yet if the religious interest were wholly subtracted from philosophy, philosophy would cease to be a matter of the most general and profound human concern, and would tend to become a matter for specialists and technical experts in the art of intellectual analysis and synthesis. And in the event of such a divorce between philosophy and religion, religion would suffer as much as philosophy. Lacking an instrument for the detection and discrimination of truth, religion would sink to the level of blind, customary observance, without rhyme or reason, and falling out of adjustment with reality would gradually lose its power to lead human life to any high fulfillment. Incidentally, it would lose its power over the minds of educated people.

Among the recognized branches of philosophy, some have a more direct religious bearing than others. Aesthetics, logic, political philosophy, and philosophy of education are only indirectly connected with religion, and are generally pursued in a spirit of religious neutrality, so that orthodox religionists and radical opponents of religion may find themselves agreeing upon questions of logic or aesthetics, while adherents of the same religious sect may find themselves differing upon questions of politics or education. Epistemology, ethics, and metaphysics, on the other hand, are subjects that bristle with religious issues. Epistemology raises the question, How and how much can we know? Ethics, How ought we to act? Metaphysics, What is the ultimate nature of things? Now there are at least four great religious concepts which fall athwart the field of philosophy at this point. The concept of revelation raises epistemological problems, since it seems to imply that certain special channels of knowledge are open to religious people, which are inaccessible to others. The concept of salvation raises ethical problems, since it defines a way of life leading to the highest good, or escape from the greatest evil. The concepts of God and the soul raise metaphysical problems, since they imply that the ultimate nature of things is not merely physical. These concepts are taken, for illustrative purposes, from the Christian religion, with which the reader is presumably most familiar; but they have their analogies or equivalents in other religions, as we shall see.

Would it be correct, then, to say that the philosophy of religion consists in a selection of the problems of general philosophy which bear most directly upon religion? Not precisely. We must distinguish between *religious philosophy* and *philosophy of religion*. Hegel's whole philosophy was a religious philosophy; but his philosophy of religion was that special part of it in which he reviewed the historical religious faiths of mankind and worked out his own conception of the " absolute " religion. The philosophy of religion resembles the philosophy of science and the philosophy of education in that it takes its departure from a certain activity, interest or function of life, scrutinizes the concepts which it presupposes, and then rises to some kind of theory or synoptic view that interprets the meaning of this activity and aims to improve it.

What is philosophy? The distinctive feature of philosophy is that it studies concepts. In other walks of human life, as in friendship, science, gardening, art, automobiling, we deal with things actual or possible or imaginary. We use concepts to deal with them, but it is the things which hold our interest, not the concepts. In philosophy, however, this situation is reversed. In philosophy it is the concepts themselves which interest us. Let us use a rough analogy to show what we mean. When I am chopping wood I do not ordinarily think much about the ax. I give my attention to the wood. But if the ax becomes dull I take it to an ax-grinder, who gives his attention to the ax and sharpens it. Now philosophy is like the ax-grinder. It takes the concepts which we use in everyday life — the concepts we use in art, religion, science, the concepts we use in friendship, education, politics — and sharpens them. Philosophy is distinguished from every other field of human interest in that it is chiefly engaged in improving our concepts.

What is a concept? A concept is a pattern. The simplest concepts are the patterns by which we recognize things when we see them. For example, in geometry we study the pattern or concept of the triangle. The actual triangles we see are things, but they have a pattern by which we recognize them. This pattern is the concept. There are chemical patterns, physical patterns, biological patterns.

It is the business of philosophy to help us get a good set of concepts for art and aesthetic appreciation, for politics and industry, for science and morality, for education and religion. Philosophy does not invent or construct these concepts; it finds them already in use, in a somewhat confused state. Philosophy helps to disentangle them, shows how they are related to one another, makes them stand out clearly. By thus clarifying our concepts philosophy not only gives us better insight into the meaning of what we are doing, but actually enables us to do it better.

It is also the duty of philosophy to search out those concepts which underlie the concepts we ordinarily use. We are generally unaware of these underlying concepts. They correspond to the axioms of geometry. They are the basic concepts on which are builded all the other concepts by which we think our world and deal with it in practical ways. Our everyday concepts are implied by these underlying ones. The searching out of these most fundamental concepts is what we mean when we say that it is the work of philosophy to explore, as well as to clarify,

criticize, and systematize, concepts. This searching out of the
most fundamental concepts is what is called metaphysics. As we
have already seen, metaphysics is one of the branches of philosophy
which most concern religion.

What is religion? It is one of the chief problems of the philosophy of religion, and *the* chief problem of Part I of this book,
to define the concept of religion as clearly as possible, on the basis
of a broad survey of religious phenomena. But a difficulty confronts us at the start: How are we to determine what phenomena
are " religious," and so deserving of our attention, unless we have
defined " religion " to begin with? There is danger here of
committing the well known fallacy of " begging the question," by
smuggling into our investigation a tacit conclusion about the very
thing we are supposed to be investigating.

There is only one way to avoid this danger: to start out with
whatever idea of religion one happens to have, and then sincerely
try to apply this definition to everything that goes by the name of
religion, until in the process of testing the original definition a
more adequate definition develops. It will never be possible to
include in any significant definition everything which anybody
might choose to call his religion. A definition which included
everything called religion would be worthless, for one of the
purposes of a definition is to distinguish what is truly religion from
what is not, and a definition that covered such a diversity would
not help us to distinguish anything. But with this reservation it
may be said that the open-minded investigator of religion should
first seek for a good descriptive definition of religion, which will
cover all instances of what is called religion so far as possible,
singling out the common traits which bind these instances together and differentiating these instances from others which do
not hold these traits in common. He should then seek those
patterns or concepts that will give order, unity, intelligible character to all these distinguishing traits of religion. Finally he
should seek to discover among these distinguishing patterns which
interpret the common characteristics of religion, that pattern
which has greatest functional significance for human living. The

investigation which began with a descriptive definition would thus end with a normative definition; that is, with a definition which would not only determine what religion has been and is, but what it ought to be and may become. Any attempt to define the proper function of anything, whether it be a physiological organ or a social institution, involves the setting up of a norm in some sense. To begin with a descriptive and end with a normative definition of religion is not begging the question. It is like casting one's net widely, and then drawing it in to see what fish 'have been caught that are worth keeping. It is like surrounding a field and then proceeding to beat the underbrush in search of quail.

As a preliminary and descriptive definition of religion, the following may be found helpful: Religion is man's attempt to realize the highest good, through coming into harmonious relations with some reality greater than himself, which commands his reverence and loyal service. This definition includes three main elements that will be found in varying proportions in all religions, and in many working philosophies of life that are religious by virtue of the function they perform in human life, even though they may not always bear the name of religion. These elements are: (1) A scale of values, or ideal of the highest good, which defines the goal toward which religion drives; (2) an idea of a higher power (or powers) which may or may not be called God, and may be purely human and social (as in Durkheim's conception of religion) but must at least represent something above and beyond the individual, to which he gives himself loyally and on which he depends; (3) a method of adjustment, whereby the religious devotee gets in touch with the higher power so as to become a channel through which its energies flow out toward the goal of the highest good.

It is of course obvious that this definition has passed through a considerable process of testing and restatement before being offered to the reader. While descriptive in character, it has passed through the second stage of elaboration, as outlined above, and already points the way toward a normative definition. It is offered as a *hypothesis* — not to take the place of an unbiased examination of the data of religious history nor to obscure its conflicting types and trends, but to enable the reader to approach these confusing facts with a provisional interpretative pattern in mind, which may be expanded or corrected as he proceeds.

What is philosophy of religion? Having described the nature of philosophy and the nature of religion we are now in a position to define the task of philosophy of religion more precisely. It resembles the task of philosophy of education in that it is concerned with a fundamental human activity, found in institutionalized form in all parts of the world, but needing to have its function redefined and its concepts clarified from time to time, in order that it may the better do its work — if, upon examination, it is found that it still has work to do. Summarizing, we may say that *philosophy of religion is that branch of philosophy which (1) inquires into the origin, nature and function of religion; (2) examines the source and validity of the claims which religion makes; (3) clarifies the fundamental religious concepts; and (4) criticizes the chief religious practices on the basis of a comprehensive survey of religious data.*

Philosophy of religion, in other words, is concerned to improve religious thought and practice by distinguishing valid from invalid methods of religious inquiry, reality from fiction in religious thought, and valuable from worthless religious practices. The philosophic clarification of a concept will often enable us to know immediately the nature of some reality in our existing world, although philosophy has done nothing but define the concept. The reason for this is that the reality in question pervades our experience so persistently that we cannot miss it once we know the pattern (concept) of it. We do not need to go out and make investigations, scientific or otherwise, or search the world in any way, to know that the world exists. We know it as soon as the concept is clarified, we know "by definition" that the world exists, because all experience is full of it. All experience cries, It is here! It is here! when once we get the right concept.

Take for example the concept of time. Until the concept is

clarified one may never know there is any such reality as time.
But once let a man have the clarified concept of time and he knows
that time runs all through his experience. So also with the concept
of friendship. One may not know that there are any such realities
as friendship and friends, even though he has experienced them
from infancy. But give him the concept and he knows immediately that he has met such realities.[1] The same is true of society,
of economic processes, of business and industry, of health and
sickness, of better and worse, and so on. The point is that there
are many kinds of reality, perhaps all the most important realities,
which thrust themselves upon us; yet we may never recognize
them, never know they exist, be vastly confused and uncertain
about them, until we get a clarified concept of them. But once we
have the concept, immediately, without need of further investigation, we know that the reality in question is an indubitable part of
our experienced world.

One of the major duties of philosophy of religion is to clarify
the concepts of religious entities so that we can discern these
realities more clearly, unmistakably, and unfailingly, as they run
through our total experience. The concepts used in religion, like
those used in politics or industry or education, are often so confused,
ambiguous, blurred, and contradictory that it would be useless to
try to set them forth simply as they are. But this blurred confusion
and tangle of vague concepts presupposes and implies a clarified
system of concepts, somewhat as the ancient Egyptian method of
measuring land implied and presupposed Euclidean geometry.
It is this clarified system of concepts which we shall be seeking.
We cannot hope to get very far in this endeavor when dealing
with such a tangled complexity of ideas and practices as the religions of man display. To complete this endeavor will require
many cooperators throughout many generations. It took many
men and many generations to develop geometry out of Egyptian
land measuring. It will take even more to bring to light the concepts which are involved in religion. But we shall hope to bring
some concepts to light that will help not only to make more
intelligible the objects and objectives of religious concern, but

also to make religious living practically more effective. By "prac- tically effective" we do not mean primarily building up the church, although that may be included; but we mean releasing in human life the potentialities of religious passion and applying this passion to the practical reconstruction of the world. Above all we mean closer connection between human effort and divine power.

How do philosophy of religion and theology differ? Much that we have said about the philosophy of religion applies equally well to theology, which is also concerned with the clarification of religious concepts and the guidance of religious practice. Yet the two are not identical. Theology, generally speaking, takes its stand within a particular religious tradition (such as the Christian or Mohammedan) and attempts to guide the further development of that specific form of religion in such a way that the truths and values it contains may be conserved and reinforced by being brought into harmony with all discoverable truths and values. Philosophy of religion, on the other hand, views the whole history of religion from a nonpartisan point of view, so far as possible, and aims to investigate the truth and value of religion in general. Philosophy of religion goes more deeply into the underlying con- cepts which are presupposed in religious living, and it may reach more loftily and widely into the concepts which are implied by religious living. It is better able than is theology to show us the deepest roots of religion and the heights of ideal religion. But theology fills out more richly, with more completeness of detail, the concepts which are operative in the actual religious living of a particular people of a particular time and place. Until a phi- losophy of religion has become translated into a theology which can carry the sentiments of a fellowship it can scarcely sustain the actual living which is religious. One must always have a particu- lar religion, one cannot have religion in general. Philosophy of religion is to theology, then, what dietetics is to cookery. One cannot live on vitamins and calories unless they are embodied in food acceptable to the culture which shapes his taste; yet the principles of dietetics underlie the practice of cookery, and are

particularly important when — as at present in religion — the old
food fails to satisfy man, and a change of diet seems required.[2]

The points of view of theology and of philosophy of religion
are not necessarily incompatible.[3] Many schools of theology teach
philosophy of religion as an essential prerequisite for the study of
theology. Where this is done the assumption is that a fair, nonpartisan survey of the general field of religion will lead to the
conclusion that *this* particular religion (let us say, Mohammedanism) is, at least for those who have been brought up in it, the
best religion, so that philosophy of religion itself points one to
the desirability of an intensive study of the history, literature, and
doctrines of this one religion. Needless to say, philosophy of
religion can make no such assumption at the start without destroying its nonpartisan character. It has no quarrel with theology, if
theology does not dogmatically refuse to listen to the claims of
rival religions. It recognizes the need in practical religious teaching of going beyond the bare minimum platform of " religion-in-
general " to a well rounded body of doctrine such as the great
theologians have elaborated. But it believes that all such further
affirmations of religious faith need to be based upon a fair objective
scrutiny of the whole field of religious phenomena and upon an
unbiased judgment of the problem whether religion is in general
good or bad, true or false, or a mixture of diverse elements needing
to be handled with discrimination.

The difference and the connection between theology and philosophy of religion perhaps come out most clearly in relation to the
fundamental religious concept, the idea of God. Theology has an
elaborate doctrine of the attributes of God, in which a wealth of
symbolism is used, drawn from a particular religious tradition and
warm with sacred associations. Philosophy of religion, in its endeavor to clarify the meaning of a concept common to many religions and to distinguish that which is certainly valid in it from that
which is dubious, gravitates toward a conception of God which,
however true it may be, strikes religious people as bare, thin, and
insufficient. To get a clarified concept of God it selects some
single part of the total pattern of God, which in its wholeness may

be infinitely complex. Yet from the point of view of philosophy of religion it may be better to have an incomplete concept of God which is nevertheless so clear and distinctive that it enables us to recognize God as surely present in human experience, than to have a very full, rich concept which is so inaccurate, ambiguous, and confused with other concepts that we can never identify God anywhere with certainty, or be sure that God exists, or develop a better idea of God by methodical testing of our original definition. Theology inevitably sympathizes with the religious demand for a fully developed concept of God, and it therefore cannot accept philosophical definitions of God without expansion and enrichment; yet a wise theology will gladly acknowledge its dependence upon the philosophy of religion for its bedrock foundation. If philosophy of religion can ascertain, by careful clarification of the concept, that God in some minimum sense surely exists, then theology can go about its necessary task of elaborating this concept in the assurance that it is not building upon shifting sand. But if theology rejects all alliance with the philosophy of religion it is likely to be haunted by the suspicion that the whole idea of God is a mere mirage and its systematic elaboration no better than the systematic delusions of the insane. This is essentially the conception of the proper relations between philosophy and theology which one finds in all rationally minded theologians, from Philo of Alexandria to Archbishop Temple. If it differs at all from traditional scholastic theology, it is in its hope that by the methods of the philosophy of religion we may actually, in the long run, *increase* our knowledge of God beyond the limits to which it is apparently confined by the authority of the ancient Scriptures and creeds.

H. N. W.
W. M. H.

NOTES

[1] M. Jourdain, in Molière's *Bourgeois Gentilhomme*, exclaims with childish delight, " *Je fais de la prose!* " as soon as the difference between prose and poetry is explained to him.

[2] See article by H. N. Wieman, " The Need of Philosophy of Religion," *Journal of Religion*, XIV, No. 4 (Oct., 1934).

[3] For a conception of theology designed to be thoroughly compatible with philosophy of religion, see the first chapter in *A Psychological Approach to Theology*, by W. M. Horton, or Chap. X in *Religious Realism*, a symposium edited by D. C. Macintosh.

BIBLIOGRAPHY

Wright, W. K.   *A Student's Philosophy of Religion*, Chaps. I, V.

Lyman, E. W.   *The Meaning and Truth of Religion*, Chap. I.

Wieman, H. N.   *The Wrestle of Religion with Truth*, Introduction and Chap. VIII.

Horton, W. M.   *A Psychological Approach to Theology*, Chap. I.

PART I

THE HISTORICAL GROWTH OF RELIGION

By WALTER MARSHALL HORTON

RELIGIOUS TOPOGRAPHY

The order in which these types and subtypes are listed is roughly in accord with the order in which they have appeared in history, except that the ancient religions of the Far East are listed in the order in which Buddhism encountered them.

I. PRIMITIVE RELIGION

Uncivilized regions in Africa, Australia, islands of the Pacific, frigid zone; small enclaves of primitive life in India, Ceylon, Indo-China, North and South America

II. ORIENTAL RELIGION (spreading eastward from India)
1. The parent stock: Hinduism (found not only in India, but as far east as Java and Bali)
2. The great sects:
   a. Jainism (India)
   b. Hīnayāna Buddhism (Ceylon, Burma, Siam, Cambodia)
   c. Lamaistic Buddhism (Tibet, Mongolia)
   d. Mahāyāna Buddhism (China, Japan)
   e. Sikhism (India)
3. Native religions of the Far East, encountered and partly transformed by Buddhism in its eastern-most extension
   a. Confucianism (China)
   b. Taoism (China)
   c. Shintō (Japan)

III. OCCIDENTAL RELIGION (spreading mainly westward from Palestine and Arabia)
1. The link between east and west: the Parsees (Bombay presidency)
2. Judaism (Palestine and urban centers in many parts of the world, especially in Russia, Rumania, Poland, Austria, Germany, and the United States)
3. Eastern or "Greek" Christianity (the Near East, Greece, the Balkans; surviving under great diffi-culties in Russia, formerly its stronghold)
4. Roman Catholic Christianity (Italy, western and central Europe, Ireland, Latin America, missions in the Orient)
5. Mohammedanism (from Arabia westward through north Africa, northward into the Bal-kans, eastward through Iran and north India to central Asia, Malaysia, and the Philippines)
6. Protestant and Anglican Christianity (northern Europe, Great Britain, North America, south Africa, Australasia, missions in Africa and the Orient)

IV. RADICAL SECULARISM

Marxism in Soviet Russia and Mexico; nationalism in Turkey, Germany, Italy; religious indifference in universities and industrial centers in many nominally religious countries.

INTRODUCTION TO PART I

NOT even the casual round-the-world tourist can fail to be impressed with the importance of religion as a factor in human civilization and history. Temples and shrines, cathedrals and mosques, pagodas and monasteries form his staple diet from Japan to Java and from Siam to Spain — so much so that he is often warned by experienced travelers not to overdo this sort of sightseeing at the start, lest he get an attack of " temple-itis " and be incapacitated for enjoying some of the rarest beauties that lie in store for him. For it seems to be a fact that men have lavished their highest artistic genius upon their religious edifices. Again in museums — which rank perhaps next to temples on the tourist's daily bill of fare — he is bound to notice how large a proportion of the significant remains of the past are religious images or relics; and this for the simple reason that they are likely to be made of stone or bronze or other durable materials, and to have been preserved with exceptional care; while the tools and conveniences of ordinary life have not been the object of such anxious concern. Or again, as he seeks to understand the manners and customs which mark off one group of people from another, our tourist is sure to have his attention continually called to certain religious observances in which a whole attitude toward life is picturesquely summed up and expressed: a Catholic workman raising his hat as he passes a church; a group of Mohammedan passengers on the forward deck of a steamer, prostrating themselves in unison toward Mecca at sundown; a frock-coated Japanese statesman bowing and clapping his hands before the shrine of the sun-goddess at Ise; a Hindu with a caste mark on his forehead, bathing in the Ganges at Benares; a shaven-headed Chinese Buddhist monk, eyes fixed in meditation, monotonously chanting a sūtra to the accompaniment of a wooden drum.

It is true, of course, that in the more "modern" industrialized part of the world the importance of religion does not so clearly appear. In the skyline of New York commerce holds the supremacy, despite the efforts of Riverside Church and the Cathedral of St. John the Divine to compete for attention. In the port cities of the Far East the advance of modern civilization and the retreat of religion seem to keep step with each other. In Canton, for example, the widening of the streets and the introduction of automobiles, radios, and moving pictures have been accompanied by the dismantling of the temples and shrines. In Russia, finally, we have for the first time a whole civilization founded upon the proposition that religion is an evil thing, to be sternly suppressed in the interest of public welfare. In view of this modern trend toward secularism and "irreligion" many observers have concluded that religion's great days belong to the past and that from now on religion must be content to play a very minor role in human affairs.[1]

It will be in a sense the major problem of this book — as it is one of the major problems which every educated man must face today — to consider whether this secularistic trend is really leading us away from religion, or is merely a transition in the form of religion; whether the whole great religious adventure of the human spirit has been a wild-goose chase, henceforth to be abandoned, or whether, on the contrary, there are essentially involved in religion truths and values without which mankind can never reach the goal of the good life. But this major problem, and the many minor ones that grow out of it, cannot be intelligently discussed without a broader knowledge of the facts concerning the world's religions than the average reader can be expected to possess at the start. It is therefore part of the task of Part I of this book to furnish a fair, impartial account of the chief historic religions which still continue to exert a significant influence upon human affairs, with just so much allusion to extinct religions as may be necessary to explain the living ones, and just so much critical comment upon the strength and weakness of these existing religious forces as may be desirable to prepare the reader for the philosophical discussions which are to follow.

The religious topography of the world is in its main outlines fairly simple:

(1). In the regions more remote from civilization — the Arctic and Antarctic regions, the heart of Africa, central Australia, and the islands of the Pacific — a primitive form of religion is still practiced which gives some clue to the probable nature of the religion of our prehistoric ancestors. Many of the more civilized portions of the world, such as North and South America, have surviving remnants of savage tribes whose religion, so far as it has remained pure, is also to be classed as " primitive."

(2). The region of eastern Asia — China, Japan, and the Indo-Chinese peninsula — is dominated by the religious influence of India. The direct influence of the Indian national religion, Hinduism, is felt as far away as Java; but the influence of India is mainly exerted through the great universal religion called Buddhism, which originated in north India, spread southward to Ceylon, northward to Tibet, and eastward to Burma, Siam, China, and Japan, and later died out in the land of its birth — or, some would say, was reabsorbed into Hinduism. In China and Japan the influence of Buddhism is less completely dominant than in Burma and Siam, for in the former countries Buddhism is superimposed on three ancient traditions — Confucianism, Taoism, and Shinto-ism — which still continue to live and thrive; but in Japan at least this struggle with rival religious forces has had a tonic effect upon Buddhism, for it is commonly recognized to be more vigorously active there today than anywhere else in the world. There are two main forms of Buddhism: Hīnayāna Buddhism, or the " Lesser Vehicle," found in Ceylon, Burma, Cambodia, and Siam; and Mahāyāna Buddhism, or the " Greater Vehicle," found in China and Japan.[2]

(3). The rest of the civilized world is dominated, so far as it has a traditional form of religion, by religious influences emanat-ing from Palestine and Arabia. Judaism, Christianity, and Mohammedanism, the three religions originating in this one small area, are perhaps best regarded as three offshoots from a common family tree, not as three wholly distinct religions.

Judaism, the oldest of the three, goes back to the same common stock of primitive Semitic religion from which Mohammedanism later sprang. Between the destruction of the temple at Jerusalem by the Roman emperor Titus in A.D. 70 and the recent inauguration of the Zionist experiment in Palestine, the Jews have been without any national home, so that it is hard to locate them on the religious map of the world; but wherever they have gone — and they have gone almost everywhere, including some of the remotest parts of China — their influence has been out of all proportion to their numbers.

Christianity, an offshoot of Judaism, spread most rapidly at first to the westward, throughout the Mediterranean area under the sway of Rome; and its two earliest types, the Eastern or Greek Orthodox and the Western or Roman Catholic, were deeply colored by the religion and culture of the two principal divisions of the Roman Empire. Later, the Greek or Eastern Orthodox form of Christianity spread to the north and east among the Slavic peoples and became the dominant faith of the Russian empire, while in its (heretical) Nestorian branch it crossed the whole continent of Asia and reached China, only to die out there, leaving scarcely a vestige of its former power. Western or Latin Christianity, centralized about the authority of the Roman pontiff, spread to the northwest, conquering the barbarian tribes of northern Europe and the British Isles, and in the thirteenth century welding all Europe into a rich cultural unity.

Meanwhile a fresh offshoot from the Semitic family tree had started in Arabia, in conscious relation and opposition to both Judaism and Eastern Christianity. The spread of Mohammedanism was the most phenomenal in the whole history of religion. To the westward, Mohammedanism captured north Africa and part of Spain from Greek and Latin Christianity, and was repulsed in France only after a great struggle. To the eastward, it recaptured Persia, traversed central Asia, and established powerful outposts in China, the Malay Peninsula, and the Philippine Islands. Through the power of the Mogul and Turkish empires, northwestern India,[3] Asia Minor, and part of eastern Europe also fell under the sway of Mohammedanism. It is expanding steadily today in central Africa.

Mohammedanism is sometimes called the " southern Reformation," to compare and contrast it with Protestantism, the " northern Reformation." As Mohammedanism replaced Greek Christianity in the Near East, so Protestantism replaced Roman Catholic Christianity in northern Germany and Switzerland, Scandinavia, Holland and the British Isles. Later, during the period of the expansion of Europe, Roman Catholicism and Protestantism ran a race for the possession of the new territories. The Jesuit missionaries were centuries in advance of the Protestant missionaries in India, Malaysia, China, and Japan, and somewhat in advance even in North America; yet the colonial and commercial expansion of the Protestant nations gave North America, Australia, and south Africa to Protestantism, while South America and Mexico were the only considerable territories which fell to Catholicism. In India and the Far East both Catholic and Protestant missions have exerted a powerful and significant minority influence upon the religious situation, whereas in the Mohammedan world they have (so far) found themselves faced by a stone wall. In Africa, Mohammedan missions are competing with Catholic and Protestant missions for the conversion of the savage tribes of the interior.

(4). It must be candidly recognized that the expansion of Europe has been a military and industrial expansion more than a religious one. Christian missionaries have often been the first to reach new and unexplored territories and penetrate forbidden regions, but the influence of the traders and the machines and the scientific ideas which came after them has generally outstripped theirs. More and more, since the birth of natural science in the sixteenth century and especially since the industrial revolution in the early nineteenth century, " Christian " civilization has been going secular. In Turkey and Russia today, western secularism has been enthusiastically proclaimed as separable from Christianity and made the basis of a frankly nonreligious culture. In many so-called " Christian " lands nationalism exerts a more vital influence than Christianity. We must therefore reckon modern secularism, based on science and the machine and motivated by nationalistic loyalties, as a fourth major stream of influence affecting the religious topography of the world. Since these four major streams — primitive religion, Oriental religion, Occidental religion, and modern secularism — have sprung up in the order named, a treatment of them in this order will enable the reader to grasp both the history and the topography of religion in a single perspective.

NOTES

1 See for example *The Religious Revolution of Today,* by Professor J. T. Shotwell of Columbia, who maintains that the whole drift of human history reveals a steady advance of secularization and a steady retreat of religion.

2 Lamaism, a corrupt form of Buddhism mingled with devil worship and magic, which developed in Tibet and spread to Mongolia and north China, is sometimes distinguished as a third type; but to this we shall give little attention.

3 The influence of Mohammedanism in northwest India is to be seen not only in the large Mohammedan population of the Punjab and other Moslem areas, but in the large Sikh population. The Sikh religion is a combination of Islam with Hinduism. See pp. 56–57 *infra.*

1.

PRIMITIVE RELIGION

I. THE PROBLEM OF THE ORIGIN OF RELIGION

RESEARCH into the religious ceremonies and beliefs of primitive peoples has been greatly stimulated in modern times by the hope of discovering in them the clue to the fascinating problem of the ultimate origin and early development of religion itself. Religion is apparently one of the distinguishing characteristics of the human species; hence anthropology, which traces the origins of the human race and the development of human culture, is concerned to discover, if possible, the earliest records and primitive forms of religion. Here, however, a formidable difficulty is encountered. The records which prehistoric man has left of himself are scanty and hard to interpret. A few rude drawings on the walls of caves; a good many ruined dwellings, with the remains of household implements, buried deep in the dust of centuries; a good many graves, usually containing ornaments and utensils as well as bones — these are practically all we have, and it is hard to discern their significance. It is far easier to trace the development of the human skull than to trace the development of what went on inside it. For this reason, anthropologists have turned their attention to those out-of-the-way corners of the earth where " our contemporary ancestors " live, believing that there is enough basic similarity between the religion of these modern " primitives " and that of our prehistoric progenitors to warrant an inference from one to the other.

A wealth of material has been gathered in the last century concerning the customs and ideas of primitive peoples — more than was ever collected before, and more than will ever be collected again, since the inroads of civilization are rapidly corrupting the purity of primitive custom and putting new ideas into the minds of savages. To this whole body of data is attached a certain suspicion that the civilized investigator may have been deliberately misled by his informants or may unconsciously have interpreted what he observed in terms of his own previous conceptions. Yet there is sufficient agreement among the accounts of independent investigators to give rise to the important judgment that *primitive religion is substantially the same the world over.* This is hardly what one would expect. It would seem as if men approaching the problem of life in widely separate parts of the world would arrive at radically different solutions — given the vastness of the problem and the diversity of human temperaments. Certain minor variations do indeed occur; but it appears that whenever human beings face life under simple, elemental conditions, they spontaneously react in about the same way and leap to the same conclusions. As Brinton puts it:[1] "The laws of human thought are frightfully rigid, are indeed automatic and inflexible. The human mind seems to be a machine; give it the same materials, and it will infallibly grind out the same product."

If this judgment about the psychological unity of man and the similarity of primitive religion, wherever found, is solidly based, then it does not seem unreasonable to add, *whenever* found, and to conclude that the religion of our primitive ancestors must have been similar to that of modern savages. All theories of the origin of religion are implicitly based upon this conclusion and stand or fall with it. Since such theories, however dubious, incorporate and interpret a great deal of genuine information about primitive religion in thought-provoking form, it may not be illogical to introduce our account of primitive religion with a discussion of some of these theories.

1. "Animistic" and "Naturistic" Theories. The first theory of religious origins to be developed on the basis of a wide induction from the phenomena of primitive religion was the theory set forth by E. B. Tylor in his great work, *Primitive Culture* (first edition, 1871), and later adopted, with modifications, by Herbert Spencer. Tylor was impressed by the universal prevalence among savages of the belief in ghosts, demons, and other spiritual beings, ranging

from the " ghost-soul " or " double " of a living man, conceived
to be capable of wandering abroad during sleep or trance, to
nature spirits or deities, conceived to inhabit trees and rocks or to
be responsible for the working of the more impressive natural
phenomena upon which human life depends. He therefore
proposed, as a minimum definition of religion, " the belief in
spiritual beings," [2] and undertook to explain how religion, thus
identified with " animism," must have originated.

He found his clue in the fact, already alluded to, that all savages
believe that the life of the body is derived from a soul or souls,
variously identified with a man's breath, or shadow, or heart, or
with the image in the pupil of his eyes; while they commonly
explain phenomena like dreams, trances, sickness, and death by
saying that the soul has left the body and gone a-wandering to
distant parts. From this belief in a material but vaporous soul,
detachable from the body, are derived (a) the universal cult of the
souls of the dead, believed to linger in or around the grave; and
(b) the universal practice of sacrificing human or animal victims
to the manes of the departed, and burning or burying with the
body various material objects designed to help the ghost on its way
or placate its wrath — lest it come back to haunt and plague the
living.

Ancestor worship was thus the original form of religion, and the
first altars were tombs. How nature worship was derived from
ancestor worship Tylor does not find it so easy to explain. Some
theory of derivation is required, for in primitive religion nature
swarms with spirits, benign or malignant, and every place or
thing has a spirit for its inhabitant. Tylor suggests [3] that nature
spirits are modeled on the human soul, and " their purpose is to
explain nature on the primitive childlike theory that it is truly
and throughout ' Animated Nature.' " Herbert Spencer, who
agrees with Tylor in the main, objects that even animals, not to
speak of children, can distinguish between animate and inanimate
objects, and explains the development of ancestor worship into
nature worship on the somewhat curious theory that ancestral

spirits were often *named after* animals or natural objects, and this led to confusion. "Thus," he says, summing up the whole theory,

> setting out with the wandering double which the dream suggests; passing to the double that goes away at death; advancing from this ghost, at first supposed to have but a transitory second life, to ghosts which exist permanently and therefore accumulate; the primitive man is led gradually to people surrounding space with supernatural beings, small and great, which become in his mind causal agents for everything unfamiliar.[4]

It is obvious that the most vulnerable part of this theory is the derivation of nature worship from ancestor worship. On this question, most later investigators have preferred to believe that nature worship has independent origins. Some, indeed, following an earlier theory of Max Müller, have held what has been called the "naturistic" theory of the origin of religion, which derives all other forms of worship from the spontaneous adoration and personification of the powers of nature.

Max Müller had no direct knowledge of primitive religion, but his studies in comparative mythology and philology, undertaken in the first half of the nineteenth century — a time when so many interesting facts came to light concerning the common origins of the Aryan "races," languages and cultures — led him to some significant conclusions about the probable origin of religion. He was struck by the fact that the names of the gods in the Hindu Vedas, like those of the cognate deities of Greek, Roman, and Norse mythology, were largely derived from common nouns designating the powers of nature. Thus Agni (*ignis*) means "fire," and Dyaus (*Zeus*) means "the bright sky." He inferred that religion must have been born of wonder and awe at the great powers of nature which surrounded primitive man on every side, full of threat and full of promise, giving him a sense of their infinity and his own dependence. How these natural powers got personified into anthropomorphic deities, Müller explained by another philological argument, more ingenious than convincing. He pointed out that the chief roots of all the Aryan languages

are found in a certain number of verbs expressing human actions.
Now let one of these verbs be turned into a noun descriptive of
some natural phenomenon, and it will describe it as "something
which acts in such and such a way." Wind, for example, is
"something that moans or whistles," or, more compactly, "the
whistler." At first merely analogical, such language came at
length to be taken seriously, and the powers of nature came to be
regarded as manlike agents of colossal stature and superhuman
force and cunning.

Müller's philological theory of personification is generally regarded today as unnecessarily elaborate. The personification of
the forces of nature is so easy and natural for unsophisticated minds
that spontaneous emotional projection seems quite sufficient to
explain it. Even modern scientifically trained people, when caught
off their guard in a crisis, curse or bless whatever thwarts or aids
them, with cheerful disregard of the question whether it is really
animate or inanimate. William James testifies that when the San
Francisco earthquake overtook him at Stanford University, and
began shaking the room as a terrier shakes a rat, he caught himself
personifying the quake as a malevolent superhuman will, bent
upon mischief and destruction.[5]

With this correction, Müller's account of the origin of nature
worship is still to be taken seriously, as is the "animistic" account
of the origin of ancestor worship. But the question remains
whether the worship of spirits, either ancestral or cosmic, is the
most primitive root from which religion has sprung. Recent
studies have tended to show that "the belief in spiritual beings"
is not the only prominent feature of primitive religion, and it is
not unreasonable to suppose that its nonanimistic features may be
the most primitive.

2. "Pre-animistic" Theories: Magic and Mana. One important
fact about primitive religion which recent anthropology tends to
stress is its intimate intermixture with magic. Sir J. G. Frazer, in
his encyclopedic work, The Golden Bough, A Study in Magic and
Religion, has advanced a theory of the origin of religion built upon
this fact. There is something more primitive than animism, he

argues, since this something is found universally, even where, as among the Australian bushmen, there is no trace of prayer, sacrifice or priesthood. "This universal faith, this truly catholic creed, is a belief in the efficacy of magic." [6]

There are two chief varieties of magic, imitative and contagious. Imitative magic is illustrated by the mimetic dance in which a certain Australian tribe portrays the witchetty grub coming out of its chrysalis — the idea being to procure the multiplication of the grub. Pouring water through a sieve as a means of rain making is another illustration. Contagious magic is illustrated by the custom of cooling the arrow which has wounded a man in order to heal the wound. The well known practice of burning (or piercing with needles) a wax image of one's enemy, into which bits of the enemy's hair and nails have been incorporated, illustrates both types of magic at once. Both types assume, says Frazer, that "things act on each other at a distance through a secret sympathy . . . by means of what we may conceive as a kind of invisible ether"; [7] so he applies to both the descriptive title, "sympathetic magic."

Magic is based upon the same elementary laws of association by similarity and contiguity which, when rightly used, give rise to modern science and technology. Nothing is more understandable or inevitable than this attempt to manipulate natural forces directly, by mere will power. Religious behavior, on the other hand, with its attempt to control these forces indirectly through propitiating the spirits that are believed to control them, is a much more devious and elaborate form of behavior. It is probable then, thinks Frazer, "that magic arose before religion in the evolution of our race, and that man essayed to bend nature to his wishes by the sheer force of spells and enchantments before he strove to coax and mollify a coy, capricious or irascible deity by the soft insinuation of prayer and sacrifice." [8] Magic gave way to religion when "men for the first time recognized their inability to manipulate at pleasure certain natural forces which hitherto they had believed to be completely within their control. It was a confession of human ignorance and weakness." [9]

Closely connected with magical beliefs and practices in primitive religion is the conception of wonder-working power, to which anthropologists have given the name of " mana." [10] This wonder-working power is believed to reside in curiously shaped rocks and other striking natural phenomena, in fierce wild animals, in courageous men, in sacred places and objects; and if rightly handled it may become a source of power to a needy individual. If wrongly handled it may work his undoing — as in the case of the young man Uzzah in the Old Testament who was struck dead as by a bolt of lightning when he put out his hand to steady the Ark of the Lord. All that is possessed of mana is taboo; it cannot, so to speak, be handled without gloves. But there are right and reverent ways of getting mana. One may, for example, get the mana (*virtus* = " manhood ") of a courageous enemy by cutting out his heart and eating it, when he has died a valorous death in battle.

The anthropologist Marett, in his book, *The Threshold of Religion,* has suggested that in the concept of mana we have a truly primordial concept which antedates both animism and magic and may be regarded as the common root of magic and religion. Magic is the attempt to make mana work by comparatively impersonal methods of manipulation (imitation, contact), while religion involves a more reverent and humble attitude toward it. Marett suggests that in certain of his dealings with mana the religious savage passes through a sense of weakness (" asthenic stage ") to a sense of triumph (" sthenic stage ") quite parallel to a modern man's passage through humility to joy and thanksgiving in his dealings with God.

When a savage launches a canoe or lays the foundation of a dwelling place, or starts forth on the chase, or samples his harvest of ripe yams — when, in short, he takes the first step in any enterprise of consequence — he is accustomed to perform a ceremony of inauguration. The moment is critical, or, in other words, he feels nervous. Therefore he performs a ceremony, the object of which would seem to be, in all cases alike, to bring him into communion with something sacred, something full of mana, that is to say, supernatural power or " grace "; for, thus strengthened, he can face the future with good hope. [11]

Whether magic and mana are really more primitive than the worship of spirits is not easy to determine, since animism, manaism, and magic are generally found side by side in primitive religion, even among the Australian tribes. But the stress laid upon magic and mana by recent anthropology has tended to break down Tylor's minimum definition of religion as " the belief in spiritual beings " and to dissipate the impression that the origin of religion has been fully explained when the origin of primitive animism has been explained. Is religion, after all, to be defined in terms of primitive intellectual concepts, or is it a dynamic attitude which can use, discard, and replace many sets of intellectual concepts while itself remaining relatively stable?

3. *Social and Pragmatic Theories.* The most monumental work on the problem of religious origins which has appeared since Tylor's *Primitive Culture* is Émile Durkheim's *Formes élémentaires de la vie religieuse,* published in 1912.[12] Accepting the general proposition that there is a more primitive form of religion than animism or nature worship and the view that the most primitive religion now surviving is the " totemism " of the Australian bushmen, Durkheim proceeds to subject this religion to minute and exhaustive analysis, in order to find its most essential elements, explain their origin, and so explain the origin of religion in general.

It is a cardinal principle for Durkheim that no explanation of the origin of religion which makes it appear to be a pure illusion can possibly be a true explanation; for nothing purely illusory could ever continue to exert such a sway over the minds and lives of men. By this test, Tylor's theory and Frazer's theory are to be rejected. It may well be, of course, that the truth in religion is not what its devotees suppose; but *some* saving truth, at least, it must contain. In other words, some at least of the "sacred " objects which are ringed about with taboos because they are thought to possess mana must really possess power communicable to needy men.

Now among the native tribes of Australia the most sacred objects are those connected with the tribal totem or emblem. This emblem is generally taken from some animal that is common in the neighborhood — the kangaroo, the cockatoo, the witchetty grub, etc.; but Durkheim is quite sure that totemism is not really a form of theriolatry or animal worship, for the reason that the animals themselves are less sacred than the totem mark which represents them. In all the most sacred ceremonies of the tribe — in the *Intichiuma* rites, when the totem animal is solemnly eaten by the tribe; in the mimetic dances designed to procure the multiplication of the animal; and in various commemorative rites portraying episodes in the history of the tribe — objects marked with the totem sign are in constant evidence. It is tatooed on the youth when he is initiated into the tribe; it is painted on pieces of wood or stone called *churinga,* which are kept in a sacred place and brought forth during ceremonies, and which convey health and strength when rubbed upon the body; it is marked upon the " bull-roarer," whose thunderous whirring sound is used to scare and subdue the uninitiate; it appears in the form of poles and flags; on certain solemn occasions it is scratched upon soil watered with blood. It is always sacred; that is, it is taboo and possesses mana. All other sacred things seem to derive their sacredness from it, by contagion or association.

What does the totem represent? Two things simultaneously: mana, and the tribe itself. That is, the totem is at once a sacramental object, representing and conveying divine power, and a patriotic emblem, signifying the tribe as a flag signifies a country.

> If therefore [says Durkheim] it is at once the symbol of deity and of society, does it not mean that deity and society are one? How could the emblem of the group have become the outward form of this quasi-divinity (mana) if the group and the divinity were two distinct realities? The deity of the clan, the totemic principle, can therefore be nothing else than the clan itself, but hypostasized and presented to the imagination under the visible appearance of the vegetable or animal which serves as totem.[18]

Durkheim is firmly of the opinion that in thus tracing the origin of the totemic principle to a *social* source, he is solving at a stroke the problem of the ultimate origin of religion and the problem of its final truth. What have the gods of religion ever done for their worshipers, he asks, which society is not capable of doing for the individual? Society it is which rightly inspires us with respect, which gives us laws and duties, and which rewards us when we obey those laws by " lifting us above ourselves " through the power of the communal life entering in to vitalize its members.[14]   All that society sanctifies becomes sacred; all that pertains to the life of the detached individual is profane; and in this distinction between sacred and profane — not in the belief in literal gods and spirits — the essence of religion is to be found.   Modern science makes it impossible to believe in animism and supernaturalism, or in any realities visible only to some alleged mystical sense; but it is still possible for us to be religious, since the essence of the most primitive religion consists in the recognition — confused by magic and superstition, but fundamentally important — that the individual is dependent on society for his being and his well-being. Society really possesses mana, communicable to the individual; and objects symbolizing society possess derived powers: this is the sustaining truth by which religion lives.   When we *together* seek aid of the gods or other supernatural powers, we get it — from one another, not from the gods.

Behind Durkheim's theory of the origin of religion there is a very definite philosophy, whose influence in France is widespread: the positivist philosophy of Auguste Comte, which rules out the possibility of knowing any realities other than those recognized in the primary sciences, beginning with astronomy and ending with sociology, and which accordingly cannot admit that there is any superhuman source of power.   In this country, a somewhat similar philosophy (radical or left-wing pragmatism) has given rise to a somewhat similar theory of the origin and nature of religion. Especially in the University of Chicago, where the influence of John Dewey's philosophy is deeply felt, a group of religious psychologists and historians has arisen who stress the practical and social nature of religion in its beginnings and in its contemporary developments.[15]   Religion, from their " pragmatic " point of view, is not to be defined in terms of animism, supernaturalism, or any other theory of the world.   It is essentially not a theory at all, but a practical social activity, " a shared quest of the good life." [16] If one asks what distinguishes it from other practical social activities in quest of the good life, the answer is that it is a form of activity which arises when " the satisfaction of immediate reactions becomes difficult or remote," [17] and which always is concerned, not with the lesser things of life, but with those "highest social values " [18] to which the group attaches supreme importance — whether they are the tangible values of food, health, and victory or, later on, the intangible values of goodness, truth, and beauty. Thrown back upon itself by failure to attain these goods directly, the group resorts to ceremonies, prayers, sacrifices, and other forms of appeal to whatever higher powers there be, in hope of attaining the desired goal indirectly. Whatever acts and beliefs appear to succeed are consecrated by social custom and become immune from criticism. Actually, the success is not due to the aid of supernatural powers, but to the vital reinforcement which comes to all the members of a group when the group as a communal whole gathers itself together. The gods are real in a sense, but their reality is a social reality, like the reality of such figures as Alma Mater and Uncle Sam, which represent the group spirit or collective mind in symbolical form. [19]

Certain types of religion lend themselves admirably to this social and pragmatic interpretation: the public religion of ancient Athens and other city-states, whose supreme deity (" Athene ") was the city itself; the official Shintō rites of modern Japan, which are essentially a worship of the state personified in the imperial family; and, some would add, Italian and German fascism, which seem to be growing conscious of themselves as religious and not merely patriotic movements. Taking the general stream of the history of religion as a whole, however, one would have to say that only a comparatively small portion of it could be fully explained on this theory. Mystical religion, for example, which thrives especially in India, often ignores social life completely, and sets the solitary individual directly face to face with ultimate Reality (Brahman) with which he endeavors to become completely merged, forgetting all social responsibilities. Most religious men, in all times and

places, would express vehement dissatisfaction with the view that
the object of their worship was nothing more than the spirit of the
social group to which they belonged. They *mean* to make contact
with the superhuman, and if there is nothing beyond humanity
that is worthy of worship or capable of responding to it effectively,
then, they would say, religion is false and we are deluded. A
theory that aims to explain the origin and persistence of " religion "
is incomplete unless it explains the origin and persistence of mystical religion, which claims to have direct contact with deepest reality. If Durkheim is right in dismissing Tylor's and Frazer's theories because they reduce religion to an illusion, then it is not
surprising that other investigators, who set greater store by the
mystical type of religion, dismiss Durkheim's theory for the same
reason.[20]

4. *Mystical Theories of Religion.* One of the earliest protests
raised on behalf of mystical religion against theories which seemed
to make religion illusory came from a student of anthropology and
comparative mythology, Andrew Lang, well known to all children
for his collections of fairy stories. His criticism was mainly directed
against Tylor and Frazer. In opposition to Tylor he asserted that
while the belief in spiritual beings *was* central in primitive religion
and did arise from dreams, trances, and visions of various kinds,
it was not based upon mere hallucinations and false inferences,
but upon veridical spiritual experiences. Calling attention to a
great body of evidence in support of the actual occurrence of
telepathy, clairvoyance, and other psychic phenomena in modern
times, Lang concluded that savages are correct in their general
belief in the existence of a spirit world, however mistaken they
may be in some of their conjectures about it. They are, in fact,
superior to the modern sophisticated scientist in their intuitive
capacity for direct contact with this higher world, though inferior
to him in reasoning powers. Lang does not specifically say, with
Bergson, that critical intelligence is a kind of disease of the mind
which makes it impossible for the modern man to see the metaphysical truth about the universe, which is revealed only to naïve

intuition; but he implies just this. Furthermore, he maintains against both Tylor and Frazer that the highest concepts of modern religion — above all the idea of one supreme God — were not built up out of primitive animism and magic by a slow process of evolutionary accretion; they were intuitively and vaguely grasped by primitive man from the start. In most surviving forms of primitive religion, notably in certain African tribes, there is what Lang calls " primitive monotheism " — the belief in a great All-Father who created the world and lives in the sky. He is to be sure not so important in popular religion as are the lesser gods of vegetation and hunting, or even the objects called " fetishes," which a man may beat if they fail to work his will, but Lang believes that these magical and polytheistic elements in present-day savage religion are marks of degeneration from an originally purer religion, instead of first stages in religious evolution.[21]

Certain features of Lang's theory recall what is known as the " primitive revelation " theory, popularized in the age of political reaction in the early nineteenth century by the French traditionalist philosophers, Joseph de Maistre and the Vicomte de Bonald. According to this view, the first men were enormously wiser than we, having been enlightened about all things by their Creator, directly, through their intuitive faculties. Vestiges of this primitive revelation still linger on in our midst in the shape of political customs and religious traditions which are unintelligible to our degenerate minds, but which we abandon at our peril — as when the French revolutionists, trying to invent a new political order, came to grief as soon as they deserted the ancient ways and the ancient faith. Not all mystics would feel obliged to hold any such theory as Lang's or de Maistre's; in fact, most of them would claim that the " inner light," as the Quakers call it, shines as clearly today as it ever did, when the right conditions are met. But they would generally unite in ascribing to primitive man a sort of faculty or end-organ of perception adapted to the apprehension of super-human realities, and would see the origin of religion in the origin of this faculty. The most scholarly defense of this view which has been made in recent years is to be found in *The Idea of the Holy,* by Rudolf Otto, a German theologian and student of comparative religion.

Otto begins, like Durkheim, with the category of the " holy or sacred " as the fundamental religious fact, whose origin and nature demand explanation; but he insists that this category cannot possibly be reduced to that of the moral, the social, the beautiful, or anything else, without denaturing its peculiar and specific quality, to describe which he is obliged to coin the word " numinous." " It is not easy," he says,

> to discuss questions of religious psychology with one who can recollect the emotions of adolescence, the discomforts of indigestion, or, say, social feelings, but cannot recall any intrinsically religious feelings. We do not blame such an one, when he tries for himself to advance as far as he can with the help of such principles of explanation as he knows, interpreting " Aesthetics " in terms of sensuous pleasure, and " Religion " as a function of the gregarious instinct and social standards, or as something more primitive still. But the artist, who for his part has an intimate personal knowledge of the distinctive element in the aesthetic experience, will decline his theories with thanks, and the religious man will reject them even more uncompromisingly.[22]

Insisting that the experience of the holy, the sacred, the " numinous," is ultimately something *sui generis,* incomparable and unanalyzable, Otto nevertheless attempts to suggest certain " elements " or " moments " in the experience. Subjectively, it is pervaded with what he calls " the creature-feeling "; in the presence of the holy one feels small and unworthy, " dust and ashes." Objectively, one is conscious of something strange and tremendous, " *mysterium tremendum,*" looming up ahead.

Further analyzed, this divine Something is found to contain the elements of " awfulness " (or uncanniness), " overpoweringness " (or majesty), " energy " (or wonder-working power), and stupefying " majesty," which Otto expresses by saying that the object of religious experience is felt to be " wholly other " than any natural object with which it may happen to be associated — lurking behind things, rather than in them. In spite of all these elements which

tend to humble the worshiper and make him keep his distance
there is also in the numinous object an element of the "fascinating" which irresistibly impels the worshiper to draw near and
come into touch with the object in spite of all his reverent fears —
an experience which often results in an access of power that thrills
him to the point of ecstasy.

In this experience of the numinous Otto finds the ultimate source
and taproot of religion. Magic and mana, souls and nature spirits,
myths and fairy tales, and even "daemons" or "numina" — gods
in the making — all these are religious only in proportion as they
partake of the quality of numinousness, and apart from it are not
religious at all. (The same might be said, indeed, of modern
philosophical conceptions of God, which, lacking the numinous
flavor, are as nonreligious and secular as brass tacks!) If we seek
the origin of this distinctive type of experience we shall find it,
thinks Otto, in the emergence at a certain stage in the evolutionary
process of a "rich potentiality of mind and spirit"[23] peculiar to
man, which renders him capable, under certain conditions, of
becoming aware of higher realities (or aspects of reality) imperceptible to animals and imperceptible by the five senses alone.
Otto calls this the "religious a priori" or "faculty of divination."
It is like those higher faculties which enable man to recognize
and value immaterial goodness, beauty and truth, when they are
presented to him; but it is higher than all these faculties, as its
object, the Divine, is higher than all other realities. If primitive
man stumbles at first in his attempt to conceive and describe what
he dimly apprehends as divine, that is only what is to be expected.
Nevertheless, in these humble beginnings of religion that same
Reality is perceived as mana, as the sacred, as the numinous, which
high religion calls God. Religion is not the survival of an initial
error; it is the progressive discovery of a truth, as man's faculties
· are gradually sharpened to perceive it.

II. GENERAL CHARACTERISTICS OF PRIMITIVE RELIGION

Already, in the exposition of these rival theories of the origin of
religion (whose relative merits the student must now estimate for

himself), the main features of primitive religion have been pretty well indicated. We have only to review them and supplement them a bit to get an idea of the place of religion in primitive society.

In a sense the whole collective life of the savage tribe may be said to be religious. It is governed by customs of the most rigid sort, affecting all the details of existence; and this body of customs is enforced by religious sanctions; i.e., to break a custom is to violate a taboo and run the risk that some mysterious power may break forth and wreak destruction upon the disobedient one. Instances are known of savages who, having unwittingly broken taboo by eating from utensils sacred to the chief or the medicine man or by some other (to us) harmless infraction of the local code, have sickened and died when they discovered their error. So powerful is the belief that the world is full of occult powers waiting to slay the breaker of tribal customs!

All the important events in life from birth to death are consecrated and solemnized by religious ceremonies. In the life of the boy the most important ceremony is that of initiation, which comes at puberty, and admits him simultaneously into physiological manhood and into the privileges and secrets which are reserved for the adult men of the tribe. At this time he is expected to pass tests of his ability to hunt and fight and to endure pain without flinching. Severe wounds and mutilations are sometimes inflicted upon him. Among the American Indians he is expected to spend a season in solitary fasting, until he sees a vision in which his personal totem is revealed to him. Only after these trials is he pronounced worthy to be taught the traditional mythology of the tribe and to become a member of the governing group. Women and children are jealously excluded from the sacred precincts and sacred lore to which men are admitted after initiation; and the awesome, thunderous sound of the bull-roarer is used to scare off the inquisitive. Girls undergo ceremonies somewhat similar to initiation, to prepare them for marriage; but even in matriarchal societies they are not admitted to powers and privileges comparable with those of the men. For both girls and boys the initiation ceremony is likely to symbolize new birth. The initiate is sometimes put through the motions of being physically born, and afterwards is fed on milk like an infant.

In addition to these ceremonies marking crises in the life of the individual there are ceremonies marking crises in the life of the tribe. There are ceremonies connected with the rebirth of vegetation and the reproduction of animals in the spring; "mimetic" ceremonies designed to make rain, or increase the supply of the totem animal, or prepare the tribe for war and the hunt; great tribal gatherings when tribal heroes are impersonated and their deeds enacted. From such ceremonies as these, drama, epic poetry, and mythology may claim lineal descent. In addition there are special ceremonies to meet special emergencies, such as epidemics of disease, crop failure, or military defeat.

While these ceremonies have a markedly social character, as Durkheim insisted, it should also be noted that they are performed with the constant objective of invoking or compelling the aid of higher powers of some sort: mana, or ancestral spirits, or nature spirits, or, on exceptionally important occasions, in some tribes, the Old Man in Heaven himself. The means employed are sometimes of a magical character. Marett thinks that magical spells preceded the use of sacrifice and prayer; yet among most primitive peoples sacrifice and prayer are also used, with the evident hope that the higher powers are amenable to gifts and entreaties. Another way of getting in touch with the higher powers is by inducing strong emotional excitement, through dancing, shouting, cutting and bruising oneself, until at length the enthusiast falls in a trance and sees visions, or speaks and acts as one "possessed." These acts are especially cultivated by the medicine man or shaman, who exerts immense influence over the practical decisions and policies of the tribe as well as over its settled social customs. He is at once a faith healer, a priest, a fortune-teller, a detective, a magician, a spiritualistic medium, and a political boss. "He is largely a trickster, but a half-believing one, nevertheless, because of the elements of his practice, chiefly suggestion and self-hypnosis, that he does not control by trickery." [24]

We have spoken as though primitive society were completely

dominated by religion. That society does indeed constitute a very close-woven fabric which all hangs together and in which certain religious patterns stand out distinctly. But it is a question whether it would not be better to call primitive society *wholly undifferentiated,* rather than *wholly religious.* It contains the beginnings of art, science, medicine, and law — indeed, of every essential element in more complex civilizations — bound up in such an inextricable union with one another that it is impossible to say where one leaves off and another begins. It is hard to tell whether certain ceremonies should be described as primitive religion or primitive drama; whether certain wonder-tales (mythology) should be described as primitive theology or primitive poetry. All sorts of distinctions with which we are familiar — such as the distinction between ethical conduct and mere etiquette — are simply not made in primitive society. If, therefore, we desire to know the nature of religion, as a distinctive form of human activity, we had better not confine our view to primitive religion — which we are at all able to recognize as " religious " only through its resemblance to later religion — but turn our attention to the process by which religion gradually emerged from the undifferentiated mass of primitive beliefs and customs, and came to have a specialized organization of its own, with a distinctive cult (prayer and sacrifice) offered to a specific sort of beings (gods) in particular places (temples, altars) by specially consecrated people (priests).

III. THE EARLY DEVELOPMENT OF RELIGION

If anthropology can tell us little about the remote origins of religion it can at least give us a few clues to its early history.

Concerning the religious habits of Neanderthal man, who lived in Europe during the cold middle period of the Old Stone Age, we know only that he laid his dead to rest with great care and ceremony. " Thus at Le Moustier the skeleton of a youth about sixteen years of age was found carefully placed in the attitude of sleep, with the right forearm under the head. A bed of flint chips formed his pillow, and close by the hand was a splendid implement." [25] The belief in life after death, which has played such a large role in religious history, thus seems to be almost as old as the human race. In some of these Palaeolithic caves, skeletons have been found with the bones painted red — which probably indicates the belief that the life principle was to be found in the blood and that bones painted the color of blood would live again. A common motive binds together this ancient practice of Neanderthal man and the later mummification rites of the Egyptians.

The first clearly recognizable objects of religious worship date from the Aurignacian culture, which follows the Neanderthal in the last division of the Old Stone Age, just after the last recession of the great ice sheet that formerly covered Europe: " rude female figures with the maternal organs grossly emphasized." [26] What these figures may have meant to the Aurignacians we cannot know; they may have been magical amulets or fetishes rather than true idols; but they are identical in every respect with the figures later found in Crete and Asia Minor, and associated with the worship of the powerful goddess of life, health, and fertility, known as the " Great Mother." It seems likely, then, that the first clear concept of deity that emerged from the primitive welter of spirits, demons, and wonder-working powers was that of a great nourishing, life-giving principle of fertility in nature. Whether the concept of an All-Father in the sky, cooperating with Mother Nature or Mother Earth in the creation and renewal of life, went along with the concept of the Great Mother in the minds of the Aurignacians, as it did in many later mythologies, we do not know; but it is not unlikely. Indeed it is probable that many other deities, associated with special places or natural forces and fulfilling special human needs, were associated with the Great Mother then as later.

With the emergence of gods at this remote period in the Old Stone Age, religion in the most familiar sense of the word may be said to have arrived. In Australian and other primitive societies, where there is neither prayer nor sacrifice and nature is conceived of as the scene of the chaotic operation of wonder-working powers (mana) which may be bent to human uses through appropriate ceremonials, it is difficult to recognize the familiar lineaments of historic religion. One wonders whether it is not better to describe these societies in the words of a contemporary anthropologist, as "magic-ridden." [27] So also with the belief in spirits and a future life, which we assume to be implied in the Neanderthal method of burial: it has nothing clearly religious about it. Animism, or the belief in spirits, may be as religiously neutral as atomism; and the provision of weapons or food for the dead may be as matter-of-fact as stocking one's cellar for the winter season. When an inanimate object (fetish), believed to be inhabited by a spirit, is beseeched to bestow certain gifts which the medicine man has guaranteed it to possess; or when the medicine man himself, believed to be temporarily spirit-possessed, is treated as an oracle and his wild mutterings reverently heeded — in both these cases we do recognize the religious character of the act, but it is religion on a very low level. It is not until certain spirits begin to rise to the stature of gods — until animism gives way to polytheism — that we feel our feet securely set upon the path of development which leads from primitive undifferentiated religion to the great religions of historic times. If we have not misinterpreted the significance of those little Aurignacian images, man had already passed from animism to polytheism by the end of the Ice Age, perhaps a quarter of a million years ago.

It is not hard to see why certain spirits came to have more religious value than others nor why, among these multiple candidates for godhood, the primacy might go to such a nature spirit as the Great Mother. The religious interest selects from among the many spiritual beings with whom the primitive world is peopled those that seem to promise the best support for the primal human needs; and these spirits are elevated to the rank of gods. Now among the primal human needs the two most basic are food and sex; and consequently it is not surprising that man should first have deified the mysterious spirit that seems to breathe upon the face of the earth in the springtime, bringing rebirth to vegetation and making the beasts of the field and forest bring forth their young.

Between the Aurignacian period in the Old Stone Age and the beginnings of recorded history in the great river-valley civilizations is a long span; but archaeology, combined with what we know of modern "primitive" religion, enables us to fill up this gap in the history of religion after a fashion. It shows that the development of religious ideas and practices is closely bound up with that of civilization. As man's changing habits of living make him more or less dependent upon this or that aspect of his environment, the forms of deities emerge from the mist at the points where human need and dependence come to the sharpest focus; and as the focus shifts new deities appear, while the old ones melt away or coalesce with the new.[28]

In the hunting stage of society wild animals are at the focus of interest, as they are today in the totemistic cults of the Australian bushmen and the American Indians. Wild animals are not notably responsive to prayer and sacrifice; and so men's efforts to control the conditions of life in the hunting stage were likely to take the form of magical rites for compelling the animals to multiply and the weapon to hit the mark. The images of bison and other animals on the walls of the oldest Palaeolithic caves — sometimes represented with weapons sticking in their sides — were probably drawn with magical intent. If, in addition to using such magical practices, Aurignacian man also prayed to the power that brought the revival of life in the springtime, he could not of course have felt the same kind of dependence upon the Great Mother that a pastoral or agricultural people later came to feel. He merely experienced a hopeful gratitude toward the mystical Something that periodically overcame the deadly chill of the slowly retreating glaciers, and brought him new supplies of food through the multiplication of wild life and vegetation.

With the domestication of animals and the dawn of the nomadic-pastoral period in social evolution, a great change comes over religion. Pastoral people are mainly dependent upon four factors for their sustenance: good weather to maintain the supply of fodder; springs and streams to serve as watering places; the health and fertility of the females of the flock and the women of the clan; the military prowess of the men, who must be able to beat off forays from other wandering nomads and, if opportunity offers, make forays of their own. We find, accordingly, that religion concentrates itself at new points corresponding to these new needs, and new deities emerge. The celestial bodies whose changes seem to regulate the changing seasons and whose regularities serve to guide the wanderings of the clan upon its long migrations; the stormy powers of wind and rain, so fickle in their behavior, so awesome in their anger, so generous at times in pouring out their benefits upon a parched and thirsty land; the spirit of fertility that seems to reside in springs and streams and shady groups of trees, where the flocks and herds congregate and give birth to their offspring; the virile power and warlike prowess that reside in bulls and rams; food and drink themselves, and the act of eating and drinking together, which brings a sense of fellowship and impregnable solidarity to the clan and prepares it to do battle with the hostile forces that threaten its existence: these are the materials out of which the nomad selects his symbols.

On the open steppes of central and eastern Asia the chief deities are those connected with the sky and air; in the desert country of Arabia and north Africa the deities are more apt to be local powers inhabiting the oases. In the former case, there are no settled shrines; in the latter case, a regular cult, with sacrifice and prayer, carried on at sacred places by a sort of priesthood, early develops. In addition to these ceremonials connected with oases and other special places there are ceremonials performed by the clan wherever their tents are pitched. Such is the strange communion meal of the pre-Moslem Arabs, described by Robertson Smith, in which a whole camel was devoured raw by the members of the clan in the light of the morning star, every vestige of the animal — skin, hoofs, and bones included — having to be bolted before the star faded out at dawn.[29] In such ceremonies as this we see the truth in Durkheim's contention that the social group itself, with the animals on which it was dependent, bound together in intimate kinship on certain solemn occasions, was regarded by our uncivilized ancestors as a sort of god, to whom every individual owed allegiance and from whom he drew strength. It was usually true, however, that the clan distinguished between the social unity of its own life and the god who was the source of this unity through his power to inspire devotion and infuse strength. In some cases indeed the god of the clan was originally a local deity to whom the clan became so attached that they carried him off, so to speak, on their wanderings. It was thus that the Hebrew nomads became attached to the God of Thunders who resided on Mount Sinai and carried him off to Canaan with them (in the " Ark of the Lord ") as their God of Battles.

The transition from a nomadic-pastoral to a settled agricultural existence was even more momentous for religion than was the transition from hunting to herding. It began in certain great river-valleys — that of the Yellow river in the Far East, those of the Nile and the Tigris-Euphrates in the Near East — where rich alluvial deposits and regularity of weather conditions made agriculture easier than elsewhere, while the need of irrigation and flood control early led to the founding of more-than-tribal units of society: city-states and empires, the first civilized communities known to history. Under these conditions man comes to have greater trust in the dependability and benevolence of the heavenly powers, though occasional droughts, floods, or insect pests drive home the lesson of human dependence. " Every step in the cultivation of the soil is accompanied by a corresponding cultivation of the powers. . . . He could not imagine that his labors of themselves would bring him crops without this concomitant. Tilling the soil is not only an art but a religion; from the breaking of the ground to the ingathering of the harvest, religious rites attend every stage." [30] Again, since human welfare now depends, more obviously than hitherto, upon good laws and good government, there comes to be a close alliance between religion and civic life. The king, upon whose power and justice the safety and stability of the state depend and upon whose favor or displeasure hang the life, liberty, and prosperity of each of his subjects, comes now to be regarded as a divine being, a son of the gods above, and the laws which he promulgates are regarded as divine decrees.

When mortal men are thus raised up into the midst of the heavenly gods, the gods themselves — originally wild, irresponsible, and monstrous, like the natural forces of wind and weather which they represent — begin to be " humanized" and even "civilized." [31] Men living in neighborhoods, towns, and cities, along the banks of a great river thronged with trading craft, are closer to their fellow men than they are to the elemental forces of nature and the wild beasts of the forest; and so they come to look upon the gods as magnified men, celestial kings and nobles, who may be approached through their priests as the king is approached through his ministers, and induced to grant favors by humble petitions, flattering laudations, and suitable gifts presented at their temples, as the king may be moved to action by similar gifts and entreaties presented at his palace. Gods who were originally represented as animals or as conventionalized natural objects (like the disk of the sun, for example) begin to take on human form, sometimes by slow degrees; and an elaborate collection of tales (mythology) grows up, recounting the story of their birth, their relationship with one another, and their miraculous doings on their occasional visits to the earth. If some of their doings seem immoral judged by the laws that govern the conduct of men, that may be set down to the fact that they were originally nature powers which know no morals; but as the sense of morality grows among civilized men the behavior of the gods is subjected to a severer censorship — and thus the gods, too, become civilized! Meanwhile, with the consolidation of tribes and city-states into great empires, the local and tribal gods tend to be subordinated to a few great gods, or perhaps to a single great god who is supreme above all the rest of the heavenly powers as the king-emperor is supreme above all other earthly powers. That is not to say that true monotheism is ever quite reached in these ancient civilizations. "Henotheism," or the belief in the supremacy of one god over the rest, and a tendency toward exclusive attachment to this god, is as far as the development reaches. Usually it is true that the worship of all sorts of local, tribal, and family deities and of all manner of ghostly and demonic spirits, together with the practice of magic and sorcery, goes on side by side with the worship of the supreme god.

This stage in the development of religion is best studied in the monuments and inscriptions of ancient Egypt, which present to us a continuous record of a flourishing river-valley civilization over a period of three thousand years, from the foundation of the First Dynasty under Menes, about 3400 b.c., to the absorption of Egypt into Alexander's empire in 332 b.c. On the religious side, this whole long history revolves dramatically about the rivalry between the sun-god, Ra (called also Horus or Aton), and Osiris, god of the Nile and of the fruitful earth.

Both the sun and the Nile, obviously, are of first-rate significance for the maintenance of life in Egypt; but the sun-god was the favorite god of the kings, while Osiris was the favorite god of the people. The kings claimed descent from Ra, and expected to rise after death from their pyramid tombs, cross the Eastern Lake, pass through the gates of the morning, and thence ascend the stairway to the sky, where they would become the associates of the sun-god and daily sail with him in his bark across the heavens.[32] Such a celestial destiny could be only for the few — for the Pharaoh, and for the exceptional favorites who could be provided with costly tombs and huge mortuary endowments, without which it was impossible to " crash " the celestial gates and be kept eternally alive by the prayers and charms of the priests. The common people did not go to the sky when they died; they went to the underworld, from which the Nile was believed to take its rise. In that world Osiris was king and judge, and assured all human beings, both rich and poor, of a resurrection like his own. For, according to a very early myth (based evidently upon the alternation of winter and summer, the recurrent rebirth of vegetation, and the seasonal renewal of the Nile), Osiris was slain by Set, the power of darkness and cold; but Isis, his wife and sister, had a son by him after his death — Horus, the sun-god, who subdued Set after a great struggle and brought his father Osiris to life again, offering in token of filial devotion his eye, which had been torn from its socket in the struggle with Set. This humanized myth had great appeal for the people of Egypt; it illustrated, in the lives of the gods, those virtues of marital attachment and filial loyalty which were most prized in Egyptian society; and the resurrection of Osiris seemed to them a pledge of human resurrection, to which they clung with eager longing. The priests of the sun, at Heliopolis, recognizing the power of Osiris, tried to incorporate the Osiris faith with the " solar theology " by raising Osiris to the heavens as one of the companions of Ra; the popular theology retaliated by making Ra visit the nether world and flood it with his rays each night on his circuit beneath the earth; while all the minor gods were made to serve as scribes or jurors or spectators in Osiris' Court of Judgment, where every human heart was weighed in Anubis' great scales, and character assessed at its true worth. To Osiris, too, was assigned the honor of being the first king of Egypt — which made the Pharaohs *his* sons, instead of Ra's.

The popularity of Osiris, as king of the underworld, reflects the extraordinary interest in the afterlife which played so dominant a part in Egyptian religion. Perhaps nowhere else, at any time, have men expended such care upon the embalming of human bodies, the building of tombs, and the maintenance of a cult of the dead. (This is probably due to the circumstance that in the dry desert sands bodies are naturally preserved for a long space of time.) Although a happy destiny in the hereafter was at first, apparently, reserved for the wealthy few who could pay for this elaborate service, it came at length to be believed that character, not wealth, was the best passport to eternal felicity, or, failing that, an appeal to the mercy of Osiris, or the knowledge of certain magical spells and charms that would enable one to " get by." The *Book of the Dead,* a sort of Baedeker's guide to the underworld, is about equally compounded of high ethics and pure magic. In the last resort, however, it was felt that the surest way of getting a favorable judgment from Osiris and escaping the gaping crocodile-jaws of the " Devouress " was to live so purely and so justly that one could honestly make the forty-two declarations of innocence which were required of every soul.

But there was another dominant note in Egyptian religion which was not so consonant with the Osirian faith: a passion for social justice in this world. In the prophetic denunciations of Ipuwer, in the tale of the Eloquent Peasant, in the Wisdom of Ptah-Hotep, all dating from the Middle Kingdom or feudal age, we have evidence of the growth of an ideal of social equity and a dream of an ideal society to come, quite parallel to Hebrew " messianism." The patron god of this messianic movement was not Osiris, god of the nether world, but the sun-god, whose beams enlighten this upper world of living mortals. There arose in the days of the Empire a messianic king, Ikhnaton, who attempted to make his realm an ideal state, and abolished the worship of all gods save one, the sun, whom he called by the name of Aton. Ikhnaton was evidently a man of highest intellectual genius and deepest religious feeling. Breasted calls him " the first individual in history," and compares the sense of natural beauty and grandeur expressed in his " Hymn to the Sun " with that of Wordsworth or Ruskin.[33] He was a true cosmopolitan and a genuine monotheist. Living in a time when Egypt had lately become aware (through her own conquests) of the great world outside, his mind expanded to the conception of a single God, symbolized by the life-giving sun, who is the " father and mother " of all men and all living creatures everywhere. He recognized the importance of the Nile (Osiris) for the Egyptians, but he saw that there was also " a Nile in the sky (rain) for the strangers," [34] which he believed was sent like all good things by the one God.

In none of the other river-valley civilizations was there so close an approach to monotheism as this. But the work of Ikhnaton was soon overturned. He underestimated the power of tradition and vested interest. After his death his successor Tutankhamen — lately unearthed from his tomb amid dramatic circumstance — was faced with a universal popular revolt against the new monotheistic faith, led by the outraged priests of Amon at Thebes; and the name of Ikhnaton was chiseled from the monuments and covered with opprobrium. Osiris and the lesser gods — jackal-faced Anubis, the ram-god Amon, the bull-god Apis, and the rest — came back into their ancient power and never lost it again while Egypt stood. The work of Ikhnaton was not wholly lost, for dispositions

and attributes were ascribed to these other gods which Ikhnaton
had ascribed to the sun; but the popular priesthood, with its traditionalism and hoary superstitions, grew steadily in power, until at
length it overthrew the monarchy and established an ecclesiastical
state, like that which Ezra and Nehemiah established in Jerusalem
after the Exile. From this period of sacerdotal supremacy are to be
dated the most magnificent temple structures that have come down
to us from ancient times; but it was a period of political decline,
which ended in the loss of national independence. When Alexander the Great got his certificate of deity from the priests of Amon-
Ra he took in exchange whatever vestiges of political power had
been left the Egyptians by the Persian conquerors who preceded
him.

The history of Egyptian religion is the connecting link between
primitive religion and the great historic religions which still survive. It begins dimly, with the establishment of the first settled
communities. It leads up to the main line of religious development
in the west. For it was " out of Egypt," many centuries ago, that
a little band of enslaved nomads made their escape, to found an
agricultural state of their own on the rocky soil of Canaan —
where they met with vicissitudes which fitted them to become the
progenitors of the dominant religious trend of the western world.

NOTES

[1] *Religions of Primitive Peoples* (New York, 1897), p. 6.
[2] *Primitive Culture* (seventh ed., 1924), I, 424.
[3] *Ibid.*, II, 184.
[4] *Principles of Sociology* (third ed., 1893), I, 420–21. Quoted by permission of the
D. Appleton-Century Co., publishers.
[5] Cf. George Foot Moore, *The Birth and Growth of Religion*, Chap. I, p. 8.
[6] Abridged edition (Macmillan, New York, 1922), p. 56. This and subsequent
quotations from Frazer's *The Golden Bough* are made by permission of The Macmillan
Co., publishers.
[7] *Ibid.*, p. 12.
[8] *Ibid.*, p. 55.
[9] *Ibid.*, p. 57.
[10] Consider the healing " virtue " that was believed to reside in the bones of the
blessèd St. Martin of Tours. (Gregory of Tours, *History of the Franks*.) The term
" mana " is used by Melanesian savages to designate a concept exactly analogous to
what is called *manitou, wakonda, orenda*, in the languages of the American Indians,
and *virtus* in Latin.

11 *The Threshold of Religion*, p. 171 (chapter on " The Birth of Humility "). Quoted by permission of The Macmillan Co., publishers.

12 English translation, *The Elementary Forms of the Religious Life* (London, 1915), by J. W. Swain, p. 206. Quotations from this work are made by permission of The Macmillan Co., publishers.

13 *Op. cit.*, Book II, Chap. VII, Sec. I.

14 *Ibid.*, Sec. II.

15 See especially Irving King, *The Development of Religion;* E. S. Ames, *The Psychology of Religious Experience;* and A. Eustace Haydon, *The Quest of the Ages.*

16 Haydon, *op. cit.*, p. ix.

17 King, *Differentiation of the Religious Consciousness*, p. 9.

18 Ames, *op. cit.*, p. vii.

19 Ames, *Religion*, p. 176.

20 For a general statement and critique of the social and pragmatic theories see C. C. J. Webb, *Group Theories of Religion.*

21 See Andrew Lang, *The Making of Religion* (critique of Tylor) and *Magic and Religion* (critique of Frazer).

22 *The Idea of the Holy*, p. 8 (Eng. trans. by Harvey, fifth impression, revised, London, 1928). Quoted by permission of the Oxford University Press, publishers. The word " numinous " is derived from the Latin *numen* (a " spirit " or " presence " inhabiting a certain place) as the word " luminous " is derived from the Latin *lumen* (" light ").

23 *Ibid.*, p. 129.

24 G. A. Coe, *Psychology of Religion*, p. 80.

25 " The Emergence of Religion," by E. O. James (Chap. I, p. 5, in *Essays Catholic and Critical*, edited by E. G. Selwyn. Second ed., New York, 1926).

26 *Ibid.*, p. 10.

27 A. A. Goldenweiser, *Early Civilization* (New York, 1922), chapter on Australia.

28 For a contemporary instance of this, see the description of the religion of the Todas in Wright's *Student's Philosophy of Religion*, Chap. III. In this primitive south Indian tribe a change in occupation has brought about a change of gods.

29 *Religion of the Semites* (Edinburgh, 1889), pp. 263-69.

30 G. F. Moore, *op. cit.*, pp. 46, 47.

31 *Ibid.*, pp. 49-57.

32 Breasted, *Development of Religion and Thought in Ancient Egypt*, Lectures III and IV.

33 *Ibid.*, pp. 334, 335, 339.

34 *Ibid.*, p. 327.

BIBLIOGRAPHY

Wright, W. K. *Op. cit.*, Chaps. II–IV, VI.

Friess and Schneider. *Religion in Various Cultures*, Chaps. I, II. (The most valuable reference for Part I as a whole. Provided with an exceptionally full bibliography and splendid illustrations.)

Moore, G. F. *History of Religions*, 2 vols. (A classic work, valuable for Part I as a whole.)

———. *The Birth and Growth of Religion.*

Hopkins, E. W. *The Origin and Evolution of Religion.*

Frazer, E. W. *The Golden Bough* (abridged edition).

Durkheim, E. *The Elementary Forms of the Religious Life.*

Otto, Rudolf. *The Idea of the Holy.*

2.

ORIENTAL RELIGION: INDIA

TO the contemporary observer, the religious life of India presents a spectacle of bewildering confusion. Sacred cows and human untouchables, noisy temples and secluded *āśrams* for silent meditation, the poetry of Tagore and the tattered multitudes bathing in the dirty waters of the Ganges, the degradation of child marriage and the lofty social passion of Mahātma Gandhi. Behind this human pageant, the pageant of the gods, no less confused and multiform. Gods high and low, benevolent and bloodthirsty. The supreme deity, three-faced: Brahmā the Creator, Vishnu the Sustainer, Śiva the Destroyer. Kālī with her necklace of skulls and her lust for bloody sacrifice, riding on a tiger. Her sinister majesty, the goddess of smallpox. A host of lesser gods, worshiped at little grotesquely carved shrines and temples, with offerings of flowers, cakes, and clarified butter (*ghī*). Hanumān the monkey-god and Ganeśa the elephant-god, affectionately worshiped for the aid they gave to epic heroes in days gone by. Rāma and Krishna, human incarnations of the high gods. Saints and holy men, in process of becoming divine by self-mortification and mystic ecstasy. And running through all this variety the conviction that somehow God is One.*

It is not easy to arrive at a sympathetic understanding of all this; and yet the effort must be made, since India is the motherland of Oriental religion, and without an understanding of India's faiths one is perpetually baffled in his contacts with the eastern mind.

---

* Note on pronunciation. The main points to remember in pronouncing the Hindu words which abound in this chapter are that the long vowel *ā* is pronounced as in *father*, the short vowel *a* like the vowel *u* in *but*, and other vowels as in German. The consonant *ś* is halfway between *s* and *sh*; the other consonants may be pronounced as in English, although there are differences which ordinary English spelling cannot indicate. The accent falls upon the next-to-the-last syllable, if it is long; otherwise upon the third syllable from the last. Thus the name of one of the great epics, the *Mahābhārata*, is pronounced *Muh-h ā-bhā-ruh-tuh*.

The best way to understand the complex situation of today is to begin with the simple religion of the Vedas, the sacred books to which orthodox Hinduism still appeals, and then to consider the steps by which this simple religion has changed into the complex phenomenon which meets the eye today.

I. THE RELIGION OF THE VEDAS

The Hindus of today are descended from a conquering race of northern invaders, tall and fair-skinned, who originally appeared in the Punjab (having come through the Khyber Pass like so many later invaders) and gradually pushed southward, driving the dark-skinned aborigines (Dravidians) ahead of them, until today these original inhabitants are mainly to be found in the extreme southern part of the peninsula. The language of the northern invaders (Sanskrit) was related to the Aryan family of languages, and their religion and customs bore a strong resemblance to those of the Greeks, Romans, Celts, and Teutons, who were offshoots of the same stock. Fustel de Coulanges, in his classic work, *The Ancient City,* has pieced together materials from ancient Greek, Latin, and Hindu literature to prove that one identical body of religious beliefs and practices underlies the laws and customs of India, Greece, and Rome.

This ancient Aryan religion had its center in the family, and its two most sacred objects were the family hearth fire and a little niche opposite the hearth (called the *cella* in Latin) where the family god was kept. The hearth fire represented the souls of the founders of the family, who were originally buried beneath the hearth. It was never allowed to go out, but carefully banked each night, revived each morning, and solemnly renewed once a year. It was fed only with certain especially sacred kinds of wood. Every family meal taken before the hearth fire was a sacrament; it began and ended with prayers to the ancestors, and offerings or libations of each food or drink were made to the sacred flame. Purity, both physical and spiritual, was required in its presence; health, prosperity, and moral power were believed to flow from it.[1] The god in the *cella* represented a nature power of some kind; and its presence, opposite the hearth fire, was a tacit recognition of the dependence of the family upon the powers above. Prayers and gifts were offered at the hearth and at the *cella* by the father of the family, who was at once its priest and its patriarchal head.

In Greece and Rome, an unbroken line of development can be traced from this early patriarchal cult to the public religion of the Roman Empire. When families joined to form a phratry, or phratries to form a tribe, or tribes to form a city-state, in each case the first act of the new community was to set up a new communal hearth fire,[2] dedicated to some ancient " eponymous hero " who was at least supposed, by a convenient legal fiction, to have been the common ancestor of all; and at the same time to set up an altar to some nature deity, who was to be the patron of the new unit, as other deities were patrons of the smaller units. Private worship survived unchanged alongside the new public worship. The temple to the patron deity of the city was a development from the family dwelling house, the little niche or *cella* gradually growing until it became the great space at the end of the temple, where a colossal figure of the god was set. When, finally, imperial Rome attempted to dominate the world, it was necessary for all these private and local cults and deities to be coordinated in a great religious system centering in the emperor, who was, so to speak, the patriarch of the whole human family. Virgil's *Aeneid* was the Bible of this new imperial cult, for it traced the origin of the imperial city to a great eponymous hero, the " pious Aeneas," who after many wanderings had brought the city gods and sacred fire of ancient Troy to Italy, thus giving a sort of common ancestry to the eastern and western halves of the empire. It goes without saying that the final resultant of this long development was a highly complicated system of private and public worship and a highly elaborate pantheon of patron deities — so complicated and elaborate that the effort to unify the world by its means finally failed.

In India the development took a different course — largely due to the fact that a priestly caste, the Brāhmans, acquired a dominating position that no priestly caste ever attained in Greece or Rome. Already at the dawn of history, when we first catch sight of the

Hindu tribes in the valley of the Indus, their members are divided into three distinct classes: warriors (Kshatriyas), priests (Brāhmans), and farmers (Vaiśyas). The Śūdra or servant class did not appear until later. The warrior class was at this time supreme, for these Aryan invaders were constantly at strife with the Dravidian aborigines, whom they were gradually beginning to push to the east and the south; but the work of the farmer and dairyman was likewise respected; and great trust was already placed in the priests for their ability to coerce or propitiate the heavenly powers, on whose good pleasure one must depend for success in battle or the prospering of the crops and herds. Every warrior chieftain had his Brāhman chaplain, without whose advice and consent he dared not take any important step. The priests were educated in regular schools, and divided into three orders: one to recite hymns of praise, another to sing chants, and a third to mutter sacred formulas connected with the sacrifice. From these three orders of the priesthood were derived the three Vedas, or books of sacred " knowledge ": [3] the Rigveda, the Sāmaveda, and the Yajurveda. [4] Since the Rigveda or hymnbook is the oldest, the most interesting, and the most elevated from the religious point of view, our account of the religion of the Vedas will be chiefly based upon it.

There were no temples in vedic times, no strict caste rules, no severe restrictions upon the freedom of women, no prohibition to eat meat or drink intoxicating liquors, no doctrine of transmigration and no pessimism, such as prevailed in later times. The sacrifices were offered under the open sky, to gods whose presence seemed so evident that no visible image of them was necessary. There were three great classes of gods: (1) gods of the bright heaven, (2) gods of the air, and (3) gods of the earth.

(1). In prevedic times the supreme god of the heavens was Dyaus (Greek, *Zeus*) who with his consort Prithivī, Mother Earth, was the progenitor of all living things and father of the gods. Now, however, Dyaus had receded into the background, and the supreme god of the heavens was called Varuna (Greek, *Ouranos,* " heaven "). From him came, ultimately, all blessings and cursings, and to his all-seeing eye the deeds of men, both good and evil, were well known. " Strike us not, Varuna! " men prayed when they knew they had done wrong.[5] With him were associated the gods Savitar, Sūrya, and Vishnu, who represent the sun in its various aspects and functions, and the goddess Ushas (Greek, *Eos*), the lovely maiden who brings the dawn.

(2). Among the gods of the air the greatest of all is Indra, the god of the monsoon. He is in fact the chief of all the vedic gods, one-quarter of the hymns being addressed to him. This fact reflects, of course, the immense importance of the wind-that-brings-the-rain to all the dwellers in the dry and thirsty land of India. Every year the dragon Vritra locked up the waters in the clouds, and for weary days, while the dark clouds hung heavy, one must wait for the coming of Indra to slay the dragon and release the rains. Indra was represented as a great warrior, accompanied by his faithful henchmen the Maruts [6] or storm-gods. So represented, he very naturally became the god of battle, who helped the Kshatriyas in their combat with the aborigines as he helped the Vaiśyas in their combat with the dragon of drought. He was represented as a wild, rollicking, blustering fellow, fond of drinking Soma, and gracious to those who gave him plenty of it to renew his strength.

(3). Among the gods of earth Soma itself, the powerful intoxicant that was offered up to Indra, occupied an important place. As food of the gods it became itself a god; to drink it made men "immortal, and immune from ill." [7] (The chants of the Sāmaveda were chiefly designed to be sung at the Soma festival.) Still more important than Soma was Agni, god of fire. Agni was originally the family hearth fire; but now that he had become the communal altar fire he had acquired new functions, while still keeping the old. As the sacrificial fire sent man's offerings up to the gods of the sky and air, Agni became the messenger between gods and men, and many of the functions of the other gods were ascribed to him. In a somewhat similar fashion Brihaspati, the personification of the magic spells of the Brāhmans, became a god of earth. Last of the gods of earth is Yama, the first man, who now rules over the underworld, " that deathless undecaying world wherein the light of heaven is set and everlasting luster shines . . . where joys and felicities combine, and longing wishes are fulfilled." [8]

In addition to all these gods (*devas*) of the heaven, the air, and the earth, the vedic Hindus worshiped their ancestors (*pitaras,* Latin, *patres,* " fathers ") thus continuing the dual family cult of the *cella* and the hearth, which they had received from their remote Aryan progenitors. In general, it may be said that their healthy, active, out-of-door life was reflected in the cheerful, hearty character of their religious beliefs and practices, as yet untinged by the asceticism and pessimism which entered so deeply into Hinduism in later periods.

II. THE RELIGION OF THE UPANISHADS
(PHILOSOPHIC HINDUISM)

After the three Vedas, the next body of Hindu literature which has high religious significance is found in the Upanishads. These mystical, philosophical discourses were written for the instruction of a special type of Brāhman who, having spent the required twelve years in study, and having spent some years as a regular married priest, had then retired for a time to the forest as a hermit (perhaps in company with his wife) and was now ready to spend the rest of his days as a homeless, solitary wanderer, thinking only of God.[9] The Upanishads were originally meant only for this limited class of holy men, as the Brāhmaṇas were meant for the ordinary married priests, and the Āranyakas for the forest hermits; but their philosophic insight and poetic genius lifted them high above these other writings and made them the favorite religious classics of the Hindu intelligentsia, down to this day.

In the Upanishads we encounter for the first time in its full-blown form what is generally known as " essential Hinduism ": (1) the belief in one great Reality (Brahman) as the ground of all existence; (2) the belief in transmigration and karma as the explanation of the apparently unjust distribution of good and ill in the world; (3) the hope of deliverance from the wearisome "wheel of rebirth" through the union of the individual self (Ātman) with the absolute Self (Brahman). Let us see how these characteristic teachings developed and what they mean.

✓ *1. Brahman.* In the later hymns in the Rigveda the suggestion was already made that behind the multiplicity of the gods was a single divine creative principle of some sort. Sometimes this is identified with Prajāpati, "Lord of Creatures," sometimes with Visvakarman, "the deities' Namegiver," sometimes with an unknowable creator:

> The gods are later than this world's production, who knows
> then when it first came into being?
> He, the first origin of this creation, whether he formed it all
> or did not form it,
> Whose eye controls the world in highest heaven, he verily
> knows, or perhaps he knows it not.[10]

Once only the honor is assigned to a god whose position in vedic religion was obscure, but who gradually climbed to the highest station of all as the power of the Brāhman priesthood increased: Brahmanaspati (Brihaspati), "Lord of Prayer," personification of the power exercised by the priests through prayer and sacrifice, esoteric learning, and magical incantation. As the Brāhman priests took to themselves a more and more exalted position in society as the ruling caste in a race that was subduing all the tribes in north India — subduing them even more through the awesome prestige of the Brāhmans than through the military prestige of the Kshatriyas — they came at length to have a rather patronizing attitude toward the ordinary gods! "Verily," it was said, "there are two kinds of gods; for, indeed, the gods are the gods; and the Brāhmans who have studied and teach sacred lore are the human gods." [11] And for all practical purposes the human gods were more worthy of reverence than the heavenly, since — if properly fed and feed — they knew how to wheedle or coerce the heavenly gods into doing your bidding and granting your desires. In fact the idea grew current that the heavenly gods were nothing but mortal beings who had acquired immortality through prayer, sacrifice, and asceticism — as any good Brāhman might hope to do in good time! But as the old gods of the Vedas thus declined and their worship became secondary, Brahmanaspati (Brahman) came to be adored as the one supreme being and to be conceived philosophically as a sort of essence diffused throughout the universe. It was now the great object of the forest-dwelling hermits (*vānaprasthas*) and wandering holy men (*sannyāsīs*) to purify themselves of the illusions of sense through abstentions and austerities of all kinds, and to concentrate their minds through various difficult postures and breathing exercises, that they might pierce through the multiplicity of transient things and apprehend the one eternal Reality, Brahman.

2. *Transmigration and Karma.* "The doctrine of *Transmigration* is that souls are emanations of the divine spirit, sparks from the central fire, drops from the ocean of divinity, that each soul is incarnated in a body times without number, that the same soul may be in one life a god, in another a man, in a third an animal or even a plant, and that there can be no rest for this soul nor relief from suffering until it finds release from the necessity of birth and returns to the divine source whence it came." [12]

In the oldest Upanishads this doctrine is announced as a piece of esoteric learning never hitherto known to the Brāhmans. It is reconciled with older views about the future life, as follows: (*a*) The average man, when he dies, having lived a life of "sacrifice, charity, and austerity," goes up by the "way of the fathers" to the "world of the fathers," the realm of Yama, described in the Vedas, and thence, after a sojourn in the moon, returns to earth to be born again according to his deserts, perhaps as a Brāhman, or a Kshatriya, or a Vaiśya. (*b*) The sage, when he dies, having learned the higher wisdom in the forest retreat, goes up by the "way of the gods" to the "world of the gods," and thence, after a sojourn in the sun, is escorted to the "world of Brahman," where he "dwells exalted for ages" and never returns. (*c*) The wicked, when he dies, "will quickly attain an evil birth, the birth of a dog, or a hog, or a [low-caste] Chandāla." [13]

In other statements of the doctrine of transmigration there are many varieties in the conception of what happens between death and rebirth. Sometimes dreadful hells are depicted, in which the wicked and ignorant are punished before receiving the further disgrace of a low form of rebirth; sometimes the soul is said to pass from one body to another, "just as a caterpillar passes from one blade of grass to another, or just as a goldsmith molds a piece of gold into another and more beautiful shape." [14] But one conception remains constant throughout: that a man's fate in his next existence is strictly determined by the total resultant of his works or deeds (karma) in this one. "In proportion as a man consists now of this or that, just as he acts, just as he behaves, so will he be born." [15]

Each life thus follows from the last and determines the next; and each man occupies the precise place in the caste system where he deserves to be — so that social change would be impious. While there is always, apparently, a chance of rising a bit in the scale next time, the hope of progress seems to have had little fascination for the Hindu mind. The whole process, in fact, gets nowhere in the end. The world periodically runs down into the nothingness from which it came, and after a period of rest called a *pralaya* is re-created exactly as it was before — each individual reappearing in his allotted caste, exactly where he was before in the wheel of transmigration — and runs down toward nothingness again, in four descending ages, through another great cycle called a *kalpa*. For the modern western philosopher Nietzsche the acceptance of this doctrine of "eternal recurrence" was the supreme test of one's ability to affirm the will to live and the will to power; for the Hindus the test was too severe. That life is evil and the world a great illusion (māyā), a bad dream from which one can only pray to be awakened, became axiomatic. An attitude of resignation toward social ills — for are they not the inevitable consequences of the iron law of karma? — and pessimism about the possibility of improving one's lot by active effort entered deeply into the Hindu philosophy of life.

√ *3. Deliverance through Union with Brahman.* If all action produces karma, if karma leads to rebirth, if rebirth is an evil to be escaped from, the conclusion follows that if there be any escape from the ills of life it is to be found in some form of *inaction*. Logically enough, therefore, was the custom followed by the sages of the Upanishads of abandoning the active life of the householder and spending the culminating years of their lives in solitary meditation upon the futility of all things earthly. But there was more than world negation in their philosophy. Running all through the Upanishads is a great hope of deliverance. " From the unreal lead me to the real! " prayed the sage. " From darkness lead me to light! From death lead me to immortality! " [16] In so praying he indicated a path of escape which still lay open when the path of action was closed: the path of philosophic speculation, dissolving the illusions of life and uniting the soul with eternal Reality.

Two great affirmations underlie the positive teaching of the Upanishads. One is the affirmation already mentioned, that Brahman is the one Reality, manifested in all things. The phrase *satchidananda Brahman,* " Brahman is reality, intelligence and bliss," was later employed to summarize the teaching of the Upanishads on this point. The other affirmation is expressed in the equation Brahman = Ātman, which asserts the identity of the soul of the universe (Brahman) with the deepest element in the human soul (Ātman), and so makes it possible for the essential part in us to take flight from the world of transient things and transient sensations to its eternal home in the eternal Being. " Children follow after outward pleasures, and fall into the snare of wide-spread death. Wise men only, knowing the nature of what is immortal, do not look for anything stable here among things unstable. . . . The wise, when he knows that that by which he perceives all objects in sleep, or in waking, is the great omniscient Self, grieves no more." [17]

Tat tvam asi, " that art thou," is the triumphant conclusion to which all the greater dialogues in the Upanishads lead up. In other words, as we might say, " Look out at the world, and discern the one Reality which manifests itself there in many forms. Then look within yourself, and discern the enduring self which is the Knower in all knowledge, the Thinker in all thoughts. Then realize that your deeper self is a part of the universal Self, the one

Reality ('that thou art') and in that knowledge find peace. Let your self become merged into the Self, as a drop of water merges with the ocean, and for you there is no rebirth. Reality, intelligence, and bliss are yours forevermore." The climax of this way of salvation leads beyond philosophic knowledge to mystic ecstasy. The Ātman cannot be known, since it is the knower; Brahman cannot be known, since knowledge implies division between the knower and the known, and in Brahman there is no division, but perfect unity. *Neti, neti,* " not this, not this," is all one can say concerning any precise conception of either Ātman or Brahman. But in some moment of mystic vision the soul of the sage, purified by fasting and meditation, may pass beyond all diversity and multiplicity and become literally one with Brahman, thus in some ineffable sense knowing the Unknowable.

This philosophic way of redemption is only one of many ways that the Hindu mind has found to escape from the wheel of rebirth. Jainism and Buddhism, which arose at the end of the upanishadic period, about 500 B.C., were rival ways of redemption which sharply took issue with the philosophic " way of knowledge " and became estranged from orthodox Hinduism. A thousand years later the same thing happened with the Sikhs. Within orthodox Hinduism, as we shall shortly see, there arose an alternative way of redemption known as *bhakti,* or " the way of devotion," which has had a far greater popular vogue than the " way of knowledge " could possibly have attained. Yet all these ways of redemption rest back upon the doctrine of the Upanishads, for they all accept the theory of transmigration, assume the emptiness of all transient beings, and find salvation not in any active attempt to transform the world, but in some method of achieving detachment from the things of time and sense. Naturally enough, therefore, the Upanishads have become a part of the Hindu sacred canon, and the term " Vedas " is sometimes used in a sense which includes them.

III. THE RELIGION OF THE *BHAGAVADGĪTĀ*
(POPULAR HINDUISM)

Philosophy appeals to the few, but epic poetry appeals to the many. In the period between 500 B.C. and 200 A.D. occurred the gradual growth of the two great epics which are to the Hindus of today what the *Iliad* and the *Odyssey* were to the ancient Greeks: the *Rāmāyana* and the *Mahābhārata*. Originally, these had to do with the exploits of two human heroes, Rāma and Krishna; and in the earliest portions of the narratives the two heroes are represented in very human fashion. Greatest of all the gods in this early period was Brahmā, the personal and more popular form of the impersonal Absolute (Brahman) of the Upanishads; but Vishnu and Śiva, who were destined to supersede Brahmā in popular estimation, were already associated with him. In the later portions of the *Rāmāyana* (the first and seventh books) Rāma became a semidivine being, the incarnation of half the essence of Vishnu, born among men for their good. In contemporary portions of the *Mahābhārata* Krishna also became a demigod. Finally, in the *Bhagavadgītā*, which was added to the *Mahābhārata* about 100 A.D., Krishna became the full incarnation of Vishnu, who was now the supreme God and the soul of the universe (Ātman). Since this is by far the most popular and influential passage in the epics, and indeed in *all* Hindu literature, we may ignore the rest, and concentrate our attention upon it.

The *Bhagavadgītā*, or " Song of the Lord," takes the form of a dialogue between the warrior Arjuna and Lord Krishna. Arjuna hesitates to give the signal for battle because he is averse to killing. Krishna teaches him how he may be, so to speak, both in the battle and above it. As a Kshatriya it is his duty to fight, as it is the duty of the Vaiśya to farm and of the Śūdra to serve. Killing is not what it seems to be, for the souls of the slain put on new bodies as a man puts on new clothes. But as Arjuna does his duty, let him do it without hatred, without hope or fear, without concern about the outcome, and let him attach himself by faith and devotion to Krishna; so shall he be delivered from all sin, and find redemption, although his calling does not permit him to devote himself to philosophic meditation, like the Brāhmans. At the close of the dialogue Krishna reveals himself in his terror and his splendor, as destroyer and sustainer of worlds and of men; and Arjuna, satisfied with the revelation, bids his soldiers advance.

The *Gītā* solved definitely the religious problem of the average Hindu, as the Upanishads solved the problem of the Brāhman intellectual. Obviously, it was not possible for the warrior, or the farmer, or the servant, to obey the rules and fulfill the duties of his caste and at the same time to practice that complete detachment from active life and those elaborate physical and spiritual exercises (known as "yoga") on which the Brāhman sages relied to secure their release from the wheel of rebirth. Must one wait to be reborn as a Brāhman before beginning to be religious? No, says the author of the *Gītā;* you can begin to be religious and to achieve your deliverance here and now, in the midst of your work. Two ways of salvation, distinguishable but supplementary, are open to you: (1) Your work itself, if done in the right spirit, without desire or hope of reward, out of pure allegiance to the requirements of your caste and station, may become your salvation; and (2) in the midst of your work, you may rise above it through the grace and power of God, who has become incarnate for your sake times without number, in his various avatars, and to whom you may become united through faith and loving devotion (*bhakti*) even if you cannot grasp him in thought. These two new ways of salvation have come to be known as karma-yoga and *bhakti*-yoga; and for the ordinary Hindu they take the place of the more elaborate yoga exercises of the holy man — regulated breathing, difficult postures, ascetic austerities, and mystic contemplation.

We may summarize, now, the religion of the ordinary orthodox Hindu. It consists primarily not in beliefs but in the faithful observance of certain ancient practices which have come down to him in the rules of his caste. If he observes these rules he is orthodox, no matter how much he disbelieves of the theory behind them; if he breaks them he is beyond the pale, though he be a saint and a scholar versed in the teachings of the Vedas, the

Upanishads and the *Gītā*. First and foremost is the requirement not to marry outside his caste — which in this case means not the Kshatriya or Vaiśya caste, but one of the many subcastes into which the main caste is divided. In the lower castes, his occupation is pretty definitely prescribed for him by his birth. Then there are all sorts of requirements about eating. A man may not eat with his wife, nor with a member of a lower caste. He may eat only certain kinds of food, prepared under the right conditions by the proper people. To accept a cup of water from a man of lower caste, or to permit even the shadow of an outcaste to fall across his person, contaminates him, and necessitates elaborate purification rites, including the swallowing of a pill composed of the " five products of the cow " — not all of which are highly palatable! Strictly speaking, he must not travel; for it is forbidden to cross the ocean, or leave India, or mingle freely with mixed throngs of people; but high-class Hindus now frequently go abroad to be educated, and the railway trains have become a necessity for all castes, so that the caste rules may be said to be suspended when one steps aboard a train.

Second to the caste regulations in the life of the orthodox Hindu are certain family ceremonies, of which the *śrāddha*-offering to the ancestors is the most important. Only a male descendant can make this offering; hence it is every man's duty to his ancestors to marry and have a son to continue the *śrāddha* rites. The central point in this ceremony — which occurs for the first time on the eleventh day after cremation, and recurs monthly for a year, and yearly thereafter — is the offering of a *pinda* or rice-ball to the deceased person who is supposed thereby to be transformed from a wandering ghost into a respectable ancestral spirit. The *śrāddha* ceremony may be considered to be the last of a series of sacramental rites which celebrate all the epochal events in an individual's existence, beginning with conception and ending with elevation to the position of ancestor. The Laws of Manu, the great Brāhmanic manual of etiquette for caste Hindus, prescribe twelve such ceremonies in addition to *śrāddha;* but the only ones now commonly observed are the name-giving and food-giving ceremony, the initiation ceremony, and marriage, corresponding to the Christian sacraments of baptism, confirmation, and matrimony. Initiation, for the three upper or "twice-born" castes, is an especially solemn ceremony. The youth, about to begin his education in a Brāhmanical school, has the Brāhmanical cord or thread hung about his shoulders, while the priest mutters sacred *mantras* which make of him henceforth a new man.

Girls, of course, are not initiated. Marriage is for them the one great ceremony. As in all patriarchal systems it is arranged by the parents in the interests of the clan. Quite commonly, in India, it takes place in childhood, though supposedly not consummated till much later — with the result that child widows, forbidden by law to remarry, constitute a not inconsiderable portion of India's population. The custom of *satī* (*suttee*) — the burning of a widow with the body of her husband — is now forbidden by law; but it remains true of the orthodox Hindu woman that her life is one of subjection: to her parents before marriage, to her husband after marriage, to his parents or to some male relative after her husband's death. In return for her self-abnegation she is honored and reverenced — and obeyed, particularly by the younger women of the household. Her world is limited, especially in the upper castes, where the custom of keeping women shut up in *purdah,* invisible to all males except those of their own household, has prevailed since the time of the Mohammedan conquest; but within that little world the authority of the wife or mother of the head of the family is practically supreme. Woe to the daughter-in-law, or the son, who dares to offend her!

These rites and customs of the caste and the family have come down, with comparatively little alteration, from the primitive religion of the prehistoric Aryans. The Brāhmans were astonishingly successful in imposing this system upon the conquered aborigines, whole tribes of whom were from time to time received into the lower castes as new subcastes; although, as we all know, a great multitude still occupy the unenviable position of outcastes and "untouchables" — unless Mr. Gandhi, by his dramatic protests, has at last succeeded in breaking the barrier that separates them from the caste Hindus and winning their admittance to certain privileges. But in the observances having to do with the worship of the gods the new prevails over the old. The orthodox Hindu begins the day, to be sure — as he takes his morning bath, preferably in Ganges water — with an ancient vedic prayer to the sun-god, Sūrya;[18] and he worships household gods handed down from his remote Aryan ancestors; but his public devotions are much more monotheistic than his private devotions, and reflect the Upanishads or the *Gītā* rather than the Vedas. If he is an educated Brāhman he probably has little to do with temple worship and cultivates some form of the Vedānta philosophy, which grew out of the teaching of the Upanishads. If he belongs to one of the middle castes he is probably either a Vaishnavite (worshiper of Vishnu) or a Śaivite (worshiper of Śiva) and frequents the temple of his chosen god. If he lives in Bengal he is very likely a worshiper of Kālī, Śiva's terrible consort, known as the "Great Mother" for all her bloodthirsty attributes. Worshipers of Vishnu, Śiva, or Kālī are exclusively attached to the one deity of their choice, and hope through "passionate devotion" to this deity (*bhakti*) to attain that same deliverance (*moksha*) which the sage attains through philosophic contemplation; but this is not generally thought to be inconsistent with the worship of idols and minor deities, for does not God manifest himself in many ways?[19] In the lowest castes, of course, the minor deities crowd out the high gods. They are in fact the survivors of the spirits, demons, and local deities originally worshiped by the aborigines; and the Brāhmans have made no systematic attempt to uproot this primitive form of religion. It is good enough for the outcastes and for the Śūdras.

IV. SCHOOLS, SECTS, AND REFORM MOVEMENTS

Modern Hindu expositors of the religion of India generally represent it as one comprehensive religious system, based upon the fundamental affirmations of the Vedas, the Upanishads, and the *Gītā,* and tolerant of infinite variations upon those unifying themes. There is much truth in this conception, as we have seen; but it is important also to recognize the range of disagreement among Hindus, and the fact that orthodoxy, as just defined, is not broad enough to include some of the most important and interesting variations that have appeared. Let us consider, then (1) the principal philosophic schools and religious sects into which orthodox Hinduism is divided, and (2) the principal reform movements which have given rise to religious communities beyond the pale of orthodoxy.

(1). Within orthodoxy, there is much difference of opinion with regard to the interpretation of the teaching of the Upanishads and the message of the *Gītā*.

During the centuries following the composition of the *Gītā*, the *bhakti* form of piety which it recommends became more and more influential; but only the Vaishnavite sect accepted the supremacy of Vishnu, which it preaches. The Śaivite sect, while practicing *bhakti* with equal enthusiasm, centered their devotion upon the Great Destroyer instead of on the Great Sustainer, and represented the divine presence in their temples by the uniform symbol of the *linga* — a rounded stone pillar which was originally a phallic emblem — instead of by the images of Vishnu in his various incarnations. Both sects worship in about the same fashion, with offerings of grain, fruit, flowers, and milk, portions of which are distributed to the worshipers; both pay religious reverence to their teachers or *gurus,* and put great trust in the magic power of sacred *mantras;* but the opinion they hold of each other may be indicated by the Vaishnavite saying that "Vishnu is the divinity of the gods; the Trident-holder (Śiva) is the divinity of devils." [20]

At about the same period when the *bhakti* sects were developing the schools of philosophy were also becoming differentiated. Six orthodox schools of philosophy are commonly enumerated, one of which, the Sānkhya, is atheistic; but by far the most influential are the various forms of the Vedānta philosophy, based upon the Vedānta-sūtras of Bādarāyana, in which for the first time the philosophy of the Upanishads was reduced to a system. The two great representatives of this philosophy are Śankara (A.D. 788–850) and Rāmānuja (*floruit* A.D. 1100). Śankara taught a completely

monistic and deterministic system, in which the unreality of the
world and of all individual souls, apart from Brahman, was un-
compromisingly affirmed. Brahmā, Vishnu, and Śiva were recognized as temporal manifestations of the one Reality, Brahman; but
like all temporal beings they were ultimately unreal. Rāmānuja,
influenced more by the *Gītā* than by the Upanishads, taught that
the ultimate reality was not to be found in the impersonal Absolute,
but in the personal god Vishnu; and that man's final destiny was
not to be lost in the Absolute, but to live forever in the presence of
God, retaining individuality and self-consciousness. Both Śankara
and Rāmānuja preached their philosophy to the multitudes, going
beyond the boundaries of caste Hinduism, as did the Vaishnavite
and Śaivite preachers; and both founded important monastic
orders which remain to this day. Rāmānuja's followers divided,
a century after his death, into two schools, on the issue of divine
grace. Both schools teach the necessity of faith in the grace of
God and surrender (*prapatti*) to its influence; but one school
teaches (like the Calvinists) that God's grace is irresistible, while
the other teaches (like the Arminians) that its efficacy is condi-
tional upon men's willingness to receive it. They are known as
the "cat" and "monkey" schools, since the cat carries her kittens,
willy-nilly, by the nape of the neck, while the baby monkey "co-
operates" by clinging to his mother. In modern times, under the
impact of western civilization, orthodox Hinduism has begun to
show itself less inflexible in its adherence to the ancient customs,
and has tolerated and even encouraged many movements which
would have been driven beyond the pale in earlier times. Notable
among these is the Rāmakrishna movement, which combines the
piety of the Upanishads and the Vedānta philosophy with a missionary zeal for social service and social reform among the low-
caste masses, and fearlessly attacks the abuses of the caste system,
child marriages, etc. The Rāmakrishna movement was nobly represented at the Congress of Religions (Chicago, 1893) by Swami
Vivekānanda, who planted the movement in America and made
a number of western converts.[21]

(2). The first great reform movements in Hinduism that burst the bounds of orthodoxy were Jainism and Buddhism, which arose about the same time, at the close of the upanishadic period. Buddhism will be considered later, more at length; but a few words must be said here about the Jains. Their founder, known as Mahāvīra or the Jina ("the conqueror"), was an older contemporary of Gautama the Buddha. Rejecting the whole Brāhmanical code of caste morality and sacrificial rites, as well as the belief in a supreme God, Mahāvīra aimed to secure deliverance from the wheel of rebirth by an exceptionally strict observance of the ascetic rules laid down for the hermits and holy men of his day. These rules are commonly reduced to five, of which all but the last are identical in Hindu, Jain, and Buddhist monastic orders: (1) *Ahimsā:* not to kill, hurt, or eat any living being; (2) not to lie; (3) not to steal; (4) to live a celibate life; (5) to be liberal and generous. Mahāvīra laid special stress on the first of these rules. Since he held the belief that not only animals, but plants and even clods of earth are living beings, the rule that no living being must be killed or eaten became for him a very difficult rule to observe. A certain amount of compromise here is inevitable, if one is to go on living at all; so the Jains are permitted to eat " beings of only one sense," including inorganic substances like salt and most kinds of vegetables; but they certainly try to be as consistent as possible in their resolution not to kill or hurt. Every Jain monk owns, among his few indispensable possessions, a straining-cloth through which he drinks his water, a veil to prevent him from inhaling or swallowing insects, and a brush with which he sweeps the ground whenever there is danger of his stepping or sitting on any living creature, even the tiniest. When attacked by man, beast or insect he must bear the pain without complaint or retaliation. It is related of Mahāvīra that when he was beaten, stoned, and tortured in many ways by contemptuous villagers who hooted at his eccentricities, he "humbled himself and bore pain" without a word, and so "bearing hardships . . . undisturbed, proceeded on the road to nirvāna." [22] The motive of all this seems to have been, in part, reverence for life, but still more, self-discipline and the extinction of all bodily passions and cravings. As a counsel of perfection, it is recommended that the Jain monk end his life by starving himself to death. To this same end Mahāvīra interpreted the fifth rule of the ascetic code more stringently than it had hitherto been interpreted. It implied, for him, not only liberality with one's possessions, but the inadvisability of having possessions. The Jain monks accordingly live in a state of extreme personal deprivation, and even the laymen are advised to set a limit to the amount of money or property that they will ever permit themselves to own. One sect of Jains, the Digambaras, has carried this principle so far that they refuse to wear any clothing whatsoever, and go about "clad in the sky."

Jain temples are easily distinguishable from regular Hindu temples. Apart from a certain amount of Hindu imagery that has surreptitiously crept into Jain architecture in a few localities, there are no images of gods in Jain temples. No gods are worshiped by the Jains. Although they do not deny the existence of beings higher than man in the cycle of transmigration, they do not look to them for aid. The only images that rightfully appear in the Jain temples are those of the twenty-four Tīrthakaras or "ford-finders" — human beings who have attained bliss (*moksha,* nirvāna) in this life through becoming completely indifferent to good and ill. The first of these lived billions of eons ago; the last was Mahāvīra, of whom it is said that " he was indifferent alike to the smell of ordure and of sandalwood, to straw and to jewels, dirt and gold, pleasure and pain, attached neither to this world nor to that beyond, desiring neither life nor death." [23] There are doubtless many uneducated Jains who worship the Tīrthakaras as gods and pray to them for material benefits; but in correct Jainist theory they are simply ideal human beings, to be venerated and imitated.

Practical-minded westerners are apt to dismiss the Jains as crazy fanatics, who in any country but India would be confined in asylums. Hopkins, in his generally admirable book, *The Religions of India,* impatiently characterizes Jainism as " a religion in which the chief points insisted on are that one should deny God, worship man, and nourish vermin." [24] If the student is tempted to concur too hastily in such a judgment, let him remem-

ber that " Mahātma " Gandhi, the most powerful religious leader
in the world today, has been profoundly influenced by Jainism,
and in his vegetarianism, his nonviolence, his voluntary poverty,
his scanty clothing, his ascetic self-discipline, and his willingness,
under certain conditions, to " fast unto death," reflects the teaching
of this radical sect. It may be possible to dismiss the average Jain
monk as a fanatic, but even the hardest-headed politician is obliged
to take Mr. Gandhi very seriously indeed.

Between the time of Mahāvīra and the time of the Mohammedan
conquest, the reforming idealism of the Hindus mainly expressed
itself in the various *bhakti* sects and movements, and in the monastic orders founded by philosophic saints like Śankara and Rāmānuja. It was from one of these monastic orders that the radical
reform movement of the Sikhs took its start. Rāmānanda, a
fifteenth-century follower of Rāmānuja, left the fold of orthodox Hinduism, giving up the ancient food laws and admitting
all castes to his order without distinction. For his heresy he
was driven out of south India, and preached the gospel in the
north, then under the domination of the Mohammedans. His
sect is still powerful among the lower and poorer castes in north
India, and through the poetry of Tulsī Dās, one of his adherents,
has exercised a great influence upon modern Hinduism. One
of his converts was a Mohammedan, the gifted poet Kabīr, who
founded a new movement, the Kabīr Panth, aiming at reconciliation between the Hindu and Moslem faiths but sternly opposing idolatry, caste, and exaggerated forms of austerity. Kabīr
in turn influenced Nānak, the founder and first *guru* (leader,
teacher) of the Sikhs.

Strict monotheism is the chief teaching of the Sikhs, as it is of the
Mohammedans; but their conception of God partakes more of the
nature of Vishnu or Brahman than of the nature of Allah. That
is, their God is not a heavenly king (with manlike passions and an
imperious will) but an all-pervading Presence. The chief Hindu
gods — Brahmā, Vishnu, and Śiva — are recognized as celestial
spirits, servants of the most high God; but idol worship is forbidden, and the idea that God could ever become incarnate in

human form, in such heroes as Rāma or Krishna, is absolutely
rejected. The light of God's presence is nevertheless believed to
be with every man who has eyes to see it, and in the *gurus* —
Nānak and his successors — it burns with exceptional clearness.
The Hindu view of the future life and the final destiny of man
is accepted, but the Mohammedan heaven is also accepted as a stage
on the way to nirvāna; and the ascetic-philosophic pathway of the
Upanishads and the Vedānta is rejected in favor of a simple life of
devotion to God and active good works. The Sikhs are encouraged to engage in the ordinary occupations of society instead of
retreating from the world, and they are not required to observe
the Hindu laws against meat-eating, etc.

The history of the Sikh movement is rather strange. Protesting
at first against all authoritative scriptures, both Hindu and Moslem,
and relying upon direct intuition of truth, it soon developed an
authoritative standard of its own. When Guru Nānak was about
to die he named one of his followers, Angad, to be his successor,
and Angad in turn did the same, the belief being that each *guru*
" blended his light with " his successor so completely that Nānak
himself literally lived on in them all. The fifth *guru*, Arjun, who
was martyred at the hands of the Mogul emperor Jehangīr, was
a poet; and he made a collection of the hymns of Kabīr, Nānak,
and the other *gurus,* which has become the Bible of the Sikh religion and is known as the *Granth Sahib* or " Noble Book." The
tenth *guru*, Govind Singh, appointed no human successor. " After
me," he said, " you shall everywhere obey the *Granth Sahib* as your
guru; whatever you shall ask, it will show you." [25] Today, in the
Golden Temple at Amritsar, the headquarters of the faith, one may
see a huge ornamental copy of the *Granth Sahib* occupying the
focus of adoration, lying upon a luxurious ottoman, fanned by
attendants as though it were a rajah, worshiped with offerings of
marigolds like a Hindu idol!

The same Govind Singh who brought about the lapse of the
Sikhs into book worship instituted severe military training among
them, in order to protect them against the persecutions of the
Mohammedans. So successfully did they defend themselves in

battle that they became from that time on, to all intents and purposes, a race of professional fighting men, fearless and loyal, and incomparable for valor in all the Indian peninsula. The British have made of them the backbone of their Indian army; and they are used as soldiers or policemen in other British colonies in the Orient, as far off as Hong Kong. They are quite distinct from both Hindus and Moslems and hostile to both. Thus it has come about that a religious movement designed to create peace between Hindus and Moslems and to obliterate caste discrimination, has only added one more unassimilable religious community to the great hodge-podge of faiths and castes which makes Indian national unity so hard to achieve.

In recent times, the two most notable reform movements which have become independent of orthodox Hinduism are the Brāhma Samāj and the Ārya Samāj. The Brāhma Samāj was founded in 1828 by Rām Mohan Rai, a believer in the eventual unity of all religions, who found in essential Hinduism, purged of caste and idolatry and interpreted monotheistically, the basis of a world religion, in which enlightened Mohammedans and Christians might be expected to join. Like the Rāmakrishna movement, the Brāhma Samāj combines Hindu reverence for the Upanishads with Christian concern for social betterment; but it is much more radical than the former in its free handling of Hindu tradition and in its attack upon the evils of caste, idolatry, child marriage, etc. Its creed is simple: " (1) That there is but one God, 'the First Without a Second'; (2) that the soul has before it an endless progress; (3) that worship or realization of God is the only duty of man." [26] It has so much in common with Unitarian Christianity that it has been not uncommon for Brāhma Samāj leaders to study in Unitarian theological schools.

After Rām Mohan Rai's death the leadership of the movement fell into the hands of the noted Tagore family, under whom it flourished greatly. Devendranath Tagore, who became active in the movement in 1841, guided it through many crises, and compiled a collection of the more monotheistic passages in the Upanishads which, under the name of *Brāhma Dharma,* became the

Bible of the society. His son is the great poet Rabindranath Tagore, in whose poetical and philosophical works — especially in *Gītanjalī* and *Sādhana* — the principles of the society are very beautifully and persuasively expressed. In 1867 a branch of the society split off under the leadership of the meteoric Keshab Chandra Sen, who claimed divine inspiration, thundered against the evils of Hinduism with exceptional daring, and came so close to professing Christianity that he alienated those who reverenced the Hindu tradition. Keshab's movement again split in two when the adored leader shocked some of his followers by permitting his daughter to be married, at the age of thirteen, to a Hindu rajah, with idolatrous rites.[27] All three branches of the society continue to be active; but the third, known as the Sādhārana Brāhma Samāj, is the most numerous.

The Ārya Samāj is much more conservative than the Brāhma Samāj, and is in fact often characterized as a " fundamentalist " movement, which upholds the infallibility of the Vedas as the Protestant fundamentalists uphold the infallibility of the Bible. It was founded in 1875 by Swami Dayānanda Sarasvatī, a passionate believer in the supremacy of Hindu over western culture, and an earnest reformer whose one aim was to restore Hinduism from its modern degeneracy to its ancient purity. Under the influence of a vedic scholar, Swami Virjānanda, he came to believe that all wisdom was contained in the Vedas, and all later books might as well be " drowned " in the river. He hated idolatry, polytheism, and pantheism as much as any Mohammedan, Sikh, or Brāhmo; but he contended that none of these evils was to be found in the Vedas. His movement has far outstripped the Brāhma Samāj in popularity, and has been very active in converting and educating the untouchables. It does not wholly oppose the caste system, but maintains that a man's position in the social scale should be determined by character rather than by birth. It has been very active in famine relief, social reform, and education. If it be asked how the Ārya Samāj schools can consistently teach sciences and other modern subjects, the reply is that these subjects help the student to see things in the Vedas which he could not see before — for example, that modern mechanical inventions are foreshadowed in the vedic hymns and that the principles of chemistry and physics are taught in them! [28] In much the same way, some Protestant fundamentalists are able to find the automobile described in the Book of Nahum or in the famous " vision of wheels " in the Book of Ezekiel. And, it may be added, the belief in the infallibility of the Vedas holds many young Hindus steady in their moral life in face of the bewildering changes now going on in ethical standards, much as the belief in the infallibility of the Bible holds some young Protestants.

V. BUDDHISM IN INDIA (ESSENTIAL BUDDHISM)

The greatest of all Hindu reform movements, Buddhism, remains to be described. With the background we now have, it should not be hard to understand, for it is thoroughly Hindu in its presuppositions and its aims — starting, like all other Hindu ways of salvation, with the theory of transmigration and karma, and aiming at deliverance from the wheel of rebirth. But of all the Hindu ways of salvation it alone has become the basis of a universal religion which has appealed to all nations and classes in the Far East, as Christianity has in the west. Hinduism is to Buddhism what Judaism is to Christianity: its indispensable foundation. Buddhism has done to Hinduism what Christianity has done to Judaism: disentangled its essential and universal from its national and local elements, and made them available, in simple and persuasive form, to men of widely different cultures. One must be born a Jew or a Hindu; one becomes a Christian or a Buddhist only by conviction.

Professor J. B. Pratt, a lifelong student of Buddhism, analyzes essential Buddhism into three main elements, independent in origin, not wholly consistent with one another, but inextricably woven together: (1) The Brāhmanical element, which Gautama the Buddha simply " took for granted from the common beliefs of his time." (The chief illustration of this was the doctrine of transmigration, but there were also various notions about " heaven and hell, the acquisition of merit and the value of various external acts," which probably appealed less to Gautama than to his disciples, but nevertheless did leak into Buddhist teaching from Hindu sources.) (2) "Gautama's own original doctrine, the Four Noble Truths, based upon direct experience of sorrow, sorrow's cause, and the purely psychical way of escape." (3) "Gautama's own great sympathetic heart, his unselfish devotion and desire to serve and save his fellows." [29] In dealing with the life of the founder, we shall observe the process by which these three elements became interwoven; and then, in tracing the development of Buddhism, we shall observe how they regained their independence to some extent, giving rise to different emphases in Buddhist teaching.

Gautama Siddhārtha, called "Sākyamuni," "the Tathāgata," "the Bhagavatī," or most commonly "the Buddha," [30] was born in Kapilavathu, a hundred miles north of Benares, about 560 B.C., and died at the age of eighty, about 480 B.C. The dates of his birth and death are somewhat uncertain, but it is clear that he was a younger contemporary of Mahāvīra, and was thus born into an age of great spiritual ferment, when rival religious sects and schools of philosophy were fiercely disputing about the way of salvation. Legend has magnified his origin, making of him a royal prince, whose birth was attended with all sorts of miraculous circumstances, and whose father, alarmed at prophecies that his son would forsake the world, endeavored to keep his mind from serious topics by building for him three palaces and surrounding him with a harem of forty thousand dancing girls. The truth seems to be that he was the son of a member of the ruling clan (the Sākyas) in a small agricultural state, and that his life had nothing extraordinary about it up to the time when at the age of twenty-five, shortly after the birth of his first and only son, Rāhula, he suddenly left his family to go out into the "houseless life" in quest of nirvāna.

The reasons for this decision are obscure. Tradition relates that the youth, having been brought up in luxury, and in ignorance of the hard facts of life, was suddenly shocked into a realization of the bitterness of man's lot by the sight of "a decrepit old man, a diseased man, a dead man, and a monk"; and on inquiring the meaning of these things determined to follow the monk in search of a solution of the problem of suffering. There is probably truth beneath this tradition. A sensitive upper-caste youth, living a sheltered and thoughtless life, would be bound sooner or later to encounter the seamier side of human existence; and the sudden realization of man's misery and mortality might well cast a pall over his mind, never to be lifted until he could face and solve the whole riddle of life. Tolstoy, the aristocratic landowner, had a very similar experience in modern times.

From this time on, we have more authentic information about Gautama's history. He went first, in search of enlightenment, to a famous philosopher named Alārā Kālāma, who led him, as he afterwards said, not to nirvāna, but only "as far as the realm of nothingness." Another philosophic teacher, Uddaka, led him "only so far as the realm of neither perception nor yet nonperception." [31] Wearied then of philosophic subtleties, Gautama gave up the upanishadic "way of knowledge" and tried the way of ascetic self-mortification, which Mahāvīra had lately been proclaiming as the way that leads to "conquest." In a grove near Uruvela he met with five ascetics, who soon came to regard him as their leader, so ruthlessly did he starve and torture his physical frame. But while they looked eagerly for the moment when he would announce victory, he — with his usual sanity and candor — recognized that he had entered upon another false path and, to their disgust and disappointment, "gave up his exertions."

Deserted by his companions, frustrated in his quest, he then sat down beneath a bo-tree to review the situation and consider what to do next. There, suddenly and unexpectedly, enlightenment came upon him. He saw the nature of the human self, the cause of human misery, and the cure of human misery; and seeing these things he was emancipated and at peace. For four weeks, tradition tells us, he sat cross-legged in meditation, working out the implications of his discovery, and pondering upon the responsibilities which it imposed upon him. He was strongly tempted to keep the great secret to himself, for, said he (according to an early record), "If I proclaim the doctrine, and other men are not able to understand my preaching, there would result but weariness and annoyance to me." It was indeed a doctrine "abstruse, intelligible only to the wise," and its very essence was a peaceful detachment from all cares and anxieties — which he would be likely to lose the moment he began to preach it! Yet when he "looked full of compassion, toward sentient beings, over the world," [32] he could not resist the call to communicate his healing discovery; and the rest of his long life was spent in tireless missionary activity. Māra, the tempter, had failed in his assault upon the Blessèd One! [33]

The Buddha's first converts, after his enlightenment, were the five ascetics who had been his companions at Uruvela. At the Deer-Park (Sarnath) near Benares he found them again; and though they shunned him at first as a renegade they consented at length to listen to his teaching, and listening were convinced. Tradition has preserved a full and probably authentic record of his first sermon, which presents the very core of the teachings of Gautama, as the Sermon on the Mount presents the central teachings of Jesus.

The sermon begins, naturally enough, with a comparison between the true way of salvation and the way by which the ascetics had hitherto been seeking it. The true way is not the ascetic way of self-mortification, neither is it the way of pleasure-seeking and self-gratification, which the worldly man pursues. It is a Middle Way between these two extremes: the holy Eightfold Path of "right belief, right aspiration, right speech, right conduct, right means of livelihood, right endeavor, right memory, right medita-"

The meaning of this Eightfold Path cannot be understood apart from the still more fundamental doctrine which the Buddha next sets forth: the Four Noble Truths, concerning suffering, the cause of suffering, the cessation of suffering, and the path which leads to cessation. We have here nothing less than a medical diagnosis of the disease from which the human race is suffering, taking up in orderly sequence its symptoms, its cause, its cure, and the method by which the cure is to be administered.

(1). The First Noble Truth: the Symptoms. "This," says the Buddha, "is the Noble Truth of Suffering: birth is suffering; de-

cay is suffering; illness is suffering; death is suffering. Presence
of objects we hate is suffering; separation from objects we love is
suffering; not to obtain what we desire is suffering. Briefly, the
fivefold clinging to existence is suffering." [34]

Western commentators have said much about the unmitigated
pessimism of this description of life. It ought to be said that what
we have here is not an attempt to "see life steadily and see it
whole," but a cool medical description of the *pathology* of human
life, an enumeration of the chief points at which human misery
does actually appear. Christianity and Buddhism are not fundamentally in disagreement, so far. Both paint a very dark portrait
of man's "unregenerate" state, before he has found the way of
salvation; both believe that there is a cure for his disease. There is
undoubtedly, however, a marked contrast between Buddhism and
many other religions in the extreme stress that the former lays
upon the weariness and futility of ordinary human living and upon
the all-pervading presence of suffering from birth to death. At
this point, the Buddha's teaching simply reflects the pessimism
which recurs like a refrain in all the religious philosophies of his
day.

| (2). The Second Noble Truth: the Cause. "This," says the
Buddha, "is the Noble Truth of the Cause of Suffering: Thirst,
that leads to rebirth, accompanied by pleasure and lust, finding
its satisfaction here and there . . . thirst for existence, thirst for
prosperity."

There is more in this diagnosis than meets the eye. The simp
way of explaining it would be to point to the observable psychological fact that *inordinate desire* ("thirst") leads to stress and
strain, invites frustration and disappointment, and is in truth the
chief root of human suffering. But the Buddha means to assert
more than this. He means to assert that a human individual is
nothing but a bundle of desires, and continues as an individual, in
this life and all subsequent lives, only so long as these desires cling
to one another and to the world of transient things. In other
words, there is no permanent soul, passing on from one existence
to another, as the Upanishads teach; there is only a collection of

impulses, which continues to exist and reproduce itself in a definite
pattern, according to the law of karma, so long as the impulsive
force of desire continues. Actually, the Buddha's psychology was
still more elaborate than this, including an intricate scheme of
" dependent origination," tracing suffering back to the nature of
birth and existence, that in turn back to desire and attachment,
sense perception and contact, and so eventually back to ignorance
of the true way of life. The gist of his teaching can be very simply
expressed, however, in the proposition that *desire is the root of all
evil.*

(3). The Third Noble Truth: the Cure. " This," says the Buddha, " is the Noble Truth of the Cessation of Suffering: it ceases
with the complete cessation of this thirst — a cessation which consists in the absence of every passion — with the abandoning of this
thirst, with the doing away with it, with the destruction of desire."

It follows in strict logic from the theory of the self as a bundle
of desires that in the extinction of passion and desire the *self* should
also be extinguished. It is one of the moot questions of Buddhist
philosophy whether nirvāna, the blissful " going out " which is the
goal of every good Buddhist's aspiration, and which Gautama himself is said to have attained, means " annihilation " or not. The
founder always refused to commit himself on this issue. He had
but one object in his teaching, he said: to bring man deliverance
from suffering; and he had observed for himself that philosophical
speculation never brings peace of r tion out rather the reverse. To
one of his followers who inquired about the condition of the spirit
after death he replied that he had deliberately taught nothing
about it, because it was not essential to salvation. He who would
not obey the teachings of the Blessèd One until he had settled such
questions would be, he said, like a man wounded by an arrow who
refused to be treated by a physician until he understood all about
the arrow and the man who shot it. He would die before the treatment began!

It is clear from such passages as this that the Buddha's teaching
is primarily concerned, as we should say today, with the laws of
mental hygiene. He is a scientist, not a metaphysician; and though

he holds certain metaphysical assumptions in common with all his contemporaries — notably the theory of transmigration — he never allows these assumptions to take precedence over the great psychological discovery which he believed himself to have made, and which he believed could be verified, in this life, by anyone who would take the trouble. Nirvāna, in other words, is first of all a state of mind, which comes to the man who has stilled his passions, detached himself from all particular ambitions, possessions, and objects of desire, and learned to look out upon all life with impartial compassion, as if from some high point of observation, above the dust and the heat. Something of its meaning can be sensed, even by the prosaic modern American, in the brooding stillness, the pervasive air of peace and serenity that inhabit the Buddhist monasteries of the Orient and live in the calm face of the great Buddha of Kamakura. It is possible to abandon the whole theory of transmigration, as some modern Buddhists do, and still see in the Third Noble Truth one of the profoundest psychological principles that have ever been discovered.

(4). The Fourth Noble Truth: the Method of Treatment. "This," says the Buddha, "is the Noble Truth of the Path which leads to the cessation of suffering: that holy Eightfold Path" — with which we are already acquainted. Considering its steps more carefully now, we note that they fall into three divisions. The first two steps, "belief" and "aspiration," simply reaffirm the necessity of accepting the Buddha's diagnosis of the cause of suffering, and turning one's hopes away from self and the usual objects of desire, toward the passionless peace of nirvāna. The next three steps — "speech," "conduct," "livelihood" — express the Buddhist code of ethics. It is a code of honesty, sobriety, kindness, and self-denial. Slander, falsehood, and frivolity are the three great abuses of speech. Unchastity, theft, and killing are the three great abuses of conduct. The most dishonorable of livelihoods is to gain money, like the Brāhman priests, by pretending to possess extraordinary holiness or supernatural powers. Especially bad — because they form insuperable obstacles to the selflessness of nirvāna — are hatred, deceit, contempt, and all the angry passions; especially good is a kindly, forgiving, peaceful disposition, which cultivates "a boundless friendly mind towards all beings." The last three steps in the path — "endeavor," "memory," "meditation" — outline a system of mental self-discipline, partly modeled on the ancient yoga system of mental concentration and mystic absorption, but particularly designed to combat self-love and inordinate desire and to encourage universal compassion. Thus, for example, one is directed, as a cure for self-love, to enumerate mentally the "thirty-two constituents of the body" and the "nine exits and excrements of the body"; as a cure for sexual passion, to consider the body of the beloved one as if it were already a putrescent corpse. On the other hand, one is to practice "filling the universe with thoughts of love." When he sees a sick dog the Buddhist should not say, How disgusting! but, What can I do to help this poor creature? [35] Because the Buddha had himself traversed this noble Eightfold Path, he could testify to the five ascetics at Sarnath concerning the bliss and emancipation that lay at the end of it. The sermon ends in a cry of triumph: "The emancipation of my mind cannot be lost; this is my last birth, I shall not be born again!"

It is obvious that — unlike original Christianity — original Buddhism is not a doctrine which is "hidden from the wise and learned and revealed unto babes." It is a severe method of mental discipline, a regime of life that is "difficult" and "rare," as Spinoza said of his *Ethics;* so that the average man — let alone the average woman — cannot be expected to adopt it. To be a perfect Buddhist it is necessary to become a monk. The greater part of the Buddha's long life was, consequently, employed in the founding and instructing of a monastic order. For nine months in the year he wandered to and fro in the "Eastern Lands" round about Benares, converting so many young noblemen to his order that (it is said) he "caused fathers to be childless, wives to become widows, and families to become extinct." Then for the three months of the rainy season he retired with his monks to some one of the monastic establishments with which the order soon became endowed, and spent the time in meditation and instruction. Applicants for admission to his order took the usual vows of the Hindu or Jain monks — nonviolence, chastity, honesty — and in addition abjured drinking fermented liquors, eating at certain times, dancing, singing, gazing at theatrical spectacles, fine clothes, perfumes, using a high or broad seat, and the possession of money. On entering the order, they repeated the formula, "I take my refuge in the Buddha, I take my refuge in the Teaching, I take my refuge in the Order." Rather dubiously, at the entreaty of his aunt Mehapajapati and his favorite disciple Ānanda, the Buddha permitted orders of nuns to be organized;[36] and he also recognized a group of lay adherents, who were not ready to leave the world and so could not reach nirvāna in the present life, but who could "acquire merit" for their next life by observing as much as possible of the teaching and by giving gifts to the order.

Gautama firmly refused, on his deathbed, to leave any instructions for the future conduct of his order. He had given them the teaching; they needed no more. "Be ye lamps unto yourselves," he urged. "Betake yourselves to no external refuge. Hold fast to the truth as a lamp. Hold fast as a refuge to the truth. Look not for refuge to any one besides yourselves."[37] He had left them a religion without a theology, and without any form of public worship — except that twice a month the vows of the order were recited, and all the monks were solemnly asked whether they had any infractions to confess. Gradually, as the doctrine spread and became popularized, a theology and a form of worship developed. The Buddha became the object of a genuinely religious veneration, as did Mahāvīra among the Jains; and he was regarded as one of a long line of Buddhas, corresponding to the Jainist "Tīrthakaras" and the Hindu "avatars." His ashes, distributed among a number of burial places, were marked by great mounds called stūpas — crowned later with a high point called a dāgoba, whose umbrella-like pinnacle still later developed into what we know as a pagoda. At first, no images were used; then, under the influence of the Greek sculpture which Alexander's conquest introduced into north India, it became customary to build temples with a huge image of some Buddha at one end, as an aid to meditation. The image was usually surrounded by symbolic figures — the lotus, the wheel of the law, and so on — and passages from the Buddhist writings were intoned before it at regular intervals. So before many centuries had passed Buddhism had lost the severely philosophical and agnostic character which the founder sought to imprint upon it, and was in a fair way to become a polytheistic cult like all the other Hindu sects.

The popular extension of Buddhism was particularly rapid in the time of Aśoka (264–227 B.C.), the great and enlightened monarch who united most of the Indian peninsula under his rule, and then, in penitence for the violence which he had used, renounced war, became a Buddhist monk, and devoted the rest of his days to promoting the welfare of his subjects and the peaceful extension of his influence through missionary activities, which resulted in the conversion of Ceylon. Needless to say, when Buddhism thus became popular, it had to accommodate itself to the needs and interests of the masses, as did Christianity under the Emperor Constantine. Again, under Kaniska, Buddhist ruler of the "Kushan" empire which flourished in north India in the first and second centuries A.D., important popular developments took place which were crystallized in the split between northern and southern Buddhism. The former called itself Mahāyāna or the "Great Vehicle" of salvation; the latter was dubbed Hīnayāna or the "Lesser Vehicle." We shall follow the fortunes of these rival branches of Buddhism outside India in the next chapter. In south India the Hīnayāna form — which was closer to original Buddhism — remained dominant as long as Buddhism continued to thrive. Fa-Hsien, the Chinese traveler who visited India in the fifth century A.D., reported that he found flourishing Buddhist monasteries all over India, the Mahāyāna being always in the minority except in the northwest. Hsüan-Tsang, two centuries later, reported an increase in the total number of monasteries, and a great increase in the Mahāyāna, which was now in the majority except in the far south. Shortly after this time, both forms of Buddhism declined rapidly in India, and by the thirteenth or fourteenth century it was practically extinct in the land of its birth.

Many causes contributed to this decline. The persistent hostility of the Brāhman priests, reinforced in north India by the hostility of Mohammedan invaders, doubtless had something to do with it. But the greatest cause was almost certainly the rejuvenation of Hinduism which took place in this period. The rise of the *bhakti* form of devotion, coupled with the work of great philosophic mystics like Śankara, enabled the Hindu tradition to make room for the values of Buddhism in a more comprehensive and appealing system, rooted in the soil of the land, and appealing to men of all classes.

The name of the Buddha is still reverenced in India; but the organization which he founded has been overgrown and re-absorbed by Hinduism, as the ruins of Angkor have been overgrown and almost hidden by the luxuriant growth of the surrounding jungle.

NOTES

[1] " Render us always prosperous, always happy, O fire; thou who art eternal, beautiful, ever young; thou who nourishest, who art rich, receive favorably these our offerings, and in return give us happiness and sweet health." " Render us rich and flourishing; make us also wise and chaste." " O Agni, thou placest upon the good way the man who has wandered into the bad. . . . If we have committed a fault, if we have gone far from thee, pardon us." (Fustel de Coulanges, *The Ancient City*, pp. 31, 34, 37.)

[2] At Athens, this was called the Prytaneum; at Rome, the Temple of Vesta.

[3] The word " Veda " means " knowledge."

[4] A fourth Veda, the Atharvaveda, was compiled much later. It consists mostly of magic charms, and did not win recognition, for a long time, as a genuine part of the sacred canon.

[5] Rigveda, II, 28.7.

[6] One of the Maruts, Rudra, under his euphemistic title of Śiva (" propitious one ") later came to share with Vishnu the supreme allegiance of modern Hinduism.

[7] Cave, *Living Religions of the East*, p. 17.

[8] Rigveda, IX, 113.

[9] These four stages in the ideal Brāhman's life are called the four *āśramas*. The term *āśram(a)* also means a secluded retreat where a group of people seeking holiness live as a community. Mr. Gandhi's *āśram* at Ahmedabad is famous.

[10] Rigveda, X, 129. 6, 7.

[11] Satapatha Brāhmana, II, ii. 2, 6.

[12] Farquhar, *A Primer of Hinduism* (second ed., 1914), pp. 39, 40. Quoted by permission of the Oxford University Press, publishers.

[13] *Sacred Books of the East*, I, p. 82. Cited in Cave, *op. cit.*, pp. 32–34, where the whole passage is reviewed.

[14] Cave, *op. cit.*, p. 31.

[15] Brihadaranyaka Upanishad, IV, iv.5.

[16] *Ibid.*, I, iii.28.

17 *Sacred Books of the East*, XV, p. 15.

18 This famous prayer is known as the *Gāyatrī*. It is taught to all initiates, and is supposed to be repeated many times daily: "*Aum*, earth, sky, heaven, *Aum*. That excellent glory of the Quickening Sun, the god, may we attain; may he stimulate our devotions." (Rigveda, III, lxii. 10.)

19 Among the more popular of these minor deities are Ganeśa, the elephant-headed son of Śiva and Kālī; Hanumān, the monkey-god, patron of agriculture; and other animal-gods such as Śiva's bull, Nandi, and the Nāgas or serpent-gods.

20 *Karma Purāna*, xxii. 43 (Farquhar, *op. cit.*, p. 104).

21 On Hinduism in America see W. Thomas, *Hinduism Invades America* (New York, 1930).

22 *Akaranka Sūtra*, I, 8, 3. (Cited in Pratt, *India and its Faiths*, p. 289.) The word "*moksha*" is more commonly used by the Jains than the word "nirvāna," but the meaning in either case is *complete selflessness*.

23 *Kalpa Sūtra*, 119 (Pratt, *op. cit.*, p. 263).

24 Boston, 1898; p. 297.

25 Cited in Pratt, *India and its Faiths*, p. 247.

26 *Ibid.*, p. 195.

27 Keshab's followers claim — rightly, I think — that the "marriage" was only a betrothal, and that whatever idolatrous rites were introduced into the ceremony were surreptitiously smuggled in by the rajah's relatives, after they had signed a written agreement to permit a purely "theistic" ceremony, and after Keshab had threatened to call off the wedding because of their recalcitrancy. See *Keshub Chunder Sen and the Cooch Behar Betrothal, 1878*, by P. K. Sen (Calcutta, 1933).

28 This reply was made to the writer by an Ārya Samāj leader with whom he conversed in Lahore. In the course of the same conversation, a disciple remarked, "If I had not held fast to the Vedas, I would have lost my morals completely when studying engineering in London."

29 Pratt, *op. cit.*, p. 394. Cf. the similar analysis in the opening chapters of his later book, *The Pilgrimage of Buddhism*.

30 Siddhārtha was his given name, which he renounced when he entered upon his religious quest. Gautama was a family surname. "Sākyamuni" means "the sage of the Sākya clan." "The Tathāgata" means "he who has arrived." "The Bhagavatī" means "the Blessèd One" or "the Lord." "The Buddha" means "the Enlightened One."

31 Cave, *op. cit.*, p. 98.

32 *Ibid.*, pp. 101, 102.

33 In the *Book of the Great Decease*, the Buddha tells his friend Ānanda how Māra, the tempter, tried to persuade him at this time that the moment had come for him to pass into nirvāna, and how he resolved not to pass away until his "true religion" had become "widespread and popular." On this basis, legend has built up the picture of a terrific cosmic conflict, in which Māra attacked the Blessèd One with a vast army of demonic powers, while all the gods hung breathless on the outcome. Cave, *op. cit.*, pp. 102, 103.

34 This and the subsequent quotations from the Sarnath sermon are from Oldenberg's translation of the *Mahāvagga* (*Sacred Books of the East*, XIII, pp. 89–102).

35 Pratt, *India and its Faiths*, p. 354.

36 When Ānanda asked the Buddha how to behave toward women, the reply was, not to see them at all. "But if we should see them, what are we to do?" — "Abstain from speech." — "But if they should speak to us, Lord, what are we to do?" — "Keep wide awake, Ānanda!"

When it was finally agreed that women should be admitted to the order, Gautama said that, if women could have been kept out, the true religion would have stood for a thousand years, whereas now it could hardly last more than five hundred!

[37] Quoted in Cave, *op. cit.*, pp. 112, 113.

BIBLIOGRAPHY

Wright, W. K. *Op. cit.*, Chaps. VII, VIII.

Friess and Schneider. *Op. cit.*, pp. 57–141.

Moore, G. F. *History of Religions*, Vol. I, Chaps. XI–XIV.

Hume, R. E. *The World's Living Religions*, Chaps. II–V.

Cave, Sydney. *An Introduction to the Study of Some Living Religions of the East,* Chaps. I, III.

Barton, G. A. *The Religions of the World*, Chaps. VIII–X.

Pratt, J. B. *India and its Faiths*, Chaps. I–XIII.

———. *The Pilgrimage of Buddhism*, Chaps. I–VI.

Farquhar, J. N. *A Primer of Hinduism*.

3.

ORIENTAL RELIGION: EASTERN ASIA

THE religious history of eastern Asia can all be treated in connection with the mission and expansion of Buddhism. As it spread toward the south, the north, and the east, Buddhism came in contact with all the national religions of the Far East. In Ceylon, Burma, Siam, and Cambodia the Hīnayāna form of Buddhism almost completely displaced the native religions, which survived only as a creeper-like growth of superstition, obscuring to some extent the pure outlines of Gautama's philosophy. In China, the Mahāyāna form of Buddhism fought a long and indecisive battle with the national religion of ancestor worship, and was forced at length to accept a position of equality with Confucianism and Taoism, as one of the "three religions" to which the Chinese people *simultaneously* subscribed, before the fall of the empire. In Japan, Mahāyāna Buddhism became for long centuries completely fused and amalgamated with the national religion, Shintoism, and even today, since their legal separation, each exhibits many traces of the influence of the other. Our discussion of the religions of eastern Asia therefore falls naturally into four sections: Southern or Hīnayāna Buddhism; the Chinese national religion; Buddhism in China; and Buddhism and Shintoism in Japan. Since the main principles of Hīnayāna Buddhism have already been discussed in connection with original or Indian Buddhism, a brief treatment of this topic will suffice.*

* Note on pronunciation. In pronouncing the Chinese words which occur in this chapter, the chief rules to remember are as follows: The consonants *t, p, k* and *ch*, in the Wade romanization, are pronounced as in English *when followed by the aspirate* ('); otherwise, *t* is pronounced like *d, p* like *b, k* like *g* and *ch* like *j*. *Ts* also sounds very much like *j*, while the letter *j* itself represents a curious sound something like *zhr*. Thus *Tao = Dow, Chu = Joo, Kuan = Gwan, Tsang = Jang,* and *Jen = Zhren*. The vowel *e* is pronounced like *u* in *bung*, the vowel *ŭ* is mute, and the combination *ih* is like *ir* in *stir*. Thus *Feng = Fung, K'ung = Koong, Tzŭ = Tz-z-z, Shih = Shir*. There are many local differences in pronunciation, so that even these rules are not universally applicable.

73

I. SOUTHERN OR HĪNAYĀNA BUDDHISM

The essential difference between the Hīnayāna and Mahāyāna forms of Buddhism is the difference between the ideal of the *Arhat* and the ideal of the Bodhisattva. The *Arhat* is the ideal monk who lives according to the precepts of the Four Noble Truths and the noble Eightfold Path, and so, becoming completely detached from all objects of desire, enters into nirvāna. There is a certain selfishness about this ideal, which is at war with another ideal equally illustrated in original Buddhism: the deep compassion for human suffering which caused the Buddha to postpone the joys of nirvāna until he had preached his doctrine to a needy world. Mahāyāna Buddhism, as expressed in its classic scripture, *The Lotus of the Good Law,* exalts this more unselfish aspect of original Buddhism into the supreme place, and sets forth the view that among the many celestial beings who have appeared to enlighten mankind the most admirable and worthiest of imitation are the Bodhisattvas, who one and all delayed becoming Buddhas and entering into nirvāna out of pure disinterested love for all living creatures, men and beasts included. In Hīnayāna Buddhism, then, it is detachment, passionlessness, at which one aims; in Mahāyāna Buddhism, it is kindness, longsuffering service, forgiving love.

It would be a mistake to suppose that these two sides of the Buddhist ideal are cleanly divided between southern and northern Buddhism. Professor Pratt relates many delightful episodes which go to prove the genuineness of the spirit of kindness and compassion among the Buddhists of Ceylon and Burma.[1] The gentle and amiable virtues appear to be nourished by Buddhism wherever it goes. Yet there is much in southern Buddhism — in its professed aims as well as in its achievements — which it would not be unfair to characterize as selfish. A monk near Kandy, in Ceylon, expressed this side of Buddhism very plainly when he said: " I have to think of my salvation only and not of

---

The rules for Japanese are much simpler: pronounce the consonants about as in English, the vowels as in German. The vowels *u* and *i* are sometimes mute; the well known dish *sukiyaki* is pronounced *s'k'yaki.* There is no accent in Japanese; all syllables are equally stressed, as in French.

other people's. You have a mother and father, brothers and sisters? Leave them all to themselves, do not think about them, but think only of your own salvation. They are ties that bind you to this world."² In Burma, the idea of " merit " plays an enormous role; and the remark is sometimes made that in this country one-half the population (the laity) is busy heaping up merit for its own salvation by supporting the other half of the population (the monks) in a lazy and self-centered existence. The remark is not without exaggeration, for the Burmese monks are much occupied with the religious education of the young people — more so than in most Buddhist countries; and yet the zeal and intelligence with which they apply themselves to this task leave something to be desired. When Buddhist peace and serenity become corrupted they easily sink into indolence and callousness. Both in Ceylon and in Burma, still more in the jungles of Siam and Cambodia, popular Buddhism has become further complicated by contact with primitive animism. Devil-dances for the exorcism of evil spirits, nat-houses for the habitation of good spirits, temples consecrated to serpent-gods called Nāgas, mingle oddly with shrines dedicated to the Blessèd One, who denied all forms of supernatural power and relied upon the scientific working of the " iron law of karma " to secure the world's salvation. Such, however, is the fate of every religion when it attempts to appeal to the masses; and time has proved that there is something in the message of Gautama which appeals to all sorts and conditions of men.

II. THE CHINESE NATIONAL RELIGION

When the first Buddhist missionaries from India penetrated into China by way of the central Asian caravan routes, in the middle period of the Han dynasty (about the time of Christ), they found themselves confronted with an indigenous state religion, based upon a combination of ancestor worship and nature worship. This native and national religion of China had then been practiced, without notable alterations, since the remote beginnings of agricultural civilization in the valley of the Yellow river; and it continued to be the dominant religion of China, in spite of Buddhist,

Christian, and Mohammedan influences, down to the fall of the empire in 1911. It is now crumbling away rapidly before our eyes — a strange and rather disturbing spectacle for one who reflects upon its venerable age and its matchless power for social control; yet in many parts of the interior provinces, remote from the western influences which stream out from the industrialized ports of Canton and Shanghai, the ancient cult and the ancient customs still prevail, substantially as they were before the dawn of history. Were they to vanish completely, overnight, it is probable that China would awake tomorrow morning to a state of utter social chaos.

The basic factor in Chinese civilization has always been the institution of the patriarchal family or clan. Living in a complicated network of courtyards, gardens, and tile roofs, surrounded by a stout outer wall, governed autocratically but benevolently by an elder, the Chinese family forms a very tough and resistant bit of social fabric, which has repeatedly shown its power to survive intact when the empire itself has gone to pieces. The basic element in Chinese religion is accordingly the private cult of ancestral spirits, which is carried on within the walls of the family dwelling house generation after generation, with the ruling elder as its only priest and the family annals as its only scriptures. This cult does not differ essentially from the ancestral worship of the ancient Greeks and Romans or that of their Aryan relatives, the Hindus; and it results in the same social attitudes and principles which prevail in all thoroughgoing patriarchal systems: great reverence for the aged and for ancient usage; subordination of the individual's freedom and happiness to the welfare of the family group; communism of possessions within the clan; and the duty of having plenty of male offspring to continue the line — implying (a) the right of taking a second wife if the first be sterile, (b) the probability of great overpopulation, and (c) the necessity of selling or killing female children in hard times. But Chinese ancestor worship is perhaps the most fully developed of all such systems; and it has expressed itself in many picturesque rites and customs which are peculiar to the land and the people.

The presence of the ancestral spirits in and with the family is represented by small wooden tablets on which the names of the ancestors are inscribed.[3] In very poor families, the tablets may be replaced by lists of names written on paper and kept in a little niche in the wall; in wealthier families the tablets may be supplemented with portraits of the deceased, and the simple niche may develop into a veritable shrine or temple. In any case, it is the duty of each member of the family to bow thrice, say a prayer, and burn a stick of incense before this niche or shrine, every day of his life. Twice a year there are more elaborate ceremonies at the graves of the ancestors, which sometimes bring divided branches of the family together from a considerable distance for a sort of Thanksgiving reunion. The graves are cleaned and set in order — a bit of sod sometimes being put on top of the mound to indicate that this has been done — and the souls of the departed are liberally supplied with food and drink, vehicles for travel, money, and all sorts of gifts and conveniences, which are usually made (economically enough) of paper, and made available for the spirits by being converted into smoke and flame. When a member of the family "plucks the flower of life" and joins his ancestors in the spirit world, the funeral ceremonies include similar burnt offerings on a much larger scale. Supplies, so to speak, have to be laid in stock for eternity; later it will be sufficient to replenish them. So the deceased is furnished with such gifts as the following: "Life-size papier-mâché servants, each with his or her name attached; bannermen with scrolls of gray, blue or black silk; papier-mâché horses, carriages, and grooms; silver and gold; a chest of books; a table lute; a set of chess; a three-sided boat manned by a boatman and his wife; a hen with chicks, and a basket of ripe peaches." [4] As the funeral procession advances, with bands of music, chanting priests, and troops of hired mourners, paper "money" is flung right and left to propitiate the demons who might do harm to the newborn spirit, while plenty of real money is spent, if available, to give all possible magnificence to his entry into the spirit land. Mourning clothes of white are worn by the family for sixty days, and for three years there may be no marriage among the sons and daughters of the deceased. For three years, while they were help-less infants, their parent had given them lavishly of his thought and care; for three years, after his death, they are to show their gratitude by thinking of him rather than of themselves.

This family cult of ancestors is the very backbone of Chinese re-ligion, as the family itself is the backbone of Chinese society; but it is supplemented, as in other patriarchal societies, with a system of nature worship not unlike that of the vedic Hindus — due allow-ance being made for differences of climate and national topog-raphy. Not unnaturally, the most popular deities are the spirits of the soil and grain, who govern the yield of rice or wheat upon which the fate of the teeming multitudes depends. Just a degree higher in augustness, and a degree lower in popularity, are the spirits of the mountains, which govern the wind and rain and so in a sense control the spirits of the soil and grain, and the spirits of the great rivers, which are anxiously propitiated in the hope of preventing the devastating floods that have cursed the land for so many centuries. High above all these — too high for the common man — are the two supreme deities, Heaven and Earth, by whose combined forces all things are ultimately determined. Heaven represents the male principle of light and warmth (*Yang*); it is worshiped at the winter solstice, when the sun's light begins to in-crease. Earth represents the female principle of darkness and cold (*Yin*); it is worshiped at the summer solstice. All things are variously compounded of the *Yang* and the *Yin* principles, and pass through cyclic changes like the changing seasons.

Popular religion had given rise to these fundamental concepts long before the religion of the Chinese state took shape; but with the appearance of the first strong imperial dynasties an attempt was made to bring the religion of the people under regular govern-mental control. Heaven was described as *Shang-Ti*, " supreme emperor," and to it was ascribed final moral and political au-thority, as well as ultimate causative power. Once a year — down to the year 1911 — the Chinese emperor solemnly paid his rever-ence to Heaven and the heavenly powers (sun, moon, stars, rain, storm) at the great circular altar of Heaven on the south side of Peking. Once a year he paid his reverence to Earth and the earthly powers (the mountains, the four seas, and the four great rivers) at the great square altar of Earth — surrounded by a trench full of water, as the earth is surrounded by the seas — located on the north side of Peking. The relations between the human and divine emperors were somewhat cold and distant, since Heaven was never conceived as a manlike being, and it was generally admitted that Heaven never speaks; yet it was firmly believed that Heaven sees all things, and sends prosperity or adversity in strict accordance with man's moral deserts.

The worship of Heaven and the other great deities being reserved for the emperor and his officials, the common people inevitably became very limited and superstitious in their religious outlook. In addition to the ancestor worship which was their private religion, and the worship of the guardians of the door or the furnace — a choice of which was permitted to them by law — they gave, and continue to give, much attention to various local deities, spirits of the ground, patron spirits of trade, of war, of healing; and above all they stand in terror of a host of evil spirits, ghosts, and demons, to get the better of which they employ all sorts of devices. Evil spirits, for some reason, travel only in straight lines; so one protects the household against them by building the roof in curving lines and seeing that every gate is protected by a screen and no two gates are in a line with each other. Further protection against the evil spirits is found in the aid of the local gods, the art of divination by lot, and the elaborate pseudo-science known as Feng-shui, or "Wind and Water," by which lucky and unlucky times and places are detected. Feng-shui is especially important in connection with funerals. Bodies are kept in the coffin for a considerable period of time, until the local geomancers have determined exactly where the tomb of this particular individual, with his peculiar qualities, will be safest from unwholesome spiritual influences. Tombs thus are not exclusively grouped in cemeteries, but dotted all over the landscape, and have become in the course of centuries a very serious impediment to agriculture, since it is necessary to plough around them in wide circles. Formerly it was

the custom, at the beginning of a new dynasty, to order all com-
moners' tombs to be leveled; but the Manchus, unfortunately, felt
too insecure to risk the wrath of the people, and so Chinese agriculture has not had a fresh lease of life since the beginning of the
Ming dynasty! Thus does religion sometimes destroy the very
values it aims to conserve.

The term "Confucianism" is generally used to describe the native religion of China. This is very misleading. Confucius
(K'ung Tzŭ, B.C. 551–478) was in no sense a religious innovator.
He was, as he himself said, "a transmitter, not a maker, believing
in and loving the ancients," and his career as statesman was mainly
devoted to restoring the good old ways as far as possible. Punc-
tilious in observing all ancient religious ceremonies, he was personally inclined to be agnostic about matters of religious belief. Like
other practical statesmen — George Washington, for example —
he was confident that Heaven watched over the fate of the virtuous
man; but he had no personal dealings with heavenly powers or
spirits. Once when he was sick a disciple asked leave to pray for
him; but although it was found to be the proper thing to do,
according to ancient custom, he still objected, "My prayer is of
long standing" — meaning that his lifelong devotion to virtue
was a better prayer than any oral one.[5] As for the future life, he
refused to answer any questions about it, though he correctly observed the rites of ancestor worship. "So long as you do not know
life," he said, "how can you know about death?"

Although not a seer or prophet in any sense, Confucius had
nevertheless a very far-reaching influence upon the ethical side of
Chinese religion. By reducing the moral rules of his people to
writing and to philosophical order, and by lending them the
authority of his acknowledged strength and rectitude of character,
Confucius became the patron and exemplar of a moral ideal
which has shown its power to persist. In his ethical system there
are two fundamental principles, *li* and *jen*. *Li* is the principle
of respect for custom, the principle of polite, ceremonial correct-
ness. *Jen* is the principle of benevolence, of just reciprocity in all
one's human relations. The man who exhibits the principles of

li and *jen* in all the five natural relationships of life — father and son, older and younger brothers, husband and wife, ruler and subject, friend and friend — is the truly "superior man" whom Confucius delights to honor. Filial piety is the cardinal virtue from which all others grow. Let one have proper respect for one's parents and observe the ancestral customs diligently; then one will have established the right attitude toward all men in every relationship. Confucius is confident of the fundamental goodness of human nature. If a man but master the great rule of reciprocity — not to do anything to anyone which he would not like to have done to himself if he stood in the same relationship [6] — then he will infallibly go right.

While the term "Confucianism" is inappropriate to describe the Chinese religion as a whole, it is appropriate to describe this system of moral philosophy. Its author became, in the course of centuries, one of the most venerated figures in Chinese family worship and state worship — a sort of beloved great-uncle to the whole nation, one might say — and many tablets, shrines, and temples were consecrated to his memory. In 1906, just before the fall of the empire, this venerable agnostic was raised, by imperial edict, to the rank of supreme deity, his only peers being Heaven and Earth! [7]

Of the other philosophers and sages who have influenced Chinese thought and life there are many who would deserve attention in a more exhaustive treatise — Yang Chu, the pessimist; Mo Ti (Mocius), the exponent of universal love; Mencius, who developed the *jen* principle in Confucius' teaching into a complete ethical philosophy, and Hsün Tzŭ, who did the same for the *li* principle; Wang Ch'ung, the materialist; Chu Hsi, the great restorer of Confucianism in the twelfth century A.D. For our purposes, however, it is sufficient to stress the significance of Lao Tzŭ, an older contemporary of Confucius, who founded a school of philosophy and a religious cult which has continued, from that day to this, as a specific ingredient in Chinese religion, quite distinct from Confucianism.

The leading idea of Lao Tzŭ was the idea of *Tao,* the "way" or "order " of Heaven which men should learn to know and express. The idea of *Tao* was not an original idea; it is found in the Confucian teachings as well; but Lao Tzŭ gives an original interpretation of it, as the mysterious Absolute Principle which is behind both the *Yang* and the *Yin,* both Heaven and Earth. " There was a Something," he says, " undifferentiated and yet perfect, before heaven and earth came into being. So still, so incorporeal! It alone abides and changes not. It pervades all, but is not endangered. It may be regarded as the mother of all things. I know not its name; if I must designate it, I call it *Tao.* . . . Man takes his norm from earth; earth from heaven; heaven from *Tao;* the *Tao* from itself." [8]

According to Lao Tzŭ, the great characteristic of the *Tao* is effortlessness: it moves all things while itself remaining unmoved. Hence the man who takes his norm from the *Tao* will be characterized above all by gentleness, humility, frugality, which are the " three jewels " of Taoist ethics. Absolute nonresistance, and faith in the power of good over evil, are part of the Taoist credo. Lao Tzŭ recommends that a man win his way like water, which is very " soft and weak," yet able to displace things that are " firm and strong." " To those who are good, I am good; and to those who are not good, I am also good, and thus all get to be good. To those who are sincere I am sincere; and to those who are not sincere, I am also sincere, and thus all get to be sincere." [9]

When Confucius was asked what he thought of this doctrine of returning good for evil, he replied: " With what, then, will you requite kindness? Requite injury with justice, and kindness with kindness." [10] When Lao Tzŭ discussed the teachings of Confucius, he remarked that all active stirring after benevolence, righteousness, and filial piety was a sad declension from the true way of nature. True goodness, he maintained, was not to be found in " doing good," but in quiet unity with the ultimate principle. The two teachers were thus fundamentally opposed to each other. The one was practical, the other mystical; the one activistic, the other quietistic. Confucius' ethics stopped with the law of retaliation — " an eye for an eye and a tooth for a tooth." Lao Tzŭ, like

Jesus, believed that it was possible for man to be "perfect," as Heaven is perfect when it sends its rain on the just and the unjust. The Confucian and Taoist influences have inevitably remained distinct.

But if Confucius could not comprehend Lao Tzŭ, still less could the multitude. When the Taoist sages, in their mountain retreats, sought to unite themselves with the eternal and unchanging through quiet meditation, the people confused eternity with long life and believed the sages to be possessed of some magic formula for becoming immortal. There grew up a popular belief that they possessed the "elixir of life" and the "philosopher's stone"; that they knew the secrets of alchemy and could transmute base metal into gold; that they could give you good luck in business, fair offspring, and many other earthly benefits, if you paid them the price. Naturally enough, there were charlatans among them who pandered to these tastes; and so Taoism began its long descent into the system of magic and exorcism which is all that is left of it at the present day. There have been great philosophers, like Chuang Tzŭ, who have maintained the doctrine of the founder in its purity and penetrated deeply into the mysteries of the one Being from which all things are derived; but popular Taoism has come to express itself mainly in (a) the exorcism of evil spirits, (b) divination and Feng-shui, and (c) worship of the guardian spirits of the city walls and moats, who protect the city's inhabitants from drought and fire and report their deeds to the lords of heaven and hell — thus determining their fate in the next world. It seems to be the common lot of mystical and metaphysical religions to degenerate into magic and superstition. Christian Platonism and Jewish Cabalism were in the Middle Ages entangled with alchemy and witchcraft in much the same way.

III. BUDDHISM IN CHINA

Buddhism made its way very slowly in China. Indeed, when one considers the practical Chinese temper and the Chinese attachment to family life, it is hard to see how a religion so unworldly and so opposed to the family virtues ever got a foothold at all on Chinese soil. It was viewed with great hostility by Confucian scholars from the start, and regarded as a dangerous rival by the Taoist priests. While it was probably known in China long before the Emperor Ming-Ti (58–75 A.D.) had his famous vision of a " golden man " and invited Indian monks with books and statues to his capital at Lo-yang, it was not until the so-called "Age of Darkness " (265–589 A.D.) that Buddhism began to take root rapidly. In this period of prolonged social chaos and political insecurity, the Chinese people seems to have become somewhat disillusioned about its own inherited principles and more than usually susceptible to foreign influences — as once again at the present day. Indian monks had already for a long time been laboring in China at the work of translating the Buddhist scriptures; now, suddenly, it became possible for them to assume a more aggressive attitude. In the year 363 A.D. a Chinese ruler, of one of the northern dynasties, Shih Chi-lung, for the first time gave permission to his subjects to receive the tonsure as Buddhist monks; and shortly thereafter it was reported that nine-tenths of the inhabitants of the northwestern provinces had been won over to Buddhism. The new religion had become naturalized and assimilated to Chinese culture.

The Hīnayāna scriptures were among the earliest to be translated, but the Hīnayāna ideal of the *Arhat* always seemed antisocial to the Chinese, and never made any headway among them. The Mahāyāna scriptures, however, with their detailed descriptions of merciful and beneficent deities — Buddhas and Bodhisattvas — and their detailed descriptions of heavens and hells, made a deep impression upon an age of helplessness and distress. The first Mahāyāna sect to win a wide popular following was the one in which these features of divine help and celestial reward and punishment received their most pronounced expression: the Chingt'u or " Pure Land " sect, founded by a converted Taoist, Hui Yüan (333–416), who was much influenced by a learned Indian teacher, Kumārajīva, a captive brought to Chang-an in 383 by a Chinese general after the sack of a city in central Asia. The chief object of adoration in this sect is not the historic Bud-

dha, Sākyamuni, but the heavenly Buddha, Amitābha, Lord of
Boundless Light, who dwells in the happy land of the Western
Paradise. It should be explained that in Mahāyāna Buddhism
every great era in cosmic history has both its historic (*manushi*)
Buddha who stoops from heaven to be born on earth, whence he
must painfully win his way back to nirvāna, and also its eternal
(*dhyāni*) Buddha, who never leaves nirvāna, but without effort
creates about himself a vast " Buddha-field " of grace and merit,
represented in Buddhist art as a spiritual effulgence flowing from
his unconscious, meditative figure like a sea of light. Now the
dhyāni Buddha of our age, Amitābha, is an exceptionally gracious
figure. Endless *kotis* of aeons ago he was a human being, a disciple
of the earthly Buddha of that age; and out of the compassion of
his heart he took a vow never to attain to Buddhahood until he
had combined the virtues of all the Buddhas and all the Buddha-
fields into his own, so that all possible divine help might be available to poor mortals who cried out to him in their distress. And
so from his Buddha-field, Sukhāvatī, the Pure Land, there now
flows out to needy men all the merit they need to balance their
guilt, all the comfort they need to carry them through the wilderness of this world; and at death he will come in person to take
them to dwell with him forever. The one real condition of salvation is to call upon the name of Amitābha (O-mi-t'o-fo in Chinese)
as trustfully and as often as possible — a condition which, among
simple people, leads to the habit of murmuring the sacred name
automatically, almost endlessly, throughout the waking moments
of the day, as a charm against all ills. There is likewise a body of
prayers and hymns — generally addressed to O-mi-t'o-fo though
sometimes addressed to certain great Bodhisattvas, like Kuan-Yin,
queen of mercy, and Mi-lo-fo, the Buddha-to-be of the next age
— all of which reminds one greatly of the *bhakti* type of piety in
India, and of certain types of Christianity in which salvation by
divine grace, through simple faith in the name of Jesus, is the
burden of the teaching.

In almost every religion a sect stressing salvation by divine grace
will be found standing in opposition to other sects which stress

salvation by individual effort of some sort. In India, as we have seen, the "cat" school was opposed by the "monkey" school, which taught the necessity of human cooperation in the work of salvation. So in China, where the Pure Land sect offered salvation freely and cheaply to the multitude and even suggested the attractive possibility of saving the souls of one's ancestors through prayers and religious services, there arose two schools which insisted upon the necessity of strenuous self-discipline: the Ch'an or " Meditation" school, founded by the Indian monk Bodhidharma about 520, and another school or group of schools of which the Lü or Vinaya sect, founded by Tao Hsüan (595–667), is typical. These two schools differ from each other in that the second group treasured the Buddhist sacred writings, and endeavored to keep in touch with the traditions of Indian monastic Buddhism through study and travel;[11] while Bodhidharma appealed from all scriptures to the direct authority of the "Buddha-nature in all men" (much as the Quakers appealed from the Christian Scriptures to the "inner light"), for the perception of which he devised a discipline of simple living and mystic meditation, similar in many respects to that of the Taoists. Finally, in the T'ien T'ai school, founded by Chih-K'ai, an older contemporary of Tao Hsüan, the theory was set forth that all these sectarian varieties of Buddhism were taught by the Buddha at different stages in his career to different groups of people, and all represented partial truths. The most inclusive truth, for this school, is set forth in the *Lotus,* which has become the basic scripture for both Chinese and Japanese Buddhism, both of which, in spite of many schools and divisions, tend to be eclectic and tolerant. Another scripture whose influence is pervasive in Chinese Buddhism is the sūtra known as "Brahma's Net," of which there is no Sanskrit original. This is the sūtra whose fifty-eight precepts are set before the monk after he has passed through the ranks of postulant, novice, monk, and saint, and is ready to become a Bodhisattva. It enjoins benevolence of the most positive and outgoing sort, expressing itself in generous deeds and in prayer for the spiritual welfare of all sentient beings, whether living or dead, animal or human.

The greatest period in the history of Chinese Buddhism was the T'ang dynasty (618–907), when Chinese culture became very cosmopolitan, and many foreign influences, including Nestorian Christianity and Manichaeism, were poured into the melting-pot. Among these influences was that of Tibetan Buddhism (Lamaism), which had become quite distinct from Indian Buddhism and developed strong demonistic, mystical, and magical tendencies. Partly stimulated by Tibetan ideas, a new school of Chinese Buddhism, the Chen Yen or "Mystery" school, which was destined to play an important part in fusing Buddhism with Taoism in China and with Shintō in Japan, developed about the year 719. The influence of Buddhism upon Chinese life, art, and culture was at its height at this time; but it never became exclusively dominant; nor did the average Chinese layman ever accept it as his whole creed. He went to the Taoist temple for certain purposes, and guided his ethical relations by the Confucian maxims, even while he prayed to O-mi-t'o-fo and paid for sūtras to be said for the repose of his grandfather's soul in the Buddhist heaven. Buddhism was one of the "three religions" of China, never *the* religion of China; and the "three religions" were embraced simultaneously, synthetically.

In the last thousand years Buddhism has suffered many vicissitudes in China. One of the late T'ang emperors endeavored to suppress it on a wholesale scale; and it never fully recovered from this great persecution. Repeatedly, monasteries have been confiscated and monastic orders secularized. Under the Mongol emperors, Genghis and Kublai Khan, the Tibetan form of Buddhism enjoyed imperial favor and established many "Lama" temples in north China. A revulsion against Buddhism followed, led by the first Ming emperor, who had himself been a Buddhist monk. Today Chinese Buddhism is in a general state of degeneracy, lassitude, and decay. The great Buddhas and Bodhisattvas — with the possible exception of Kuan-Yin — are no longer objects of great popular trust or veneration, though there are signs of a superstitious worship in the little side chapels, where one may pray for earthly benefits like rain, or long life, or the birth of a man-child. In central China, under the leadership of an educated monk, T'ai Hsü, there is going on what is known as the " Buddhist revival." In that region at least — especially at Hangchow — the temples are likely to be kept in fairly good repair, while in north China they are falling into desuetude, and in Canton the images have all been thrown down by municipal order. Only the future can determine whether Buddhism is dying today in China or not. All external appearances indicate that it is.

IV. BUDDHISM AND SHINTOISM IN JAPAN

The Japanese have always been known as an uncommonly hospitable folk, both in the social and in the intellectual sense. Apart from certain periods of antiforeign revulsion, induced by their having imported more new ideas and customs than they could properly assimilate, they have generally shown themselves singularly eager to learn and appropriate whatever was attractive in any other culture with which they have come in contact. During the period since the Meiji Restoration in 1868, the Japanese have assimilated modern western ideas with startling rapidity and thoroughness; but previous to that time, the main influences which shaped their culture came, naturally enough, from China, either directly or by way of Korea. Among these influences Buddhism was the most important. It became, in fact, so integral and so central a part of Japanese life that, down to the Meiji era, Japan might fairly be described as a Buddhist nation — at least in the same sense in which certain western nations have been described as " Christian." Even today, since the official revival of Shintō and the official disestablishment of Buddhism, it may still be said that Buddhism is more vigorously alive and active in Japan than in any other country in the world. Our account of Japanese religion must therefore concern itself primarily with Buddhism, while noting the interactions between Buddhism and other religious tendencies, especially with Shintō, the ancient national religion.

The introduction of Buddhism into Japan coincides with the beginnings of genuine civilization there, in the sixth century A.D. Previous to this, the Japanese were a primitive, hardy, uncultured race of warriors, fishermen, and farmers, gradually unified under the leadership of the Yamato clan, whose chiefs have borne the title of emperor (*Tennō*, or in poetic parlance *Mikado*) since the beginnings of recorded history in the islands. All that we know of Japan before the sixth century is contained in the *Kojiki*, or " History of Antiquity," a collection of narrative legends published in 712 A.D.; the *Nihongi*, or Japanese " Annals," published in Chinese in 720; the *Kogoshūi*, or " Gleaning from Ancient Stories," published in 807; and the *Engishiki*, or ritual code, compiled in the ninth century and promulgated in 927. It is hard to tell what is really ancient and primitive in these books and what has already been affected by Chinese ideas.

The purely native part [12] of the elaborate body of myth and legend contained in these old collections begins with the descent of the cosmogonic deities Izanagi and Izanami over the " bridge of heaven," and the creation of the first island of Japan out of the sea foam stirred up by Izanagi's jeweled spear. On this island, then, the god and goddess alighted, and from their union came forth the other islands in the archipelago, together with the gods of the plains and mountains, trees and food, earth, water and fire. The god of fire's birth proved fatal to Izanami, and she descended to the underworld, followed by Izanagi, who was forced to flee without his mate when — contrary to her warning — he looked upon her decaying body. Out of the things he discarded in his flight, and the water with which he cleansed himself from the impurities of the underworld, other gods were formed.

Among the next generation of deities the two most important proved to be Amaterasu no Ohokami, the sun-goddess, and Susa no wo, the god of the stormy sea and the underworld — whence, no doubt, the still more stormy phenomena of earthquakes and volcanic eruptions were believed to come. The rivalry of these two is the theme of many myths. Susa no wo visits his sister in heaven on a promise of good behavior, but lets loose the " piebald colt of heaven " in her rice fields and commits other misdemeanors, until she withdraws in a rage to the rock cave of heaven, leaving the world in darkness, and has to be lured forth by stratagem. For this

Susa no wo has his beard and his nails plucked out, but nevertheless establishes his son as ruler of the islands, until at last, by order of all the gods, Ninigi, the grandson of the sun-goddess, is established in his place, and becomes the founder of the dynasty of the emperors, " coeval with heaven and earth." With Ninigi's grandson Jimmu Tennō, the first human emperor, who came over from Kyushu to conquer the central island at a date traditionally reckoned as 660 B.C., the age of the gods comes to an end and the age of men begins.

Although this mythology provides an excellent background for the cult of the imperial family, which is so central a feature of modern Shintō, there is reason to believe that neither emperor worship nor ancestor worship was a part of original Shintō.[13] The ancient national religion which still prevailed in the sixth century A.D. was a pure nature worship, paid to the various " high powers " [14] on whose favor or disfavor the precarious lot of the inhabitants of these storm-swept and mountainous islands seemed to depend. Among the heavenly deities the greatest was of course Amaterasu, the sun-goddess; among the earthly, Inari, the rice-god, whose messenger and symbol is the fox. Originally these powers seem to have been worshiped directly in their natural shapes, as living beings but not as human-like persons. Mount Fuji, for example, was not merely the residence of a god; it *was* a god. Indeed, it may be said that the earliest deity of the Japanese was simply their whole natural environment: " the sun, the moon, seas, rivers, mountains, trees, and herbs, and the Great-Eight-Island-Country, i.e. the Land of Japan itself." [15] In a sense — in spite of all the anthropomorphic myths that have grown up about the *kami* — this most ancient form of the Shintō faith is also the most modern; for a love for the land is the most deeply rooted of all sentiments in Japan; and Shintō deities are never represented by anthropomorphic images, but only by symbolic objects called *shintai* or " god-bodies," in which wonder-working power (mana?) is supposed to dwell, and from which this power can be communicated by contagion, and transported, so to speak, in other sacred symbols, such as the curious zigzag strips of folded paper known as *gohei,* to be found at every Shintō shrine. The commonest Shintō "god-bodies" are the mirror, the jewel, and the sword, representing the three gifts which the sun-goddess gave to her "heavenly grandchild," Ninigi. Another form of symbolism which was formerly quite prominent in Japan was phallicism. Contrary to the opinion of certain western writers, the use of phallic emblems had nothing to do with obscene rites. The phallic gods were not gods of fertility, but protecting powers, guardians against ghosts, demons, "dogs of Hades," and other dark forces; and their huge symbols, set at the crossroads — whence they have now been removed by order of the government — were meant to bar the way to all such malignant beings.

Upon this primitive nature worship there was now superimposed, in the sixth century, the whole cultural tradition of China, with especial emphasis upon Confucian ethics and Buddhist theology.

Confucian influence was evident in the growth of the ideal of filial piety, in the general organization of society, and in the development of ancestor worship. This last took deep root in Japan, and took a nationalistic form which it never had in China; for in Japan, on account of its very insularity, patriotic sentiment could become intense and fervent as it never could in a vast, loosely governed country; and the Japanese emperor thus came to focus upon himself all the filial piety which in China has remained dispersed among innumerable ancestral lines. The *Kojiki* and *Nihongi* represent a deliberate revision of Japanese mythology undertaken by imperial decree in order to reinforce this sentiment of loyalty at a time when it was still nascent and feeble.

Along with all these Confucian influences came the still more powerful influence of Buddhism, which was adopted wholesale by the official rulers of Japan very much as Christianity was adopted by the Teutonic and Celtic chieftains at about the same period — because it was associated in their minds with an obviously superior type of civilization. Soga, the imperial minister who embraced Buddhism when its mysterious symbols were first imported from Korea, seems to have understood it about as little as

Clovis understood Christianity; but he was in favor of adopting the civilization of the mainland, and was sure that one had to take the gods of the foreigners with their customs. His rivals warned the emperor against provoking the wrath of the native gods, and, a pestilence ensuing shortly after Soga had set up his weird foreign image of Buddha, his temple was ordered burned and the image pitched into a canal. Forty years later, however (593 A.D.), the Soga family became the power behind the imperial throne, and under the regency of the enlightened Prince Shōtoku Taishi the policy of foreignism triumphed completely. Troops of scholars were dispatched to the great centers of learning in China, very much as they were dispatched to Europe and America by the Emperor Meiji in recent times; and they brought back with them an exact and detailed knowledge of the new religion. Its assimilation in Japan was enormously facilitated a century and a half later by the vision of the monk Gyogi, who was sent by the emperor to the shrine of the sun-goddess at Ise to determine whether a plague which was then raging could best be abated by returning to the old gods of the land, or — as the Buddhists advised — by building a colossal image of the *dhyāni* Buddha Vairochana (Japanese, Biroshana, Lochana, or Dainichi) in his capital at Nara. Gyogi claimed to have been told by the sun-goddess herself that " the sun *is* Biroshana." This initial identification of a Shintō with a Buddhist deity was afterward extended until all the Shintō gods were accommodated in the Buddhist pantheon as Buddhas or Bodhisattvas. Thus for about a thousand years, from the eighth to the eighteenth centuries, Buddhism and Shintoism in Japan were merged in a single religious system, which is generally known as Ryōbu Shintō, " the Twofold Way of the Gods."

All of the main schools of Chinese Buddhism reappeared in Japan, and developed new characteristics. During the early or Nara period of Japanese Buddhism, it was mainly the scholarly, bookish type which prevailed, naturally enough. The Hosso, Kegon, and Ritsu sects, whose temples still survive at Nara — alongside the Todaiji temple with its colossal image of Biroshana — have never attained wide popularity.

Soon after the capital was moved to Kyoto in 794 two great religious leaders, Dengyō Daishi (767–822) and Kōbō Daishi (774–835), returned from study in China and transplanted successfully to Japanese soil the Tendai (T'ien T'ai) and Shingon (Chen Yen) sects, which still remain the groundwork of Japanese Buddhism. Dengyō's monastic establishment, located on Mount Hiei, overlooking Kyoto, grew into a veritable city, with hundreds of temples and many thousands of monks, drawn largely from the aristocracy and exercising a great influence over the politics of the capital. Kōbō's establishment, as befitted the more esoteric character of his sect, was located on a secluded high mountain, Koya-san, some miles to the south of the capital; but from its mysterious precincts it exerted a great fascination upon many young nobles, who retired there from the cares and conflicts of the world, and were at last buried there in the great cemetery — which, from the number of emperors and statesmen whose tombs it contains, is often called " the Westminster Abbey of Japan." It was largely under the influence of Dengyō and Kōbō Daishi that Buddhist theology was expanded to take in all the Shintō gods, and Buddhist ritual was developed into a solemn " high-church " ceremonial which impressed the Jesuit missionaries as a sort of devil's parody of their own high mass. Shingon theology was artistically summarized in two great *mandalas* or charts: the " Diamond Mandala," representing the eternal world of " indestructibles," at the center of which sits Dainichi (Biroshana) the supreme Buddha, surrounded by ring after ring of lesser Buddhas, each in turn surrounded by a ring of Bodhisattvas; and the " Womb Mandala," representing this temporal and transient world of the six material elements, whose reality and power is wholly derived from the other world, but where the Shintō deities are given places of honor. Tendai theology is more metaphysical and less mystical; but, like Shingon theology, its general tendency is pantheistic and hospitable, and its practical effect is to sanctify all the ancient customs of Japan as temporal expressions of eternal truths. No wonder that many young aristocrats found it possible to pursue simultaneously a monastic and a political career, so that the monasteries became at length centers of temporal power and wealth and a serious menace to the state.

The most rapid popular expansion of Japanese Buddhism took place in the period from the tenth to the thirteenth centuries, when the Pure Land teaching was introduced and spread like wildfire among the people. The Pure Land monks differed from the Tendai and Shingon monks very much as the mendicant orders (Franciscans and Dominicans) differed from the older Christian orders of monks: they went out among the people as active evangelists, instead of living a secluded and self-centered life. Greatest of these evangelists were Hōnen Shōnin (1133–1212), founder of the Jōdo sect, and his disciple Shinran (1173–1263), founder of the Jōdo Shin Shu or "True Pure Land" sect. Both were originally adherents of Tendai, but abandoned its elaborate philosophy, ritual, and "good works" for a gospel of simple faith in the blessed name of Amitābha (Japanese, Amida). Hōnen encouraged the Chinese custom of frequently repeating the name of Amida, though insisting that its saving effect consists not in "vain repetition" but in the spirit of humble dependence upon divine grace. Shinran went further, and declared that faith and trust are themselves works of divine grace, the repetition of the sacred name being purely an expression of gratitude. To express his belief that secular life was no obstacle to salvation he broke his monastic vows and married. In this and many other respects his life and teachings remind us strangely of Martin Luther, as the Jesuit missionaries to Japan were the first to note.

Meanwhile, with the rise to power of the shōguns and their feudal retainers and the transfer of the seat of authority from Kyoto to Kamakura, a new class in society, the bushi or knights, became prominent, and a new sect of Buddhism won many adherents among them. This was the Ch'an or Zen sect, introduced from China by the monk Eisai (1141–1215) just about the time when the imperial dynasty was defeated by the shogunate (1185). Its stern self-discipline and taciturnity contrasted strikingly with the voluble, emotional piety of the Pure Land sects, and fitted in admirably with the temper of the warrior class. Thus it came about that a composite ethical ideal, *Bushīdo,* derived partly from Zen meditation and self-restraint, partly from Confucian propriety, and partly from ancient Japanese military codes, came into being, which bears a strong resemblance to the medieval code of chivalry. This has continued to color the morality of the whole samurai class, even since the abolition of feudalism, and through them to give a certain air of self-possession and martial self-devotion to the whole nation. The pervasive influence of the Zen sect is also to be seen in the prevailingly sober and modest character of Japanese art, architecture, and household furnishings; and two very character- istic national customs, tea ceremony and symbolic flower arrange- ment, are said to have been introduced by members of the sect.[16]

Another sect of a highly patriotic character was founded a cen- tury later by Nichiren, the "Buddhist prophet" (1222–82). He was a fisherman's son, educated in the great Tendai monastery on Mount Hiei, above Kyoto, where he learned to love the *Lotus* scripture and to judge all things by its standards and its prophecies. To his keen, severe, and honest eyes, the world which he met when he left the slopes of Mount Hiei and made his way to the capital of the shōguns at Kamakura seemed honeycombed with evil and ripe for destruction. All that he saw went to confirm his belief that the world was now entering upon the last of the three stages of degeneration sketched out in the *Lotus.* Religion and politics were equally corrupt. In the political order, it was a monstrous thing that the heaven-ordained emperor should have been defeated and overthrown by upstart feudal princelings; but this, thought Nichiren, was a divine punishment for the acceptance of false religious teachings. Against the Shingon sect, the Zen sect, and especially the Pure Land sects, he spoke out with bitter vehemence, declaring that they had displaced the true Buddha, Sākyamuni, and put imaginary Buddhas in his place. Unless religion could be reformed in head and members he predicted that Japanese society would go from bad to worse and fall prey to a foreign invader. For his invectives Nichiren suffered the usual fate of prophets. He was banished, and barely escaped execution. But the Mongol invasions, which threatened to fulfill his dire predictions, brought him back into favor for a time — like Savonarola after the French invasion of Italy. He seems to have regarded himself as a great Bodhisattva, sent by heaven to restore the true faith and save Japan. As such he was accepted by a multitude of followers, who to this day exemplify much of the ardent spirit of the founder as they repeat his words: " I will be the Pillar of Japan. I will be the Eyes of Japan. I will be the great Vessel of Japan. Inviolable shall remain these oaths." Naturally enough, their attitude toward other Buddhist sects is more intolerant than is the usual Buddhist attitude, and their attitude toward foreign influences, such as Christianity, tends to be one of outspoken hostility.

Since Nichiren, no new sect of first-rate importance has emerged in Japanese Buddhism; but throughout the age of the shōguns the principal sects already mentioned continued to advance in power and influence, under the protection of the secular authorities. Like the Christian monastic orders in the age of feudalism they often became so wealthy and powerful that they were a social menace. It was the Emperor Shirakawa (1073–86) who declared that there were three things he could not control: the waters of the river Kamo, the fall of the dice, and the monks of Buddha. The dictator Nobunaga, five centuries later, found that he could not pacify the land and make an end of civil war without attacking the monasteries, which at this time had become armed citadels, feudal strongholds which took sides in all the political struggles of the day. So he dealt a terrific blow at the most powerful of them all, the great Tendai establishment on Mount Hiei. Three thousand temples and monasteries were burned in one immense holocaust, and thousands of monks perished by fire or by sword. From this blow the Tendai sect has suffered ever since, though its scripture, the *Lotus,* continues to be *the* classic scripture of Japanese Buddhism.

Nobunaga went so far in his opposition to Buddhism as to encourage Jesuit missionaries in their endeavor to introduce a rival religion; but the Tokugawa shōguns, whose dynasty he had been instrumental in raising to supremacy, soon came to regard Christianity as a still greater menace to their power; and in their endeavor to detect and extirpate the Christians they required that all their subjects be registered as members of some Buddhist sect. Under this system of state patronage, coupled with severe controls and requirements, Buddhism throve numerically and languished in spirit. The priesthood was well paid — and ill respected. Thus the way was paved for the reform movement of the eighteenth and nineteenth centuries which, beginning in a revival of interest in ancient Japanese culture, of the period previous to Chinese influence, led at last to the undoing of the synthesis between Buddhism and Shintoism and the replacement of Buddhism by " Pure Shintoism " as the religion of the state.

The downfall of the shōguns and the restoration of the emperors, in 1868, was the occasion of a vast upheaval in the religious system. Buddhism had become identified with the feudal order, and seemed likely to perish with it. Buddhist images and Buddhist influences were zealously eliminated from the Shintō shrines — even, in many instances, to the aesthetic curve in the entrance gate or *torii* — and for a few years Shintoism was the only legally recognized religion. Later religious liberty was declared, and a distinction was made between " official Shintō," an allegedly non-religious national cult in which all Japanese must to some degree participate, and " sectarian Shintō," which is admittedly religious but not required. Sectarian Shintō takes many forms. Especially at the Inari shrines, dedicated to the god of rice — and rice-wine — a very primitive type of polytheism is practiced. Side by side with this popular and superstitious religion of the people there have lately sprung up many Shintō cults of a highly refined and spiritualized sort, having at least some germs of a more than national outlook. Prominent among these are Tenrikyo, which practices religious healing somewhat in the manner of Christian Science, and Konkokyo, a monotheistic sect which subordinates all the Shintō gods to a supreme " Heaven-and-Earth-Including-Deity," ruling not only over the Japanese but over all the sons of men. Other Shintō sects exalt the ancient principle of " purity " or " sincerity " — originally connected with the avoidance of ritual impurities — into an ethical principle of universal scope. Thanks to these contemporary examples, Genchi Kato is able to show that Shintoism has evolved through all the known stages of religious development, from primitive animism and nature worship to spiritual mono-theism.[17]

Contemporary Japanese religion, like contemporary Japanese life in general, presents a strangely assorted mixture of elements old and new. As taxicabs and ancient two-wheel vehicles jostle each other in the streets of Ōsaka and primitive agriculture crowds up close to the very walls of modern factories in many a small provincial town, so all sorts of religious tendencies vie with one another for possession of the Japanese soul. Among them all, the various Buddhist sects are probably the most powerful; for the rude shock of disestablishment in 1868 seems to have given Japa-nese Buddhism a new lease of life. Modern Christian missions have certainly been among the most powerful factors in stimulat-ing the rebirth of both Buddhism and Shintoism; both have borrowed much from Christianity, including hymns, forms of organization like the Y.M.C.A., and an interest in social service. All these competing religious influences are held within certain bounds, however, by the firm restraining hand of the national cult (official Shintō), which aims to subordinate and assimilate every element in Japanese life to the one supreme end of national greatness. Perhaps the chief religious issue in Japan today is whether the national cult is indeed to become the one religion, by suppressing or taming all more than national tendencies in Bud-dhism, sectarian Shintō, and Christianity, or whether these tend-encies are going to be able to subdue and internationalize the as yet unconquered Japanese spirit. Just at present it looks as though the former might be the likelier outcome. Love of their beautiful land and loyal devotion to her sun-descended rulers are still the principal elements in the religion of the Japanese.

NOTES

[1] See *India and its Faiths,* pp. 417–423.

[2] *Ibid.,* p. 392.

[3] In ancient times, especially during the ceremonies at the beginning of the four sea-sons, the ancestors were represented by " personators," who sat stiffly in their respective places in the shrine, and received the offerings and prayers of the family with solemn mien.

[4] Nora Waln, *The House of Exile*, pp. 108, 109. The funeral described is that of an elder, hence exceptionally magnificent.

[5] For the translation and interpretation of this often misinterpreted remark I am indebted to Professor Lyman Cady of Cheeloo University. Legge translates, "My prayer has been for a long time" (*Analects*, Bk. 7, chap. 34).

[6] In the *Great Learning* (X, 2) the cardinal principle of Confucian ethics is summarized as follows: "What a man dislikes in his superiors, let him not display in the treatment of his inferiors; what he dislikes in his inferiors, let him not do in the service of his superiors; what he hates in those who are before him, let him not therewith precede those who are behind him; what he hates in those who are behind him, let him not therewith follow those who are before him; what he hates to receive on the right, let him not bestow on the left; what he hates to receive on the left, let him not bestow on the right: this is what is called 'The principle with which, as with a measuring-square, to regulate one's conduct.'"

[7] On the worship of Confucius, see George Foot Moore, *History of Religion*, I, 20–22.

[8] *Ibid.*, p. 50.

[9] *Ibid.*, pp. 52, 53.

[10] *Ibid.*, p. 36.

[11] Among the many Chinese travelers who braved the dangers of the overland route to India, or the still greater dangers of the water route, the most famous were Fa-Hsien, whose trip began in 399 A.D., and Hsüan-Tsang, a seventh-century traveler whose journey became the basis of a sort of Arabian Nights book of adventure, *The Journey to the West*. From these Chinese travelers we have most of the information now extant concerning the decline and fall of Buddhism in India.

[12] There is also an account of the birth of heaven and earth out of chaos by simple gravitation, and of the emergence of other cosmogonic deities previous to Izanagi and Izanami, but this appears to have been borrowed from China.

[13] See Moore, *History of Religion*, I, 110–111, where this conclusion is based upon a comparison of the *Kojiki* and *Nihongi* with the *Engishiki*.

[14] *Kami*, the Japanese word for deity, means anything or anybody to which or to whom one "looks up" as to a superior being. Cf. the Latin *superi*.

[15] G. Kato, *A Study of Shintō, the Religion of the Japanese Nation* (Tokyo, 1926), p. 10.

[16] See Okakura Kakuzo, *The Book of Tea*, for a very poetic and discerning account of the philosophical and religious significance of tea ceremony. Cf. the following sentence from a lecture of Professor Anesaki's in Pratt's *Pilgrimage of Buddhism*, p. 491: "Fans, kakemonos, calligraphy, the Japanese smile, the sternness of expression, everything now known as peculiarly Japanese, was the product of Zen, directly or indirectly."

[17] Kato, *op. cit.*, Chap. XX.

BIBLIOGRAPHY

Friess and Schneider. *Op. cit.*, pp. 42–55, 141–213.
Moore, G. F. *Op. cit.*, Vol. I, Chaps. I–VII.
Hume, R. E. *Op. cit.*, Chaps. VI–VIII.
Cave, Sydney. *Op. cit.*, Chap. IV.
Barton, G. A. *Op. cit.*, Chaps. XI, XII.
Pratt, J. B. *The Pilgrimage of Buddhism*, Chaps. VII–XXXI.
Soothill, W. E. *The Three Religions of China.*
Anesaki, M. *History of Japanese Religion.*
Kato, G. *A Study of Shintō, the Religion of the Japanese Nation.*

4.

OCCIDENTAL RELIGION:
PARSIISM, JUDAISM, ISLAM

I. THE WATERSHED BETWEEN EAST AND WEST: PERSIA

IN the vicinity of Bombay there live about one hundred thousand members of a religious community that contrasts sharply with the surrounding Hindu population: the Parsees. They are practically the sole surviving adherents of the ancient Persian religion, commonly known as Zoroastrianism. When Persia fell under Mohammedan rule after the battle of Nahawand in 642 A.D. most of those who wished to remain true to the old faith fled the country and took refuge in this part of India, where their descendants have prospered greatly and become one of the most respected and influential elements in the population.

One would hardly imagine, from a hasty comparison between the modern Parsees and their Hindu neighbors, that they sprang originally from the same ancestral stock and had the same religion; yet such is the case. The remote ancestors of the Parsees came from the same plateau country north of the Hindu Kush mountains whence came the Aryan invaders of north India. Their religion was substantially identical with the religion of the Vedas, as is evidenced by the fact that many of the vedic gods appear in some form — often as demons — in the Persian scriptures. Yet from this common source in primitive nature worship the two religions have diverged more and more. The ancestors of the Hindus, moving southeastward through the Khyber Pass into a subtropical and well watered land, sank more and more into a dreamy, meditative, unworldly religion of resignation and absorption in the one Reality. The ancestors of the Parsees, moving southwestward over barren steppes and deserts, were forced to take a more active and militant attitude toward their world. To them nature was not a vast enfolding life into which man could sink and be at rest; it was the scene of a great conflict between good and evil forces, in which man must bear an active part if the good was to triumph.[1] All that we commonly mean by the "western" spirit of active combat with destiny, in contrast with the "eastern" spirit of quiescent resignation, is already embodied in the contrast between the Parsees and their Hindu cousins. There in the plateau country behind the Hindu Kush the religious "watershed" between Orient and Occident may be located: one stream flowing eastward through India and Indo-China to China and Japan; another from the same source flowing westward through Persia, Arabia, and Palestine to fertilize the whole western world. If the Hindus were the original Orientals, the Persians were the original Occidentals.

That is not to say that Persia is the fountainhead of Occidental religion in the same sense that India is the fountainhead of Oriental religion. From India to Japan a single great stream of religious development flows, to which the national cults of the countries through which it passes have become at times hardly more than tributaries. In the west, the main stream takes its rise in Palestine, and Persian religion is merely tributary thereto; yet as the first country in which a distinctly Occidental type of religion flourished on a large scale, Persia occupies a place of exceptional importance; and the Parsee faith accordingly demands a degree of attention out of all proportion to its numerical strength.

The prophet Zoroaster (or Zarathustra), whom the modern Parsees regard as the founder of their religion, is almost certainly an historical character, but the dates of his birth and death and the details of his career remain in considerable doubt. He probably lived during the seventh century B.C., which would make him a contemporary of the later pre-exilic Hebrew prophets. While his Hebrew contemporaries were still groping their way, step by step, toward ethical monotheism, Zoroaster seems to have arrived at it in a single flash. According to his own statement in the Gathas — the oldest and most interesting part of the classic scripture known as the Avesta — he had the true religion revealed to him directly by the supreme god Ahura Mazda, into whose pres-

ence he was conducted by the archangel Good Thought; and after
a series of visions had prepared him for his task, he spent the rest
of his days summoning men to take sides with Ahura Mazda in his
great conflict with the principle of falsehood and evil in the world.
After years of fruitless endeavor the prophet at length converted a
king (or chief) named Vishtaspa, who began the work of over-
throwing the old priesthood and the old gods — now regarded
as evil demons — and setting up a new moral code in terms of the
new revelation. According to tradition, Zoroaster perished at the
hands of his enemies in his seventy-seventh year — whether murdered by priests of the old religion or killed in a religious war with
the unbelieving Turanians, is not clear.

   The central idea of Zoroastrianism has never greatly altered
since the time of the prophet. It is the idea of a cosmic conflict
between the forces of good and the forces of evil, the one host led by
Ahura Mazda, who created the world through his Word of Wisdom, the other led by an evil principle which is sometimes simply
called the Lie (*Druj*) but which later theology generally personified as Ahriman, the "Enemy," a conception parallel to the
Hebrew-Christian concept of Satan or the "Adversary." It is
customary to cite this as the classic example of religious dualism.
The dualism, actually, is not complete, for the evil principle in
Zoroastrianism is not coeternal with the good. It was in the good
principle, not in the evil, that Zoroaster found his answer to the
problem of creation; and there runs through the whole history of
his religion an ardent expectation that in the end good will
triumph over evil. In comparison with the mystical monism of
the Hindus, however, the Persian creed is certainly dualistic; it
tends to give to its adherents an attitude of military aggressiveness
and moral strenuousness quite foreign to the Hindu temperament.
Life, to the Parsee, is a chance to participate in the cosmic conflict
on the side of the good; to help to turn the tide in that great battle;
and, as a faithful soldier, to win praise and rewards from his divine
leader when he enters into the life hereafter. Three days after
death, at the bridge of separation, the soul of the righteous, led by
his conscience in the shape of a fair maiden, passes safely over the

bridge to the place of endless light, while to the soul of the wicked the bridge becomes narrow as a razor-edge, and he falls into the place of endless darkness.

A popular compendium of the Parsee faith sums up its distinctive tenets in three simple affirmations: " (1) The Existence of Mazda, the All-Wise Lord; (2) the Immortality of the Soul, or the Life Hereafter; (3) our Responsibility for our thoughts, words, and actions." " If you will always keep your thoughts pure, that is, if you will think of nothing but what is true and proper, and if after such true and good thoughts you will speak nothing but the truth, and if after speaking nothing but the truth you will do nothing but what is good and righteous, then Ahura Mazda will reward you for all that, and you will pass a happy life." [2] According to this strenuous creed, there is no divine grace which aids a man in the struggle between the worse and better elements in his own nature; " every man is his own savior." Zoroaster is simply the prophet through whom Ahura Mazda has revealed the true way of life and defined the conditions which must be met if salvation is to be earned. This is almost precisely the position taken by the deists and other religious rationalists during the eighteenth century Enlightenment. The deists, in defining what they called "natural religion " in contrast to orthodox Christianity's emphasis upon " the grace of God," unconsciously reverted to the simple creed of the Parsees: " God, freedom, and immortality." It must be admitted that Parsees have not always been so severely monotheistic as this creed would suggest. In the period when the later portions of the Avesta were written they reverted to polytheistic nature worship, of which some vestiges still remain in their reverence for the sun, fire, earth, and water.

The code of ethics implied in the Parsee creed has varied somewhat from age to age. To Zoroaster himself, the chief moral imperatives were those required to support the values of a simple pastoral existence: respect for and kindness to domestic animals, especially the cow and the dog; vigilance and courage in warding off the attacks of wild beasts and human enemies; truth-telling and generosity in one's dealings with fellow believers; personal purity to maintain one's strength and courage at a high pitch. When a settled agricultural life took the place of a pastoral life, it became the duty of good Zoroastrians to destroy noxious weeds and animals; and they had the satisfaction of knowing that in so doing they were dealing a blow at Ahriman and his demons, while in making two blades of corn grow where one grew before they were extending the domains of Ahura Mazda. (The attitude of the Parsees is thus the reverse of that of the Jains, for whom all forms of life — including snakes and weeds — are equally sacred.) As the Persian empire rose to power and magnificence, cultural values were added to this simple ethical code. In the Vendidad, three kinds of good deeds are singled out for especial praise: " (1) to help the poor; (2) to help a man to marry . . . ; (3) to give education to those who are in search of it." [3] The modern Parsees are perhaps the most charitable and well educated element in the Bombay population, poverty and illiteracy being practically unknown among them.

The Parsee ritual is picturesque and distinctive. It is based upon reverence for fire, earth, and water as good gifts of the wise Lord. Ahura Mazda is present in all places and his power is manifested in all good things, but the Parsee feels his presence especially manifest in the fiery beams of the sun and in the ever burning fire which is the central object in all Parsee temples. As he enters the temple, the worshiper is given by the priest a pinch of ashes from the fire, which he applies to his forehead, reminding himself that his body, like the fire, is a transient creature of God, destined to become dust and ashes, but resolving to spread while he lives the aroma of good deeds as the sacred fire spreads the aroma of sandalwood. There are no regular services of worship and instruction at these fire temples; the Parsees go there individually when they please, and gather there collectively only on rare and special occasions; but every evening they assemble in large numbers on the western water front of Bombay to repeat old avestan prayers and purify their minds in the presence of that most glorious symbol of Ahura Mazda, the setting sun. Perhaps their strangest ritual observance is connected with their reverence for earth and water, which forbids them to defile the purity of these elements by burying their dead in the ground or committing them to the sea, as unbelievers ignorantly do. The bodies of good Parsees are accordingly exposed in great amphitheaters known as Towers of Silence, where they are soon plucked clean of flesh by the vultures, and the skeleton hygienically dried by the scorching Indian sun — after which the crumbling bones are tumbled into a central pit and dispersed as clean dust with streams of water.

In the course of the centuries the ritual element in Zoroastrianism has come to smother and conceal its moral and religious elements to a considerable extent — as is apt to happen in all " religions of law and good works." Many modern Parsees regret this loss, and are endeavoring by improved methods of religious instruction to revive the consciousness of the inner meaning of their time-honored observances. Whatever the future may hold for this little band of survivors, nothing can destroy the significance of the Parsee faith in the history of Occidental religion; for at two crucial periods in the development of the Hebrew-Christian tradition — after the Babylonian Exile and during the conflict of religions in the late Roman Empire — it came into direct touch with Persian ideas, which thus became a part of our whole western heritage. The story of the three Magi (i.e., Zoroastrians) who brought precious gifts to the Christ child at his birth is symbolic of the fact that a profound affinity exists between this oldest form of Occidental religion and all later and more highly developed forms.

II. THE BEGINNINGS OF THE HEBREW TRADITION: MOSES AND THE PROPHETS

In every large urban center in the world today are to be found representatives of the most rudely buffeted but most persistently self-perpetuating of all religious groups: the Jews. They are always conspicuous because of their high degree of group solidarity, their faithful preservation of certain peculiar manners and customs, and their outstanding success in all lines of endeavor where keen intelligence is required: as merchants and bankers, as lawyers and physicians, as scientists and philosophers, as statesmen and social reformers. In spite of their conspicuous success — or rather *because* of it — their position is always somewhat precarious, for in all parts of the world they have met with jealousy, opposition, and cordial dislike in proportion to the degree of eminence to which they have attained; and in most parts of the world they have experienced downright persecution. Driven from place to place by the changing tides of fortune they have become wanderers upon the face of the earth, forever looking for a promised homeland, forever disappointed when they think they have found it. A strange people, compounded of oddly contrasting traits, as they themselves are the first to admit. Yet whether one likes or dislikes the Jews one is bound to recognize that the main line of religious tradition in the west flows through them, as the main line in the east flows through the Hindus. Whatever we in the west have come to regard as of eternal value is bound up in some way with the history of this " eternal people."

The ancient Semitic ancestors of the modern Jews originally practiced the sort of religion common to most primitive kinship groups, worshiping the personified natural forces and objects with which their welfare seemed to be most intimately connected.

Among the dwellers in the hills and plains of the " land of Canaan," where agriculture was the chief means of livelihood from a very early date, the principal object of worship was a goddess of fertility, called in Hebrew Asherah (Phoenician, Astarte), whose symbol was the evergreen tree, usually represented by a simple wooden pole (itself known as the " Asherah ") which stood on each hilltop or " high place " where her worship was carried on. Beside the pole on the hilltop stood an upright stone (*Mazzebah*) representing the male consort of the goddess. This male god was master (Ba‘al) of the bit of territory surrounding his place of worship; the rainfall and fertility of his domain were supposed to be dependent on the sacrifices which were poured upon his stone.

Among the half-nomads who lived along the fringe of the fertile land the principal objects of worship were the spirits that were believed to gather about the wells and springs where the people watered their flocks, and about certain trees like the terebinth and the tamarisk that remained green and shady on the arid borders of the desert. Farther out in the sands, the tent-dwelling nomads worshiped the moon, by whose cool and friendly light they could travel about and live in the open as they never could in the scorching heat of the day. Sacred to them were also certain animals like the camel, the locust, etc., which were sometimes taken as the totem of a tribe. The Hebrew Passover feast seems to be descended from primitive celebrations at which the totem animal (or, later, the firstlings of the flocks and herds) was eaten raw and whole (hoofs, bones, and all!) under the light of the full moon, every vestige having to be consumed before sunrise. One may perceive that such ceremonials, crude and revolting as they look today, helped to establish a powerful sense of solidarity between the members of the tribe, in which the moon, the animal allies, and all friendly powers of nature seemed to participate. To this enlarged kinship group loyal and reverent devotion was really due; and to see in such worship nothing but superstition is to betray a want of historical imagination.

The primitive sense of loyal kinship gave way to a deeper sense of moral responsibility among the Hebrew branch of the Semites, owing to dramatic events which befell a certain clan or tribe of their connection. Forced to go down to Egypt for food in a time of famine, this tribe became enslaved there, and escaped only after a considerable lapse of time through the initiative of a great patriot, Moses, whose strangely impressive figure, half veiled in the mists of antiquity, stands forth first in the line of Hebrew religious leaders which culminates in Jesus, the Christ.

Moses had received an Egyptian education, and might have passed his life in luxury had he been content to forget his kinsmen. Instead he cast in his lot with them and was driven into exile. The place of his exile was probably the volcanic region just beyond the Gulf of Akaba, the shallow northeastern arm of the Red sea. The god of this region, Yahweh, was a god of thunder and lightning and military might, believed to dwell in the interior of an active volcano, Mount Sinai. The exiled patriot married a daughter of Jethro, a priest of Yahweh, and became a devotee of the cult.

Brooding over the plight of his people and the might of his god, Moses seems to have become convinced that here was power adequate for their deliverance. Lifted above all fear by an exalted sense of mission he returned and demanded the release of the captives; and this being refused, led them forth by night, following the glow and smoke of Sinai as a beacon. The Egyptians pursued; and to the awe and wonder of the cowering slaves were overwhelmed and drowned by returning waters at a spot on the Gulf of Akaba where they themselves had lately passed over dry-shod.

Whether this marvelous deliverance was due to the "strong east wind" mentioned in one biblical account, or whether it was due to a raising and subsidence of the sea bottom such as frequently accompanies volcanic eruptions, it made an indelible impression on the Hebrew slaves. Arrived at the foot of Sinai, they made a solemn covenant with its god of thunder, vowing to be as faithful to him as he had been faithful to them, and to obey his commandments (interpreted by Moses) as the condition of his continued guidance and protection. Departing from the region, they took with them stones from the sacred mountain, enclosed in a box or "ark," as emblems of his presence with them. Their relation to Yahweh, being thus based upon an oath of fealty and a debt of gratitude, was from the start a more *ethical* relationship than that of other tribes to their gods; and Yahweh himself, as champion of the weak against their oppressors and ordainer of just laws to regulate their behavior toward one another, was a far more ethical god than his neighbors and rivals.

The subsequent history of all the Hebrews was written from the point of view of this Yahwistic tribe, and presents a long series of misadventures — from the Wilderness Wandering to the Babylonian Exile — which they themselves believed to be due to their wavering loyalty to Yahweh, who permitted them to fall into disaster whenever they failed to keep their side of the contract made at Mount Sinai. Humanly enough, they forgot their deliverer pretty regularly in times of prosperity, and remembered him again, ruefully, in times of adversity. Their religious leaders took advantage of each recurrent spasm of repentance to issue new warnings concerning the nature and will of Yahweh, which might serve to prevent future sins and future calamities. Now it is easy to see that not all of the sufferings of this much-tried people were really due to their sins. It was not because Yahweh was angry at their sins, but because of the rise and fall of Egypt, Assyria, and Babylonia that the inhabitants of Palestine encountered such a series of political calamities and humiliations. Located on the " bridge " between the valleys of the Nile and the Euphrates, they were caught between contending armies as often as the political equilibrium of the Near East was disturbed. But as time went on the sentinels of Yahweh, from their exposed position on that bridge, began to view the world with deeper insight into the actual cause-and-effect relationships which govern its events, and to ground their appeals upon principles of social justice which still apply to modern nations, in spite of all the changes of the centuries. If the God of Moses sometimes seems as fanciful a figure as Pêlê, the volcano-goddess of the Hawaiians, it is impossible so lightly to dismiss the God of the reforming prophets who lived before and during the Babylonian Exile. In their teachings, as skeptical a mind as Matthew Arnold's found evidence of a real " power not ourselves that makes for righteousness," whose ways and laws no man or nation can safely disregard.

It is a significant fact that Elijah, the first great reforming prophet, came from the open desert east of the Jordan river. The pastoral Hebrews to the east and south of Palestine had remained closer to the simple ways of the desert and truer to the religion of Yahweh than their relatives who had settled down to an agricultural life in the central hills and plains. Particularly after the unification of the country under David and Solomon a process of rapid assimilation went on between the religious and social systems of the Canaanite inhabitants (Amorites, Jebusites, etc.) and the Hebrew conquerors, until Ba'al-worship and private land tenure — with their evil accompaniments, sacred prostitution and the enslavement of the poor by the rich — had overlaid or displaced the worship of Yahweh and the old communal property system which prevailed in the desert. The northern half of the country had revolted against the south after the death of Solomon, in the endeavor to go back to a simpler and juster regime; but the northern kings soon reverted to Canaanitish ways; and the climax came when King Ahab married a Phoenician princess, Jezebel, who introduced the worship of Melkart, the Ba'al-god of Sidon, and encouraged her husband to invade the traditional property rights of his subjects.

It is hard to say whether Elijah was more moved to indignation by the worship of foreign gods or by the illegal requisitioning of Naboth's vineyard; the honor of Yahweh and the rights of the poor were completely interwoven in his mind. Driven from the country for his denunciation of the king, he went back — symbolically enough — to Mount Sinai to recoup his strength, and returned thence, like Moses to Egypt, as the leader of a revolutionary movement that resulted in the massacre of all the priests of Ba'al and eventually swept the ruling dynasty from the throne. In his primitive ferocity the God of Elijah resembles the God of Moses; yet it is recorded that when Elijah went to Sinai he listened for the voice of God in the earthquake, wind, and fire, and heard nothing that spoke to his soul until, in the ensuing silence, he heard a " still small voice." That famous phrase, whatever it may originally have meant, foreshadows the spiritualization that the conception of God was to undergo at the hands of the great galaxy of prophetic figures which burst suddenly and amazingly into view in the eighth and seventh centuries B.C.

Amos, the first of these prophets to leave his message in writing, was like Elijah a half-nomad, living on the borders of the southern desert and viewing the settled civilization of the Northern Kingdom with clear-eyed disdain. Like his predecessor, he took the side of the poor against the rich and denounced the corruption of justice in tones of indignation; but he exceeded Elijah in the range of his vision. It was enough for Elijah that Yahweh and his ways should be made supreme *among the Hebrews;* but it never occurred to him that the sway of Yahweh extended beyond those boundaries. Amos dared to assert that Yahweh punishes *all* forms of social oppression, whether among the Israelites or among their neighbors, with even-handed justice; and he prophesied that the Northern Kingdom would soon be destroyed in consequence of its social iniquities.

Amos' revolutionary insight was taken up and developed by a long line of successors. Hosea, the last prophet of the Northern Kingdom, was as conscious of impending disaster as his grim predecessor had been; but under the influence of domestic tragedy he came to the conception that the punishment was disciplinary, not vindictive, and God's love — like Hosea's own love for his unfaithful wife — was always eager to heal and restore the erring people at the first sign of repentance. When the Northern Kingdom fell the prophetic line passed over to the Kingdom of Judah, and the message of Amos and Hosea was taken up by Isaiah and Micah. Their preaching was more successful than that of the northern prophets. They succeeded in convincing many of their compatriots that in the maelstrom of political forces which threatened to engulf the little kingdom, they should put their trust not in chariots, horses, and political alliances, but in faithfulness to Yahweh and his law of justice. In alliance with certain priests of Yahweh the prophetic party cleansed the temple at Jerusalem of all idolatrous rites, and inaugurated a program of humanitarian legislation. A wave of reaction almost immediately drove them out of power and kept them in retirement for half a century; but they used their enforced leisure to elaborate a whole new code of law for the kingdom, to which they attached the name of Moses; and in 621 B.C., when King Josiah came to the throne, this new code, which we now know as the Book of Deuteronomy, became the basis of drastic reforms. The priestly element in these reforms — doubtless strongly seconded by the king, in the interest of national unification — is to be seen in the attempt to destroy the village shrines and center all worship in the temple at Jerusalem. The prophetic element is to be seen in the prevailing note of concern for all oppressed or unfortunate people. " Thou shalt not pervert the judgment of the stranger, nor of the fatherless, nor take a widow's raiment to pledge: but thou shalt remember that thou wast a bondman in Egypt, and Yahweh thy God redeemed thee thence." [4]

Among the supporters of this program, at first, was the prophet Jeremiah, last of the great pre-exilic prophets; but as time went on and new calamities loomed up he became convinced that no amount of temple ritual and no amount of social reform could insure the safety of little Judah. In his teaching the tie between the religion of Yahweh and political nationalism was completely severed. He was prepared to face the inevitable, give up political independence, accept Babylonian rule, and make of religion henceforth a personal relation between the individual and his God. But his cosmopolitan message was not acceptable to his compatriots. Left behind after the great deportation to Babylon in 586 B.C., as one likely to exert a calming influence on the remaining populace, he unsuccessfully tried to check an uprising, and was carried off to Egypt by the fleeing rebels — there, according to tradition, to meet his death at their hands. With his death the first main division of Hebrew history — sometimes called the "Yahwistic" period — came to an end, and the age of Judaism begins.

III. THE DEVELOPMENT OF ORTHODOX JUDAISM

Modern orthodox Judaism was born in ancient Babylon. It is the religion which has come down, unaltered in its essential principles, from that "faithful remnant" of the deported Judeans who remained true to the God of their fathers when he seemed to have deserted them. They were probably few in number, but their influence has persisted, while the many who adopted Babylonian manners and beliefs have vanished from our view, along with multitudes of other Jews in later times who have conformed to their local environment and permitted themselves to be "assimilated." The outstanding characteristic of the orthodox Jew, from that day to this, has been his capacity to resist assimilation and run true to type.

The basis of this persistent type was laid during the years of the

Exile by a group of priests and prophets under the ruling influence of the priest-prophet Ezekiel. To him and his fellows the disaster which had come upon their people seemed primarily due to moral and religious rather than to strictly political causes. The people had been false to their God. They had permitted his holy temple and his holy city to be defiled with immoralities and idolatries, in express disobedience to his commands given to Moses. The promises given to Moses had thereby been rendered null and void, and the presence of God had departed from his violated sanctuary — as Ezekiel saw in a famous vision — leaving the people helpless before the assault of their enemies. But now let the people repent them of their sins, let them become a holy people, cherishing the commandments of God, and God would return to them in exile, and in due time restore them to their native land. The whole history of the Hebrew people, first sketched by prophetic historians in the early days of the divided kingdom, began now to be re-written [5] to indicate this theory; and an elaborate code of ritual purity was drawn up, to keep the temple and people holy and unde-filed thenceforth in the sight of God, if he should deign to give them another chance. This was all for the future, since formal ritual worship of the one God might be offered only in his one chosen place, in Jerusalem; but meanwhile they could at least as-semble on every Sabbath day to study God's law and plead for deliverance. These weekly assemblies were the beginning of the synagogue, in which Jewish religion now centers.

Deliverance came with a speed and decisiveness that did much to confirm the faithful remnant in their audacious trust in God. Cyrus the Great began his career of conquest, and the power of Babylonia rapidly waned before the power of Persia. An anony-mous Jewish prophet, the so-called " Second Isaiah," [6] hailed Cyrus as the Lord's " Anointed One " (Hebrew, Messiah), who would restore the Jews to Palestine and inaugurate a glorious new age in which the influence of God's Suffering Servant, Israel, would penetrate the whole earth and bring all nations to the worship of the one true God. The first part of this prophecy was immediately fulfilled; when Cyrus took Babylon in 538 B.C. he liberated the

Jews and permitted them to return at once to Palestine, if they pleased. But the second part of it was not so easily accomplished. The little group of returned exiles had set their ideals so high that when they got back to Palestine they found none to cooperate with them; indeed, they refused to have much to do with their relations who had been left in the land, since they had intermarried with the heathen and were no longer " pure and holy," as the new code required. The little community managed after considerable prophetic exhortation to rebuild the temple; but the nations of the world showed no signs of flocking there to worship; and the Jews found it hard to worship there in peace themselves, since their economic and political position was most insecure. At last, under a decree of Darius the Great, a Jewish official in the Persian court named Nehemiah was sent out as governor of Judea; and he, with his associate Ezra the Scribe, in the year 444 B.C., after rebuilding the walls of Jerusalem, established orthodox Judaism as the official religion of a little political protectorate which, with one brief period of independence, lasted on through many vicissitudes under various foreign suzerainties, until the destruction of Jerusalem in 70 A.D.

During the whole of this " period of the Second Temple" the main effort of the priests and scribes who dominated public policy was to preserve the ritual purity of the people and encourage strict obedience to the code of holiness which had been drawn up in Babylon, and which was later elaborated into the so-called " Priestly Code." This code was a complex one, in which general moral requirements were united with all sorts of special injunctions, binding only upon Jews. They must be circumcised, they must keep the Sabbath strictly, they must eat only *kosher* food, they must carefully observe the Passover and the other great festivals, they must bring sacrifices duly and rightly to Yahweh three times a year at Jerusalem, they must not mingle socially — still less matrimonially — with heathen Gentiles or corrupt Samaritans. As time went on, the institutions of the temple and the synagogue tended to drift apart somewhat; one religious party, the Sadducees, was headed by the priests who clustered about the

temple at Jerusalem, while another, the Pharisees, was headed by
the scribes who expounded the law in the synagogues. But both
parties were at one when the purity of Jewish institutions was
threatened by foreign influences. When Antiochus Epiphanes,
one of the Greek kings who succeeded Alexander the Great in the
Near East, attempted forcibly to Hellenize the Jews and destroy
their religious institutions, the whole people rose in rebellion, and
under the leadership of the Maccabees, fighting against incredible
odds, established an independent Jewish state which lasted for
eighty years (143–63 B.C.). The line of native princes who ruled
this state eventually became so secularized and corrupt that the
Pharisees in despair invited the Romans to intervene. A series of
revolts against Rome then ensued, led by various " messiahs " who
announced that the ancient dream of the "kingdom of God "
was at length to be realized. At last Rome's patience was exhausted; so in 70 A.D., amid scenes of frightful carnage, she destroyed Jerusalem and thoroughly dispersed the Jews. So ended
the Jewish temple and kingdom — but not the Jewish hope of a
kingdom of God on earth. Throughout the years of their wandering, and especially since the rise of Zionism in the nineteenth century and the Balfour Declaration of 1917, the Jews have continued
to cherish the hope of a national home in Palestine, and a national
destiny in which the whole religious destiny of mankind is somehow involved. Arab massacres will not destroy this hope. It is
evidently eternal.

The disappearance of the temple brought one decisive change in
orthodox Judaism. It made an end of the influence of the priests
and Sadducees and put the future development of the Jewish
faith entirely in the hands of the scribes and Pharisees. Now the
Pharisaic party had always been noted for its tendency to define,
expand, and apply the Jewish law through constant interpretation and reinterpretation, until it was made to cover every
conceivable contingency. Already before the Dispersion their
rabbis had accumulated a great mass of traditional opinions and
legal precedents, which had acquired an authority almost equal
to that of the Law itself. Freed from all opposition, this tend-

ency began to run to great lengths. For every text of Torah—
i.e., of the Hebrew Bible, especially the "five books of Moses"
with which it begins — there grew up a body of interpretation known as the Mishna. For every passage of Mishna, there
grew up a body of further elucidation known as the Gemara.
The Mishna, plus the Gemara, is called the Talmud ("Teaching "). In the Babylonian Talmud, completed about 500 A.D., the
Gemara is three times as lengthy as in the Palestinian Talmud,
completed about 220 A.D., and it is the lengthier version that has
become authoritative. Needless to say, the Talmud contains elements of very unequal worth, heaped together in great confusion;
and it became necessary in the end to compile simplified outlines
of the Talmud, in the endeavor to reduce it to its essential principles. The most influential of these outlines was written by Moses
Maimonides, the Thomas Aquinas of medieval Judaism, who
reduced his findings to thirteen cardinal principles, which are still
commonly recognized as essential to orthodox Judaism. The first
five of these principles assert the existence, unity, incorporeality,
priority, and eternity of God the Creator, and repeat the Mosaic
injunction to worship no other being whatsoever. The next four
assert the divine origin and absolute immutability of the Law
revealed on Mount Sinai to Moses, and deny that any supplementary revelation will ever come from God. The last four assert that
God knows the works of men, that he will reward or punish them
according to their observance of his Law, and finally that when
Messiah comes to inaugurate God's kingdom on earth there will
be a general resurrection of the dead who will be judged according
to their works.

Although the modern orthodox Jew lays considerable stress
upon this simple creed, as formulated by Maimonides, he is distinguished — unlike the orthodox Christian — by what he *does*
more than by what he *believes*. In the orthodox synagogue service
the high point comes when the scroll of the Law is solemnly
brought forth from the shrine in which it is kept and carried to
the desk where the lesson for the day is to be read. Faithful
obedience to the practical prescriptions of the Law of Moses, as

illustrated in the rest of the Bible and defined in the Talmud, is the great mark of Jewish orthodoxy. If a man keeps the Sabbath and the great festivals, if he abstains from forbidden foods and forbidden defilements of every sort, if he studies the Law eagerly and tries to walk precisely in the way that it marks out, in all his human relationships, then he is an orthodox Jew, even though he may have doubts and mental reservations upon theological questions. There are even some ultra-modern rabbis who claim to be orthodox though they deny the existence of God; but the rank and file of orthodoxy would reject their claim to the title. The typical orthodox Jew believes as firmly as Ezekiel or Ezra in the divine origin of Torah, and he expresses his allegiance to these divine teachings in much the same sort of conduct which the founders of orthodoxy prescribed in the days of the Exile and the Second Temple — save that he keeps the Feast of Lights (*Chanukah*) to celebrate the deliverance under the Maccabees, no longer worships in a temple, and in many ways adapts the ancient Law to fit new conditions, along the lines laid down in the Talmud. Whether the Jewish Law is or is not strictly "immutable," as Maimonides claimed, it has at any rate produced a type of life and conduct that is stiffly resistant to changes of environment.

IV. REFORM MOVEMENTS IN JUDAISM

The foregoing account of the development of Judaism has purposely ignored all tendencies moving counter to the orthodox emphasis upon strict national exclusiveness and strict obedience to immutable law. Yet counter-tendencies have always been present, even within the pale of orthodoxy, and from time to time they have expressed themselves in separatist reform movements.

It is easy to recognize such tendencies in the great pre-exilic prophets, with their emphasis upon universal moral principles; less easy to recognize them in the teachings of the priests and scribes who ruled Judea after the Exile. Christian scholars, who naturally sympathize with the former more than they do with the latter, have tended to idealize the religion of the prophets and disparage the religion of the priests and scribes — as if the whole period after the Exile was a period of growing narrowness and blindness, from which early Christianity abruptly recovered, through a revival of the long-lost religion of the prophets. A more objective examination of the evidence indicates that there was much " priestly " ritualism and narrow exclusivism in the teaching of the prophets, and much " prophetic " cosmopolitanism in the period of the Second Temple. The Book of Ruth — an idyllic tribute to a foreign woman from whom King David was said to be descended — was written during this latter period as a protest against the law forbidding mixed marriages; and the Book of Jonah was written to prove that God is concerned with the salvation of foreigners as much as he is concerned with the salvation of the Jews. Both these books got into the orthodox canon of sacred scripture, as did much of the so-called " Wisdom Literature " (Proverbs, Ecclesiastes), in which the Greek emphasis upon practical prudence largely replaces the emphasis upon ritual holiness as the criterion of the good man. A still larger body of literature, known as " apocalyptic " because of its claim to " unveil " the course of coming events, got left out of the canon — with the exception of the Book of Daniel — but exercised a considerable influence upon orthodox opinion. Largely through the medium of this literature Persian dualism and Persian faith in a future life came to be factors in Jewish thought. The earlier prophets ascribe evil as well as good to the will of God,[7] and have no hope of individual immortality — except for a kind of ghostly existence in Sheol (Hades) which is far worse than outright annihilation; but in the period between the Old and New Testaments it became common to ascribe evil to the work of an evil spirit, Satan or Beelzebub, who rules on earth as God rules in heaven, and even the Pharisees, pillars of orthodoxy as they were, adopted the Persian belief in a future life with rewards and punishments. In early Christianity all these new liberal tendencies united with the ancient prophetic tradition, to issue in the first great reform movement in Judaism — a movement so important that it deserves a chapter by itself.

But not all the antilegalistic, anti-exclusivistic spirit in Judaism passed into the Christian movement. It showed itself repeatedly in subsequent centuries, in revolts against the authority of the Talmud. In 762 A.D. Anan ben David attacked the Talmud in Babylon, its seat of greatest authority, and led a band of reformers to Jerusalem, where he attempted to found a religious community upon pure biblical truth uncontaminated by the doctrines of men. The Karaite sect which he founded was widely influential for a century, and still numbers a few adherents. In the eighteenth century a movement of a more enthusiastic character broke out in central Europe under the leadership of Baal Shem-Tob, a faith healer and mystic who was much influenced by the pantheistic theosophy of the cabalistic books.[8] Baal Shem-Tob claimed that prayer to God and merciful kindness toward men were more important than study of the Law. "All that I have achieved, I have achieved not through study but through prayer," he once said; and he scornfully defined a Talmudist as "a man who through sheer study of the Law has no time to think of God."[9] Through his love and trust of outcasts and sinners, this eighteenth century dissenter won many joyful converts and followers, like his English contemporary John Wesley; and his sect, the Chassidim — still numerous in central Europe — reverences him and the leaders who have succeeded him as literal manifestations of God.

Modern Reform Judaism, a more widespread movement than either of the preceding, dates from the time of Moses Mendelssohn, the eighteenth century emancipator who procured the release of the Jews in many European centers from the ghettos in which they had been confined for centuries. In negotiating with Napoleon and other statesmen, he and his associates argued that the Jews were not a separate race or nation, to be treated like enemy aliens, but a group of religious believers, capable as any others of being good citizens of their respective nations. Reform Jews have always taken their stand upon this platform. They have found the essence of Judaism, not in the strict observance of peculiar ceremonies and customs, but in the central idea of Hebrew prophecy: "The One Only and Holy God, whose kingdom of truth, justice, and peace is to be universally established at the end of time."[10] They point out

— quite correctly — that " legalistic nationalism " and " prophetic universalism " have always existed side by side in the Hebrew tradition, and while they gratefully recognize the service that orthodoxy has rendered in preserving the Hebrew message through centuries of persecution, they argue that it is now time, in a more tolerant world, to throw down the protective barriers and let the message stand forth in a form that all the world can appreciate and accept.   Accordingly, they tend to handle the whole Hebrew tradition with the utmost freedom, retaining what seems of permanent value and abandoning the rest.   At first, they were inclined to identify the permanent truth with the original Torah, contrasting its divine authority, like the Karaites, with the merely human authority of the Talmud.   Later, like the liberal Protestants, they came to discriminate between divine and human elements in the Bible itself.[11]   The resultant creed may be summarized as follows:

Negatively, many of the purely nationalistic elements in Judaism are abandoned, such as (1) belief in the coming of a personal messiah, (2) all laws relating to sacrifice, the priesthood, and Palestine, and (3) belief that at the advent of messiah all the dead will rise in Palestine.   All references to these are expunged from the prayer-book, and the synagogue service is greatly simplified, the vernacular being used instead of Hebrew in most parts of the service.

Positively, the essentials of prophetic religion are affirmed in their most universal form: (1) That God is the educator and Father of all men; (2) that Israel is God's witness on earth; (3) that this is not a privilege but an obligation, since all men are God's children; (4) that the Dispersion, far from being a calamity, was a providential means of spreading true religion among all nations, and bringing in the messianic age of peace and brotherhood; (5) that man is not innately sinful, but innately good.   Although the legal element in Judaism is subordinated, the Law is reverenced as a temporal expression of eternal moral and religious truth, and many elements of it are observed by Reform as well as by Orthodox Jews.[12]

Reform Judaism had its greatest period of expansion and influence during the period of toleration and general prosperity in
the nineteenth century, especially in the United States. American
Reform Jews have sometimes expressed the belief that America,
and not Palestine, is the real Promised Land.[13] But the success of
the emancipated Jews during the nineteenth century provoked a
wave of reaction. As inveterate internationalists, pacifists, and
cosmopolitans, the Jews became objects of suspicion and hatred to
an age in which nationalistic feeling was growing apace; and because of persecution in Germany, pogroms in Russia, and the Drey-
fus case in France, there grew up a new defensive nationalism
among the Jews, expressed in the Zionist movement. Theodor
Herzl in his book *The Jewish State* (*Judenstaat*), published in
1896, urged that Jews should admit they were a nation as well as a
religious body and colonize some unoccupied territory, preferably
in Palestine.

Reform Jews ardently opposed Zionism at first. " We consider
ourselves," they said, " no longer a nation but a religious community, and therefore expect neither a return to Palestine nor a
sacrificial worship under the sons of Aaron nor the restoration of
any of the laws concerning the Jewish state." The Zionists replied
that "without a nucleus of Jews forming a Jewish nation and
permitted to develop its own peculiarly Jewish culture unham-
pered by a superior enveloping culture, the Jewish religion will be
lost to the world." [14] The Zionist view of the matter has steadily
gained during the period of increasing persecution which has ensued. Lord Lansdowne's offer of land in east Africa for a Jewish
colony was rejected, but Lord Balfour's declaration of the British
government's determination to establish a " national home " for
the Jews in Palestine was welcomed with enthusiasm, and Palestine
has now become once more a center of Jewish learning, Jewish
colonization, and Jewish influence. Many Reform Jews have become Zionists; but the chief support of the movement comes from
Orthodox Jews and from another group that terms itself Conservative. According to Louis Minsky,[15] the trend toward conservatism
is now the unifying trend in American Jewry. Since the secession

of the conservatives from the Reform synagogue in 1886, their movement — now organized in the United Synagogue of America — has led a large proportion of Jews of all parties to the position that if Judaism has in it the seeds of universal religion and universal morality, it is nevertheless inevitably a nation and a culture as well as a religion and must behave as such.

V. MOHAMMEDANISM

Jews often refer to Christianity and Mohammedanism as " daughter religions " of Judaism. Some liberal Jews even refer to them as " divinely appointed emissaries and agencies " for the universal dissemination of the truth which Judaism embodies in a particular national culture; though they add that both Christianity and Mohammedanism have corrupted this truth in certain respects, and Judaism must accordingly maintain its separate identity " till all the heathen have learned to worship God as the spirit of holiness in man, instead of seeking him in the blind forces of nature or of destiny." [16] Whatever one may think of this view, it must be evident at once that these three religions are much more closely related than, let us say, Confucianism, Buddhism, and Shintō. Christianity is at least as closely related to Judaism as Buddhism is to Hinduism; and one might even maintain that Judaism, Catholicism, and Protestantism are cognate forms of one and the same religion, at three different stages of development. The relation of Mohammedanism to Judaism is a little more obscure, but still very close. One might describe it as a product of cross-fertilization between Judaism, Christianity, and the ancient Semitic religion from which both had originally sprung. Let us examine the origins of Mohammedanism a bit more closely to see how this is so.

The prevailing religion of Arabia in the year 570 A.D., when Mohammed the Prophet was born in Mecca, was that same primitive cult of sacred trees, stones, springs, and mountains which had prevailed among the Semitic nomads since the days of Abraham, Isaac, and Jacob. Especially sacred was the whole region around Mecca, known as the province of the Hejaz (pilgrimage) where multitudes came every year to worship at the sacred mountain

Muzdalifa, to drink of the sacred "well of Ishmael," Zem Zem, and to make the sevenfold circuit of the shrine called the Kaaba, where the famous Black Stone,[17] sacred to the god Hobal, was kept. Mecca was also the chief station on the most favored caravan route from the Mediterranean to the Indian ocean; and its leading family, the Koreish, earned a substantial competence by combining custody of the Kaaba with a thriving trade, carried on with pilgrims and caravans. It had, so to speak, a vested interest in the continuance of primitive idolatry and superstition.

Meanwhile more elevated religious ideas were beginning to ferment in the Arabian mind. On the borders of Arabia there dwelt many tribes of Jews and Christians, who lived much like the other Arabs and came in constant contact with them, but despised their superstitious rites and regarded them as " heathen." There is some evidence that the old animistic religion had begun to crumble away, undermined by these monotheistic influences, and that some Arabs had gone so far as to embrace Judaism or Christianity; but it was not until the appearance of Mohammed that the movement toward monotheism attained any considerable proportions.

Mohammed was a member of a collateral branch of the Koreish clan, the Hashimites, who were excluded from the control and profits of the Kaaba by their more powerful kinsmen and so reduced to the unenviable status of " poor relations " — which meant, of course, that there were constant bickerings and frequent bloody encounters between the two branches of the family. An orphan at an early age, he was brought up by his maternal uncle, Abu Talib, who trained him as a camel driver and on at least one occasion took him on a journey to Syria. This was the only education he received. He never learned to read or write, and always frankly confessed himself to be an ignorant man; but he seems to have picked up, from contact with the Jews and Christians, a somewhat garbled and simplified version of Bible history, which made a great impression upon him.

The first turning point in Mohammed's fortunes came when, at the age of twenty-five, he entered the service of a rich widow, Khadijah, as head driver of one of her caravans. She was fifteen years older than he, but became deeply attached to him, married him, and bore him one or two sons and four daughters. (The fact that none of his sons, by this or subsequent marriages, lived to manhood, had important consequences for his later career and for the whole history of Mohammedanism.) Khadijah encouraged Mohammed in the sense of religious mission which gradually grew upon him. Retiring to a cave outside Mecca, in a wild and deserted region, he gave himself over to periods of brooding upon the degraded state of his people. From time to time he was startled with visions and voices, which he was inclined at first to ascribe to evil spirits, but which his wife bade him trust as the divine answer to his search. At last the visions and voices became clear, and Mohammed came back to the city with the first of a long series of communications from the angel Gabriel, proclaiming that there was but one God, and that a day of " smiting " was at hand for those who continued in idolatrous practices. It is impossible to say just what this original message was, for it is impossible to date with accuracy the various suras (chapters) of the Koran, in which Mohammed's revelations were set down haphazard from memory after his death; but the gist of his message is undoubtedly contained in the famous one hundred and twelfth sura:

> In the name of the merciful and compassionate God.
> Say, "He is God alone!
> God the Eternal!
> He begets not and He is not begotten!
> Nor is there like unto Him any one! "

Mecca was anything but a favorable place for the proclamation of a monotheistic faith; but Mohammed privately preached the truth as he had seen it in his visions, and for twelve years labored to convert his kinsmen, with only slight success. Khadijah always believed in him, and he very soon made converts of a few of his close relatives, including his son-in-law Ali, but after three years he had only fourteen followers. The conversion of Abu Bekr, a prominent merchant, brought the movement to public attention, but the scorn and suspicion of the Koreish at this attack upon the religion which gave them their revenue made Mohammed's position increasingly insecure. At last, after the death of Khadijah and of his uncle and protector Abu Talib, his position became impossible, and he made his escape to the friendly city of Yathrib (Medina) where he already had a group of followers. From this flight (Hegira) to Medina, in the year 622 A.D., the Mohammedan calendar is dated; for it proved to be the beginning of the triumphant progress of the new faith.

The city of Medina was predisposed to accept monotheism, through the presence of many Jews and Christians in the vicinity. Mohammed came into close and sympathetic relations with them for a time, and made a strong bid for their support. He represented himself, not as the bearer of a rival revelation, but as the restorer of the pure faith of their common ancestor, Abraham, the last of a line of heavenly messengers of whom the greatest were Adam, Noah, Abraham, Moses, and Jesus. He instituted the Jewish Day of Atonement as a fast day for his followers, ordered them to turn their faces toward Jerusalem when they prayed, and related that he himself had been carried in a vision to the site of the temple in Jerusalem, where he was received into the company of the holy prophets of old, and thence ascended through the seven heavens to the throne of God, who told him that his followers must pray five times a day — in imitation of the Jewish custom on the Day of Atonement. Even to those Jews and Christians who would not accept the authority of his new revelation he spoke courteously at first: " Say, I believe in the book which God has sent down; and I am bidden to judge justly between you. God is our Lord and your Lord; we have our works and ye have your works; there is no argument between us and you. God will assemble us together and unto Him the journey is." [18]

It would seem that Mohammed's hope at first was to unite Jews, Christians, and Arabs in allegiance to the one God, and that he tried for a time to achieve this through religious comity, much as the Sikhs in later days achieved comity between Mohammedans and Hindus within their fellowship. But the Jews soon ceased to look to him as a possible messiah, and the Christians never took him seriously — perhaps because his matrimonial adventures grew

more and more amazing in the last ten years of his life.[19] Turning
then to his own Arab folk for support, and appealing to them in
the name of Allah to unite, Mohammed found better success.
After a period of military skirmishing with the Meccans, who were
assisted by the Jews, the Holy City at length fell into the Prophet's
hands, was magnanimously treated, and became the center of a
monotheistic movement that spread like wildfire among the Arabian tribes. The images of the old gods were smashed, and the
Kaaba was reconsecrated to the worship of Allah, which has never
ceased to be offered there, five times daily, ever since. Even before
the Prophet's death (eleven years after the Hegira) this pan-Arab
movement was already threatening the safety of the Byzantine and
Persian empires, and a long train of hostilities had begun, which
was to end in its triumph over both. The Mohammedans claim
that they never fought unless first attacked, but they certainly never
shirked a fight.[20] Idolaters who opposed them were killed unless
they became converts; Jews and Christians, unless they were converted or paid tribute, suffered the same fate. Through Palestine,
Egypt, and north Africa the advance spread westward, until
it reached France by way of Spain, and there it was checked.
Through Persia it spread eastward, until Moslem influence reached
as far as the Malay Peninsula and the Philippines. The center of
a vast empire, exceeding the Roman Empire in scope, was established at Bagdad in Mesopotamia, and there Mohammed's successors, the caliphs, ruled as secular kings, while at the same time
they served as religious leaders of the faithful. This empire,
after rendering signal services to science, art, and literature, was
overthrown by the Mongols; but the Mongols themselves were
converted to the Mohammedan faith, and founded two Moslem
empires of their own: the Turkish empire, to which the control of
the caliphate passed, and the Mogul empire in north India. So a
considerable portion of mankind is unified today in the faith that
"there is no God but Allah, and Mohammed is his prophet."

It is impossible to explain the success of Mohammedanism as due
to military prowess alone. It spread, in large measure, because of
its great popular appeal, based on its simplicity, definiteness, and

practicability. Any child can understand the beliefs and precepts of Mohammed; strong men find in them a challenge to their moral fiber, while at the same time nothing is required that is hopelessly beyond the strength of the weakest. The whole creed is summed up in the name Islam, by which the followers of the Prophet prefer to designate their own faith. It implies an attitude of absolute loyal devotion to the one God, an act of " submission " by which a man accepts God's will as his own, and so is " at peace " with God.[21] God is conceived as the absolute determiner of destiny, omnipotent in the full sense of the word; but of all his ninety-nine " names " or attributes those most often mentioned in the Koran are " the Merciful," " the Compassionate." God's way is easy, not difficult; he does not desire to burden any soul beyond its power; and to the wrongdoer it may be said, " Seek pardon of your Lord and be turned to him; verily my Lord is merciful, loving." [22]

The moral code of Islam is accordingly very simple. Against three traditional practices of the Arabs the Prophet laid down an absolute veto: drinking, gambling, and burying female children alive. Marital relations were standardized by setting a limit of four wives, and restricting the power of divorce hitherto possessed by the husband, while extending the rights of the wife. Apart from this, as Jastrow says, " fair dealings with one's neighbors and kindness towards animals may be said to sum up the chief virtues, though they must be supplemented by the performance of the religious duties and the obligation to have one's children instructed in the teachings of Islam." [23] The chief religious duties are five in number, and are known as the " five pillars ":

(1). *Shahâda,* witnessing to the faith that God is one.

(2). *Salat,* prayer five times a day. Prayer with the Moslems is a highly standardized and impressive public exercise. Five times a day the muezzin steps out upon the minaret of the mosque, and gives the call to prayer: " God is great [*Allah akbar*]. I bear witness that there is no God but God. I bear witness that Mohammed is the Apostle of God. Come hither to prayers " — adding, in the morning, "Prayer is better than sleep." In the mosque the leader stands in front of the worshipers, facing Mecca, and the congregation follows his changing postures, through cycle after cycle of kneeling, prostration, and standing erect, like a military company engaged in setting-up drill. The prayers have little in them of personal petition or aspiration, they are essentially " humble acknowledgment five times daily of Allah's greatness and of his supreme control of everything." [24]

(3). *Zakat,* paying the poor-tax. This was originally an expression of the duty of charity. "Prayer," one of the caliphs is said to have remarked, " carries us half-way to Allah, fasting brings us to the door of his palace, but alms-giving procures us admission." Later, the paying of this tax was required by law and charity made to consist in what was given over and above the minimum.

(4). *Saum,* or keeping the fast of Ramadan. This ancient Arabic month of truce was substituted for the Jewish Day of Atonement as the date of the annual fast after Mohammed abandoned his hope of converting the Jews. The fast of Ramadan is a very strenuous one; neither food nor *drink* of any kind must be consumed between sunrise and sunset, for a whole month — which is a very considerable hardship in hot countries. This is one of the really " steep " requirements of Islam, which help explain its appeal to virile and militant races.

(5). The *Haj,* or pilgrimage to Mecca, which every good Moslem must make once in his life. The rites performed at Mecca resemble closely the immemorial practices of Arabian religion, but purified of idolatry and sanctified in the name of Allah. Whatever one may think of these rites, there can be no doubt that the pilgrimage to Mecca is the most powerful bond of unity in the Moslem world. It is sometimes said that Islam is the only religion that has completely solved the race problem. It is a fact that men of all races and nations successfully ignore these distinctions because of the unifying influence of a common faith in the one God and his Prophet, and a common center of pilgrimage to which all thoughts go out five times a day.

Sectarian divisions exist in Islam, but are not so deep-going as in most religions. The chief division, between the Sunni or " follow-

ers of tradition " and the Shi'ites or " partisans," is due to a difference of opinion over the proper succession in the caliphate. When
the Prophet died, in the eleventh year after the Hegira (633 A.D.),
he left no son to succeed him, and fierce disputes broke out in
consequence. The Shi'ites declare that the caliphate should have
gone at once to the Prophet's son-in-law Ali, instead of going first
to Abu Bekr, Omar, and Othman, so they refuse to recognize the
legitimacy of the first three caliphs, and they make of Ali — who
was murdered, and replaced in authority by the Omayyid line
of caliphs, soon after he came to the throne — a veritable incarnation of deity. This idea of a human incarnation of God is applied by the Shi'ites also to the Imams or "leaders," descended
from Ali; but it is rejected altogether by the Sunni as an idolatrous
notion. The Sunni differ also from the Shi'ites in the authority
they ascribe to a body of tradition which has grown up to interpret
the Koran, very much as the Talmud has grown up to interpret
the Hebrew Bible. In recent years a considerable revolt against
this tradition has burst out in Arabia under the leadership of the
talented chieftain Ibn Saud, whose program of faithfulness to the
Koran, and the Koran alone, reminds one of the Karaite movement
in medieval Judaism and the Protestant movement in Christianity.

Theological dispute among Moslems has chiefly centered upon
the problem of free will versus predestination. In strict logic, it
is hard to reconcile human freedom or initiative with the doctrine
that God's will determines whatever comes to pass; but as a matter
of fact, there have always been many predestinarians who have
defended the freedom of the human will, asserting that part of
God's foreordained plan was that man should actively take the
initiative in carrying out his fate. Both fatalism and free will can
be justified by appealing to the Koran. In the expansive thrust of
the first few centuries of Moslem history, and in the active cultivation of the arts and sciences by the medieval caliphate, one may perhaps see the outworking of one side of the logic of Islam; while in
the stagnation of subsequent centuries one may see the outworking
of its other and more fatalistic side. The popular doctrine of
kismet, which sees in every adverse circumstance or hampering

limitation an embodiment of the will of Allah, has certainly tended to prevent the advance of civilization by promoting an attitude of passive resignation. In so far as Islam has thus succumbed to fatalism it may be said to have gone back upon the initial step toward western activism that Zoroaster took so long ago, and reverted to the passivism of the Orient. But the great changes now going on in post-war Turkey, where a fresh start in civilization has been made with the abandonment of the caliphate and many ancient traditions, make it conceivable that Islam may yet again, as so often in the past, exhibit the characteristic marks of Occidental religion.

NOTES

[1] Cf. the opening chapter of Rabindranath Tagore's *Sādhana*, where the Hindu and Greek attitudes toward nature are similarly contrasted.

[2] *A Catechism of the Zoroastrian Religion* (Bombay, 1911), p. 16.

[3] Pratt, *India and its Faiths*, p. 325.

[4] Deut. 24: 17, 18.

[5] The historical criticism of the Hebrew Bible is an exceedingly complicated study, but one outstanding and important result of it can be briefly indicated: The so-called "Five Books of Moses" (Pentateuch) with which the Bible opens are not really the oldest books, but comparatively late; the narratives and laws which they contain, although they incorporate some ancient traditions, have been subjected to a process of re-editing that continued long after the return from Babylon. In order of composition, the Law (Pentateuch) did *not* precede the Prophets; it was the Prophets who preceded the Law.

[6] So called because his prophecies have become incorporated in the book of the prophet Isaiah (chaps. 40 ff.), having in all probability been first written on the blank end of a scroll bearing a copy of that earlier prophet's writings.

[7] Cf. Amos 3:6: "Shall there be evil in a city, and the Lord hath not done it?" (The meaning of this verse is, however, somewhat in doubt.)

[8] The cabalistic literature-attempts to extract a "deeper meaning" from the Bible by means of acrostic anagrams and other strange devices, and reads into the sacred text a kind of Neo-Platonic mysticism.

[9] See *Jewish Encyclopedia*, art. "Baal Shem-Tob."

[10] See Kaufman Kohler, *Jewish Theology*, Chap. III, "The Essence of the Religion of Judaism."

[11] See *Hastings Encyclopedia of Religion and Ethics*, art. "Liberal Judaism."

[12] See *Jewish Encyclopedia*, art. "Reform Judaism."

[13] E.g., Mary Antin and Ambassador Morgenthau.

[14] See Kemper Fullerton, "Zionism," *Harvard Theological Review*, 1917.

[15] "The Trend toward Unity in Judaism," *Christian Century*, Dec. 2, 1931.

[16] Kaufman Kohler, *op. cit.*, Chap. LVII.

[17] Probably a meteoritic fragment.

[18] Sura XLII, 14.

[19] Mohammedans ascribe his ten or more marriages to a desire to make charitable provision for widowed women; or to make peace through matrimonial alliances. Non-Moslem critics are apt to accuse him of growing sensuality. A desire for a son who

might succeed to his authority was undoubtedly a powerful motive with him, as with Henry VIII of England.

[20] See Mohammed Ali's *Muhammed the Prophet,* and the introduction to his *Translation of the Holy Quran,* pp. cviii-cxii.

[21] The ideas of making one's peace and of bowing submissively (*salaam*) are both contained in the word *Islam.*

[22] Sura XI, 90.   Ameer Ali's translation cited in Atkins, *Procession of the Gods,* p. 439.

[23] See Montgomery, *Religions of the Past and Present* (Philadelphia, 1918), p. 290.

[24] *Ibid.,* p. 230.

BIBLIOGRAPHY

Wright, W. K.   *Op. cit.,* Chap. X (Judaism).

Friess and Schneider.   *Op. cit.,* Chap. VII (Judaism).

Moore, G. F.   *Op. cit.,* Vol. I (Zoroastrianism), Vol. II (Judaism, Mohammedanism).

Hume, R. E.   *Op. cit.,* Chaps. IX–XI (Zoroastrianism, Judaism, Mohammedanism).

Cave, Sydney.   *Op. cit.,* Chaps. II, V (Zoroastrianism, Islam).

Barton, G. A.   *Op. cit.,* Chaps. V–VII (Zoroastrianism, Judaism, Mohammedanism).

Pratt, J. B.   *India and its Faiths,* Chaps. XIV, XV (Mohammedans, Parsees).

Oesterley and Robinson.   *A History of Israel.*

———.   *Hebrew Religion.*

Browne, Lewis.   *Stranger than Fiction: A Short History of the Jews.*

Cohen, Israel.   *Jewish Life in Modern Times.*

Macdonald, D. B.   *Aspects of Islam.*

Nicholson, R. A.   *The Mystics of Islam.*

5.

OCCIDENTAL RELIGION: CHRISTIANITY

CHRISTIANITY has been for many centuries the dominant religion of Europe; and since Europe is the chief center from which science, commerce, and general culture have emanated in the last three hundred years, Christianity is now the dominant religion of the civilized world.[1] Its adherents, according to one much cited tabulation, number 557 millions, as against 230 million Mohammedans, 217 million Hindus, and 137 million Buddhists;[2] and these adherents are mainly found in the civilized portions of Europe, North and South America, Africa and Australia, with many strong outposts in Asia.

I. RELIGION IN THE ROMAN EMPIRE

It was not always so. Nineteen hundred years ago the civilized world was mainly comprehended within the bounds of the Roman Empire; and the crucifixion of Jesus, called the Christ, had recently occurred within that area without creating the slightest stir of sympathy in the minds of civilized men. Judea was always a turbulent province, and more than one of her many would-be messiahs had been put to death by order of the authorities. Regrettable, but necessary, if law and order were to be maintained. Certainly it did not recommend a religious sect in the eyes of good Roman citizens to learn that its founder had been executed as a rebel, and that the superscription on his cross had described him as king of the Jews. So they were inclined to believe the worst of this group of Jewish fanatics called Christians (literally, " Messianists ") when they began to appear in considerable numbers in all the great cities of the empire, causing riots in the synagogues with their new teachings, and holding secret meetings where, it was whispered, they ate the flesh of infants and indulged in every form of immorality.

Tacitus, one of the first secular historians to mention the Christians by name, is inclined to clear them of the charge of having set fire to the city of Rome, and he blames Nero for a cruelty in dealing with them which, he says, " filled every breast with compassion," turning public opinion in favor of the victims; but he regards the faith of the Christians as " a dangerous superstition," and refers to the " pernicious tendency " of their morals, which " called for the hand of justice." [3] Pliny the Younger, in his famous letter to the Emperor Trajan, shows himself better informed about the new sect but no less unsympathetic. He had investigated the rumors about cannibalism and immorality and found them to be false. The Christians did nothing worse at their secret meetings, he reports, than to sing hymns to Christ as a god and partake of ordinary harmless food; and their moral code bound them to abstain from crimes like theft, adultery, or breach of faith. But they refused to offer incense and wine before the image of the emperor and the statues of the Roman gods, or to curse the name of Christ when commanded to do so; wherefore he remanded them to prison and sentenced some of them to death, believing that " their pertinacity and inflexible obstinacy certainly ought to be punished." [4] To him and other Roman officials, refusal to worship the emperor and the gods meant atheism and anarchism, which could not be tolerated.

The old Roman gods who were thus dramatically defied by the new upstart religion were the same Aryan nature gods hymned in the Vedas and denounced by Zoroaster. Jupiter, their king, was a sky-god, identical with the Greek Zeus and the vedic Dyaus. At the beginning of the Christian era educated men did not believe in these gods or in the legends about them except in a highly sophisticated sense. Philosophic reflection had gone a long way toward monotheism in Greece and Rome, as in India. The two chief schools of philosophy, the Platonists and the Stoics, agreed in regarding the different gods as various manifestations of one and the same universal deity, who to the Platonists was mysteriously exalted above the world, accessible only to thought and mystic ecstasy, while to the Stoics he was the indwelling reason or soul of the world. The Epicureans departed still further from the ancient faith and adopted a thoroughly materialistic view of the world, relegating the gods to a distant Elysium where they were quite out of touch with the affairs of mortals. But whatever their philosophic opinions might be, educated Romans continued to offer public sacrifice before the images of the gods, since these were the patron gods of the state, and to do them reverence meant to pledge allegiance to the state. Just so, the modern educated Japanese performs the ancient Shintō rites as an act of patriotic devotion, whether he believes in the Shintō gods or not. He likewise, and for the same reason, pays divine honors to his emperor, whether he believes the story of the descent of the imperial family from the sun-goddess as literal history or as picturesque legend. The Romans paid divine honors to their emperor in much the same spirit.

Since this traditional religion of the state was rather cold and formal, giving little satisfaction to the cravings of the individual soul for personal self-realization, it was combined, in many instances, with a second or supplementary religion of a more private and personal nature, usually promising the devotee salvation from the woes and corruptions of this life, and a blessed immortality in some future state of existence. There were many salvation cults of this sort, some of them old and respectable like the Orphic and Eleusinian Mysteries, some of them recent importations from the east like the Egyptian cult of Isis and the Persian cult of Mithras. Prominent in many of them was the ancient myth of a god who dies in the winter and rises again in the spring, through union with whom — effected through sacramental meals and baths and participation in dramatic representations of the sacred story — the devotee is released from mortality and corruption and rises with his Lord to the immortal and spiritual plane. The prevalence of these cults bears pathetic testimony to the drabness and general flatness of life under Roman rule and to the widespread longing for immortality. They were tolerated by the state, so long as they confined their attention to the future life and did not dabble in politics — very much as Buddhism has been tolerated as an other-worldly supplement to the state religions of China and Japan.

The position of Judaism in the Roman world was exceptional. The Romans made every attempt to respect the national religions of the peoples they had conquered, knowing that any assault upon them made the task of government needlessly difficult. Usually, all they found necessary was to admit the national gods of their subjects into the Roman pantheon, in return for which courtesy the subjects were glad to worship the Roman gods and do homage to the emperor as a divine being. But the national religion of the Jews was strictly and intolerantly monotheistic, and idolatry in any form was forbidden to them. The Roman government was therefore obliged to exempt the Jews from worshiping the Roman gods; and they were permitted to pray *for* the emperor, to their own God, instead of praying *to* the emperor as a divine being. The dogmatic assurance of the Jews, that their God and theirs alone was real, thus received public, legal recognition; and while no doubt the bulk of the Roman populace regarded them as narrow-minded fanatics, there were many wistful religious seekers in that skeptical age who were strongly attracted to the Jews by that same dogmatic intolerance which others found so obnoxious. Most educated men, as we have seen, were convinced monotheists; but so long as they continued to perform the ancient polytheistic rites they felt somewhat abashed in the presence of the genuine, consistent monotheism of the Jews. Even before the dispersion of A.D. 70 every large city in the empire had its Jewish synagogue and Jewish settlement; [5] and about every synagogue clustered a circle of interested Gentile inquirers. A few of these actually became proselytes; but the majority of them were as much repelled by the requirement of circumcision and the national laws and customs of the Jews as they were attracted by their monotheistic creed. It was among these half-convinced inquirers — *sebomenoi,* as they were called in Greek — that the new Christian message found its first large group of Gentile converts. In order to understand its appeal to them and its eventual triumph we must now look more closely at its content.

II. THE MESSAGE OF JESUS

The Christian message, or " gospel," as it was called,[6] was not at first addressed to the world, but to the Jews alone. When the Founder of the Christian movement sent out his twelve disciples on their first preaching mission, he is reported to have said to them: " Do not go among the Gentiles, rather make your way to the lost sheep of the house of Israel. And preach as you go, tell men, ' The reign of heaven is near.' . . . Truly I tell you, you will not have covered the towns of Israel before the Son of Man arrives." [7] Their preaching, dealing as it did with the speedy coming of the " reign of heaven " and its herald the messiah (" Son of Man "), would certainly not have been intelligible to Gentiles. To Jews, on the other hand, it was news of the most exciting import, for they were eagerly hoping, in the distressful decades which preceded the disastrous events of A.D. 66–70, for some form of divine deliverance from their foreign oppressors.

Many of them, of course, looked for a messiah in the shape of a new Judas Maccabaeus, who would lead a popular uprising against Rome and succeed against insuperable odds because the hand of the Lord was upon him. Others, perceiving that military tactics had no hope of success against the Roman legions, looked for a more strictly supernatural form of deliverance: the Son of Man coming on the clouds of heaven, clad with divine power, to purge the earth of wickedness and set up God's kingdom of peace and righteousness. It seems clear that, of the two forms of messianic hope just mentioned, Jesus' followers favored the latter. They consistently refused to participate in violent revolutionary activities, both at the time of the great revolt of A.D. 66–70 and at the time of Bar-Cochab's abortive uprising in A.D. 132; and they entertained for many years the expectation of a miraculous divine intervention in human affairs, which would make an end of the present evil age and inaugurate the reign of God.

But the message of Jesus cannot be adequately summarized in any ready-made formula current at the time. Phrased in the language of Jewish apocalyptic, he presented a view of the ideal relations between God, myself, and my neighbor which has captured the imaginations of men in many different times and places. Full of reverence for the Jewish law and the Jewish prophets, he so reduced them to their essential principles that in effect he disentangled the universal from the national elements in Judaism. To most of his Jewish contemporaries Jesus did not appear to belong to any of the recognized religious parties; he impressed them as a dangerous innovator, who handled Moses and the prophets with a freedom that argued either ignorance or disloyalty. Such an innovator could not be a prophet sent from God, much less the messiah; God could not thus contradict himself.

It is not easy to give a logical summary of the teaching of Jesus. He was not a philosopher, like the Buddha; he preferred to speak in poetic parables and startling paradoxes. But the prevailing thought that runs through these sayings is unmistakable: the patient and impartial love of God for all his human children, evil as well as good; the holy wrath of God against all such as harden their hearts against their neighbors and are indifferent to the sufferings of " even the least of these "; the need of having compassion and forgiveness toward one's enemy, if one would share in the forgiving love of God; the hopeful state of the worst evildoer if he humbly accepts God's forgiveness and becomes as a child again; the hopeless state of the most respectable " pillar of society " if he allows wealth or position or self-righteous contempt for the malefactor to cut him off from his less fortunate fellow men. To a people distraught with hatred of Roman rule Jesus said that they should do good to their persecutors, and if compelled to go a mile out of their way by Roman exaction, go an extra mile out of pure good will. In short, men were to be " perfect," like God himself — perfect in patience, magnanimity and readiness to forgive; then they might confidently expect God's kingdom to come speedily and his will to be done " on earth as it is in heaven." For those who would not enter into this kingdom through the " strait gate " of lowly humility and forgiving love, destruction lay ahead; when judgment came they would find themselves in " outer darkness." Jesus not only taught and preached God's gracious love; he seemed able somehow to convey it, personally, to those who stood most in need of it. Contact with him brought hope to the poor and unfortunate, health to the sick, and transformation of character to wrongdoers whom society had put beyond the pale. Encouraged by these manifestations of divine power breaking into the world through his ministry, he seems to have been convinced that Satan's dominion over mankind was shaken and the arch-fiend ready to fall " like lightning from heaven." Yet he had no illusions about the easy success of his mission. In many of the leaders of the organized religious life of his people he recognized a proud self-sufficiency which could not stoop to acknowledge a need of repentance, and his message to them was accordingly one of woe and denunciation.

The cloud of opposition gathered thickest over the capital city of Jerusalem, where the Pharisees, guardians of the law, and the Sadducees, guardians of the temple, both had their headquarters. Representatives of both parties came down into Galilee to spy upon the new prophet and report upon his heresies. Herod Antipas, tetrarch of Galilee, was informed about the doings of this follower and successor of John the Baptizer — the man whom he had arrested and put to death — and Jesus was warned that he must escape, or Herod would kill him. But Jesus would not be silenced. Opposition and misunderstanding only convinced him the more deeply that he had a message which all Israel, yes, all the world must hear; and as he studied prophecy, meditating upon the place of his own mission in God's plan of salvation, the conclusion seems to have forced itself upon him that he had a central and tragic role to play in the coming of God's kingdom. John was the great forerunner, the last harbinger of the kingdom, and he himself was God's Messiah — not the conquering prince who was expected by the Zealots, but the Suffering Servant of Second Isaiah, of whom it was prophesied that the nations should say, " He was wounded for our transgressions, he was bruised for our iniquities; the chastisement of our peace was upon him, and with his stripes we are healed." [8]

The feast of the Passover was near. Jews from all over the world would be in Jerusalem for this great annual gathering. Herod would go up from Galilee and the Roman procurator from Caesarea, to police the Holy City during the festival and nip seditious activities in the bud. This was the setting which Jesus chose for the last act in the drama of his life. In the presence of all his countrymen and all the Roman world, in public defiance of his enemies, he would proclaim his divine mission and seal it with his blood. Until the moment was ripe, he kept in hiding; then, swiftly and secretly, he made his way from Galilee to Jerusalem, followed by his dismayed disciples, who could not see why he should court destruction. "It cannot be," he exclaimed, "that a prophet perish out of Jerusalem!" [9]

Riding upon a borrowed colt and hailed with shouts by his admirers, he made his appearance before the city gates at the beginning of Passover week. For several days he taught publicly in the temple, where he began his work of protest and reform — to the great delight of the populace and the great annoyance of the authorities — by overturning the tables of the money-changers who plied their sharp trade in the temple precincts. Many attempts were made to catch him in some treasonable or blasphemous utterance, but he evaded every trap. More and more plainly, in parable after parable, he announced that since God's good news of the kingdom was rejected by the leaders of the chosen people, the message must now be given to those who would hear it. "Therefore I say unto you, The kingdom of God shall be taken from you, and given to a nation bringing forth the fruits thereof." [10] Finally, on the eve of the Passover, after a last supper with his disciples — still solemnly and affectionately commemorated in the most impressive of all Christian rituals — Jesus was betrayed into the hands of his enemies by a treacherous disciple, who seems also to have disclosed to the Jewish Sanhedrin the secret of his messianic claims. The Roman procurator, Pontius Pilate, took him for nothing worse than a harmless fanatic, as also did Herod, to whom his case was referred; but the Sanhedrin, backed by a turbulent mob, demanded his crucifixion and got it. About three o'clock on the afternoon of the Passover, after praying for the forgiveness of his persecutors and calling upon his God in an agony of despair, Jesus gave a loud cry and expired.

These events have been recounted in some detail because they have left an indelible impression upon the Christian mind. More than his teachings, more than his healing miracles, more than all his life, filled as it was with acts of kindness and compassion, it is the voluntary death of Jesus in which the clearest expression of his love of mankind, love like that which he himself attributed to God, has been seen. "Greater love hath no man than this, that a man lay down his life for his friends." [11] The cross has remained, and rightly so, the great Christian symbol. In it the church has seen the presence of God himself, making atonement for the sins of mankind through the suffering of his well beloved Son. "*Felix culpa!*" she has said; "fortunate was the sin that could occasion so great an act of redemptive love; and hard is the human heart that can refuse a redemption bought at such a price!"

III. THE MESSAGE OF THE APOSTLES

Needless to say, the "glory of the cross" was far from evident at first to the frightened disciples of the crucified prophet. From a naïve confidence in his mission which had caused them, we are told, to dispute among themselves as to which of them should be his prime minister in the kingdom he was about to set up,[12] they were suddenly pitched into blank bewilderment and utter discomfiture by his arrest and condemnation. Not one of the twelve dared show his face at the place of execution; only a group of the "ministering women" who had followed the Master from Galilee looked on from a distance, and tried to mark the location of the tomb in which he was laid.[13] But when the disciples reassembled in Galilee after their precipitate flight their despair was soon changed into hope. First Peter and then other members of the circle had visions of the living presence of their Master; and this, combined with the testimony of the women, who had found only an empty tomb when they sought the body of Jesus to embalm it, convinced all the disciples that God had raised him from the dead. Returning to Jerusalem, they publicly preached the messiahship of Jesus, and predicted that he would shortly come again on the clouds of heaven as King and Judge.

The "descent of the Holy Spirit" — which came upon the disciples in one of their meetings, not long after the return to Jerusalem, and frequently recurred from that time on — convinced them that though Jesus was now in heaven, "at the right hand of God," he continued to live in their midst through this strange power which emanated from him. Sometimes the Spirit showed itself in healing miracles, such as the Master had worked, sometimes in prophetic utterances, sometimes in a kind of ecstatic babbling, known as "speaking with tongues," which had to be interpreted by other members of the group; but most characteristically it showed itself in a sense of a common sustaining life running through the whole fellowship, uniting them intimately with one another. So truly did they consider themselves "members one of another" that they turned all their worldly goods into a general fund which was distributed "unto every man according as he had need" by business officers known as "deacons." They believed that this communal life of theirs, "in the unity of the Spirit and the bond of peace," was a type of what all life was to become when Jesus the Christ returned to reign.

Nineteen hundred years have now passed, and some sections of Christendom are still reckoning times and seasons and scanning the heavens for signs of the second coming of Christ; but it occurred to some of his followers quite early — for example, to the author of the Gospel of John, the latest of the four Gospels — that in a sense the descent of the Spirit was the second coming of Christ and the beginning of the reign of God among men. As time has gone on, the hope of a partial and piecemeal coming of Christ's kingdom, in and through the fellowship of those who are touched by his Spirit, has tended to replace the early expectation of his sudden advent on the clouds of heaven to usher in the end of the world and rule for a thousand years in Jerusalem. Those who hold to the ancient view, known as Adventists, Chiliasts, Pre-Millenarians, etc., are now regarded as heretics, though they have much of the New Testament on their side.

It did not occur to the Jerusalem fellowship that anyone could be a member of their group without being first of all a good Jew and keeping the Jewish law. The very name, *ecclesia,* which they gave to themselves, shows that they regarded themselves as the chosen people, the true Israel. Only circumcised Jews were at first expected to apply for baptism into this special inner circle. But the Holy Spirit, it seemed, decreed otherwise! It fell, with power too evident to be denied, upon uncircumcised heathen in places like Caesarea, and it seemed to have more affinity for the souls of unorthodox, Hellenized Jews of the Dispersion than for those of correctly educated Jews of the mother country! Very early in the Book of Acts [14] we hear of certain " Grecians " who were conscious of their difference from the " Hebrews " in the church; and it appears that the first severe persecution of the church by the Jerusalem authorities was directed mainly against these, while the apostles, who kept the Jewish law, were relatively unmolested. " Therefore," says the chronicle, " they that were scattered abroad went everywhere preaching the word " [15] — among other places, to Samaria, Phoenicia, Cyprus, and Antioch. While they generally made their first approach through the Jewish synagogues, it is reported that at Antioch certain " men of Cyprus and Cyrene " took it upon themselves to preach to other " Grecians " like themselves; and they must have had great success, for it was here at Antioch that the first strong Gentile church sprang up. Significantly enough, it was here that the disciples were first called " Christians "; here first, it would seem, they became sufficiently independent of Jewish manners and customs to be distinguishable from other Jews.

The question whether converted Gentiles should be required in any sense to keep the Jewish law was the first serious doctrinal problem the Christian church had to face. James, the brother of Jesus, and one of the " pillars " of the Jerusalem church, maintained staunchly that one could not please God without keeping his law, revealed unto Moses; and his party (the so-called " Judaizers ") sent out emissaries to the Gentile churches to urge their members to be circumcised. His great adversary in this controversy was a Hellenistic Jew from Tarsus named Paul, who had been dramatically converted in the very midst of a campaign of persecution against the Christians in Damascus, and who had since given himself ardently to the task of converting the Gentile inquirers in many cities of Asia Minor. To Paul, who had failed to find religious peace in keeping the law, the very essence of his newly found faith consisted in the replacement of all outward legal requirements by a right inward disposition and a right relationship to the Spirit, from which good conduct could be trusted to flow. He argued that faith in Christ had now superseded the law and made it unnecessary. Peter, the chief pillar of the Jerusalem church, showed considerable vacillation, at one time eating freely with uncircumcised Christians and then reversing his stand under criticism; but with his aid a compromise was effected, which provided that Gentile Christians need not be circumcised, but need only refrain from idolatry and observe certain features of Jewish practice, such as abstention from " blood " and " things strangled," which seemed to be required by common decency. This compromise set the Gentile church free for a great mission to the Roman world; while the Jewish Christians, known as the Nazareans or Ebionites, were completely lost sight of after a few generations.

The apostle Paul is sometimes referred to as the " second founder of Christianity." This title would be fully justified by the decisive part he played in the controversy over the Jewish law. Had Christianity not succeeded in cutting itself loose from Judaism at this point it would never have been able to spread, as it has, from one country to another across the western world. But the apostle was not only instrumental in helping the new movement to drop certain hampering limitations; he was also instrumental in giving to its message a new form, more congenial to the Greco-Roman mind. Christianity as he presented it was still an apocalyptic message about the speedy coming of the " end of the age "; but it was also, more and more predominantly toward the end of his ministry, a message about personal salvation from the guilt and power of sin, realizable here and now by all who would permit themselves to be touched by the Spirit of the living Christ and incorporated in his body, the church. For the Jewish Christians, Jesus was simply the Messiah, the divinely anointed herald of the coming kingdom of God; for Paul and the Gentile Christians, he was not only the Messiah, but the divine Saviour, who had taken human flesh, died as man and risen as God, in order that those who were mystically united with him through the Spirit and the church might die with him to sin and rise with him to newness of life. The letters of Paul, while they contain no formal system of theology, have served as a thesaurus of religious concepts for all later times. Particularly influential have been his conception of Christ as the "second Adam" — "as in Adam all die, even so in Christ shall all be made alive" — and his interpretation of the two chief Christian sacraments: baptism as dying and rising with Christ, the Lord's Supper as a remembrance of his sacrificial death and as a spiritual feeding upon his broken body and shed blood. At every point his teaching roots deeply in Jewish tradition and in the life and message of Jesus; but as a Hellenistic Jew he was able to clothe the gospel in forms congenial and persuasive to the pagan mind.

Gibbon, in the fifteenth chapter of his *Decline and Fall of the Roman Empire,* lists the following causes of the rapid growth of the Christian movement:

1. The inflexible, and, if we may use the expression, the intolerant zeal of the Christians, derived from the Jewish religion. . . . 2. The doctrine of a future life, improved by every additional circumstance [16] which could give weight and efficacy to that important truth. 3. The miraculous powers ascribed to the primitive church. 4. The pure and austere morals of the Christians. 5. The union and discipline of the Christian republic, which gradually formed an independent and increasing state in the heart of the Roman Empire.

In the light of our analysis of the religious tendencies of the Roman world, it may be possible for us to give a simpler and more unified answer to the problem Gibbon raises, while granting much weight to the five factors he singles out. Christianity spread rapidly in the Roman world because it combined the moral and social values of Jewish ethical monotheism with the mystical and otherworldly values which men sought in the private salvation cults, and summed up all these values concretely in the person of its Founder. No other religion offered such a rich combination of values.

One element alone was at first lacking: Christianity appeared to be indifferent to the civic virtues and the cultural values for which the old state religion still stood, in spite of its decadence. But when the Christian movement gradually came to permeate every class in society, in spite of frequent persecution, it came at length to constitute what Gibbon calls " an independent and increasing state in the heart of the Roman Empire "; and the Emperor Constantine had the wit to see in this " Christian republic " a better means of conserving the unity and culture of his empire than the old state religion, on whose artificial restoration the Emperor Augustus had staked his hopes. So, in 313 A.D., the Edict of Milan was issued, granting toleration to Christians, and within a few years Christianity had become the state religion of the empire. Instead of being destroyed by the lightnings of divine wrath, as the early Christians prophesied, Rome had been undermined and conquered from within by the pervasive influence of the new religion.

IV. CATHOLICISM

The oldest Christian bodies now in existence are the Greek or Eastern Orthodox Church and the Roman Catholic Church. The Greek Orthodox Church perpetuates the ancient association of churches which had its chief strength in the eastern or Byzantine half of the Roman Empire, and its chief centers in Jerusalem, Antioch, Alexandria, Greece proper, and Constantinople. It has spread to the northeast and northwest from Constantinople, so that its Slavonic and Rumanian branches are now very important. Until the Bolshevik revolution the Russian Orthodox Church led all the rest. The Roman Catholic Church perpetuates the far more centralized ecclesiastical organization of the western or Latin half of the empire, whose destinies have always revolved, inevitably, about that of the imperial city of Rome. Its influence spread northeastward and northwestward from Rome until it embraced the whole of western Europe, and then traveled far afield, to Latin America and many more distant regions, in the wake of the great movement of colonial expansion led by Spain and Portugal. Until their formal separation in A.D. 1054 the Greek and Roman churches formed one body, commonly known as the Ancient Catholic Church. We shall therefore first consider the general characteristics of Catholicism, as embodied in this Ancient Catholic Church, before taking up the distinctive characteristics of the Eastern Orthodox and Roman Catholic churches.

1. General Characteristics of Ancient Catholicism. Ancient Catholicism had certain distinguishing characteristics, namely, apostolicity, orthodoxy, unity and catholicity, and holiness.

(1). Apostolicity. The first and most significant mark of Catholicism, both ancient and modern, is its claim to be the faithful continuator of the original church, founded by God himself through his chosen emissaries, Jesus and the apostles.

As early as A.D. 96, when the letter known as First Clement was written, we find a bishop of Rome exhorting the church at Corinth, in truly Catholic style, to beware of unauthorized wandering prophets and to hold firmly to that sound and regular order of worship, ministry, etc., which had come down from the apostles in unbroken descent. "The apostles," says Clement, "preached the gospel to us from the Lord Jesus Christ, Jesus Christ was sent from God. Christ then is from God, and the apostles from Christ. . . . They appointed their firstfruits, having tested them by the Spirit, as bishops and deacons of those who should believe." This is the doctrine of "apostolic succession" as it always has been professed by Catholics.

(2). Orthodoxy. The criterion of apostolicity began quite early to be used as a means of settling doctrinal disputes and of excluding from the fellowship of the church certain "heretics" whose views seemed to the great body of Christians to be extreme and subversive. As the movement spread far and wide in the Roman world it no longer proved workable to leave its guidance to the unpredictable promptings of the Spirit. The Spirit appeared to be prophesying in too many contradictory voices! How was one to tell the difference between true and false teaching without some external and objective test of orthodoxy (literally, "right opinion"), such as the test of apostolic origin already mentioned?

It was Irenaeus, bishop of Lyons, who first clearly formulated the principles of Christian orthodoxy, in his book *Against the Heresies,* written about 180 A.D. In his day two contrary forms of heresy were abroad: that of the Gnostics, who despised the Jewish elements in Christian tradition and interpreted Christ as a kind of pagan demigod who was never really born and never really died; and that of the Montanists, who had reverted to primitive Jewish Christianity and were expecting the immediate second coming of Christ. Against all such extreme tendencies, in the interest of peace and harmony in the church, Irenaeus defined Christian orthodoxy as that sound teaching contained in the canonical books of the Old and New Testaments, handed on from the apostles to their duly ordained successors, the bishops of the church, and formulated for the laity in a little creed (now known, in an amplified form, as the Apostles' Creed) which every catechumen was required to memorize and recite at the time of his baptism.

The Apostles' Creed still forms the groundwork of Christian orthodoxy. Against the Gnostics' denial of the God of the Old Testament it affirms faith in "God the Father Almighty, Maker of heaven and earth." Against their denial of the real humanity of Jesus, it affirms faith in "Jesus Christ his only Son our Lord, who was born . . . , suffered . . . , buried . . . , arose . . . , ascended . . . , cometh to judge." In conformity with common Christian conviction and in protest against certain subsequent heresies it concludes by affirming faith in "the Holy Ghost, the Holy Catholic Church, the communion of saints, the forgiveness of sins, the resurrection of the body, and the life everlasting." At the Council of Nicea (325 A.D.) the relations of the Son and the Holy Ghost to the Father were more closely defined, in opposition to the Arian heresy, and it was affirmed that Christ was the incarnation of a divine Being, the eternal Son or Word of God (Logos), who was no mere subordinate agent of the Father, but "of one substance" (*homoöusios*) with the Father. Later, at the Council of Chalcedon (451 A.D.), the relation of the divine and human elements in Christ was defined in opposition to the Nestorian and Monophysite heresies; and it was affirmed that Christ had two natures, each perfectly distinct from the other yet perfectly united in one person who was both God and man. This compromise formula failed to reconcile the two heretical extremes, and they seceded from the orthodox church. Nestorianism, which had its chief strength in Syria, spread eastward to Persia and China, and still survives in Mesopotamia. It teaches the complete duality between the human Jesus and the divine Word of which he was the bearer. The Monophysite creed, which teaches the complete metaphysical identity of the human Jesus with the divine Word, is still professed in the Coptic churches of Egypt and Abyssinia, with which the Armenian and Syrian "Jacobite" churches are affiliated. The Eastern Orthodox, Roman Catholic, and Anglican churches all accept the Apostles', the Nicene, and the Athanasian creeds, embodying the decisions of the early ecumenical councils, as having established the true line of orthodoxy connecting modern Christianity with the apostles. For the Greek and Anglican churches the authority of such an ecumenical council of duly ordained bishops, successors of the apostles, is supreme. For the Roman Catholic Church, it is exceeded only by the authority of the bishop of Rome, who as St. Peter's successor is chief of bishops as St. Peter was chief of apostles. "Thou art Peter," said Christ, " and on this rock I will build my Church; and the gates of hell shall not prevail against it. And I will give unto thee the keys of the kingdom of heaven; and whatsoever thou shalt bind on earth shall be bound in heaven; and whatsoever thou shalt loose on earth shall be loosed in heaven." [17] When the Roman pontiff speaks *ex cathedra,* defining orthodox doctrine as the official head of the church, his decisions are regarded by good Roman Catholics as infallible and beyond appeal.

(3). Unity and Catholicity. The Pauline conception of the church as the body of Christ implies that there can be but one body, as there is but one Head, although the members may be many and diverse. The idea of a " catholic " or " universal " church, extending "throughout the world," is therefore a native and almost inevitable Christian idea. It was in the service of this idea that the early fathers of the church combatted heresy and defined orthodoxy.

The principles of unity and catholicity were first clearly stated in their natural relations by Cyprian, bishop of Carthage from 248 to 258, in his treatise *On the Unity of the Catholic Church,* where he urged that it was just as necessary to salvation to belong organically to the one true church as it was to hold the orthodox faith. An orthodox schismatic is lost as surely as an unorthodox heretic, for "he cannot have God for his father who has not the church for his mother. . . . If anyone could escape who was outside the ark of Noah he also may escape who is outside the church." The unity of the Catholic Church is for Cyprian embodied in the consensus of apostolically descended bishops, especially when met in ecumenical council. At one time he was willing to see it still more graphically represented by the bishop of Rome, successor of St. Peter, chief of the apostles; but following a dispute with the aforesaid bishop he abandoned this position! Already in his writings, however, the foundations of papal theory are laid.

(4). Holiness. The New Testament term for the collective membership of a church was "the saints" (*hagioi*), or more literally, "the holy ones." [18] Inferentially, a universal church composed of saints, bound together in "the unity of the Spirit and the bond of peace," was itself a holy institution, from which sanctifying power might be expected to flow forth to all who came in touch with it. Actually, of course, the holiness of the church became increasingly difficult to discern the more its membership grew and the more its activities spread out into contact with secular society. While persecution lasted, there was a powerful guaranty that no unholy or insincere person would risk his life by becoming a Christian; but as soon as the church was tolerated by the state, still more when it was officially recognized, multitudes thronged into its fellowship whose claim to holiness was very slight indeed. If the church was to maintain its holiness, it became imperative that a line be drawn between merely nominal, "respectable " Christians, and those who really meant to be holy. Hence arose the distinction between the " saint " and the common man, and the tremendous development of monasticism, with its ascetic and mystical tendencies.

Monasticism means no more, in its root notion, than to " keep oneself unspotted from the world ";[19] asceticism, no more than to practice moral endurance and self-control as an athlete practices physical endurance and muscular coordination; mysticism, no more than to close one's mind to all sense impressions in order to become conscious of the presence of God.   Taken in this elementary sense, the monastic ideal may be said to represent one side of the Christian ideal as surely as the ideal of the *Arhat* represents one side of the Buddhist ideal; but taken in isolation from the active ethical virtues (" visiting the fatherless in their affliction "), it is less congenial to Christianity than to Buddhism, as the history of monasticism itself bears witness.

After an initial wave of enthusiasm for the completely eremitic (hermit) life and a certain amount of morbid interest in cases like that of St. Simeon Stylites, who spent his life on top of a pillar, the monastic movement swung over for the most part to the cenobitic (communal) life, and the rules of monastic orders required, in addition to the three great vows of poverty, chastity, and obedience, a certain amount of useful work and study.[20] Finally, in the Franciscan and Dominican movements of the Middle Ages, monasticism left the cloister and went out aggressively to transform, by preaching and by deeds of mercy, the world from which at first it had fled.   In these so-called " mendicant " orders the New Testament balance between the active and contemplative virtues was restored.

Meanwhile it should not be forgotten that even in his solitary contemplations the monk's object was not only to save his own soul, but to help his fellow men as well. As he followed the mystic way, beginning with ascetic purgation, proceeding through the stage of mystic illumination toward the final goal of ecstatic union with his God, the Catholic saint believed himself to be earning " merit " which could be added to that central store of sanctifying power known as the " treasury of merit," and thence dispensed by the church to the needy. The chief asset, so to speak, on which the treasury of merit could draw was the sacrifice of Christ upon the cross; but every saint who disciplined himself in holiness added his bit of merit and his bit of saving power to the great reservoir.

Through the sacraments (or mysteries, as they were called in the east) the members of the church had access to all the wealth of holiness created by Christ and the saints. Baptism and the Lord's Supper or eucharist still remained the two principal sacraments. The first inducted the sinner into the new life of holiness and brought him into contact with the saving power (" grace ") resident in the church. The second nourished and sustained the new life thus begun, through the sanctifying power of the body and blood of Christ. In addition to these, five other sacraments came into general usage in the Catholic Church: confirmation, by which baptismal vows made in infancy were publicly accepted and confirmed in adolescence; holy orders, by which the " religious " life was embraced, if one chose the harder path leading to priesthood or monkhood; matrimony, by which the secular life of the family was sanctified, if one chose the easier path of the common Christian; penance, the " second plank " by which a Christian who sinned after baptism might be rescued and restored to fellowship, upon acceptance of whatever penitential works or gracious indulgences his confessor might see fit to prescribe for his case; and finally, extreme unction, by which the soul was prepared at the point of death for what might await it in the next life — whether for the temporal punishments and purification of purgatory, or, in exceptional cases, for immediate bliss in heaven. Thus from birth to death, and after, the sacraments of the church surrounded and sustained the life of the Christian and nourished him in holiness. That genuine holiness was genuinely transmitted in multitudes of instances will be denied only by those who dislike the type of character produced.[21]

2. *The Eastern Orthodox and Roman Catholic Churches.* The Ancient Catholic Church, united by so many ties and uniform in so many of its fundamental principles, lasted on as a single

church until the Middle Ages, but at length split into an eastern or Greek and a western or Roman church. The causes of the split were mainly political and historical, though differences in theology and practice contributed to the growth of misunderstanding. The Roman Empire was divided, soon after Christianity became its leading faith, into a western section, of which Rome was the capital, and an eastern section, of which Constantinople was the capital. The Eastern or Byzantine Empire maintained its existence until it fell before the Mohammedan Turks in 1453; and it always kept the church subservient to the state — partly because the state was strong, and partly because the leadership of the church was divided among the patriarchs of Constantinople, Alexandria, and Antioch. The Western Empire had a very different fate. Rome was sacked by the Visigoths in 410 and by the Vandals in 455. The last Roman emperor, a puppet monarch named Romulus Augustulus, was deposed in 476; but long before this time the whole of the west had been inundated by streams of barbarians from the north, who put an end to civilization in that part of the world for a period of many centuries, generally known as the Dark Ages. In this crisis, the one institution that stood firm was the Christian church, under the practically undisputed leadership of Rome, the one most important city in this part of the empire. The Roman Catholic Church not only defended and propagated the Christian faith among the barbarians, but preserved the record of pagan culture in its monasteries, and gradually brought back the whole of western Europe to the level of civilization again. Throughout the Dark Ages and the Middle Ages the Roman papacy played a leading part in the political life of the world. Eventually, it was clear, a break [22] was inevitable between the state-dominated church of the east and the state-dominating church of the west.

Since the eastern and western halves of the Roman Empire first began to drift apart, there has been little change in the doctrine and practice of the Eastern Orthodox Church. The solemn chants and the incense of her beautiful ritual have been floating up steadily for fifteen hundred years toward the tall domes of her stately sanctuaries, as if adoration of God and pointing man's thoughts away from earth were her sole and sufficient tasks. The Roman Catholic Church has been too actively engaged with the problems of politics and civilization to remain so otherworldly or so static. How much she has developed may be seen from a comparison between the Catholicism of St. Augustine, the greatest of the ancient Latin fathers, and the Catholicism of the medieval and modern church.

The religion of St. Augustine has been compared by Friedrich Heiler, in his great work, *Der Katholizismus,* to a pyramid whose base is founded upon the Scriptures, especially the Book of Psalms and the Epistles of St. Paul; whose sides are constituted by the Roman doctrine of the authority of the visible church; and whose apex is the Neo-Platonic ideal of mystic ecstasy as the culmination of the religious life. The biblical and Neo-Platonic elements in the teaching of St. Augustine are most clearly expressed in his *Confessions* — the greatest religious document which has come down to us from Latin Christianity — while his teaching about the church was classically formulated in *The City of God.*[23]

When St. Augustine died in 430 A.D. as bishop of Hippo in north Africa, the Vandals were battering at the gates of the city. For centuries after, the Roman Catholic Church labored at the task of enlightening and disciplining the many tribes of northern barbarians who had overrun the world. Not only were the actual invaders slowly civilized and Christianized, but missionaries pushed out beyond the frontiers of civilization to carry the gospel to northern Europe. St. Patrick (d. 461) was mainly instrumental in planting Christianity in Ireland; St. Columba (d. 597) carried the cross from Ireland to Scotland; St. Boniface (d. 754), a British monk, became the apostle to Germany, and before his death at the hands of the barbarians had welded the whole missionary enterprise into a unified movement with headquarters at Rome. As feudal society began to rise out of the ruins of Roman society the Roman Church became an active participant in its organization and administration. Bishops of the church became secular officials. Charlemagne was consecrated by the pope in 800 A.D. as ruler of the

Frankish empire; and a claim to papal supremacy in temporal affairs was thus set up, which was fiercely contested between emperors and popes for centuries thereafter. By the thirteenth century — called "greatest of centuries" by some Catholic historians — Europe had been lifted again, under the leadership of the church, to a high plane of civilization; and there came a great flowering of religious architecture (Gothic cathedrals), religious literature (Dante), religious philosophy (scholasticism), and noble religious living (the Franciscan movement), which marks perhaps the high point in the history of the influence of Christianity over western civilization.

In medieval Catholicism, elements of the most diverse sort were mingled and blended as in a rich mosaic. In the *Summa Theologica* of St. Thomas Aquinas, greatest of the scholastics, the philosophy of Aristotle furnishes the groundwork of a great reconciliation between Greek and Hebrew thought, while the pagan "cardinal virtues" (courage, wisdom, temperance, and justice) are made the indispensable foundation for the Christian "theological virtues" (faith, hope, love). In Dante's *Divine Comedy* the pagan poet Virgil, representing human reason, guides his Christian successor through two-thirds of his long pilgrimage; and even in the *Paradiso* the conception of the heavenly spheres is borrowed from Aristotle and Ptolemy.

Along with the influence of classical Greece and Rome, the influence of the northern peoples combined to make medieval Christianity a very different thing from ancient Latin Christianity. The warlike spirit of the Celts and Teutons was refined and disciplined by the church, but not wholly mastered; and so emerged the ideal of chivalry, a strange but beautiful and appealing perversion of the religion of the Prince of Peace. Old barbarian customs and superstitions lingered on, transmuted but not destroyed, in the medieval church. The Christmas festival in northern lands gathered to itself the ancient northern reverence for the holly, the ivy, the mistletoe, and the evergreen tree. The austerities of Lent were interrupted and followed by popular carnivals of a pronouncedly heathenish character. The popular belief in the wonder-working powers of the bones of the saints — a belief which turned the tomb of St. Martin at Tours and the tomb of Thomas à Becket at Canterbury into rich sources of revenue — is very characteristic of the Middle Ages.

Most significant of all, perhaps, was the elaborate development of the penitential discipline in this period: a great system of laws, penalties, rewards, and indulgences, designed to control and moralize an unruly people. Protestants regard this " religion of law and good works " as a kind of reversion to Jewish legalism and a betrayal of the Pauline gospel of free grace; but the taming of the barbarians practically necessitated some such reversion to legalism. St. Augustine had said, " Love God and do as you please "; but that was dangerous doctrine to preach to savages! Meanwhile a higher way was held out for the saint. According to St. Bernard (d. 1153), the saint's progress involves four stages, leading progressively toward completely disinterested devotion: first I love myself; then I learn to love God because of what he does for me; then I learn to love God for his own sake; and finally I love myself for God's sake.[24]

Beside the relatively simple and closely knit religion of St. Augustine, the religion of the medieval church looms up as at once vaster, more magnificent, and more heterogeneous, like a great Gothic cathedral in which the Augustinian element is but a small Romanesque side chapel. This heterogeneity, this " complex of opposites," as Harnack calls it, was at once the beauty and the weakness of medieval Catholicism. For a century or two the medieval synthesis held together as a thing of beauty; then it began to go to pieces with the decline of the feudal system, to which it was closely bound. All authorities, Catholic and Protestant, are agreed that by the fifteenth century the church was in a lamentable state of decay, needing to be reformed " in head and members."

Modern Catholicism, which dates from the Council of Trent (1545–63), was dominated from the start by a demand for consistency, unity, and order, urged with special force by the soldier-saint Ignatius Loyola (d. 1556), founder of the Jesuits. Both in opposition to the Protestants and in opposition to the disintegrative tendencies of modern civilization, the Roman Catholic Church has become a disciplined army of conservatism, fighting against all forms of social and intellectual chaos with stubborn courage and tenacity. The principle of comprehensive hospitality, which made medieval Christendom such a charming crazy-quilt, has been replaced by the principles of authority and continuity. Unity has triumphed over catholicity. This change may be understood in part as a natural consequence of the Protestant Reformation, which took the more venturesome and self-assertive spirits out of the Catholic fold, leaving the leadership of the older church in conservative hands. Today, it can be fairly said that the great appeal of Catholicism is to those who feel the need for a strong central authority and a uniform code of faith and conduct, as a bulwark against the disturbing diversity and uncertainty of modern thought and the bewildering flux and disorder of modern society. The great representative of this group is John Henry Newman (d. 1890) whose *Apologia Pro Vita Sua,* describing his conversion to Rome, has done more than any other modern book to create understanding and respect for Catholicism in the English-speaking world.

V. PROTESTANTISM

In the later Middle Ages many attempts were made to reform the church. Although directed primarily at specific abuses, these protests led in many cases to open repudiation of the authority of the Roman pontiff and its replacement by some other authority, such as that of the Bible or of an ecumenical council. Abortive revolts of this sort were led by John Wyclif (d. 1384) and John Huss (d. 1416); but the first successful revolt was led by Martin Luther (d. 1546), who is by common consent designated as the father of the Protestant Reformation.

The religious experience of Luther was strikingly similar to that of St. Paul and St. Augustine. As an Augustinian monk, he had tried feverishly to escape from the fear of hell by penances and austerities and all manner of " good works "; yet he found no peace of soul, no power of self-mastery, until Staupitz, his wise and kindly superior, advised him to read St. Paul and cast himself upon the mercy of God. Reading the apostle he suddenly saw that the Christian gospel was addressed to just such sinners as himself; and it promised salvation, not upon the condition that they first earn it by will power and good works, but upon the sole condition that they have faith to receive the unearned grace of God. Seeing this, he was changed from a cringing slave, cowering before the divine wrath, into a bold and aggressive man, so confident of the divine mercy that no mortal could intimidate him thenceforth. This conversion experience, which took place in the seclusion of the monastery, implicitly undermined the whole penitential discipline of the Roman Catholic Church; for it happened without benefit of clergy, without the aid of the sacraments, nothing standing between Brother Martin and his God save an open Bible.

If Luther's experience resembled St. Augustine's in its total abandonment of self-reliance and complete trust in the grace of God, the outcome of his conversion was decidedly different. St. Augustine's conversion enabled him to abjure a life of sexual indulgence and embrace the rigors of a monastic life; Luther's conversion led to a revulsion against all ascetic austerities as needless and harmful. Everything connected with monastic life and the penitential discipline became obnoxious to him; and though he protested at first only against certain abuses like the sale of indulgences, he was led at last, in the heat of debate, to denounce the whole system and reject the authority of the pope, by which it was supported. The double standard of morality and the religion of good works thus fell to the ground at a single stroke. " It looks like a great thing," said Luther, " when a monk renounces everything and goes into a cloister, carries on a life of asceticism, fasts, watches, prays, etc. On the other hand, it looks like a small thing when a maid cooks and cleans and does other housework. But because God's command is there, even such a small work must be praised as a service of God far surpassing the holiness and asceticism of all monks and nuns. For here is no command of God. But there God's command is fulfilled, that one should honor father and mother and help in the care of the home." [25] The import of these words was demonstrated when Luther renounced his monastic vows and married a nun.

| Luther was of course accused of encouraging moral laxity — as the apostle Paul had been before him. Salvation by faith alone, apart from good works, sounded like an invitation to " sin, that grace may abound." Luther's answer to the charge was straightforward. Good works, he said, are the inevitable fruit of Christian faith. We cannot do enough good works to *deserve* our salvation; but when God saves us *without* our deserving it, we are impelled by gratitude to praise God and do good. " Oh, faith is a living, busy, active, mighty thing. It is impossible that it should not always be doing good. It asks not whether good works should be done, but before one asks it does them, and is always doing them." [26] The man of faith does not give alms to earn merit for himself, but out of disinterested love for a fellow man in need.

The doctrine of salvation by faith alone (*sola fide*) became one of the two cardinal principles of the Protestant Reformation. It reduced Christianity to simple terms, which the average man could understand and test for himself without professional religious guidance. Since this message was contained in the Bible, it became a second cardinal principle of the Reformation that Scripture alone (*sola Scriptura*) was the final test of religious truth; and every man could claim the right of private judgment as to what the Bible really taught.[27] The primacy of the clergy over the laity was thus destroyed, and the priesthood of all believers became a favorite Protestant teaching.

As might be expected, the exercise of the right of private judgment led to the founding of a great multitude of Protestant denominations, each claiming to be the truly biblical church. In the United States alone, there are no less than a hundred seventy-four different Protestant denominations. It would be more confusing than enlightening to try to give an account of all these minor divisions; but it may help to bring order out of chaos to note the fact that there were three main types of Protestantism which appeared at the time of the Reformation; that in the eighteenth century the Evangelical movement brought an important realignment of forces; and that in the nineteenth century a trend toward unity developed, which is now overcoming many old differences.

1. The Three Original Types of Protestantism. The three original types of Protestantism were the conservative or Lutheran, the Puritan or Zwinglian, and the radical or Anabaptist. The Lutheran and Episcopalian churches trace their descent from the Conservative Reformation; the Presbyterian and Reformed churches, from the Puritan Reformation; the Mennonites, Quakers, Congregationalists, and Baptists, from the Radical Reformation.

(1). The Conservative Reformation. Though it was Luther whose bold defiance of the pope launched the Reformation, he was far from approving rebellious and revolutionary activities as a matter of principle. The more he saw of the extreme consequences which some men drew from his teachings, the more conservative he grew. The logic of his heroic stand at the Diet of Worms seemed to point to complete religious liberty and political democracy; but in dealing with the "Zwickau prophets" at Wittenberg and later with the Peasants' Revolt he consistently took sides with the established authorities against all disturbances of the peace. In his first pronouncements on the sacraments, he seemed to imply that they were no more than symbolical ways of preaching the Word of God; but when Carlstadt preached against the mass, abolished the use of pictures, and denied the necessity of all sacraments, the attack revived Luther's loyalty to the good old ways and led him to champion the real presence of Christ in the eucharist. The principle to which he appealed was that, though the Bible was the norm of Christian faith and practice, it was not necessary to abandon all nonbiblical elements in Catholicism, if they were edifying and if they were not expressly forbidden in Scripture.

The Lutheran churches of Germany and Scandinavia, and the Church of England, which was reformed upon similar general principles, are accordingly much closer to Catholicism than the churches which adopted the Zwinglian principle and condemned everything not expressly commanded in Scripture. Their services of worship are highly ornate and liturgical, like the Catholic, but preaching is somewhat more important, and Latin is replaced by the vernacular of the country. Their government is hierarchical like the Roman Catholic, and state-controlled like the Greek Orthodox. In Germany, the ruling prince took the place of the bishop and governed the church through a consistory; in England and Scandinavia, bishops and archbishops were appointed by the state; in America, state control has given way to self-government. Theologically, the Augsburg Confession, to which all Lutherans subscribe, and the Thirty-Nine Articles of the Church of England, are very conservative documents. Melanchthon, who drew up the Augsburg Confession, hoped that it might be acceptable to Roman Catholics, while John Henry Newman, just before going over to Rome, made an attempt to interpret the Thirty-Nine Articles as entirely Catholic. Many overtures toward renewed understanding with Catholicism have been made by Lutherans and Episcopalians. They agree with the Greek Orthodox and Roman Catholic churches in officially recognizing the authority of the three great creeds of the undivided church: the Apostles' Creed, the Nicene Creed, and the Athanasian Creed.

(2). The Puritan Reformation. The Swiss Reformation, under Zwingli and his successors, differed from the German in its whole spirit and temper, as Luther himself recognized when he met Zwingli at Marburg. It fought against different elements in Christian tradition. It was not the "religion of law and good works," but the " idolatrous " side of medieval Catholicism — its use of images, its belief in the wonder-working power of sacred objects, its worship of the Blessed Virgin and the saints — that roused the ire of Huldreich Zwingli; and he thundered against these practices like an Old Testament prophet in the name of the jealous God of Sinai. If Luther's religion was predominantly Pauline and antilegal, Zwingli's was predominantly Hebraic and antipagan. Luther sought inward peace of mind; outwardly, he was willing to conform to the established order of society. Zwingli sought to create a new social order deserving to be called the kingdom of God; inwardly, he had passed through no such profound experience as Luther, though he formally accepted the Lutheran doctrine of salvation by faith. Ezekiel or Ezra would have understood him easily. The directive force of the whole Puritan movement, from that day to this, has been the ancient Jewish dream of an ideal commonwealth, peaceful and prosperous because governed strictly in accordance with the expressed will of God, made known in his Word. In the light of that hope Calvin governed the godly city of Geneva, John Knox crossed over from Geneva to claim Scotland for Jehovah, Oliver Cromwell overthrew the Stuart monarchy in England, and the disappointed Puritans left England to find the heavenly city in the New World.

Theology has always been a matter of prime importance in the Presbyterian and Reformed churches; and by tradition they are staunchly Calvinistic. In the Westminster Confession, which is the most typical of all Puritan creeds, the irresistible power of God and the helplessness of man are affirmed, as in Calvin's *Institutes,* in the most uncompromising terms. " By the decree of God, for the manifestation of his glory, some men and angels are predestinated unto everlasting life and others foreordained unto everlasting death." [28] This is only just, it is maintained, for all men since Adam are totally depraved, and deserve eternal punishment. If God condemned us all to hell it would be perfectly just; if he determines to save an elect few, out of pure grace and for no merit of their own, and if we are among the elect, we can but marvel at his mercy and serve him faithfully all the days of our life. This theology, with its apparent denial of human freedom, would seem to lead to fatalistic inertia; as a matter of fact, it has developed an intense vigor of character, a sturdy independence of mind, which has been the consistent foe of all kinds of tyranny. Morally, it has made for severe self-discipline, as in the well known Puritan injunctions against Sabbath-breaking, dancing, card-playing, and theater-going. Sobriety, frugality, industry, and a sense of concern for the public morals have been generally characteristic of this type of Protestantism. The Presbyterian or Synodical form of church government has had much influence upon the development of similar forms of representative government in the secular state. This could hardly fail to be the case, for the Puritan ideal of the state is a theocracy, in which the church (on behalf of God) exerts a dominating pressure upon public affairs. In their forms of worship the Presbyterian and Reformed churches are extremely bare and simple by comparison with the Lutheran and Episcopalian churches. Altars, priestly vestments, stained glass, and, in the old days, any music other than Psalm tunes, seemed to them to savor of popery and pagan idolatry. Needless to say, the various forms of Puritan austerity have tended to be softened with the lapse of time.

(3). The Radical Reformation. The most consistent of all the reformers in their application of the principles of religious liberty, private judgment, and direct access to God, were the Anabaptists, or "rebaptizers," so called because they insisted upon a change of heart as a necessary condition for church membership, and administered "believers' baptism" (adult baptism, usually by immersion) to those who joined their circle. It is impossible to generalize much about the Anabaptists, since they sprang up in many different parts of Europe, were forced to meet in secrecy on account of the persecution of other Protestants, and never fully agreed among themselves; but two types of Anabaptism should be carefully distinguished: the violent type known as Obbenites, exemplified by the group which seized the city of Münster in 1532 and established a communistic theocracy, and the pacifist type, exemplified by the Mennonites.

The Mennonites — named after Menno Simons (d. 1561), one of their earliest leaders — are the modern successors of a group of dissenters who broke off from Zwingli's congregation at Zurich in 1523. Only those are admitted to their society who have experienced the "new birth" and are prepared to renounce worldly things completely — including military service, the taking of oaths, and the holding of public office. Each of their congregations is completely self-governing, and there is no ordained ministry, their elders and bishops being regarded as elected representatives of the laity. They practice "believers' baptism" (by pouring, not by immersion), and foot-washing as a part of the Lord's Supper; but they hold these rites to have only a symbolical value, as emblems of inner purification. Their ideal is to reproduce the New Testament church as exactly as possible in the modern world; and they therefore frequently live in secluded communities, discouraging intermarriage with other people. One sect, the Amish, refuses to use such modern conveniences as buttons and razors.

Closely akin to the Mennonites in many ways are the Quakers, or more correctly, the Society of Friends, founded by George Fox in 1647. Although their connection with the original Anabaptists is obscure, there can be no doubt that they represent that religious tradition, in perhaps its most consistent and attractive form. Their characteristic teaching is the doctrine of the " inner light," whereby every man is capable of communing directly with the Spirit of God. For them, the supreme authority is not the Scriptures, but " the Spirit in which the Scriptures were written." This Spirit, they believe, makes the mind of Christ known to them in their meetings, when they reverently wait in silence together until the Spirit moves them to speak. Like the Mennonites, they object to military service, oath-taking, and an ordained ministry; but unlike them they object to *all* sacraments, while on the other hand they are more willing than the Mennonites to participate in civic affairs and mingle with other people. Perhaps for this last reason they have made a deeper impression upon the general public and are widely respected for their serenity of mind, their loyalty to their principles, and their active advocacy of great social reforms.

The largest and best known of the denominations which have sprung from the Anabaptist Reformation are the Congregationalists and the Baptists. Both are descended from the English Independents, who are known to have been in frequent communication with the Dutch Anabaptists. They share with the Mennonites and Quakers the advocacy of an autonomous local church and a " regenerate " church membership. According to Robert Browne, who founded the first Independent Church in 1580, " Christians are a company or number of believers who, by a willing covenant, made with their God, are under the government of God and Christ, and keep his laws in one holy communion." [29] According to this definition, infants cannot possibly be Christians; yet Browne encouraged the practice of infant baptism as an expression of the desire of Christian parents that their children might be " offered to God." ³⁰ This led at length, about 1612, to a schism among the Independents, some of whom — the modern Baptists — renounced infant baptism as inconsistent with their principles and adopted immersion as the correct form of adult baptism. American Congregationalism was the product of a fusion between the Pilgrims of Plymouth, who were Independents, and the Puritans of Boston and Salem, who were dissatisfied members of the Church of England. The Puritans adopted the Independent form of church government after the union, but the Pilgrims seem in turn to have been influenced by Puritan theocratic ideas; for the Massachusetts Bay Colony granted no tolerance to Quakers or Baptists, and enforced religious uniformity with a heavy hand. Roger Williams, fleeing from their persecution, founded in 1638 a Baptist community in Rhode Island — the first American colony to grant complete religious toleration. The Baptists have consistently advocated the complete separation of church and state — which has become the prevailing American policy.

2. *Later Realignments in Protestantism.* When the American colonies were first settled the original alignment of Protestantism still prevailed. The Conservative Reformation was represented by the Episcopalians of Virginia and scattered Lutheran colonies in New York, New Jersey, and Delaware. The Puritan Reformation was represented by the Puritans of Massachusetts, the Dutch Reformed of New York, and the Scotch-Irish Presbyterians of the south. The Radical Reformation was represented by the Pilgrims of Plymouth, the Baptists of Rhode Island, the Quakers of Pennsylvania, and a few small Mennonite settlements.

Before the end of the eighteenth century the whole religious map of America was altered by a great religious movement, a veritable second Reformation, commonly known as Pietism or Evangelicalism. This movement started in Germany toward the end of the seventeenth century, under the leadership of Philip Jacob Spener (d. 1705). Lamenting the aridity of the theological disputes which were agitating the Lutheran churches in his day, Spener founded circles for Bible study and prayer known as *collegia pietatis*. Through him and his successors, German piety came to take at once a more practical and more mystical turn, expressing itself in a multitude of charitable works as well as in devotional study and prayer meetings. Most of those who joined the Pietist movement stayed in the Lutheran Church; but one group, the Moravians, under the leadership of Count Zinzendorf, founded a religious community of their own at Herrnhut, and sent missions throughout Christendom. It was through an encounter with some of these Moravians, on his first visit to America, that John Wesley, the founder of Methodism, experienced that deepening in his religious life which impelled him to " take the world for his parish." Between the preaching of Wesley and his great associate Whitefield, and the independent outburst of the " Great Awakening " under Jonathan Edwards in New England, the whole English-speaking world was deeply stirred and changed in the eighteenth century. Especially in America, periodic revivals of religion came to be the prevailing manifestations of the Protestant faith, and to be " soundly converted," after " conviction of sin " and " full surrender," came to be the indispensable mark of a Christian. Not only were several new denominations, such as the Dunkards, the Methodists, the Evangelicals, the United Brethren, brought into being by this movement, but most of the older denominations were transformed in their characteristics. The Baptists became as " Evangelical " as the Methodists; the Presbyterians and Congregationalists joined only a trifle less zealously in the promotion of interdenominational revival meetings; and even the Episcopalian Church came to have a powerful " Low Church " or "Evangelical " wing. Only the extreme ritualists to the right and the extreme rationalists to the left refused to join the Evangelical movement. At least in America, Protestant unity was almost an achieved fact.

Under these circumstances, it was not surprising that many movements for church unity sprang up in the nineteenth century. One of the earliest of these was the general movement for a nonsectarian, creedless, evangelistic Christianity which resulted, paradoxically enough, in the birth of two new denominations: the Christians, and the Disciples of Christ. Both grew out of attempts to unite Christians upon a nontheological basis, with the New Testament as their only charter and a common experience of Evangelical conversion as their chief bond of sympathy. Both had their chief success in the middle west and the far west, where denominational loyalties are weakest. The Christians have recently united with the Congregationalists; the Disciples, however, still remain a separate body, distinguished by certain practices like baptism by immersion and the regular celebration of the Lord's Supper each week. More successful movements for unity were those which resulted in the United Evangelical Church of Germany, the Reunited Church of Scotland, and the United Church of Canada. Collaboration in missionary work abroad — one of the great results of the Evangelical revival — has resulted in many movements for comity on the mission field, the most remarkable of them being the movement for organic unity between Episcopalians, Presbyterians, and Congregationalists in south India. American Protestants are now functioning as a united body, for many practical purposes, through the Federal Council of Churches. Through the International Missionary Council, the International Y.M.C.A. and Y.W.C.A., the World's Student Christian Federation, the World Alliance for International Friendship through the Churches, and most especially through the world conferences on Life and Work (Stockholm, 1925; Oxford, 1937) and Faith and Order (Lausanne, 1927; Edinburgh, 1937), they now participate in a world-wide ("ecumenical") movement for Christian unity which already includes the Eastern Orthodox Church and hopes eventually to come to some understanding with the Roman Catholic Church. At the recent Oxford and Edinburgh conferences, steps were taken to give an organ and a voice to this movement in a World Council of Churches, roughly corresponding to the American Federal Council.

Whether the independent spirit of Protestantism can ever be reconciled with the authoritative claims of the papacy seems very problematical. It is at least significant that Protestants have begun to realize that independence can be bought at too heavy a price, and that many precious religious values were sacrificed in the Protestant revolt; while the Catholic Church now permits to her philosophers a much greater freedom in scientific investigation and in reformulation of old truths than in the days when the Inquisition was at its height. In the Middle Ages the Protestant spirit found scope within the universal church in the form of monastic and mendicant orders with diverse rules. It is conceivable that if we can once more unite our world about some commonly acceptable philosophy of life — without which we shall never again have a great flowering of culture and art — we may be able this time to do it by free consent, without violent compulsion, making full room for individual differences of opinion and temperament, thus combining the advantages of Catholicism and Protestantism. If contemporary political developments are any indication, mankind will continue, for a long time to come, to choose between the values of freedom with disunity and unity by dictatorship. Yet the close complexity and delicacy of our interdependence would seem to indicate that both these alternatives will rapidly become impossible. If these two ways should prove to be impracticable in such a complex world as ours, another pair of alternatives presents itself — and they seem to be the only others. Either we must learn to live together with harmony and cooperation, which means common acceptance of certain basic principles; or else we shall destroy our civilization and sink to a level of lesser interdependence where freedom with disunity on the one hand and dictatorship on the other once again become practicable alternatives.

NOTES

1 The truth of this statement does not perhaps seem so obvious today as it did during the latter part of the nineteenth century, when the power and prestige of European civilization were at their height. Then, the inferiority of Oriental civilization and the Christian character of Occidental civilization were more easily taken for granted. Now, in the wake of a disastrous war which weakened and humbled the western powers, it is no longer clear that the Orient is in all respects less " civilized " than the Occident; while the civilization of the west is seen to contain many powerful " pagan " or " secularistic " tendencies, which often dominate the Christian element and even threaten to extinguish it. Nevertheless, it remains true, so far as objective statistics can settle the matter.

[2] Hume, *The World's Living Religions* (New York, 1924), p. 14. Hume also lists 250 million Confucianists; but religion in China is now in a state of rapid decay and radical transformation. The Columbia University Press recently (1935) gave out the estimate that out of every hundred persons 38 were Christians, 19 Confucianists or Taoists, 12 Hindus, 11 Mohammedans, 10 animists, 8 Buddhists, one Shintoist, and one Jew. The statement is somewhat misleading, since it ignores the vast numbers of people who are alienated from their historic faith or merely nominal adherents; but as a rough estimate of the relative strength of the chief historic religions it deserves attention.

[3] *Annals*, XV, 44 (A.D. 64).

[4] Letter 96, A.D. 111.

[5] Cf. Bevan, *Christianity*, p. 9. "The Jews were now everywhere a people to whom their numbers alone would have given importance. The Roman Empire was Jewish to a greater degree than the United States today."

[6] The New Testament word is *euangelion*, "good news." For our knowledge of early Christianity we are entirely dependent — apart from a few slight contemporary references such as the above-cited passages from Tacitus and Pliny — upon early Christian literature, and chiefly upon the New Testament itself. The canon of the New Testament was formed upon the assumption that all of its books were written by or at the dictation of the twelve apostles, or the apostle Paul. Modern historical criticism casts doubt upon this assumption. Its most important conclusions are (1) that the earliest and most authentic New Testament writings are the genuine epistles of Paul; (2) that the epistles to the Hebrews, to Timothy, and to Titus are not Pauline; (3) that the Gospel and epistles of John are probably not by the apostle John, but by some later author of great religious genius, who had not known Jesus in person and does not quote his words exactly; (4) that the Gospels of Matthew and Luke are dependent for their main *narrative* upon the Gospel of Mark (which may have been based upon the recollections of the apostle Peter), while their account of the *teachings* of Jesus is derived from some early collection of his sayings.

[7] Matt. 10: 6, 7, 23 (Moffatt's Translation).

[8] Isa. 53:5.

[9] Luke 13:33.

[10] Matt. 21:43.

[11] John 15:13.

[12] Mark 9:34; Luke 22:24; etc.

[13] We apparently owe our account of the crucifixion to a young man named Simon of Cyrene, who was impressed by the soldiers to carry Jesus' cross when he fell under its weight, and who later became a Christian. The story of the crucifixion in the Gospel of John, according to which Mary, the mother of Jesus, was standing at the foot of the cross, with two other women and one of the disciples, is inconsistent with the earlier and more reliable evidence of the other three Gospels.

[14] Acts 6:1.

[15] Acts 8:1, 3.

[16] Gibbon obviously refers to the report of the actual resurrection of Jesus, in which Christians saw the assured promise of their own future resurrection.

[17] Matt. 16:18, 19.

[18] For example, the Epistle to the Romans (15:26) alludes to the church at Jerusalem as the "saints which are at Jerusalem."

[19] Jas. 1:27.

[20] In the west many monastic orders developed. In the east the rule of St. Basil is universal, which forbids strong drink and uncanonical reading in addition to the restrictions of the west.

[21] The list of the seven sacraments just given is that of the Roman Church. In the Greek churches there are also seven sacraments or " mysteries," but chrismation after baptism takes the place of confirmation, confession takes the place of penance, while unction is administered to heal the sick instead of being given at the point of death.

[22] The break, when it finally came, was technically based upon a long-standing dispute over a theological term, the famous *filioque*. When the Western Church adopted a creed asserting that the Spirit proceeds from the Father *and from the Son* (*filioque*), this seemed to the Eastern Church to deny that God the Father was the sole ultimate Source. Besides this, there are many minor differences between the two churches: the priests of the Eastern Church (except bishops) need not be celibate; *both* the bread and the wine in the eucharist are given to the people, including infants; the sign of the cross is made in a different fashion; and the whole liturgy differs from the Roman mass. But all these are subordinate to the main difference: the Roman papacy claims an *authority* which the Eastern Orthodox Church refuses to recognize — an authority superior to that of ecumenical councils in matters of doctrine, and extending beyond the sphere of doctrine into the moral and political spheres. The Roman Catholic Church, through her supreme pontiff, successor to Peter, prince of the apostles, and heir of the prerogatives of the Roman emperors, not only claims supreme control over the sacraments upon which man's salvation depends, and infallible authority to define the doctrines which he must believe, but also claims supreme right to govern the behavior of men and nations. The Eastern churches, on the other hand, are closely bound to the national state in those countries where they exist. In czaristic Russia, the Orthodox Church was so fully an arm of the state that the destruction of czarism almost inevitably entailed the destruction of the church. In the words of Harnack, the Orthodox churches are " nationalistic," while the Church of Rome is " imperialistic."

[23] The germinating center of St. Augustine's gospel was a conversion experience of the Pauline type, which released him from a terrific inward conflict between the " flesh " and the " spirit." (*Confessions*, Bk. VIII, 11: " Thus I understood, by my own experience, what I had read [in St. Paul], how the flesh lusteth against the Spirit and the Spirit against the flesh.") As this experience brought him into deep concurrence with the apostle's teaching concerning the helplessness of man to save himself by his own efforts, and the necessity of a complete surrender, in faith, to the grace of God, this central part of his teaching has been very influential with Protestants, who also follow the Pauline pattern. Indeed, Protestants have been readier than Catholics to follow some of the extreme theological deductions which the ardent saint drew from his experience of the grace of God: the total depravity and utter inertness of the human will, until the grace of God takes hold of it to change it; the predestination of some men to salvation, and the equally certain predestination of others to damnation. But it must be emphasized that the religion to which St. Augustine was converted was a religion of the Catholic type, in which Neo-Platonic asceticism and mysticism were blended with the worship of the God of the Old Testament, and the authority of the Roman Church was all-determinative. No one did more than he to support that church's authority, in civil as well as religious matters. His *City of God*, with its doctrine that the church represented all that was of lasting worth in civil society, and could survive the impending death of ancient civilization, mapped out the career of the church for a thousand years after his death.

[24] See the chapter, " The Quality of Love in St. Bernard," in Taylor's *The Medieval Mind*.

[25] *Works*, V, 100. See McGiffert, *Protestant Thought Before Kant*, p. 33.

[26] *Works*, lxiii, p. 125. McGiffert, *op. cit.*, p. 39.

[27] The *sola fide* is known as the " material principle " of the Reformation; the *sola Scriptura*, as its " formal principle."

[28] Westminster Confession, Chap. III, section 3.
[29] See McGiffert, *op. cit.*, p. 134.
[30] *Ibid.*, p. 135.

BIBLIOGRAPHY

Wright, W. K.   *Op. cit.*, Chaps. IX, XI–XIII.
Friess and Schneider.   *Op. cit.*, pp. 298–457.
Moore, G. F.   *Op. cit.*, Vol. II (Christianity).
Bevan, Edwyn.   *Christianity* (Home University Library).
Harnack, A.   *What is Christianity?*
McGiffert, A. C.   *Christianity as History and as Faith.*
Guignebert.   *Christianity.*
Atkins, G. G.   *The Making of the Christian Mind.*
Richards, G. W.   *Christian Ways of Salvation.*
Lyon, W. H.   *A Study of the Christian Sects.*
Allen, A. V. G.   *The Continuity of Christian Thought.*

6.

MODERN RELIGIOUS TENDENCIES

THE description of Protestant Christianity in the preceding chapter fails in one important respect to cover all the facts. It fails to take into account the widespread prevalence in Protestantism of a set of tendencies generally known as " liberalism " or " modernism." During the last century or two, these tendencies have steadily increased in power, evoking at the same time a mounting wave of opposition and reaction, until they have created a new division between conservatives and liberals, cutting horizontally across the old vertical divisions between the denominations and separating many members of the same denomination much more sharply from one another than from members of other denominations who share the same convictions on these new issues.

The significance of this situation will not be grasped if it is treated as an isolated phenomenon, confined to Protestantism or even to Christendom. The tendencies in question are most clearly visible in Protestantism, and especially in the so-called " liberal Protestant " churches — Unitarian, Universalist, and the others — but there has been a resounding controversy over modernism in the Roman Catholic Church, and in all the world religions similar tendencies have simultaneously appeared.[1] Evidently, we have here to deal with a single great magnetic disturbance of some sort, felt throughout the world, but affecting different religious groups in different degrees, according to their distance from the radiating center (or centers) and their ability to insulate themselves against the powerful currents proceeding thence. The nature of this disturbance may be inferred from the fact that it appears almost immediately wherever what we call " modern western civilization " begins to make its way, and is wholly absent only in the remote regions where westernism has never penetrated. The one source of all characteristically " modern " religious tendencies is to be found in a new and unique type of secular civilization, enormously dynamic and aggressive, which first began to show its distinctive traits in Europe some time in the sixteenth or seventeenth century, but which became influential on a world-wide scale only after the Industrial Revolution of the late eighteenth and early nineteenth centuries. In order to understand the nature of modern religious tendencies, we must first investigate the nature of modern western civilization, trace its origin, and endeavor to discover the secret of its power to transform whatever comes within its sphere of influence.

I. WHAT IS MODERN WESTERN CIVILIZATION?

A compact description of modern western civilization will be found in the following passage from Professor C. A. Beard's *Whither Mankind: a Panorama of Modern Civilization:*

What is called western or modern civilization by way of contrast with the civilization of the Orient or medieval times is at bottom a civilization that rests upon machinery and science as distinguished from one founded on agricultural or handicraft commerce. It is really a technological civilization. . . . It rests fundamentally on power-driven machinery which transcends the physical limits of its human directors, multiplying indefinitely the capacity for the production of goods. Science in all its branches —physics, chemistry, biology, and psychology — is the servant and upholder of this system. The day of crude invention being almost over, continuous research in the natural sciences is absolutely necessary to the extension of the machine and its market, thus forcing continuously the creation of new goods, new processes, and new modes of life.

For the present, machine civilization is associated with capitalism, under which large-scale production has risen to its present stage, but machine civilization is by no means synonymous with capitalism — that ever changing scheme of exploitation. . . . The acquisitive passion of the earth's multitudes for the goods, the comforts, and the securities of the classes is . . . likely to survive capitalism as we know it. Few choose nakedness when they can be clothed, the frosts of winter when they can be warm, or the misery of bacterial diseases when sanitation is offered to them. . . .

Though machine civilization has here been treated as if it were an order . . . it in fact differs from all others in that it is highly dynamic, containing within itself the seeds of reconstruction. Machine civilization based on technology, science, invention, and expanding markets must of necessity change — and rapidly. The order of steam is hardly established before electricity invades it; electricity hardly gains a fair start before the internal combustion engine overtakes it. There has never been anywhere in the world any order comparable with it, and all analogies drawn from the Middle Ages, classical antiquity, and the Orient are utterly inapplicable to its potentialities, offering no revelations as to its future.[2]

In this description of modern western civilization three chief elements are to be noted: (1) a mode of production, by machinery; (2) an underlying ideology, science; and (3) a social order, at present known as capitalism, but already in process of transformation under the stress of forces too great for it to contain — so that, as in the case of Russia, it might cease to be capitalistic without ceasing to be " modern " or " western."

It is one of the favorite doctrines of Karl Marx that in every transformation of civilization *production-mode* is the really determinative factor, new ideology and new social structure following inevitably upon basic change in the economic process. The recent history of civilization in the Orient seems at many points to substantiate this thesis; as, for example, in Japan, where the introduction of machinery has drastically changed the mentality of the nation and led to a series of rapid social changes, from feudalism through capitalism to something very like fascism. Yet when one tries to trace the early history of modern western civilization he is almost obliged to disregard this Marxian doctrine and give the primacy to ideology; for without modern science, neither modern technology nor modern capitalism is comprehensible at all; and the modern scientific mind had been at work for several centuries before it began to produce that series of useful mechanical inventions which has transformed the economic life of the world. A good Marxian might doubtless find connections between the economic condition of sixteenth century Europe and the discoveries of Copernicus and Galileo; but in the interest of simplicity and brevity, we shall trace the origin of modern civilization directly to those discoveries and to the mental travail which led up to and followed from them.

That every event has its cause is a fundamental assumption of modern science; so it would be most unscientific to represent science as having sprung full-grown from the head of Copernicus or Galileo, like Athene from the head of Zeus. There must have been a cause for its appearance in the west rather than in the east, and among the men of the Renaissance rather than among the men of the Reformation. That reason is not far to seek: the influence of Greek philosophy.

Bertrand Russell has packed a great deal of truth into one sentence when he says, " Western civilization is derived from three sources: the Bible, the Greeks, and Science — the last operating chiefly through machines." [3]   As machinery sprang from science, science sprang, he suggests, from the previously existing tendencies of western culture; and as between " the Bible " and " the Greeks," whose reconciliation and union had gradually been accomplished in Christian thought, it was undoubtedly the latter, not the former, which was the chief progenitor of modern science. Ancient Greek philosophy was scientifically unproductive because it despised things and facts and devoted itself too largely to deductive speculation; but in the time of the Renaissance, when there was a great revulsion against medieval contempt for the world, a group of thinkers arose who combined the deductive and mathematical forms of thought inherited from the Greeks with an insatiable curiosity about concrete facts; and so modern science was born, with its characteristic method of rising inductively from facts to laws, and descending deductively from laws to new facts — a method " already complete," as Russell remarks, " in the writings of Galileo." [4]

If the science upon which modern civilization is based were identifiable with " scientific method " this account of its origin might suffice, and all the credit for it would have to be entered on the Greek side of the ledger. The Hebrews never rivaled the Greeks in inquisitiveness about the origin and nature of things, nor grasped the idea of an ordered cosmos ruled by inherent necessity. But they did have one fundamental idea that the Greeks never grasped, and which has become basic to the modern " scientific spirit," if not to " scientific method ": the idea that the existing world is not fatally ordained to repeat itself, but is capable of becoming radically better. The Greek mind was dominated — even in the philosophy of Plato, Aristotle, and the Stoics — by the astrological notion that human history is but the reflection of the eternal circlings of the stars, and comes evermore back to the same point, as often as the configurations of the heavenly bodies repeat themselves. The Hebrew mind was schooled by the messianic hope to the idea of an open future in which anything might happen, however new and strange.

Now it is impossible to mistake in the writings of some of the pioneers of modern science — especially Francis Bacon — what might fairly be called a "messianic" or "apocalyptic" strain. Bacon's *New Atlantis* stands as truly in line with the prophetic visions of Isaiah, Daniel, and the Apocalypse as with Plato's *Critias*. For Bacon, however, the new age is to be ushered in not by a divine emissary from heaven, but by the inevitable increase of human knowledge and power, once the true method for investigating nature's secrets has been discovered. The idea of human perfectibility and progress, the most characteristic idea of the scientific era, appears clearly in Bacon. It is an idea half Greek, half Hebraic; and if it could never have been derived from the Bible alone, it could never have sprung from any source other than the Hebrew-Christian tradition. The Orient knows nothing of it.

The progress of modern science did not take place, of course, in a social vacuum. The way was prepared for the coming of capitalism by a long series of social transformations which at first had little to do with the results of scientific investigation. The first of these took place in the later Middle Ages, when the unity of feudal society, with the manor as its basis and the papacy as its crown, began to be undermined by the growth of the towns and the development of the trade guilds. These guilds were rigidly regulated at first by the canon law of the church, and by self-imposed codes which forbade "usury" (taking interest),[5] "forestalling" (buying outside the recognized market), "engrossing" (cornering the market), and "regrating" (selling above the market price). These codes also set up standards of craftsmanship and fixed " fair " wages and prices. By themselves, these " burgher " craftsmen and traders could never have won the position of eminence to which they have attained in modern " bourgeois " society. But by taking advantage of the rising force of nationalism, and supporting the king against the pope and the feudal nobility, they early won their independence of feudal and ecclesiastical control, especially in France and England, and obtained a power over the organs of government which they have never lost — unless the present generation may be said to have witnessed the beginnings of its downfall.

This power was first strongly consolidated as a consequence of the commercial revolution which resulted — after 1492 — from the inflow of vast quantities of gold and silver from newly discovered mines in America and the development of colonial expansion and exploitation. Having become independent of the church and the nobles and indispensable to the monarch and the people, the merchant class now proceeded to exact from the crown all sorts of constitutional privileges and immunities and to dictate the foreign and domestic policy of the state. The policy generally preferred up to the latter part of the eighteenth century was what is known as mercantilism — a form of economic nationalism in which the state took over the function of regulating trade formerly exercised by the municipal guilds, and fostered the interests of the commercial classes by bounties, public works, and especially by tariffs and foreign trade concessions, designed to give the nation victory in its perpetual struggle with competitor nations, for a " favorable balance " of exports over imports and a resultant surplus of bullion in the treasury.

It is a historical accident of considerable importance that the beginnings of mechanical invention in England (which brought about what is called the Industrial Revolution) happened to coincide with a reaction against the mercantilist system and a growing demand for a governmental policy of " hands off " (laisser faire) in relation to business. The mercantilist policy, although originally dictated by commercial interests, had proved self-defeating. Abroad, it had resulted in the loss of the American colonies; at home, in a bureaucratic regulation of trade that grew increasingly irksome and suffocating. Adam Smith, in his *Wealth of Nations,* gave classical form to the new doctrine of free competition. Borrowing certain conceptions from the French physiocrats and adapting them to English conditions, he argued that the public good would be most effectively secured under a system of " natural liberty," in which the government would protect property rights against foreign aggression or domestic fraud, but otherwise leave every man " free to pursue his own interest in his own way, and to bring both his industry and capital into competition with those of any other man, or order of men." [6] It was under this regime of noninterference that power-driven machinery first made its appearance and began its clanking march to the position of supremacy it now occupies in western civilization; while scientific research, hitherto motivated by disinterested curiosity, began to be more and more controlled by the interests of technological development.

What followed would have astonished and dismayed Adam Smith. Sympathy was the first principle of his moral philosophy, and a sympathetic interest in the welfare of the working class was one of his personal concerns; but the age which took him for its guide put aside human sympathy, for the most part, in favor of mechanical efficiency. Great factory towns sprang up, where human necessities and conveniences were turned out in vast quantities, at surprisingly cheap rates — made possible by cheap labor. Railways and steamships carried these products to the ends of the earth, and brought back raw materials to be poured into the roaring mills. The whole globe was made into a neighborhood through the invention of the telegraph and the telephone; while over the unexploited areas of this shrunken planet the military forces of the industrial nations scurried about staking out commercial concessions, and presently transformed Asia and Africa into appendages of Europe. Economic imperialism, the child of nationalism and industrialism, was born. Competition for markets, colonies, raw materials, and trade routes led to competition in armaments — to which, as to all these tasks, science lent a hand — and the stage was set for the magnificent pyrotechnics of the World War, in which a century of progress in applied mechanics found its brilliant culmination.

From the point of view of men's mastery over nature, this was the first century in all human history; from the point of view of social welfare or individual happiness, the results must be viewed with mixed emotions. Potentially, man's victory over poverty has now been secured, for methods of production have been devised which make it physically possible to feed, clothe and house, in comfort and even in luxury, the entire population of the globe; while from a mechanical point of view, the problem of distributing these benefits, and others — such as improved sanitation — to all parts of the world is entirely solved. But in spite of this industrialism brings great evils in its train wherever it goes: unwholesome living conditions and low wages for the workers in factory towns; insecurity of employment, so great as to make serfdom or slavery seem preferable; the concentration of wealth and power in the hands of a few; conflicts between capital and labor, in which the farmer and the general public always lose; conflicts between nations, in which the whole world suffers and the victors are as badly crippled as the vanquished. Truly, this civilization of ours is the best and the worst that has ever been known!

Whatever one may think of modern western civilization no one can ignore it. Whatever it touches is changed; and religion is no exception. In the sphere of religion, its transforming power is attributable to two main causes: (1) the influence of scientific ideas, directly or through the medium of philosophy, upon theological doctrines, and (2) the general effect of changed living conditions upon all traditional forms of religion, which are made to seem somehow anachronistic and irrelevant in their new environment, even when no special point of weakness in them becomes the object of an attack. We shall observe the effects of these causes first in Christendom, where modern civilization took its rise, and then in the Orient, where it has appeared more recently.

II. LIBERAL RELIGIOUS TENDENCIES IN CHRISTENDOM

The direct influence of science and changed living conditions upon Christian thought has been most evident in the last fifty or sixty years, when a conscious attempt has been made by Christian thinkers to apply scientific method to the study of the history and psychology of religion, and to adjust theological teaching to its changed environment. In the earlier part of the scientific era, the attitude of the church toward science and invention was one of indifference — hardening into hostility when, as in the case of Galileo, the results of investigation clashed with the commonly accepted assumptions of Christian theology. Through the medium of general philosophy, however, Christian thought has been kept in pretty close touch with scientific and cultural developments. Theology is always obliged to wrestle with contemporary philosophical tendencies, if only for the sake of defending herself against them; and modern philosophy is distinguished from all other periods in the history of thought by its predominant interest in science and social change.

Bacon and Descartes, often cited as the founders of the two chief schools of early modern philosophy, were pioneer exponents of scientific inquiry, and the difference between their schools (empiricism versus rationalism) amounted mainly to a difference of emphasis: whether precedence should be given to the inductive and experimental or to the deductive and mathematical side of scientific method. In Immanuel Kant, the central figure of modern philosophy, the two earlier schools were merged; but he bequeathed to his successors a new problem, on which they split into two new schools: the problem, namely, whether scientific knowledge really gives us the ultimate truth about things as they are in themselves, or a partial and limited truth about things as they appear to us. The philosophers of the eighteenth century Enlightenment — men like Voltaire and Diderot — had assumed that the same process of cool scientific reasoning which led Sir Isaac Newton to his great discoveries could be applied to the solution of all the tangled difficulties of morals, politics, and religion.

Kant's *Critique of Pure Reason* — coupled with the disappointing results of the Enlightenment — convinced the nineteenth century that scientific reasoning could never penetrate the ultimate mysteries of the universe, nor solve any of those questions, so numerous in the realm of morals, politics, and religion, where judgments of *value,* as distinct from judgments of *fact,* were concerned.   In the idealistic or " romanticist " school of philosophy, which prevailed in the first part of the nineteenth century, the attempt was made to reconcile scientific reason with religious faith and intuition by assigning to science the realm of things as they appear, and to religion the realm of things as they really are.   In the positivist or " agnostic " school which prevailed in the latter part of the century, a similar division of territory was made — with the important difference that the realm of ultimate reality was now described as " unknowable."   Attention was thus turned away from the realm of " insoluble" mysteries to the realm of partial but " positive " knowledge which science was then so rapidly opening up, and which was believed to be sufficient to meet all really practical and soluble difficulties.

The first distinctively " liberal " Protestants were the Unitarians. Appearing in Poland and Hungary in the sixteenth century, they reflected at first the prescientific humanism of that period.   The two Socini, who were their most distinguished leaders, were believers, like Erasmus, in a simple ethical interpretation of Christianity, shorn of all irrational superfluities.   Like him, also, they believed in man's ability to find salvation by his own free will, without supernatural aid or grace; and it was as a corollary of this faith in the dignity of man that they were led to discourage the worship of Christ and deny the doctrine of the Trinity.   Driven from Poland by the Catholic revival in 1661, the Socinians or " Polish Brethren," as they were called, fled to Holland, whence their influence, combined with that of the Arminian Remonstrants (against Calvinism), passed over into England and New England.

Anglo-American Unitarianism took its definitive shape during the scientific Enlightenment of the eighteenth century, when the significance of the work of Copernicus, Galileo, and Newton first took hold of the popular imagination, and philosophic thought claimed to be guided exclusively by the principles of reason, nature, and humanity. There were three parties to the somewhat acrid religious controversies of that age: the supernatural rationalists, the deists, and the skeptics or atheists. All three parties agreed that religion's function was to furnish an incentive for morality; and that no religious teaching should be upheld which in the face of cool scientific scrutiny proved to contain anything irrational, unnatural, or inhumane. The first two parties agreed that there were three great truths, rationally indisputable, on which " natural religion " was founded: (1) There exists a God, who must be supposed to have made the world very much as a skilled jeweler makes a watch; (2) it is God's will that man should live a virtuous life; (3) there will be a future life, in which God will reward virtue and punish vice. For the deists, this simple creed seemed quite enough to support morality; and they derided the teachings of the Bible as irrational and immoral. The supernatural rationalists, on the other hand, argued that the Bible contained many inspiring teachings beyond those of natural religion, and it was right to accept those teachings (in so far as they did not contradict reason) since the prophecies and miracles of the Bible proved it to be a book come down from God. The skeptics, meanwhile, of whom David Hume was chief, derided both the other parties, and cast doubt upon the principles of natural as well as of revealed religion.[7]

The Unitarians were at this time to be numbered with the supernatural rationalists, accepting the Bible and believing in its miracles as heartily as Archbishop Tillotson or Bishop Butler, but interpreting it more radically, so as to exclude many traditional Christian doctrines. A creed that is still popular in Unitarian churches reflects very clearly the rational and optimistic temper of the eighteenth century: " I believe in the fatherhood of God, the brotherhood of man, the leadership of Jesus, salvation by character, and the progress of mankind onward and upward forever." In American Unitarianism the period of supernatural rationalism lasted through the first third of the nineteenth century. William Ellery

Channing was the chief spokesman of the movement during this period, and it was under his leadership that the Unitarians split off from the orthodox or Calvinistic Congregationalists. From about 1835 to 1885, under the leadership of Theodore Parker, the movement entered upon a second phase, in which it was strongly influenced by German idealistic philosophy, and gave up all emphasis upon the supernatural, but remained convinced of the supremacy of the Christian religion. Since 1885, it has sought more and more to establish relationship with liberal movements in other religions — the Brāhma Samāj, for example — and has embraced wholeheartedly the implications of the scientific spirit and method, whatever may be their consequences. The most recent consequence has been the rise of what is called the " new humanism," which takes a negative or agnostic attitude toward belief in God and in immortality, replacing these ancient beliefs with a very modern faith in the possibility of indefinite progress through social cooperation and scientific research. Ethical monotheism is still the heart of religion to many Unitarians; but a large group of them are now convinced that the essential thing in their creed is that faith in the dignity of man which was already prominent in Socinianism, coupled with a faith in progress through science, first kindled by the eighteenth century Enlightenment and deepened by the scientific triumphs of the late nineteenth century. In this pilgrimage of faith — or of doubt — from supernatural rationalism through romantic idealism to scientific agnosticism and the religion of humanity, the Unitarians have been but a step behind the boldest philosophers of modern times, blazing a trail which has been followed, with more caution and circumspection, by liberals and modernists of many other sects and cults.

The only other liberal sect which reflects the spirit of the eighteenth century Enlightenment is Universalism, whose distinctive tenet, the eventual salvation of all,[8] was the expression of a rationalistic and humanitarian protest against Calvinistic election and eternal punishment. Founded about 1770 by the Reverend John Murray of Good Luck, New Jersey — later of Gloucester, Massachusetts — the Universalist Church has never won a large membership, but its principles have been accepted by the Unitarians and by many adherents of other denominations, who have felt the force of the argument that a loving and omnipotent God cannot allow any of his children to be lost. Meanwhile the Universalists have been influenced by the Unitarians and by the general current of liberal religion in the nineteenth century. Some have recently gone so far as to become adherents of the new humanism — which means that in their case the original Universalist hope of a happy immortality for all has been replaced by the hope of a happy future for mankind on this planet.[9]

The great century for liberalism in religion was the nineteenth century. Not only did a great many liberal sects or cults make their appearance, but, more significant still, the liberal movement invaded the orthodox churches by an almost imperceptible process of peaceful penetration, so that when, a few years ago, the conservatives in several of the larger American denominations endeavored to set up doctrinal standards that would rule out the liberals, they found the liberals strongly entrenched in positions of leadership. In the eighteenth century liberal religious thought was promoted mainly by " freethinkers " and " infidels," at whom organized religion looked askance; in the nineteenth century it was promoted — especially in Germany — by highly respected clergymen and theologians. Of these the two most notable and influential were Friedrich Schleiermacher (1768–1834) and Albrecht Ritschl (1822–89).

Schleiermacher is known as " the father of modern theology." Like St. Paul, St. Augustine, and Luther, he had passed through a severe inward struggle before arriving at his final religious convictions. Brought up as an adherent of the Moravian Brethren, the strictest of all the pietistic sects, he came in contact as a university student with the rationalistic philosophy of the eighteenth century, and the whole intellectual superstructure of his faith was swept away. But at the moment when his skepticism reached its negative climax he became conscious that the religious sentiment still was deeply rooted within him and refused to be eradicated. " When God and immortality vanished before my doubting sight, religion still remained." This realization had important consequences for him. It implied that religion was not primarily a matter of belief, as the eighteenth century had supposed; it was primarily a matter of feeling, a matter of experience, a deep emotional attitude or sentiment which was so much a part of human nature that it was bound to persist in some form, no matter what one's philosophy might be. Exulting in this discovery, and finding much to confirm it in the new philosophy of romanticism, with its disparagement of reason and its exaltation of feeling and intuition, he issued a book which started a veritable revolution in religious thought: *Discourses upon Religion, Addressed to the Educated among its Despisers* (1799). Religion, he urged, is no more to be confused with any definite code of morality than it is to be confused with any specific set of beliefs. It bears fruit in knowledge and in conduct, but it is something deeper than either: a " sense and taste for the infinite," a feeling of oneness with the universe, "life in the endless nature of the whole." [10] By this definition, as Schleiermacher clearly saw, many of those who are denounced as infidels by the orthodox — Spinoza, for example — should rather be saluted as men who were religious in the deepest and truest sense.

The *Discourses on Religion* do not represent the mature theology of their author, but they set forth boldly and clearly an idea which was destined to become the most characteristic religious teaching of nineteenth century liberal theology: the idea of the immanence of God. The eighteenth century deists had represented God as if he were wholly external to the world, as a mechanic is external to the machine which he has made and operates. Schleiermacher, like Goethe, Wordsworth, and many others of his contemporaries, defends the opposite idea, that God dwells within the world as its soul, or its unifying principle. In this he was undoubtedly influenced by the pantheism of Spinoza, for whom he expresses warm admiration; but there is this great difference between them, that the universe of Spinoza is fixed, static, and mechanical, while the universe of Schleiermacher is conceived vitalistically, as a living, growing organism. It is a world of law, as Spinoza and all the

natural scientists maintain, but at the same time it is a world of
marvels and miracles, since all that occurs in it is in a sense God's
work. Schleiermacher's attitude toward miracles is very characteristic of modern liberal theology. " Miracle," he says,

is only the religious name for event. Every event, even the most natural
and common, is a miracle if it lend itself to a controllingly religious interpretation. To me all is miracle. In your sense of the word only something
inexplicable and strange is a miracle, which to me is none. The more
religious you were the more miracles you would find everywhere. All conflict over particular events, as to whether they are worthy to be called miracles
or not, impresses me painfully with the feeling that the religious sense of
the disputants is very poor and needy.[11]

Schleiermacher's ripest work is his great survey of *The Christian
Faith,* first published in 1821–22. It is a much more conservative
work than the *Discourses,* since its author had now recovered, on a
new basis, much of the faith which he had lost in his younger days,
and since he now no longer spoke as an individual, but as interpreter of the faith of the Christian church; but it is based upon the
same radical principle which first emerged in the *Discourses:* that
religious feeling or experience is primary, and religious dogma
secondary. All is grist for his mill that can be presumed to be an
expression, however remote, of genuine religious experience; and
the great texts of the Bible, as well as the creeds of the churches, are
profusely quoted; but the effort is always made to sift out the pure
wheat of essential experience which underlies the text or the creed,
and separate it from the mere intellectual chaff with which it is
mingled. A great deal that Schleiermacher affirms about God is
directly derivable from the elementary " feeling of absolute dependence," which he considers basic in all religions. A good deal
more is derivable from the general Christian experience of redemption from sin through fellowship with Christ. In still other parts
of Schleiermacher's theology, he speaks as the interpreter of specifically Protestant religious experience, and one catches distinct
echoes of his early Moravian training. But everywhere the principle is the same — Christian experience the test of Christian belief.
Sin and salvation are what they are experienced *as*. God and

Christ must possess just those qualities which must be attributed to them in order to account for the experience which we have of them. Ever since Schleiermacher, modern liberal theology has generally aimed to begin with religious experience, and return to religious experience, avoiding all vain speculations that cannot be put to that test.

Albrecht Ritschl is by no means so original or so important a thinker as Schleiermacher; but he illustrates very well the religious temper of the late nineteenth century, when the romantic stress upon poetic feeling and intuition had given way before the mounting prestige of natural science, and when nature, in the light of Darwinian evolution, seemed " red in tooth and claw " — no longer the fair " garment of God " which the romantic writers had adored. Ritschl finds the basis for his theology in experience, like Schleiermacher, but in a different sort of experience, moral instead of emotional. Here he follows in the footsteps of Kant, who claimed the right to believe in God, freedom, and immortality because moral action, as he sees it, presupposes or " postulates " these great assumptions. Ritschl goes beyond Kant, however, in affirming that at one point in our world, and only one, we may pass from faith to sight and actually meet God face to face. Not in nature — which to Ritschl, as to most of his puzzled contemporaries, seemed only a great enigma — but in the person of the historic Jesus of Nazareth, and here alone, was God actually to be met. What we seek when we seek God is " victory over the world "; what we find when we meet Jesus is victory over the world. Jesus then " has the value of God to us," and in this practical sense he is divine. Such a view answers none of the metaphysical puzzles about the " two natures in one person " which early Christian theology has handed down; but it does make the whole scheme of Christian thought revolve about the person of Jesus. This practical, ethical form of modern theology has had a great influence in America, where it chimes in with the pragmatist movement in philosophy, and the general American tendency to stress useful ethical activity at the expense of deep feeling or precise thought. It goes very commonly with a strong emphasis upon the need of a social application of Christian principles — as in the teaching of Walter Rauschenbusch.

The influence of liberal Protestantism as represented by Schleiermacher and Ritschl may be seen at work, to various degrees, in all the more important Protestant denominations. The influence of Schleiermacher and other German romanticists was mediated to the English-speaking world through the writings of Coleridge, Carlyle, and Emerson; the influence of Ritschl, through a host of theological students who flocked to the German universities in the later years of the nineteenth century. In most recent Protestant theology, the two streams of influence will be found mingled together, so that their contradictions and their extreme divergencies from traditional Christianity are somewhat neutralized. In the "modernist" movement in the Roman Catholic Church, however, and in various religious cults outside of the commonly recognized denominations, these same two tendencies have appeared more isolated from each other, and with far more radical consequences. In these more radical movements, the Schleiermacher or " divine immanence " type of thought seems regularly to gravitate toward a consistent idealistic monism, which is often called " pantheistic " by its critics; while the Ritschlian or " ethical theism " type of thought tends to gravitate toward a religion of humanity, like that of Auguste Comte or the new humanists, in which there is little place for belief in God or immortality.[12]

Among modern religious cults of the first type, the most important is unquestionably Christian Science. No brief account of it can do justice to its indubitable power of appeal or adequately handle the numerous delicate points of controversy which it raises; but an abbreviated description of its underlying philosophy can easily be given, since it is a very clear and consistent expression of the doctrine of the immanence of God. Perhaps the most concise statement of this philosophy is to be found in the " scientific statement of being," printed in the chapter called " Recapitulation " in *Science and Health,* the authoritative textbook of Christian Science: "There is no Life, Substance, or Intelligence in matter. All is Mind. Spirit is immortal Truth; matter is mortal error.

Spirit is the real and eternal; matter is the unreal and temporal. Spirit is God, and man is His image and likeness; hence, man is spiritual and not material." [13]

The connection of this idealistic philosophy with the art of spiritual healing, for which the Christian Scientists are best known, may not appear at first glance. It may be set forth in a double chain of propositions which recur in various forms in the many editions of *Science and Health:* God is all-in-all; God is good; therefore, all is good, and evil is nonexistent. God is all-in-all; God is mind; therefore, all is mind, and matter is nonexistent. It follows that bodily illness is doubly unreal, since it is material and since it is an evil; and to attack it with drugs and *materia medica* is to attack error with error. The true remedy for all supposed ills — sin and death as well as sickness — is to realize their unreality, through unity with God, the one all-inclusive Reality, the one all-embracing Mind.

The name "Christian Science" is significant. Christian Scientists claim to be *Christian* in that they believe the Bible teaches, when properly (i.e., spiritually) interpreted, the same system of idealistic monism expounded in *Science and Health;* and they claim that the art of spiritual healing discovered by Mary Baker Eddy in 1866 was the same art discovered and practiced by Jesus, but lost for many centuries. Jesus was a man by whom the Divine Idea, Christ, was first apprehended and scientifically demonstrated. Modern Christians, in so far as they grasp and live by the "scientific principle of being" now rediscovered and more fully expounded by Mrs. Eddy, may expect to work miracles as marvelous as those of Jesus; for these miracles were not supernatural, they were the expression of a higher law, which may now be comprehended and demonstrated with all the certainty of a proposition in geometry. It is in this sense that Christian Scientists claim to be in possession of a *science* — not identical with mere natural science, which deals with material unrealities, but comprehending all spiritual reality in a unified, logical system whose truth is "demonstrated" every time it heals disease by scattering the errors of mortal mind.

To the question, Is Christian Science pantheistic? Mrs. Eddy replied: "Christian Science refutes pantheism, finds Spirit neither in matter nor in the modes of mortal mind." [14] There is certainly a strong contrast between the nature-pantheism of Walt Whitman and other nineteenth century poets, who found God ever present in the material universe as its living soul, and the world-negation of Christian Science, which sees no trace of God in anything material. If Walt Whitman is a typical pantheist, Mrs. Eddy is not. He says, "All is God"; she says, "God is All"; and there is literally a whole world of difference between these two propositions. For an analogy to her "acosmic pantheism," or "theopantism," as it is sometimes called, one would have to go to the mysticism of the Upanishads or the Christian Neo-Platonists.

For a religious analogy to the pantheism of Whitman one might better go to that widely diffused but loosely organized cult known as "New Thought," which resembles Christian Science in its interest in spiritual healing, but differs from it in recognizing the partial, relative reality of the material world and the partial, relative truth of secular natural science. Historically the two cults are closely related. An influential event in the New Thought movement was the splitting off, from the original circle of Christian Scientists, of a group of people who objected to what they considered the too dominating and autocratic rule of Mrs. Eddy, and preferred a looser organization. They likewise believed in employing frankly, in their spiritual healing, those methods of suggestion and hypnotism by which Phineas P. Quimby, a faith healer of Portland, Maine, had originally helped Mrs. Eddy back to health, prior to her discovery of a deeper and more metaphysical method of healing in 1866. In more recent times, the New Thought movement has become much more interested in the development of various techniques of psychotherapy and mental self-help, such as Pelmanism; but Christian Scientists feel that all such methods smack too much of "mortal mind," and characterize them as "malicious animal magnetism" — a sort of diabolic black art which spreads error instead of quenching it with divine truth. As time has gone on, Christian Science — being held to its original principles by a strong centralized government — has tended to become more and more isolated from the regular Christian denominations and from contemporary secular thought; while the New Thought movement has tended to become a part of the general stream of liberal Christianity. Between the idealistic "New Theology" of R. J. Campbell [15] and the principles of New Thought, as defined in the official account given in Hastings' *Encyclopedia of Religion and Ethics,* there is so much similarity as to amount almost to identity. Both carry the idea of the immanence of God to great lengths; both bring nature, man and God into such close organic unity with one another as to verge upon a fully pantheistic position; both find great difficulty, in these more pessimistic days, in presenting a convincing view of the place of evil in the divine scheme of things. It is hard to believe, today, that our economic ills will automatically melt away if we only " hold the right thought " and keep " in tune with the infinite."

There is no modern religious cult of the Ritschlian or " ethical theism " type which equals Christian Science or New Thought in popularity or general influence; but there are many smaller cults and movements which illustrate this trend very clearly. The oldest of these is the religion of humanity, founded by Auguste Comte, in the first half of the nineteenth century.

Comte's positivist philosophy had led him to dismiss all theological and metaphysical beliefs about superhuman beings and forces, as survivals from prescientific mentality; but he was interested in promoting social progress, and experience seemed to show that it would not come about by scientific thinking (sociology) alone, but that some form of worship was necessary to give the emotional stimulus for sustained idealistic endeavor. The object of this worship Comte found, not in a nonexistent deity, but in an idealized humanity. His system was unkindly described by Huxley as " Catholicism minus Christianity "; and the epigram had some point, for Catholic emblems and usages were freely used and diverted to humanitarian ends. A new calendar of saints was set up, composed of inventors, philosophers, and social reformers; and in the chancel of the church appeared an image of the Sistine

Madonna, as a symbol of ideal humanity. The cult still has some followers, in France, England, and Latin America.

Closely akin to Comte's positivism, in its strong humanitarian emphasis, is the Society for Ethical Culture, founded in 1876 by Felix Adler of New York City. Adler was himself a believer in the reality of a superhuman Being, though he insisted that this Being was plural and not one. "The object of religious devotion," he said, "is the infinite holy community, the spiritual universe. . . . The family, the vocation, the nation, are subgroups of this, lesser entities. Even mankind itself is but a province of the ideal spiritual commonwealth that extends beyond it." [16] Since, however, the basis of membership in the society was found in ethical purpose rather than in metaphysical conviction, and since the only form of worship Adler recommended was that of "concentrating attention on the spiritual need of the fellow beings with whom we are in daily touch," [17] the ethical and social side of the cult has tended to crowd out the mystical and superhuman. One of the leaders of the movement, Dr. Stanton Coit, has sought to counteract this tendency by developing a highly mystical conception of the national state as a living spirit, with which we may freely commune in prayer, and to which we owe allegiance in gratitude for benefits received and for our very existence as persons.[18] Generally speaking, however, the meetings of the society would be more accurately described as public lectures on humanitarian themes than as services of worship.

The most recent of the humanitarian cults is that very considerable movement among Unitarians, liberal Jews, and other intellectuals, which is known as the new humanism. Since the founding of the First Humanist Society by Charles Francis Potter of New York City in September, 1929, the increase in the number of independent humanist societies has not been very noticeable; but as a sort of informal grouping or school of thought among left-wing religionists, humanism has won a considerable following; and in the spring of 1933 this group issued a "Humanist Manifesto," signed by John Dewey, Harry Elmer Barnes, and thirty-two others, including Jews, Unitarians, Universalists, and, significantly enough, two representatives of the Society for Ethical Culture. Along with many beliefs and attitudes common to various types of liberal religion, the " Manifesto " contains some pronouncements that set its signers rather sharply in opposition to other liberals, as for example:

Fifth: Humanism asserts that the nature of the universe depicted by modern science makes unacceptable any supernatural or cosmic guarantees of human values. . . .

Sixth: We are convinced that the time has passed for theism, deism, modernism, and the several varieties of " new thought.". . .

Ninth: In place of the old attitudes involved in worship and prayer the humanist finds his religious emotions expressed in a heightened sense of personal life and in a cooperative effort to promote social well-being.

In other articles it is stated that humanism makes no " distinction between the sacred and the secular," discourages " sentimental and unreal hopes and wishful thinking," and envisages a " socialized and cooperative economic order," a " shared life in a shared world," in place of the existing acquisitive and profit-motivated society. " Man is at last," it concludes, " becoming aware that he alone is responsible for the realization of the world of his dreams, that he has within himself the power for its achievement. He must set intelligence and will to the task." [19]

The line which divides the new humanists from the socialists, the communists, and other secular advocates of humanitarian reform, is rather difficult to draw, and is perhaps more verbal than real. The word " religion " is for them a good word, whereas it is a bad word to the communists and a matter of indifference to most socialists; but it is associated with " no uniquely religious emotions and attitudes," and is in fact simply identical with " the quest of the good life," which every human being inevitably carries on as best he can, with the aid of his fellows. This seems to be the logical outworking of the extreme ethical and social emphasis in religion, and forms a natural connecting link between liberal Christianity and the various secularistic and antireligious movements which are next to be considered.

III. RADICAL SECULARISM AND CONSERVATIVE
REACTION IN CHRISTENDOM

At the Jerusalem meeting of the International Missionary Council in 1928, a conviction found clear expression for the first time which had been gradually dawning for some time in the minds of the leaders of the Christian churches: that the chief contemporary rivals of Christianity are not to be found in the other long established religions, such as Buddhism or Mohammedanism, but in certain "secularistic" trends of modern civilization which threaten to undermine all the existing religions, replacing them with what some would call new religions and others would prefer to call substitutes for religion. Of these new secular religions, or substitutes for religion, the most aggressive in their attack upon Christian institutions are *communism* and *nationalism*.

The challenge of communism to Christianity is of course most visible in Russia. There, one of the oldest, largest, and most powerful of all the Christian communions, the Russian Orthodox Church, has been overthrown, and religion of every sort has become a sort of tolerated evil, like alcoholism, confined as far as possible to confirmed addicts, forbidden to be taught to the youth, and constantly combatted by a vigorous state propaganda. The reasons why Russian communism is so determinedly antireligious are to be found, in part, in the historic alliance between the Russian Church and the czaristic regime. Much of the illustrative material in the Soviet antireligious museums is devoted to proving the "counter-revolutionary" tendency of the church. But if this were all, the revolutionary government would be disposed to favor those religious sects and movements which support the new communistic economy, such as the so-called "Living Church" movement among the Orthodox. Until 1929, such movements were favorably treated and began to spread with some rapidity; but at this juncture the right of propaganda was withdrawn from all religious bodies, and they were forbidden to perform any act of social service or engage in any activities whatsoever except public worship. Even the holding of prayer meetings was forbidden. Nothing less than the desire to extirpate religion completely can explain such a policy. Such is, quite frankly, the aim of the Soviet government; and it finds the ultimate justification for this attitude in the writings of Karl Marx, upon which the communist program is based. To Marx, the whole religious outlook on life, with its belief in the goodness of God, its hope of a future life, and its preaching of such " virtues " as kindness and humility, seemed a kind of " opium " with which the exploited masses of mankind had been drugged to keep them content with their unjust lot. Lenin, the leader and adored hero of the Bolshevist revolution, thoroughly subscribed to these views; and his statement of the communist attitude toward religion may be taken as authoritative. He says:

Religion is one of the forms of spiritual oppression, lying everywhere on the masses of the people. . . . The helplessness of the exploited classes in their struggle with the exploiters just as inevitably generates faith in a better life beyond the grave, as the helplessness of the savage in his struggle with nature produces faith in gods, devils, miracles, etc. To him who works and is poor all his life, religion teaches passivity and patience in earthly life, consoling him with the hope of a heavenly reward. To those who live on the labor of others, religion teaches benevolence in earthly life, offering them a new cheap justification for all their exploiting existence and selling tickets to heavenly bliss at a reduced price. Religion is opium for the people.[20]

In spite of this outspoken antireligious animus on the part of the communist leaders, it has frequently been noted by outside observers that communism itself bears many of the marks of a religion. A matter of definition is involved here, which is of the greatest interest for any one who would frame an adequate philosophy of religion at the present day. Our own final definition of religion must be deferred to the next chapter, when we shall be in a position to review all the historical data; but it may be said at once that upon any generally acceptable definition, communism must at least be said to have much that is " religious " about it. Even more than the new humanism — which calls itself religious — it resembles a militant religious movement. It has a prophetic forerunner in Karl Marx, and a heroic founder in Lenin, whose images

have replaced those of the Virgin and the saints in the so-called
" icon corners " in Russian homes, and whose writings are the
sacrosanct basis of communist orthodoxy, from which no " devia-
tion " is permitted. It has a definite way of salvation for mankind,
which it preaches to all the world with missionary zeal and is prepared to follow with utter devotion, even at the cost of great suffering. It trusts that its program will ultimately be accomplished,
in spite of all the evil machinations of the bourgeois, because reality, embodied in the dialectic of history, is ultimately on its side;
and it believes itself to possess, in the shape of science, technology,
and the power of cooperative effort, " means of grace " that make
the sacraments and prayers of the church look futile and superstitious by comparison. It is observable outside Russia that the
embracing of the communist faith often has upon a man the
effect of a religious conversion, galvanizing his energies, disciplining his life, and filling him with fervent hope.

   If it is correct to describe communism as a religion there can be
comparatively little doubt about the religious character of nationalism. Patriotism and religion, God and country, have been associated from very early times, as we have seen. Only a few universal
religions, like Buddhism, Christianity, and Mohammedanism,
have ever decisively parted company with nationalism, and they
have repeatedly relapsed into bondage to it. Whenever a universal
religion begins to weaken, the ancient worship of the gods of the
clan and the soil — *Blut und Boden,* as they are called in Germany
today — begins to revive. It may be seriously questioned how
much of the religion of the average respectable citizen of modern
England is really Christianity and how much of it is British patriotism. The sentiment he has for the Church of England is part of
the deep tie which binds him to the soil of England and makes
all old English landmarks and historic institutions dear to him.

   The development of the " corporate " or " totalitarian " state in
Italy and Germany, in recent times, has simply rendered explicit
the conflict between Christianity and nationalism which has
troubled sensitive consciences in Christendom ever since the modern nations won their absolute sovereignty in defiance of the

papacy. In every western country, during the period of international rivalry and imperialistic expansion leading up to the World War, the claims of the state over the citizen came near to touching the absolute.

The recent Supreme Court decision in which Professor D. C. Macintosh of Yale was denied American citizenship because, although no pacifist, he refused to promise to fight in an unjust or oppressive war, shows how little standing the Christian conscience has in the American Constitution. Italy and Germany have simply given to this modern absolutism of the state a more coercive and more patently religious form, more nearly parallel to the emperor worship which was demanded of the early Christians and which is still obligatory in Japan. In Catholic Italy, the fascist cult has been resisted by the papacy, which has won for Catholic believers legal title to certain inalienable religious liberties within the framework of the state. In Protestant Germany, where the church has been politically compromised ever since the reformers accepted the principle of *cuius regio eius religio,* the state has attempted to assume a more nearly complete control of religious affairs, and there are many who feel that the very existence of the Christian church is imperiled as it has not been since the northern peoples were converted from paganism. One party, represented by the " German Faith Movement," is openly making war upon Christianity and proposing to replace it by a patriotic religion based upon the teachings of the great German philosophers from Eckhart to Nietzsche. The "Confessional Synod," at the opposite extreme, is taking its stand upon the historic Protestant confessions of faith, and claiming exemption from political control on the ground that its gospel is wholly nonpolitical. The "German Christians," midway between the two, aim at a reconciliation between historic Christianity and German nationalism in a church which shall be national and politically active without ceasing to be Christian.[21] Whether this reconciliation between historic Christianity and German nationalism is possible seems dubious to their opponents. Christianity can make room for the contributions of national and racial groups within its conception of the kingdom of God, and it can lend its blessing to patriotic devotion as it does to family loyalty and other powerful human motives; but it cannot allow the national state to become solely or supremely authoritative over the church without turning its back on its own sources and denying its Founder.

Beset in this fashion, both from the communist left and the fascist right, by political and social forces which threaten to destroy it, contemporary Christianity is beginning to exhibit marked symptoms of conservative reaction. The liberal leaders who brought the Christian church in the eighteenth and nineteenth centuries into such close and friendly relations with modern science, modern philosophy, and modern humanitarianism are now being denounced as traitors who have seriously compromised the Christian cause. The first manifestation of this reactionary swing came before the war, in 1907, when Pius X launched his two encyclicals, the *Lamentabile* and the *Pascendi gregis,* against the Catholic modernists. This action resulted within a few years in the excommunication or submission of all pronounced liberals in the Roman Catholic fold. Just before the war, a conservative movement known as fundamentalism began to gather headway among various Protestant bodies in the United States. Attaining its greatest strength between the years 1921 and 1926, it succeeded in blocking the ordination of many liberal theological students, procuring the dismissal of some liberal teachers from denominational colleges, and enacting laws in several states against the teaching of Darwinian evolution in public institutions. In the Presbyterian, Baptist, and Episcopalian churches, it made a determined attempt to capture the denominational machinery and exclude from the ministry all those who were " unsound on the fundamentals." [22]

In recent years the strength of fundamentalism has waned, but a new conservative movement in Christian thought, known as the "theology of crisis," originating in Switzerland, has come to be widely influential in Germany, Scotland, Denmark, Holland, and to some extent in America. The leaders of this movement, Karl Barth and Emil Brunner, differ from the American fundamentalists in having already passed through liberalism in the course of their religious pilgrimage. They have no quarrel with the attested findings of the natural sciences and are somewhat radically critical in their attitude toward the Bible. But they believe that Schleiermacher and Ritschl have betrayed the Christian church into a compromising alliance with rationalistic philosophy and humanitarian ethics, from which it must be extricated if it is not to become completely secularized; and they accordingly define their leading principles in diametrical opposition to those of nineteenth century liberalism. Divine revelation instead of human religious experience, transcendence instead of immanence, crisis and catastrophic judgment instead of gradual progress, have become their watchwords. It is noteworthy that many former liberals, while rejecting this sweeping program of reaction, are equally convinced with the Barthians that Christianity must be disentangled from its alliance with secular culture,[23] and they applaud Barth for his courageous stand against the German government's attempt to "coordinate" the church. Evidently, another great turn in the history of Christianity is at hand; but it is too soon to predict the exact direction it will take.

IV. MODERN TENDENCIES IN OTHER RELIGIONS

We have analyzed in detail the interactions between Christianity and modern civilization, since it was on the soil of Christendom that modern civilization took its rise, and its influence upon Christianity has been more profound and far-reaching than upon any other religious tradition. But the effect of modern civilization upon other religions has likewise been very extensive, and it will cast much light upon the situation in which we find ourselves if we briefly survey the main cultural areas, noting the similarity and difference between the religious tendencies which prevail in the west and in the east. Everywhere there are to be found three groups: (1) The radical secularists, ardently in favor of modern science and modern culture, scornfully opposed to old religious superstitions; (2) the liberals, who believe that many elements in modern civilization and foreign religious teachings can be harmoniously combined with the ancient religious heritage; and (3) the conservatives, who fear lest the ancient verities be corrupted by modern ideas and modern manners.

In the Islamic world — to begin with that section of the east which is contiguous to Christendom — the development of radical secularism is most advanced in Turkey. Since the abolition of the caliphate in 1924 and the disestablishment of Islam as the state religion in 1928, a wholesale process of westernization has gone on, while old Moslem customs and institutions, such as Friday worship and the dervish orders, have been abolished and expropriated without compunction. Needless to say, this does not imply any admiration for Christian ideas, but only for the scientific and material aspects of western culture. The liberal tendency in Islam is best represented by the Ahmediyya movement, which carries on an aggressive propaganda in the English-speaking world through the *Islamic Review,* published in Woking, England. It is willing to contemplate very considerable departures from ancient practice, provided only that they keep in line with the spirit of Islam, which modern Moslems are as able to determine as their ancestors. In the words of the Prophet, " Whatever Muslims find good, that is good with God." The conservative tendency has its headquarters at the great Mohammedan University of Al Azhar at Cairo, Egypt, where in spite of certain recent modern importations into the curriculum the memorizing of the sacred text of the Koran still forms the main substance of education. A theologian of this university recently described the unveiling of women in Turkey as " a great setback to the nation . . . a great catastrophe, contrary to the book of God and the regulations of his Prophet." [24] To the outside observer, it seems as though the crust of ancient Islamic custom were now thoroughly broken up, and the religion of the Prophet could no longer preserve itself by a policy of immobility, but only by a resolute facing of the new situation in the light of basic principles.

In India, the whole religious situation is linked up with the rising movement for national independence, which gives unusual strength and prominence to the conservative effort to maintain the ancient Hindu heritage in the face of the western influences fostered by the British government. Nowhere, perhaps, is western civilization in its scientific and technical aspects so unpopular as in India. When Mr. Gandhi, in 1920, wrote: " The last war has shown as nothing else has the satanic nature of the civilization that dominates Europe today. . . . Europe today is only nominally Christian. In reality it is worshiping Mammon " — he woke an answering chord in many Indian hearts. To those who agree with him, not only western imperialism and western greed, but western machinery, science, and medicine seem devices of the devil. Let India return to her ancient religious seers and preserve the social order her life requires if she wishes to save her soul! Under these circumstances, the liberal religious movement of the Brāhma Samāj, led by the Tagores, which was so popular among educated Hindus a generation ago, has come to seem like a form of treason against India's national integrity, and its progress has been slackened, while the Ārya Samāj or " fundamentalist " movement has gained ground. Meanwhile, for some years back, the leadership of the Indian National Congress has been divided between Mr. Gandhi's party of religious nonviolence and a rising young secularist party which declares that India will never be united or independent until all religions are destroyed. The influence of Russian communism is very evident in this, the first radical antireligious movement that India has ever seen. It may perhaps already be predicted that unless Mr. Gandhi succeeds in reforming Hinduism and reconciling it with the better elements in western culture, the secularistic movement is destined to outstrip him.

In China, the situation is in some respects the reverse of that in India. Secular western civilization is as eagerly sought as it is angrily resisted in India; and religious conservatism is hardly evident at all. Dr. Braden remarks that " China has known no such militant, aggressive conservative defense reaction as has appeared in some other religions." [25] Strong movements exist for the revival of Buddhism and Confucianism, but they are of the liberal, not of the reactionary type, aiming to recover certain valuable elements in an admittedly decadent tradition, and — in certain circles — to combine them syncretistically with Christianity.

Meanwhile the antireligious and anti-Christian campaigns of communist and other groups, and the rise of nationalism as a kind of secular religion, with Sun Yat Sen as its titular deity, have put all religions in China somewhat on the defensive. The whole religious status of contemporary China is most unstable. Waves of enthusiasm for this or that religious or antireligious movement sweep over the land from time to time. China seems ready to turn to any faith that will save her in her need, as she will turn to any political alliance that will deliver her from her enemies. Western science and machinery she knows she must have to rescue her from poverty. Confucianism still lives, and will live, as an ingrained ethical attitude, even though its institutions are in decay. Christianity, Taoism, and Buddhism offer visions of far horizons, while communism — already in possession of large districts in the interior — offers a radically different vision. Many contemporary critics, pointing to the ascendancy of Christianity in the present ruling group in the Nanking government, offer the opinion that China will be either Christian or communist within the next half century.

Japan began in 1868 to traverse the cycle of westernization upon which China has but recently entered. It seems now to have run its course, and to have been succeeded by a movement of nationalistic reaction. Japanese civilization is rationalized, industrialized, and militarized after the western pattern; but a deep need now manifests itself for the assimilation of the new ways to the old. Liberal syncretism, embracing any and every idea that seems good, is still the prevailing tendency of Japanese life; but the movement is evidently back to a profounder appreciation of the ancient traditions as the core of life to which all new elements must be related. Shintō, as the oldest element in Japanese tradition, seems likely to prevail over all others, especially since the exigencies of the political situation require the government to keep patriotic loyalty constantly at the boiling point. Radical secularism exists, both in the form of anarchic individualism — expressed in the *mobo* and the *moga* * who make night life gay in the great cities — and in the

* Japanese slang for "modern boy" and "modern girl."

form of communistic agitation against the economic injustices of a heavily overpopulated and socially stratified society; but both forms of secularism are combatted by the state in continual campaigns against what it regards as "dangerous thoughts." Christianity has played a great part in Japan during the period of westernization, but is now threatened with the twin perils of being frozen out as something "foreign" or so forcibly adapted to the Japanese national mold as to lose its identity. Since Japan is likely to dominate a large section of eastern Asia in the near future, the prediction already made about China may have to be changed. Japan may restore the Buddhist-Confucian tradition in China as she has done to some extent in Korea. Or we may see China divided into a Christian, a Buddhist-Confucian, and a communist area.

However much the development of religion may vary from country to country in the next generation on account of local differences in religious tradition and social structure, certain general influences seem to be at work today throughout the whole world. One of these is the influence of scientific modes of thought upon the magical and miraculous elements in all religions, which it seems to purge away as with a powerful antiseptic. Another is the liberalizing influence of different religious traditions upon one another in a world grown small and interdependent through improved means of transportation. Another is the pressure of economic change upon old social structures, which is forcing religion either to retreat from the social arena altogether, or to take a hand decisively in the task of rescuing mankind from poverty, social injustice, and international war. The questions which religion must answer if it is to survive and flourish in the near future have to do with the truth of the fundamental concepts upon which religious thought is based, and with the effectiveness of the means by which religion seeks to promote the growth of the individual and the progress of society. These questions will be considered in Part II of this book. But there is one preliminary question which underlies the rest: What is religion? Our survey of the living religions of the world has given us much light upon the question, and we shall accordingly treat it in chapter 7 as the culmination of our investigation so far, and the indispensable preface to what follows.

NOTES

[1] The evidence for this assertion will be found conveniently summarized in Prof. C. S. Braden's *Modern Tendencies in World Religions,* to which reference will be made later in this chapter.

[2] C. A. Beard, *Whither Mankind?* pp. 14, 15. Quoted by permission of Longmans, Green and Co., publishers.

[3] Cited by Beard, *op. cit.,* p. 63. The whole chapter is remarkably illuminating.

[4] *Ibid.,* p. 64.

[5] See Randall, *Making of the Modern Mind,* p. 90.

[6] *Ibid.,* p. 327.

[7] Neither the deists nor the skeptics of the eighteenth century left behind them any organized movement, though the deists exerted a great influence, through men like Voltaire, Thomas Paine, Franklin, and Jefferson, upon the American and French revolutions and upon the general current of political thought.

[8] This is expressed in Art. II of the brief " Winchester Profession," adopted in 1803: " We believe that there is one God, whose nature is Love, revealed in one Lord Jesus Christ, by one Holy Spirit of Grace, who will finally restore the whole family of mankind to holiness and happiness." Cf. also the following from the " Statement of Essential Principles," adopted in 1900: " 4. The certainty of just retribution for sin. 5. The final harmony of all souls with God."

[9] Cf. the report of the new Universalist declaration of faith in the *Christian Leader,* XXXVI (Dec. 16, 1933), 1576: " We avow our faith in God as Eternal and All-Conquering Love; in the spiritual leadership of Jesus; in the supreme worth of every human personality; in the authority of truth, known or to be known; and in the power of men of good will and sacrificial spirit to overcome all evil and progressively establish the kingdom of God."

[10] See McGiffert, *The Rise of Modern Religious Ideas,* pp. 65, 66.

[11] *Discourses on Religion,* quoted in McGiffert, *op. cit.,* p. 203.

[12] Cf. the case of Alfred Loisy, one of the most eminent of the Catholic modernists, who became an adherent of Comte's religion of humanity after his excommunication from the church. See his book, *La Religion,* and his autobiography, *My Duel with the Vatican.*

[13] Nineteenth ed., revised, 1886, p. 406. The first edition was published in 1875, and later editions vary considerably; but the Recapitulation chapter generally recurs, being a confession of Mrs. Eddy's views prepared for " learners."

[14] *No and Yes,* p. 15.

[15] R. J. Campbell was the eloquent preacher at the City Temple, London, in the early days of the twentieth century, when his *New Theology* was published. Later, he repudiated certain features of the book, entered the Anglican Church, and has recently come forth again from practical retirement, as a defender of conservative theology.

[16] *An Ethical Philosophy of Life* (New York, 1918), p. 343.

[17] *Ibid.,* p. 352.

[18] See his book, *The Soul of America.*

[19] See the *New Humanist,* Vol. VI, No. 3 (May–June 1933), pp. 1–5.

[20] See Chamberlain, *Soviet Russia,* p. 306.

21 For differing views of the German church situation see Anders Nygren, *The Church Controversy in Germany;* Adolf Keller, *The Church and the Revolution;* and Paul B. Means, *Things That Are Caesar's: The Genesis of the German Church Conflict.* The situation changes so rapidly that no book is strictly up to date.

22 A much cited formulation of the " fundamentals," that of the Presbyterian General Assembly in 1910, includes the following five points: inerrancy of the Bible, the virgin birth, the substitutionary theory of the atonement, the bodily resurrection and ascension, and the miracles of Christ.

23 See, for example, *The Church Against the World,* by H. Richard Niebuhr, Wilhelm Pauck, and Francis Miller.

24 See C. S. Braden, *Modern Tendencies in World Religions,* p. 219.

25 *Ibid.,* p. 112.

BIBLIOGRAPHY

Friess and Schneider. *Op. cit.,* pp. 458–96.

Braden, C. E. *Modern Tendencies in World Religions.*

Randall, J. H., Jr. *The Making of the Modern Mind.*

Beard, C. A. (editor). *Whither Mankind?*

McGiffert, A. C. *The Rise of Modern Religious Ideas.*

Smith, G. B. *Current Christian Thinking.*

Shotwell, J. T. *The Religious Revolution of Today.*

Aubrey, E. E. *Present Theological Tendencies.*

Keller, Adolf. *Karl Barth and Christian Unity.*

———. *Church and State on the European Continent.*

Dawson, Christopher. *Christianity and the New Age.*

Berdyaev, N. *The Fate of Man in the Modern World.*

Bennett, John. *Christianity — and Our World.*

7

THE NATURE OF RELIGION
IN THE LIGHT OF ITS HISTORY

IT will be remembered that we started, in the foreword, with a preliminary definition of religion, designed simply to mark off the field of study and cover all the relevant facts. Religion, we said, is *man's attempt to realize the highest good, through coming into harmonious relations with some reality greater than himself, which commands his reverence and loyal service.* In the course of our historical survey, we have seen what an endless variety of religious ideas and practices may be covered by such a descriptive definition. The " highest good " may mean anything from physical health, wealth, and power to the passionless peace of nirvāna. The " great reality " may be found in the form of primitive ghosts, gods, and demons, or in the pantheistic Absolute, or in the living God of the Hebrew prophets, or simply in the continuing life of the human race. The method of " coming into harmonious relations with " this Being may vary all the way from magical incantations or human sacrifices to Evangelical conversion or Quaker silence.

If the test of a good descriptive definition of religion is to omit no form of religion from consideration and to make no prejudicial distinctions among them, our definition may be said to have passed this test fairly well. It applies equally to primitive animism, to the Oriental religions of resignation, to the Occidental religions of combat and hope, and even to the " antireligious " creed of Russian communism. But obviously, so broad a definition as this one can serve us no longer. We are about to inquire what religious tendencies are true as over against the false, and good as over against the bad. On the basis of our present definition, we should be obliged to say, Both. Indeed we should have to admit that almost all the views expressed about " religion," from the violent denunciations of the dogmatic atheist to the ardent panegyrics of the Catholic apologist, could be justified by pointing to something that comes within our definition. Plainly, it is necessary at this point to become more discriminating and more normative in our treatment of religion, to distinguish among various types and aspects of this multiform phenomenon that we have described, and single out those which are of lasting truth and worth from those which may be regarded as " superstitions " — i.e., in the original sense of that much misused word: belated " survivals " of religious ideas and practices whose significance is transitory or nugatory.

It will be the object of this normative conception of religion to define the sense (if there is a sense) in which men of our own time ought still to be religious in spite of all the legitimate objections that can be made against the religions of the past, and to mark out the lines along which religion must develop in the future if it is to fulfill its proper function and exert an increasing influence for good. It will not be necessary to incorporate in this conception any completely detailed set of conclusions concerning the specific problems to be discussed in Part II. Such problems may be regarded as secondary to the primary problem, whether — as we commonly put it — there is " anything in religion." A decision to become an adherent of a particular political movement is usually based upon a general conviction of " something in it," which precedes assent to all of its special teachings and may survive in spite of radical divergence from many of them. Just so, a conviction that there is something fundamentally sound in religion despite all its aberrations, must precede and lead up to such themes as God, prayer, and immortality, if these later phases of the discussion are to mean anything at all. To one who is convinced that all religion is rotten at the core, such topics represent only so many occasions for abusive or derisive comment.

It may help the reader to form his own conclusions upon this basic issue of the soundness of religion if he is first presented with a review of the contrasting opinions of modern philosophers concerning the nature and lasting worth of religion, followed by a summary of the results of recent investigations in the historical science of religion and the empirical psychology of religion, by which these philosophical opinions may be corrected or corroborated.

I. RIVAL PHILOSOPHIES OF RELIGION

The problem of the nature of religion can hardly be said to have entered modern philosophy until the latter part of the eighteenth century, when philosophy became " critical " and self-conscious beneath the embarrassing scrutiny of Immanuel Kant. Hitherto, the concept of religion had been left unexamined, like many another common notion; and it had been uncritically assumed that religion was simply a set of theological doctrines, which could be rationally tested like the propositions of Euclid, and the truth or falsity of religion thus determined. During the eighteenth century, as we have seen, opinion differed widely concerning the truth of religion. Some philosophers, like John Locke, asserted that reason could justify all the doctrines of " revealed religion " — some of them to be sure only indirectly, on the ground that they were supernaturally vouched for by rationally authenticated prophecies and miracles. Other philosophers, of the deist school, such as Voltaire, asserted that only the three great doctrines of " natural religion," God and duty and immortality, could be rationally justified; and they poured contempt upon revealed religion as a mere invention of " priestcraft " to keep the people in order. Still other philosophers, like David Hume, found as little rational justification for belief in natural religion as for belief in revealed religion, and asserted that only a blind faith could save one from complete skepticism on such matters. But no one thought of questioning the assumption that a man's religiousness was to be measured by the number of theological propositions which he could simultaneously embrace. Religion, in other words, was a matter of credulity; irreligion, a matter of incredulity.

Kant questioned that assumption, along with many other current notions; and by so doing he may be said to have created the philosophy of religion. He doubted the validity of all the rational arguments by which religion was supported in his day, and so far as

" pure reason " was concerned, arrived at a skepticism as complete as Hume's. But having arrived there, he positively declined to be considered an irreligious unbeliever, for he found in himself another faculty than reason, the moral will, by which he was indissolubly bound to religion and through which he reached a new sort of faith in the essential truths of religion, which had nothing to do with mere credulity. Kant was not a credulous man; he was in fact almost morbidly incredulous of all commonly accepted opinions. But one thing remained ineradicable in him, from his pietistic upbringing: nothing could prevent him from listening to the voice of duty, whenever it spoke. That was to him the " categorical imperative," which must be obeyed, whether it pleased him or not. In the *Critique of Practical Reason* Kant argued that when obeying the call of duty we must be allowed to assume or " postulate " whatever was logically involved in such an act of obedience; and he found the three great faiths of natural religion involved in it: moral freedom, because " we ought " is meaningless unless " we can "; immortality, because the moral law requires nothing less than moral perfection, which cannot be achieved unless we have all eternity to progress toward the goal; God, because the moral law bids us seek to promote that perfect correspondence of virtue with happiness which is called the " highest good " or the " kingdom of God," and the kingdom of God is only realizable if our finite human efforts are reinforced by the Cause of all nature. In his *Religion Within the Bounds of Mere Reason* Kant went on to justify, on similar moralistic grounds, many of the doctrines of revealed religion, such as the doctrine of original sin — " radical evil," as he called it — and offered a definition of religion which sums up his whole position very neatly: "Religion," he said, " is the recognition of our duties as divine commands." [1]

Kant's moralistic conception of religion has found advocates throughout the subsequent history of modern religious thought. Fichte, his immediate successor, described the religious attitude as follows: " Joyfully and without restraint to do what each one ought to do without doubting and troubling oneself about the consequences." [2] The difference between morality and religion, in other words, is simply the difference between doing one's duty anxiously, as if all depended on oneself, and doing it gladly and hopefully, in full confidence that the universe is somehow on the side of the right. Höffding, in his *Philosophy of Religion,* found the fundamental axiom of religion in " the axiom of the conservation of value," i.e., the moral faith that the world supports our highest values, and " no value perishes out of the world." [3] Matthew Arnold defined religion in a famous phrase as " morality touched by emotion," and God as " a power not ourselves that makes for righteousness," [4] a power not to be discovered through rational reflection upon the processes of nature, but only through obedience to the moral law. Cardinal Newman — a great intellectual skeptic and a great moral believer — once wrote, " Were it not for this voice speaking so clearly in my conscience and my heart, I should be an atheist, or a pantheist, or a polytheist when I looked into the world." [5] Albrecht Ritschl defined religion as " victory over the world," adding that we win this victory when we follow the path of life marked out by Christ, and so, by a process of " value-judgment," find in him the God we could never find in nature. William James and other members of the pragmatist school were following in the footsteps of Kant when they urged that we should not wait for rational argument to prove the truth of religious faith, but should will to believe whatever it seemed morally best to believe, and see whether the practical consequences of such moral faith did not justify the venture.[6] An excellent contemporary representative of the Kantian school in the philosophy of religion will be found in John Baillie, who defines religion as " a consciousness which comes to the dutiful, to the loyal, to those who are true to the highest values they know, that in being thus dutiful and loyal to their values, they are doing what they were meant and appointed to do, and are putting themselves in line with the Eternal and have His backing behind them." Elsewhere, he defines religion more simply as " confidence in the goodness of reality and the reality of goodness," or in Kant's own words, " trust in the promise of the moral law." [7]

There is another important school of the philosophy of religion

which agrees with Kant in distinguishing religion from the mere
acceptance of theological propositions on rational grounds, but
which also distinguishes it from morality much more sharply than
the Kantian school, and finds the taproot of religion in the realm
of the feelings. This is commonly known as the aesthetic, mystical, or romanticist school; and its founder is Schleiermacher, the
great theologian and philosopher whose definition of religion as
" the feeling of absolute dependence " has already come to our
attention. He had his forerunners and satellites in the remarkable
group of literary geniuses who founded the Romantic movement
of the late eighteenth and early nineteenth centuries — men like
Rousseau and Chateaubriand in France, Wordsworth and Coleridge in England, Herder and Goethe in Germany — but although all these men agreed that religion was a " sentiment," akin
to the poet's melting mood in the presence of a sunset, none of
them was able to express this idea so philosophically as Schleiermacher.

"Religion," says Schleiermacher,

vindicates for itself its own sphere and its own character only by abandoning
entirely the provinces of science and practice; and when it has raised itself
beside them, the whole field is for the first time completely filled and human
nature perfected. Religion reveals itself as the necessary and indispensable
third, as the natural complement of knowledge and conduct, not inferior
to them in worth and dignity.[8]

Not that it is unrelated to knowledge and morality; the realm of
feeling underlies them both, and in it the universe is continually
making upon us deep unconscious impressions, from which our
truest scientific intuitions and our noblest moral impulses both take
their rise. But religion is essentially the receiving of these deep
impressions and its characteristic symptom is the experiencing of
a sublime emotional thrill — " like a bridal embrace " — as the
impression strikes home. Since the universe is one and our absolute dependence upon it is inescapable, all religion is essentially
one; yet since its vast life impinges upon us from many angles,
religions are many. Every particular religion springs from a
unique intuitive feeling, in which the whole universe is mirrored

from a special angle. This theory made Schleiermacher exceedingly tolerant of other religions, and led his followers to interest themselves impartially in the description and classification of various types of religion.

Schleiermacher's conception of religion has been still more influential than Kant's. Even among those who reject his peculiar aesthetic and mystical emphasis, the idea that the essence of religion consists in yielding oneself gratefully and trustfully to something above and beyond oneself, on which one depends, has become current coin. (The reader will readily recognize the influence of this idea on the definition offered in the foreword.) But in addition to this more diffused influence, Schleiermacher's line has been continued in a well recognizable school of thought which still finds religion best expressed in the act of worship and notes the close analogy between worship of the holy and admiration of the beautiful. So, for example, Seeley in his *Natural Religion* (1882) remarked, "The true artist is he who worships, for worship is habitual admiration . . . enthusiastic appreciation. . . . Wherever, therefore, art is, there is religion."[9] Auguste Sabatier, in his *Outline of a Philosophy of Religion* (1897), sought to correct Schleiermacher's too passive concept of religion by combining it with Ritschl's active "victory over the world"; but his definition of religion still reminds one chiefly of Schleiermacher's: "It is a commerce, a conscious and willed relation into which the soul in distress enters with the mysterious power on which it feels that it and its destiny depend. This commerce with God is realized by prayer. Prayer is religion in act — that is to say, real religion."[10] In contemporary religious thought, the school of Schleiermacher is best represented by students of mysticism like Rudolf Otto, whose idea of religion as the numinous "creature-feeling" has been reviewed in chapter 1, and especially by Georg Wobbermin, who calls himself a "Schleiermacher-Jamesian" — reminding us that our versatile American philosopher was not only a Kantian pragmatist but also very much of a mystic, and carried on the task, which Schleiermacher began, of analyzing the psychological types of religious experience. Wobbermin's expansion and correction of Schleiermacher's definition of religion, in the light of a wide study of variant types, is as follows:

> For us the nature of religion is the relationship of man to an over-world in which he believes and of which he has intimations in his faith, on which he feels himself to be dependent, in whose shelter he knows himself to be secure, and which is the goal of his heart's most ardent yearning. . . . The feeling of dependence is the fundamental religious feeling and it allows itself to be differentiated into the two polar opposite and conflicting feelings of security and ardent yearning, in order that it may overcome this oppositeness.[11]

The notion of the overcoming of oppositeness which appears in Wobbermin's definition is derived from Hegel, the founder of a third extremely influential school of the philosophy of religion. Hegel was for some years a colleague of Schleiermacher at the University of Berlin; and they carried on a continual dispute over the relative place of feeling and thought in religion. Hegel did not deny that the religious consciousness begins with feeling, nor that in this religious feeling the deepest truth about the universe is somehow confusedly contained; but he insisted that mature religion must pass beyond feeling to thought, and so become one with philosophy. Religion, he argued, is peculiar to man; but feeling is common to man and the brutes; hence religion cannot have its true seat in the feelings, but only in the reason, which elevates man above the brutes. Religion, then, is to be defined not only as the relation of the finite spirit to the Infinite, but — in its mature form — as the knowledge which the finite spirit has of the Infinite, or still better (since for Hegel man's knowledge of God is identical with God's knowledge of himself) religion is " God's self-consciousness."

Hegel's *Philosophy of Religion,* published in 1832, after his death, represents the culminating point of his whole system of philosophy. The root idea of this system is the idea already alluded to: that all reality is an endless process of becoming, in the course of which pairs of opposites (thesis, antithesis) are continually appearing, only to be reconciled in a higher synthesis which becomes the starting point for new developments. The supreme illustration of this is the cosmic process whereby God, or "the Absolute," sets the world of nature over against himself, only to overcome this opposition through the development of the human spirit, whose highest insights are at once natural and divine. Hegel represents the history of religion as the gradual discovery by man of his oneness with the Absolute. In the nature religions of the ancient east, man had not yet become conscious of the distinction between spirit and nature, and so bowed before natural forces to which he was himself superior. In the Hebrew religion of "sublimity," the Greek religion of "beauty," and the Roman religion of "utility," man bowed before manlike deities of "spiritual individuality," which nevertheless were still represented as standing over against the worshiper, exalted in the heavens. Finally, in Christianity, the "absolute religion," man realized his oneness with the Being revealed in both nature and spirit, and so entered into his full dignity as the son and heir of the Infinite and the Absolute. This is the mature religion of "old age." Idealistic philosophy and spiritual religion are thus treated as identical in meaning.[12]

Hegel's strong emphasis upon the rational content of religion looks at first sight like a reversion to eighteenth century rationalism and an undoing of the work of Kant and Schleiermacher. On closer examination, however, it will be found that Hegel gathers up the teachings of his predecessors in a new synthesis. Will and feeling are recognized as "moments" in the development of the religious consciousness, or elements in the religious attitude, which however must pass on to the stage of rational clarification before religious maturity can be attained. Rationality, for Hegel, means something much more "concrete," much less abstracted from life, than the eighteenth century type of rationality. Hegel's "absolute religion" is the fulfillment of will and feeling as well as of thought; and it concretely embodies all the achievements of the historic or "positive" religions, instead of being divorced from history like the "natural religion" of the deists. Since Hegel, it has been a philosophical commonplace that religion involves the whole man, and not merely his intellect, his feelings, his will, or any other single aspect of his psychology. Since Hegel, also, it has been common practice for philosophers to arrange the historic religions in a developmental or evolutionary series, of which ideal religion is the natural culmination. Hegel's own arrangement has been severely criticized, on the ground that it cramps the facts of the history of religion to fit into a preconceived philosophical scheme; but in the attempt to refute or improve Hegel many semi-Hegelian schemes have arisen, and the study of comparative religion has been enormously stimulated. Among later philosophies of religion which bear the marks of Hegel's influence, Pfleiderer's *Philosophy of Religion on the Basis of its History* (1878), John Caird's *Introduction to the Philosophy of Religion* (1880), and Edward Caird's *The Evolution of Religion* (1894) may be mentioned. As a contemporary Hegelian definition of religion, the following from Professor J. E. Turner's *Development of Religion* is typical: "The response of humanity, taken as a real whole or explicit unity, to the universe, likewise taken as a whole." [13]

Although the Hegelian school did in a sense synthesize the results of previous philosophies of religion and carry them to a new pinnacle of vision, it overemphasized the rational element in religion; and its claim to possess, in its speculative interpretations of the meaning of religious dogmas, nothing less than absolute and final truth, provoked a reaction resulting in the rise of a fourth school, which we may call the naturalistic or agnostic school.

Among the so-called "left-wing Hegelians" there were men like Feuerbach and Karl Marx, who carried their naturalistic reaction so far as to deny the truth of religion altogether. For Feuerbach, religion was a subjective illusion; for Marx, the "opium of the people." This illusionistic conception of religion has received reinforcement in recent times from Freudian psychology,[14] which describes religious dogmas as rationalizations or escape mechanisms built on wishful thinking. But it has not been characteristic of the naturalistic school as a whole to denounce religion in such wholesale terms. That school has always resisted religion's claim to possess supernatural knowledge concerning ultimate or transcendent realities, and it has insisted that the world in which religion operates must be the natural world of modern physical and social science; but within that world it has commonly ascribed to religion a function of the highest human importance: the encouragement and stimulation of the individual, and the unification of society, through the upholding and worshipful celebration of certain supremely significant social values. Especially since Darwinian modes of thought have become prevalent religion has been conceived by this school as one of the ways in which man has adapted himself to his natural and social environment. Typical of this attitude is George Burman Foster's book, *The Function of Religion in Man's Struggle for Existence.*

It is impossible to point to any single great work on the philosophy of religion which embodies the principles of naturalism and agnosticism as classically as Hegel's *Philosophy of Religion* embodies the principles of speculative idealism. Naturalistic philosophers have generally preferred to speak of the "science of religion" instead of the "philosophy of religion" — partly because Hegel had made the latter term his own. But strewn through their works will be found many important discussions of the origin, nature, function, and future of religion. Especially significant, as pioneer statements, are Auguste Comte's rough draft of a "religion of humanity," and John Stuart Mill's essay, "The Utility of Religion," in which he considers "whether the idealization of our earthly life, the cultivation of a high conception of what it may be made, is not capable of supplying a poetry, and, in the best sense of the word, a religion, equally fitted to exalt the feelings, and (with the aid of education) still better calculated to ennoble the conduct, than any belief respecting the unseen powers." [15]   Another important naturalistic document is Guyau's *Non-Religion of the Future* (*L'Irreligion de l'avenir*), which, in spite of its title, provides for the survival of the central element in religion in the shape of "ideal sociology," and even permits theology to survive as metaphysical speculation, provided only that it does not lay claim to dogmatic authority. In Herbert Spencer's *Synthetic Philosophy* religion is described as an evolu-

tion from primitive animism, which in turn (as we have seen in
chapter 1) is derived from the misinterpretation of dreams; yet a
permanent function for religion is found in the contemplation of
that cosmic mystery which science can never dispel, and a great
truth is discerned behind its multiple errors: the truth that the
power which wells up within us as consciousness is somehow
ultimately akin to the power expressed in the order of nature.[16]
In contemporary philosophy, the naturalistic philosophy of religion is perhaps represented at its best in Julian Huxley's *Religion
Without Revelation,* in John Dewey's *A Common Faith,* and, most
systematically, in E. S. Ames' *Religion.* Let Professor Ames define religion for the whole school:

> Religion . . . is the cherishing of values felt to be most vital to man's
> life and blessedness, by means of ceremonial dramatization, expressive sym-
> bols, and doctrinal beliefs. These values and their representations change
> with the economic and cultural life. . . . Today the most advanced so-
> cieties are absorbed in the values of scientific knowledge, of universal human
> welfare, and in search for the means of control by which these may be made
> imaginatively dynamic and inspiring. The attainment of knowledge, de-
> velopment of personality, and the enjoyment of the fullest possible experi-
> ence are the characteristic religious values.[17]

Naturalism, which here is treated last in our sequence of philosophies of religion, is not to be regarded as the last word on the subject in any but a chronological sense. All the other philosophies
of religion previously treated have their contemporary representatives, and carry on a vigorous polemic against naturalism; while
the outstanding fact in the present religious situation is a widespread reaction against all these philosophies, on the ground that
they minimize or destroy the uniqueness of the Christian revelation. Emil Brunner's *Philosophy of Religion* (much influenced
by the teaching of Karl Barth) is a good example of this contemporary reaction. It is so exclusively concerned with the problem of Christian revelation that it falls quite outside the category
of the philosophy of religion as hitherto conceived in modern
religious thought.

II. HISTORICAL TYPES AND PSYCHOLOGICAL VARIETIES
OF RELIGION

In the latter part of the nineteenth century, the philosophic debate over the nature and truth of religion began to be checked and controlled by a vast body of scientific data hitherto unavailable. Stimulated in part by Hegelian theories concerning the evolution of religion, in part also by naturalistic Darwinism, with its immense curiosity about the origin and evolution of human institutions, anthropologists and Orientalists began to cultivate the history of religion in a genuinely disinterested and scientific spirit, as an important natural phenomenon deserving the same careful study that was being given to other aspects of human culture. Foremost among the pioneers of this new " science of religion " was the Orientalist and comparative philologist, Max Müller, to whom we owe the publication of the great series of translations known as the *Sacred Books of the East,* begun in 1879. His *Lectures on the Science of Religion,* published in 1872, was the first important work to bear that title. Next after Müller must be mentioned the Dutch savant, C. P. Tiele, whose *Elements of the Science of Religion* (two volumes, 1897 and 1899) have remained classic. In the field of primitive religion, the three classic works (already reviewed in chapter 1) are Tylor's *Primitive Culture* (1871), Frazer's *Golden Bough* (second edition, 1900), and Durkheim's *Elementary Forms of the Religious Life* (1912). Meanwhile the history and literature of Judaism and Christianity — especially the Bible — were being subjected to intensive scrutiny by a host of eminent scholars. The most distinguished American savant in the whole field of the historical science of religion was the late George Foot Moore of Harvard, whose *History of Religions* (two volumes, 1913 and 1919), *The Birth and Growth of Religion* (1923), and *Judaism* (1927) are still readable and reliable.

In the closing years of the nineteenth century the science of religion, which hitherto had been exclusively historical, was enriched and supplemented by the founding of a new science, the psychology of religion. The pioneers of this new science were three Americans, Professors E. D. Starbuck, G. A. Coe, and J. H. Leuba, all of whom published for the first time about 1899. Three years later appeared the book which remains in many respects the greatest work in the field: William James' *Varieties of Religious Experience.* The subsequent progress of the science may be briefly summarized as follows:

First period, 1899–1910. Prominent problem, psychology of conversion. Chief method, the questionnaire. Representative book, James' *Varieties of Religious Experience.* Definition of religion: " Feelings, acts, and experiences of individual men in their solitude, so far as they apprehend themselves to stand in relation to whatever they may consider the divine."

Second period, 1910–20. Prominent problem, religion and social morality. Chief method, " folk psychology." Representative book, Ames' *Psychology of Religious Experience.* Definition of religion: " Consciousness of the highest social values."

Third period, 1920– . Prominent problem, religion and ultimate reality. Methods varied and complex. Representative book, Pratt's *Religious Consciousness.* Definition of religion: " The serious and social attitude of individuals or communities toward the power or powers which they conceive as having ultimate control over their interests and destinies." [18]

The first outstanding impression which emerges from the science of religion, both in its historical and in its psychological branch, is the manifoldness and inexhaustible variety of religious phenomena. Religion occurs in all sorts of forms and all sorts of contexts. It accommodates itself to all the varieties of social system, from tribal communism to modern industrialism; all of the different world views, from primitive animism to scientific naturalism; all kinds of moral codes, from the irrational taboos of the savage to the utopian social ideals of the modern humanitarian; all sorts and conditions of men, however diverse in temperament and training. It appeals to many different motives, seeks many different ends, uses a great variety of devotional practices and forms of worship. The inescapable conclusion from all this is that no simple definition or description of religion, based upon some single line of historic development or some single element in human psychology, and no categorical judgment about the

" truth " or " falsity " of religion, can possibly cover the facts presented by the science of religion.

Religion, then — like politics, education, art, family life, and other persistent human interests — contains both truth and falsehood, good and evil, beauty and ugliness. The opinions of all the rival schools of philosophy — including the Marxian opinion that religion is a drug and ought to be suppressed — have at least something to support them in some of the many forms of religion. But to pass wholesale judgment upon religion is as unintelligent as to pass wholesale judgment upon art or politics. It is necessary to discriminate between the types and varieties of religion, as we discriminate between the types of art and the varieties of political system. The science of religion can aid us at this point, by its attempt to classify religious phenomena into certain well marked historic types and psychological varieties.

The most influential historical classification of religions is that of Tiele. In his article, " Religions," in the ninth edition of the *Encyclopedia Britannica,* he ranged all religions under the following heads, in the order of their historic origin: Primitive naturalism, animism, national polytheistic religions, nomistic religions,[19] and universal religions. Later, in his *Elements of the Science of Religion,* he superimposed upon this a general division of all religions into *natural* and *ethical,* and asserted that the transition from the former to the latter was the greatest turning point in the history of religion. In nature religions (which include all but the last two of the historic classes) the values sought are natural goods like food or protection from enemies, the deities are more or less clearly personified natural forces, and the method of propitiating them is either magical coercion or a combination of gifts and cajolery — *do ut des.*[20] In ethical religions (further described as " spiritual " religions, or " religions of revelation ") the values sought are ideal values like personal purity or social justice, the will of God stands sharply over against the world of things as they are, and religious adjustment requires an inward change in moral attitude — " what doth the Lord require of thee but to do justly and love mercy and walk humbly with thy God? " Among ethical religions, only Buddhism and Christianity qualify as universal; Islam, on account of its strong legalism and its close tie-up with Arabian nationalism, is classified, along with Confucianism, Brahmanism, Parsiism, and Judaism, as a *national* nomistic religion.

Tiele's classification has been sharply criticized, like every other classification that has been proposed. Morris Jastrow, Jr., for example, in his book *The Study of Religion* (1902), finds in animism not a form of religion, but a form of primitive philosophy; and he objects to the idea that any religion can be called universal, since all have become entangled with particular forms of culture and civilization — Buddhism with that of the Far East, Christianity with that of Europe. Tiele's classification is indeed oddly compounded. Several of the types of nature religion are described in terms of a widely accepted differentiation of seven stages in the development of the idea of deity: Pre-animism or manaism, animism, totemism, ancestor worship, polytheism, henotheism, monotheism. This purely intellectualistic classification is then crossed with two other types of classification, in terms of the predominance of natural or ethical values and in terms of the contrast between national and international religions. In spite of its illogical character, Tiele's classification admittedly covers most of the facts; and some features of it appear in most contemporary discussions. Fairly representative of contemporary thought is John Oman's classification of religions into primitive, polytheistic, mystical, ceremonial-legal, and prophetic.[21] Oman's first two types coincide with Tiele's first three; his ceremonial-legal type is identical with Tiele's nomistic type. His mystical type is a significant addition, calling attention to the fact that from national polytheism two diverse paths of religious development open out, the first or mystical path leading to pantheistic " absorption in the One," as in philosophical Hinduism and esoteric Buddhism; the other path leading to monotheistic " victory over the many," as in prophetic Judaism and Christianity. Ethical religion, in other words, is not the only ultimate form of universal spiritual religion, as Tiele seems to suggest; it is only one of two sharply contrasted types of spiritual religion; mystical religion is the other.

The psychology of religion has greatly added to our appreciation of the variety of religious phenomena, as the title of William
James' *Varieties of Religious Experience* itself suggests.   The first
conclusions to which the new science led were that religious individuals differ greatly in their susceptibility to sudden conversion
experiences and dramatic mystical experiences.   Starbuck discriminates between gradual religious awakening and two types of
sudden conversion, which he calls the "volitional" and "self-
surrender" types.   James discriminates between the "healthy
minded" religion of the "once-born," free from struggle and
agony, and the more tragic religion of the "twice-born," who
must pass through desperate inward division and conflict before
they can win personal integrity.[22]   Professor J. B. Pratt, in his
elaborate study, *The Religious Consciousness,* distinguishes four
"typical aspects" or "temperamental kinds" of religion, which
are perpetually contending for the mastery, but each of which
leads to disaster if it becomes absolutely supreme: the traditional,
the rational, the mystical, and the practical or moral.[23]   With these
classifications from the point of view of individual psychology
may be compared Professor William Adams Brown's classification from the point of view of social psychology: imperialistic,
individualistic, sectarian, democratic.[24]   Professor Brown's imperialistic type coincides largely with Professor Pratt's traditional-
istic type, and finds its perfect expression in the Roman Catholic
Church.   The rationalistic, mystic, and moralistic types are very
apt to express themselves in characteristic forms of individualistic
protest against tradition and authority.   They may, on the other
hand, express themselves less individualistically, as denominational movements, claiming independence of external control, ex-
hibiting either sectarian intolerance or democratic tolerance in
their attitude toward other movements.   On the whole, Professor
Pratt's four types have proved more applicable than any other
psychological classification.   They are closely reflected in Professor E. W. Lyman's recent book, *The Meaning and Truth of
Religion,* where the highest and most creative type of religion is
described as an ethical but not exclusively moralistic religion,
whose central ethical concern is reinforced by strong rational,

aesthetic, and mystical elements harmoniously interpenetrating. Professor Lyman's aesthetic type is a valuable addition to Professor Pratt's list.

It is important to note that the chief psychological types appear in all the great historic religions, and establish kinships between men of different faiths. These kinships, when strongly marked, sometimes exert a lateral pull that exceeds the vertical pull of tradition. Mystics like Śankara in India and Meister Eckhart in Christendom are closer to each other in many respects than they are to their co-religionists. Rationalistic Hindus of the Brāhma Samāj feel more at home with liberal Christians than with orthodox Hindus. In the Bahai movement, a practical interest in world peace has brought together men of many different faiths in a common fellowship. If similarities of psychological type thus bring together men of different religions, differences of psychological type often divide men of the same religion. Professor Pratt's four psychological types can all be illustrated, singly or in combination, among the Christian denominations, and close analogies for each can be found in Buddhism. Chinese Buddhism in its flourishing period represented a rich variety of interpenetrating types, like medieval Catholicism. Japanese Buddhism, with its sharp divisions, is more like Protestantism. The Shingon and Tendai sects, with their aesthetic ritualism and many-sided traditionalism, resemble the Episcopalian Church; the Zen sect, with its practice of silent mystic meditation, resembles the Quakers; the Nichiren sect, with its moral and social passion, resembles the Puritans; the Shin and Jodo sects, with their union of moral zeal and mystical piety, resemble the German Pietists and English Methodists; while certain modern Buddhist reform movements — represented by such a periodical as the *Young East* — are as rationalistic and moralistic as Unitarianism or the new humanism.

In addition to psychological differences, many other causes — sometimes of a historic, social, and economic nature — underlie the phenomena of denominationalism.[25] Persistent theological problems are of course not to be overlooked. Under many superficial differences of phraseology, the concepts of God and of salvation appear in all religions, and wherever they appear they give rise to similar problems, which are resolved in much the same way, independently, in different parts of the world. In Occidental religions theism is dominant, but pantheism and agnostic humanism have been persistent counter-tendencies; in India pantheism is dominant, but there are important theistic and atheistic counter-tendencies; in the Far East, since Confucius, humanism has been very strong, but pantheism and theism have never died out. Although polytheism has everywhere tended to be superseded by some more unified world view, the problem of the One and the many still remains as a cause of theological division. The adoration of the one God as revealed in many living avatars and material symbols is defended by Hindus, but fiercely denounced as idolatry by the Moslems. Catholics and Protestants differ in much the same way over the question of saint worship and image worship.

Another persistent problem on which division arises in all religions is that of grace and free will. Does man's salvation depend in part upon his own free will and good works, or must he cast himself absolutely upon the mercy and grace of the higher powers? Catholicism, Brahmanism, southern Buddhism, and many other forms of religion believe it is possible for man to " work out " his salvation and " merit " his eternal bliss; but there have been representatives of the opposite view in every important religious tradition — the so-called " cat " school in Hindu thought, the Pure Land school in Buddhist thought, and the Paul-Augustine-Luther school in Christian thought. Sometimes, as in Islam and in certain forms of Calvinism, the emphasis upon divine grace has been so all-controlling as to destroy belief in human freedom altogether; sometimes, as in modern humanistic religion, the emphasis upon human effort has been so strong as to crowd out belief in God.

The longer a religion endures the more likely it is to develop sectarian divisions and theological disputes that run parallel to those in other religions. Thus with the passage of time religions become at once more different and more similar. More different,

since all the differences of individual psychology, social organization, and national culture become imprinted upon them. More
similar, since they together experience the steady inescapable pressure of trying to deal with a common reality and are forced to
wrestle with common problems. These similarities are none the
less significant when they express themselves, as described above,
in similar differences, which agitate and divide religions along
parallel lines. If, then, the first impression to be derived from a
survey of the science of religion is one of inexhaustible variety,
the final and profounder impression is one of underlying unity. In
spite of the clear-cut differences between the historic religions, the
long story of their growth, decay, and rebirth is pervaded by many
unifying tendencies, which permit us to treat the history of religion as a single complicated process. The conception of " high
religion " which we propose to formulate in the concluding section of the present chapter will represent our attempt to discern
the more excellent forms of religion which emerge in this process.

III. SUPERSTITION AND HIGH RELIGION

Let us begin with a definition of superstition, since it is much
easier to define superstition than to define high religion. Superstition, in present-day parlance, has a very narrow and specific
meaning. To call a person " superstitious " means that he believes
in good and bad luck, trusts in talismans and omens, carries a
rabbit's foot, and never starts a journey on Friday the thirteenth.
But the word superstition, in its broader meaning, connotes every
form of religious belief or observance which has survived through
sheer inertia, after its futility has been thoroughly exposed. Belief
in luck, omens, or talismans certainly comes under this category,
but it is far from being the only form of superstition. Let the
reader review the description of primitive religion given in chapter I, and he will realize that belated survivals of primitivism are
present in every religion, at least in its popular form. There is a
continual warfare between these widely diffused popular superstitions and all the higher forms of religious faith. Let high religion
lose its grip or relax its vigilance for a moment, and superstition

immediately emerges from its underworld to make a bid for supremacy. In times of religious conflict and uncertainty like the present there is an alarming growth of superstition. The human soul appears to abhor a religious vacuum; and if the educated religious leaders of the world cannot offer us a rational faith that is convincing and inspiring we are apt to resort to superstitious quackery. Since the World War, many sociologists have commented upon the rapid spread of superstition among the better educated classes in society, which were supposedly immune to its ravages.[26]

Among the forms of superstition clearly describable as " primitive survivals " are the following:

(1). Magic in all its many forms, including witchcraft and sorcery. It is of the essence of magic that it aims to get us what we want simply and easily, by some mysterious short-cut, in defiance of all natural and moral laws. To believe that by touching a sacred object, kissing a sacred image, mumbling a sacred name or formula, making a sacred gesture, wearing a sacred symbol, one can advance one's private designs, escape danger, and triumph over one's enemies, is to believe in magic. There is a great deal of magic, obviously, in contemporary Taoism, Buddhism, and Hinduism in their more popular forms. To the Protestant it seems that Catholicism is full of magic; the Catholic can retort that there is nothing more purely magical than the popular Protestant belief in a mysterious connection between strict sabbath-keeping and good crops.

(2). Eudaemonism, or the pursuit of selfish advantage by religious means. In magic, the mistake consists in employing inappropriate means; in eudaemonism, it consists in prostituting the whole high technique of religious worship to unworthy ends. The two are closely associated. It is only slowly that men learn to seek ideal ends disinterestedly, accepting any personal benefits that may accrue as incidental by-products. " Seek ye first the kingdom of God and his righteousness, and all these things shall be added unto you."

(3). Idolatry, or the literal worship of sacred objects, whether natural or artificial. This is of course to be carefully distinguished from the use of visible symbols as an aid in the worship of higher deities. That can be defended on sound psychological grounds. Genuine idolatry occurs when the tree, or the mountain, or the fetish, or the sculptured image, is treated as if it were itself the source from which the blessings flow. When Egyptian priests built hollow idols so that they might creep inside and give audible answers to the prayers of their devotees, they encouraged superstitious idolatry. Among the densely ignorant masses in contemporary India and contemporary Mexico, there is a great deal of idolatry no less superstitious than that of ancient Egypt. In a wider sense, it is idolatry to revere anything as divine when it is less than the highest conceivable good. Many would feel that the modern totalitarian state is demanding worship in this sense.

(4). Polytheism, or the worship of local, departmental, tribal, or national deities. This is to be distinguished from the recognition of multiple aspects or manifestations of a single unified divine Being. In genuine polytheism, each deity or spirit is anchored to a particular shrine or region, performs particular functions unlike those of other gods, and fights for his favorites against other peoples and their gods. This general description applies to many varieties of polytheism, from primitive animism and ancestor worship up to that highly elaborate form of national polytheism known as henotheism, in which one god is selected for supreme adoration, while the existence of other gods is still admitted. One of the startling results of the World War has been that many modern people, under stress of strong patriotic feeling, have reverted from monotheism to polytheism, abandoning the universal God of Christianity for the old tribal deities of " blood and soil." Actually, of course, this sudden reversion is only the climax of a process of religious disintegration which has long been undermining genuine Christianity, and substituting the worship of Mammon or Mars or, since Freud, the worship of the libido (Venus) for the worship of God in Christ.

(5). Divination, or the revealing of the divine mystery of human destiny through certain mechanical signs and portents. Oracles and soothsayers, omens and auspices, have been persistent religious phenomena from the earliest times.   The ancient Greeks placed great trust in the divine wisdom of the oracle of Delphi, where a priestess under the influence of poisonous vapors rising from the depth of a certain cavern made strange responses to men's questions.   The Romans never went to battle without consulting the auspices, and determining from the flight of birds, the appearance of the entrails of slaughtered animals, and other equally illuminating signs, whether the issue of the fight was destined to be favorable.   Both the Greeks and the Romans believed profoundly in astrology.   Modern Chinese are accustomed to determine lucky days and lucky places for marriage and burial by means of the elaborate system of divination known as " Wind and Water " (Feng-shui).   In Mohammedan countries, great precautions are taken to avoid the " evil eye."   Our own popular lore about black cats, broken mirrors, moon-over-the-left-shoulder, and the like, to which the word " superstition " is ordinarily applied, belongs under this head.   If the vogue of palmistry, astrology, and other forms of fortune-telling continues to increase, we shall soon be as superstitious as the ancient Romans.   This is not to rule out the possibility that spiritualistic mediums and other psychically gifted persons may possess supernormal knowledge, even concerning the future; but it has surely been demonstrated by this time in the experience of the race that to abandon the clear light of reason and conscience and submit completely to the guidance of the lurid light that comes from mysterious hunches and portents, is to lead a miserable and slavish existence, unworthy of a human being.

Already in defining superstition we have been implicitly suggesting the general direction of the line of development which leads away from superstition, toward high religion.   It is in brief the line which leads from what Tiele calls natural religion toward what he calls ethical religion.   This does not mean that ethical progress is the only driving force in religious development.   All three of the elements in Plato's great trinity of ideal interests — the rational interest in truth, the moral interest in goodness, the aesthetic interest in beauty — as soon as they become consciously differentiated, react upon religion. The rational interest operates to purge religious ideology of logical inconsistencies and to bring it into harmony with known truth. The ethical interest operates to eliminate from religious theory and practice all that is morally shocking or repulsive, and to exalt all that makes for personal nobility and social well-being. The aesthetic interest operates to refine away the crudities and vulgarities of religion, and develop worship into a fine art to which all the other fine arts minister. Between these ideal interests and the religious interest a fruitful interaction is set up, each aiding all the others and being itself aided in turn. The net result of this process is the universalizing of religion; for all the ideal interests tend toward unity and harmony, both in theory and practice, and what they have refined is freed from merely local and temporal peculiarities, to pass henceforth as common currency in every time and place. The classic utterances of high religion spring out of particular religious traditions; but they go home to the hearts of all peoples, and draw them into fellowship with one another. This is true of certain teachings of Plato and Confucius, most true of certain teachings of the Buddha and the Christ.

If high religion is rational, ethical, and aesthetic, this does not mean that it is opposed to all traditionalism and mysticism. High religion is not " high and dry." The attempt has been repeatedly made by religious reformers to invent a religion wholly composed of rationally certified truths, sound moral maxims, and aesthetically pleasing techniques of worship. The attempt has always failed, and always will. Religions cannot be manufactured to order. They must be grounded deeply in historic tradition and in mystical apprehension of that plenitude of being which always outruns man's power of comprehension. This is the real justification for religious conservatism. It sometimes darkens reason, flouts morality, and outrages aesthetic good taste in its stubborn insistence upon time-honored and seemingly irrational beliefs and practices; yet it is often right — perhaps on other grounds than it supposes. The Chinese physicians who treated heart disease with powdered toad were right, we now perceive, for we have discovered that powdered toad contains adrenalin. Some day it may be discovered that religious conservatives have sounder reasons for insisting, let us say, upon the sanctifying power of the blessed sacraments or the healing power of Our Lady of Lourdes than rationalistic criticism has yet been able to discover. Meanwhile the dim perception of these traditional and mystical values and verities makes it unwise to seek religious unity and universality too hastily. A world religion in which the existing religious traditions were absorbed and blotted out, as certain syncretistic cults propose, would be poorer than our existing religions, and not richer. Not abstract unity, as in a mathematical science, but rich and catholic unity-in-difference, is the ideal of high religion.

In the ideal religion of the future we must therefore expect to find elements derived from all the great types of religion which we have successively reviewed. When their superstitious elements are purged away, even the most primitive and local forms of religion will be found to contain at least some elements of lasting worth, deserving to be incorporated in the universal religion of mankind. If nature is conceived less magically and animistically by modern man than by his primitive ancestors, he is none the less dependent upon her bounties; and he must not allow the complicated mechanism of urban industrial life to destroy in him completely that fresh sense of grateful dependence upon wonder-working natural forces which is the beauty and strength of primitive religion. "The sun, the moon, the stars, the seas, the hills and the plains "[27] must continue to be objects of religious reverence, though we no longer fancy them to be haunted by spirits and gods. Chinese filial piety and Japanese national loyalty likewise have their place in high religion, for it is only through practicing these simple natural loyalties that the highest religious loyalty can be learned. But it is above all, of course, in the great universal religions of the east and the west, Buddhism and Christianity, that we see the unmistakable traits of high religion. Detachment from transient and material goods, resignation to inevitable ill and suffering, loving compassion for all living creatures, is the everlasting message of the Buddha; and no one is religiously mature who has not heard and heeded it. It is not destroyed but fulfilled by the more aggressive and hopeful message of the Christ. In ancient times it was observed that good Stoics or Platonists made the best Christians; in the modern east it is often remarked that good Confucianists or Buddhists make the best Christians. There is a very real sense in which one must first experience natural human loyalty and Buddhist disillusionment before one can appreciate the meaning of Christian love, or serve "the kingdom of God and his righteousness" with adequate devotion.

In the ideal of the kingdom of God — the culminating concept of western religion — there is perhaps to be found the bridge which connects historic religion with the various forms of radical secularism which seem today to be threatening to displace or destroy religion. In so far as any form of radical secularism, such as Marxian communism, looks forward to an age of justice and peace in which all human beings of every race and class are to participate, it reflects the ancient Hebrew dream of the kingdom of God, for which the Founder of Christianity gave his life. Karl Marx has not unfairly been described as "a Hebrew prophet in the guise of a modern materialist"; and his ideal of a "classless society" has many points in common with the ideal of the kingdom of God. Materialism is not necessarily opposed to the kingdom of God at every point. Materialistic science and mechanical invention are capable, under the right conditions, of implementing this ancient ideal rather than destroying it. A high-flown idealism which ignores the material basis of life and deals out fine phrases when food and shelter are needed, is worse than many kinds of materialism. But against what is known as practical materialism — the subordination of all ideal values to the accumulation of material goods and the elaboration of efficient techniques — the ancient ideal must always protest, as it protests against all narrow and exclusive forms of nationalism and racialism. "Man shall not live by bread alone."

The whole course of our discussion heads up, then, in a conception of ideal religion, based upon the general description of religion already offered, but more specific in its content. If all religion drives toward some ultimate good, ideal religion drives toward that comprehensive goal which in traditional Hebrew-Christian parlance is called the kingdom of God. A good nonpartisan description of this goal is to be found in the following definition of the supreme ethical principle, in Professor E. W. Lyman's *Meaning and Truth of Religion:* " The fullest development of every human personality through the cooperative creation of a world-wide community of persons." [28]   It is understood, of course, that in the ideal of "fullest development" there are to be included not only the highest ethical goodness, expressed in deep natural love and loyalty, but all imaginable values, aesthetic, intellectual, and mystical, richly interacting, in such a way as to issue in an endless growth of meaning and value.   If this is the goal of ideal religion, the deity of ideal religion must be defined as that Reality wherein and whereby the fullest personal development, the completest world community, and endless growth of meaning and value are attained; while the cult of ideal religion would consist in the act of connecting with this deity in such a way that divine power may fulfill itself more abundantly in the world, for the actualization of supreme good.

To sum up: The purpose and goal of high religion may be defined as *the progressive reorganization of the world into a system of mutually sustaining activities humanly appreciated,*[29] *whereby the endless growth of meaning and value is fostered.*   Its God is the *Being whereon the accomplishment of this aim ultimately depends.* Man worships rightly when he makes this Being the object of his supreme loyal devotion, and makes himself a channel through which its power pours forth toward the above defined goal.

In Part II the deeper implications of these historical findings will be developed and presented in their bearing on religion today. Also there will be considered the conditions and methods which men must set up whereby high religion may be enabled to perform its ideal function more effectively.

NOTES

[1] See McGiffert, *The Rise of Modern Religious Ideas*, pp. 62, 63, 128–35.

[2] *Ibid.*, p. 135.

[3] *Ibid.*, p. 69.

[4] *Literature and Dogma*, pp. 17, 38, etc.

[5] *Apologia Pro Vita Sua*, p. 241.

[6] See McGiffert, *op. cit.*, pp. 136–39. Compare William James' conception of the relation between religion and morality with that of Fichte and Matthew Arnold: " This added dimension of emotion, this enthusiastic temper of espousal, in regions where morality strictly so called can at best bow the head and acquiesce." (*Varieties of Religious Experience*, p. 48.)

[7] Baillie, *The Roots of Religion in the Human Soul*, pp. 112, 127, 130.

[8] See McGiffert, *op. cit.*, p. 65.

[9] *Ibid.*, p. 68.

[10] Sabatier, *op. cit.*, p. 27 (English translation). Quoted by permission of Harper and Bros.

[11] Wobbermin, *The Nature of Religion*, pp. 181, 182 (English translation by Menzel and Robinson, 1933). Quoted by permission of Thomas Y. Crowell Co.

[12] See Hegel, *Philosophy of Religion*, I, 261–69 (Speirs' translation).

[13] Cited in his later book, *The Nature of Deity*, p. 216.

[14] See Freud, *The Future of an Illusion*.

[15] Mill, *Three Essays on Religion*, Essay II. For Comte's religion of humanity, see the *Positivist Catechism*.

[16] See especially " Religious Retrospect and Prospect " in *Principles of Sociology*.

[17] Ames, *Religion*, pp. 32, 33. Quoted by permission of Henry Holt and Co.

[18] Walter Marshall Horton, *A Psychological Approach to Theology* (Harper and Bros., 1931), p. 31, note. Quoted by permission.

[19] This division includes Confucianism, Brahmanism, Judaism, and other religions in which a national system of law and custom is treated as sacred.

[20] The significance of this ancient Latin formula is, in effect, " I give thee this sacrificial gift as a trading proposition; now give me, O Powerful One, the boon for which I beseech thee."

[21] Oman, *The Natural and the Supernatural*, Chap. XXI, " Classification of Religions."

[22] For Starbuck's and James' types, see James' *Varieties*, Lectures IV–X.

[23] Pratt, *The Religious Consciousness*, Chap. I.

[24] Brown, *Imperialistic Religion and the Religion of Democracy*.

[25] See H. Richard Niebuhr, *The Social Sources of Denominationalism*.

[26] Cf. Ellwood, *Reconstruction of Religion*, p. 22; and a remarkable article in *Harper's Magazine* for March, 1935, entitled " Written on Friday," which deals with the recent spread of superstition in fashionable American private schools.

[27] Tennyson, " The Higher Pantheism."

[28] Pp. 85, 86.

[29] In this conception of the goal of high religion the authors of this book substantially agree. Beyond that point, their views diverge in many respects. The author of Part II is solely responsible for the views therein expressed, as the present author is solely responsible for Part I.

BIBLIOGRAPHY

McGiffert, A. C. *Op. cit.*, Chaps. IV–VII.

Baillie, J. *The Roots of Religion in the Human Soul*, Chaps. I–III.

Sabatier, A. *Outlines of a Philosophy of Religion*, Book I.

Wobbermin, G. *The Nature of Religion,* Part I.
Lyman, E. W. *The Meaning and Truth of Religion,* Part I.
Ames, E. S. *Religion,* Chaps. I–VIII.
James, Wm. *The Varieties of Religious Experience,* Lectures II, IV–VII.
Pratt, J. B. *The Religious Consciousness,* Chap. I.
Oman, J. *The Natural and the Supernatural,* Chap. XXI.
Morgan, W. *The Nature and Right of Religion,* Chaps. I, II, XI.

PART II

CONTEMPORARY GROWTH
OF RELIGION

By HENRY NELSON WIEMAN

INTRODUCTION TO PART II

THERE are times when philosophy of religion is of paramount importance to religious living. There are other times when its contribution is negligible. We have reached a time when we believe that religion cannot be restored to health and power without the aid of philosophy of religion. Aids of other sorts are unquestionably necessary, but philosophy of religion is the one which is indispensable. The current conditions which make the services of philosophy so urgently needed are to be found first in religion itself, and second in the general state of culture today.

Religion today has outgrown the forms of appreciative apprehension by which the individual was able to discern the realities which commanded his high devotion. There is a difference between knowing in the abstract that something is real, and apprehending it in those forms of appreciation whereby one feels the sovereign lure of its worthfulness. The latter requires forms of appreciative apprehension. "Patterns of thought" is the term by which Shailer Mathews was wont to call the forms of appreciation which are required for the vitality of religious living and which must change from age to age to meet the changing mentality of men. Forms of appreciative apprehension which enable the people of one culture, age, temper, to discern the worthfulness of, say, a king, or the democratic way, or God, do not and cannot disclose to people of a different culture anything that stirs equally profound response. This is true in all areas involving any deep loyalty. Forms of apprehension which render apparent to one person the dearness of a home, of a locality, or of a person, may not reveal any such commanding value to another. Two people can look at the same thing, and one see in it a worth of supreme importance while the other sees nothing of the sort. The difference is that one has forms of appreciative apprehension fitted to himself and to the matter in question, while the other does not. All this applies to religious living. When the once-accepted forms of appreciative religious apprehension become unsuited to the mind and feeling of a people the vitality of their religion declines.

Since the forms of religious apprehension are so important in religious living, it is only natural that society should have recognized this fact in its organization of religious thought and practice. Now theology is that intellectual discipline which systematizes and operates with the forms of appreciative religious apprehension in its work of distinguishing between truth and error and between the real and the unreal. In this it is different from philosophy of religion. The latter does not use the appreciative forms of apprehension. It uses the cold tools of intellectual inquiry without regard for the symbols and patterns which express the ardor of religious devotion. Theology, therefore, seems to most people to be closer to religious living than does philosophy of religion. There comes a time, however, when theology finds itself frustrated. It is when the symbols and patterns of devotion, the forms of appreciative apprehension which it supports, no longer fit into the categories of current intellectual understanding. Then the people can no longer use these particular forms to lay hold on reality and distinguish truth from error. As long as intellectual inquiry can clothe itself in the established forms theology can do its work very well. But when this is impossible, theology finds itself withered or paralyzed. Its hand has lost its cunning. It can no longer grip reality. Yet with tenacious but blind faith it holds fast to the forms of appreciation for the sake of the adoration they inspire, and so, perforce, becomes increasingly uncertain that there is anything in reality to be thus evaluated. It is the fate of theology to become increasingly uncertain except as it dogmatically claims to know without any attempt at rational justification.

If our analysis is correct, the time when philosophy of religion must step in to save religion is when theology's grip on religious reality begins to weaken and fail because the forms of apprehension by which it reaches after this reality have become unusable by the modern mind. When the illumination of theology can no longer keep the supremely important matter of all human living before the conscious awareness of men, philosophy of religion must set its searchlights and floodlights to work, else the reality will slip away entirely out of our grasp into the darkness of the unknown.

It is true that when the object of religious devotion is presented by philosophy it does not display those warm and alluring features which quicken the depth of emotional response. This is inevitable because of the nature of philosophy and of its methods as distinguished from theology. Therefore the work of philosophy of religion is never in itself sufficient for religious living. Actual religion as lived must have its forms of devotional commitment. It can never be merely an intellectual grasp of what is most important. It requires not only knowledge; it requires profound evaluation expressed in a way of living. *But one must be assured that there is something out there to be evaluated and lived for.* Once doubt has arisen, the only justifiable assurance one can ever have must be attained through intellectual labor, whatever else may also be required. If this intellectual labor cannot be done by using the established forms of appreciative religious apprehension, it must be done without them. Today, unquestionably, we have reached a time when the symbols of religious devotion do not fit into the instrumentalities of intellectual inquiry. Therefore we have reached a time when philosophy rather than theology must do the intellectual job of setting forth the realities of religious concern. After this job is done, or concomitantly with it, though not prior to it, the forms of appreciative apprehension must be developed which will enable people to commit themselves in absolute and enthusiastic allegiance. On this account we hold the work of philosophy of religion to be peculiarly urgent at this time, so far as concerns the fate of religion.

But the times are ripe for philosophy of religion on other grounds. The general state of culture calls imperatively for its service. Our civilization has reached a stage where it is exceedingly difficult for many people to find any reality which seems to have that supreme worthfulness which commands devotion and imparts zest and meaning to the movement of life. There is a soul-sickness of our time which has caused a great thirst. So famished are men that they turn to communism or fascism or Barthian transcendentalism or anything else which seems to promise life-giving devotion and ardor. Men have lost the sense of supreme devotion and they will remain desperate until they find it again. For commitment to some greatest is the deepest need of human nature.

The stages through which civilization passes in reaching the state in which it becomes so difficult to find a worthy devotion can be briefly sketched, for they have been experienced before.

The culture which has prevailed throughout most of human history has been one in which men dealt first-hand with the riches of concrete existence. To get food and shelter and companionship and to satisfy the other elemental needs, they had to live close to earth, close to sticks and stones and houses and plants and animals. Above all they had to live in small compact groups, consisting of much the same people bound together for a lifetime. Such a group shared a rich accumulation of appreciations, sensitivities, loyalties, attachments, and all these were transmitted to each individual, for the most part unconsciously. In this sense and in this way, we say, men dealt first-hand with the riches of concrete existence in the form of fellow personalities and groups, plants and animals. All that they needed to be kept sensitive and imaginative was supplied by art and myth and a manifold lore. The chief problem of living was that of finding sufficient relief from the burden of toil and ill health, routine and narrow preoccupation, to enable them to respond to goods and goals intimately involved in their daily living. For it is here in the concrete existing world, and here only, that men can find the quenchless zest and the ardor that spring ever anew.

As civilization advanced the burdens and limitations of primitive life have been progressively removed, at least for a great many. But then a new difficulty arose, one quite as serious as insufficient food, ill health, and such material hindrances. Intellectual abstractions and technical devices began to intervene between the heart and mind of the individual on the one hand, and the concrete fullness of men and things, animals and plants, on the other. Whenever and wherever there are developed these abstractions in the form of ideals, programs, and classifications, and these devices in the form of techniques and instrumentalities, they are made for efficiency. Hence they are so fashioned and used as to carry the very minimum of sentimental attachment and of appreciative response. They are tools to use, and do not indicate ends to serve and enjoy in the immediate situation. For example, an individual uses money to get food and shelter. Money makes it unnecessary for the majority of us to work upon earth and plants, and with animals and men, in close all-round association, to satisfy needs. When one travels he does so by some rapid conveyance which gets him to his destination without his walking through sunshine and rain and dealing with people and things in an intimate and appreciative way. Zip! he is there. So it is with all the rest of the daily practices of life.

Perhaps we can illustrate this impoverishment which comes with civilization by considering the case of communication. The more civilized man becomes, the more efficient he is in communicating by means of abstractions. He conveys his meaning to others by using well defined concepts instead of the symbols which carry great wealth of emotional response, appreciative attachment or revulsion. These primitive emotional expressions are intellectually very vague because they point to the concrete fullness of experience rather than to finely demarcated distinctions and categories. The civilized man wants intellectual clarity. Therefore he tends to abandon these deeply emotional symbols and substitute well defined concepts in their place. But as his concepts become more accurate they become more abstract. The most striking example is that picture of the world given us by physics which reduces it all to mathematical units. To a lesser degree the same statement applies to all our ideas as philosophy and science refine and clarify them and make them more efficient as tools, but leave them increasingly shorn of reference to that matrix of existence which surges about us, which pervades us, and which awakens in us the deeps of emotion and propulsion for living.

In theory these intellectual abstractions and technical devices might be used to bring us ever richer experience of neighbor and nature and of each concrete situation that we enter. But in actual practice that is not the way they work, at least not at first. Those who gain wealth and power use them to separate themselves from intimate and appreciative dealing with concrete situations by depending on the service of underlings. Further, the underlings are prevented from appreciative attachment to persons and things, plants and animals, because they are themselves used as tools. Their work is narrowly specialized. They are thrust here and there. Attachments are broken before they can be fully developed. Worst of all, they learn to live by the use of the unemotional abstractions and technical devices employed by the wealthy, but with even more impoverishment because they do not have other outlets which the privileged enjoy.

When this state of culture arises men in places of leadership can attain great power of achievement. Individuals and groups are no longer held by deep attachments and devotions and so are easily mobilized to serve the abstract ideal and program of the leader. By means of abstractions and techniques these leaders cut their way through the warm, pulsing, and pervading matrix of connections which might bind them to their fellow men and to all the mental and submental, organic and inorganic world about them. They thrust their way to their chosen objectives without responding in any profoundly appreciative manner to rich community with neighbor and nature. They do mighty things without any sense of great values involved or emerging, and without deep devotion.

Such civilized living and striving provide their own excitements and advantages, but when men begin to live so they come at last to miss the progressive enrichment of life that rises from response to the unpredictable creative synthesis of concrete situations which always overflow and ofttimes submerge our abstract ideals and pre-established programs. If civilized man were not so efficient, if he were not so idealistic and so preoccupied with his chosen goals, if he were not so able to subordinate the emerging richness of the concrete situation to the abstract outline of his own program and so able to counteract every influence that might submerge his

scheme beneath the riches of the concrete fullness of persons and
events — then his life would not be so impoverished. But civilization has made him too strong. He plans too well. He presumes
to shape the world to his will rather than subjecting his will to a
higher loyalty which reaches after a wealth of goodness beyond
the compass of the human mind. He is able to fend off the unforeseen and uncontrolled fullness of experience that floods into appreciative human awareness when it is open and responsive. Thus
he passes by unaware, unresponsive, untouched. He is too strong
— or shall we say too arrogant. He is too unreligious.

In more primitive conditions where man is weak, when the
armor plate of efficient techniques and conceptually clarified goals
and programs does not enclose him, he is compelled to respond
to men and things in ways that he did not intend. He has his own
great difficulties and limitations, which we have already noted.
But they are the exact opposite of those of the civilized man.

We do not mean to suggest that man should go back to primitive
conditions. We are only saying that there is a soul-sickness which
increasingly threatens civilization, from which man can be delivered only by the right use of techniques and abstractions. But this
right use requires religion, and religion functioning in a certain
way. It is this way of salvation which the philosophy of religion
should set forth.

When progressive enrichment begins to fade from the life of
the civilized man after the fashion we have described, he looks
around to see what has become of the values which once filled his
days and made life abundantly worth living. Sometimes he turns
inward and says that all the good of life is to be found in states of
consciousness. Value is simply the experience of satisfaction; it is
the way we feel. He says, There is nothing out there in the objective world which is good or bad except as I experience it so.
Hence value is just my own inner state.

This flight to subjectivism, however, is intolerable for some persons and perhaps, in time, becomes more and more so for all. The
cause for this protest is easily explained. When one turns his attention upon his own inner states to find happiness and thereby di-

verts his appreciative awareness away from sky and field, friend and poem, the goods of life grow pale and wan. A grayness settles down over all things and living becomes anemic. Out there in the concrete world is the fountainhead of all value: it is not in subjective states of consciousness. But civilized man cannot turn (or at least does not yet turn) to the unpredictable fullness of concrete things and persons. He has himself and his situation too much under the control of his techniques, his programs, and his ideals.

What, then, shall he do? In desperation he may turn from subjectivism to transcendentalism. If he cannot find the good of life by turning within, and if he will not appreciate and serve the concrete situation beyond what it offers for his chosen objectives, there is only one place to turn, and that is to some transcendental realm. So after the Sophists comes Plato. After Hume and Berkeley come Kant and Hegel. After Schleiermacher and Ritschl and the "theology of religious experience" come Barth and Brunner, Tillich and Niebuhr.

The movements of civilization which we have traced can be seen in specific instances of history. We see them strikingly in the developing culture of Greece. First the Greeks lived close to the concrete world and were deeply appreciative of it. But then began the alienation of the human heart and mind from this fullness of existence through the use of slaves, technical devices, and intellectual abstractions. The Sophists then arose with their flight to subjectivism. All right and wrong, truth and goodness, are made by man; as man thinks and feels and appreciates, so is the world good or bad; in his own mind he must find all the values that are to be found. However, this attitude became intolerable. So Plato and his followers fled in the opposite direction to the transcendental. No doubt there are many Platos in the dialogues, but this transcendentally inclined Plato certainly is one. The Neo-Platonists and other sects moved further still in this direction, until the body and all physical things were held to be vile.

The same cycle can be seen in the modern world. In the late Middle Ages there was profound appreciative awareness of concrete existence. Lewis Mumford in his *Techniques and Civiliza-*

tion sets this fact forth very vividly. But intellectual abstractions and technical devices increased with the beginnings of physical science and the Industrial Revolution. Then occurred the flight to subjectivism led by Descartes and later the flight to transcendentalism led by Kant.

In religious thought and life we see similar manifestations of the struggle of the human spirit to find the breath of life — the good that makes life worth living — ere it be suffocated by its own abstractions and techniques. The turn to inner states of consciousness is represented by such current terms as these: "feeling of absolute dependence," "the value judgments," "the sense of the holy," and the "inward ho" (of Rufus Jones). More recently the opposite swing is seen in the turning of men to "the Absolutely Other," to "the Unconditioned" which is beyond all existence but which is the only rightful concern of all our meanings and devotions, to "the absolute ideal of love" which stands beyond all existence, condemning all concrete reality as miserably unworthy.

We said in the beginning that in theory the abstractions and techniques of civilization *might* be used to open the appreciative awareness of men to the riches of the unpredictable good found in the creative synthesis of each concrete situation. Instead of estranging men from the mothering matrix of existence they might be used to do just the opposite. But this reversal of the current practice of civilization cannot be accomplished without the aid of a philosophy of life which is also a philosophy of religion. We have pointed out that before the estrangement of men from the riches of the concrete situation, a philosophy of this sort was not needed. Men's problem then was of a different sort — the technical one of mastering the difficulties of existence. But when this early technical problem began to yield, the difficulty of estrangement arose. This later technical problem does require a philosophy to overcome it. We say it must be a philosophy of religion. It must be a philosophy which directs human consciousness to whatever is supremely worthful in each concrete situation. To be fully appreciative of this, however, man must make absolute commitment in advance to the unpredictable best that can be discovered in each situation. (In the older forms of appreciative religious apprehension we called this "surrender to the will of God.") The outstanding thinkers who are developing this kind of philosophy for us in the secular world are Bergson, Dewey, and Whitehead. In the religious world the men who are moving in this direction are John Macmurray, B. E. Meland, Charles Hartshorne, Gerald Heard, Charles Ellwood, and others. Work has gone far enough to justify the statement that religion is growing.

We are today, then, in one of those rare moments of history when the saving power of an adequate philosophy of religion is desperately needed. It is needed for the saving of articulate, formulated religion and, what is much more important, for the continuous growth of culture. Collapse and destruction await us unless we can recover the healing balm and the renewal of life which can be found in apprehending the reality in our midst which sustains and leads to higher fulfillment when life is shaped to meet its requirements. Whether any philosophy of religion now in existence, or to be brought forth soon, is able to render such a great service may be problematical. But at any rate we have before us the need and the task. It would seem that disloyalty must be charged to anyone who does not do what he can to meet this need — anyone, that is, who makes any pretense at all to equipment in this field. Therefore the present book is offered as an attempt to make a contribution to this end.

I am deeply indebted to a number of people who have recently opened my eyes to the truth, not so much by their philosophical acumen as by the kind of religious living which they revealed. These perhaps, for the time being, should remain nameless. Professor Fred Howes of Montreal has read the chapter, "Method of Religious Living," and I am deeply indebted to him for his helpful comments. After the manuscript was completed my wife, Dr. Regina Westcott Wieman, read it all most carefully and made many comments of great value. The book is markedly improved because of her help.

8.

NEW GROWTHS IN RELIGION

HERE we see before us the tree of religion growing through history. It has many branches, twigs, and leaves. Many of these can be removed without hurting its life. Innumerable forms and manifestations of religion are not essential to it. But through the main trunk there flows that which is essential. As the various branches of religion develop, they sometimes lose that sap of life which gives vitality. Then there is a withering at the top and new shoots must spring forth from the central trunk to carry its power.

Growth of religion in our times shows many instances of withering and of vigorous shooting forth of new branches from the main body. Which of these new shoots will be the carrier of religious vitality in the future? That is a question many are asking. In order to try to answer it we shall examine the nature of these new branches.

As religion emerged into modern times it found itself in a new and rapidly changing culture. This new culture was created by scientific findings, scientific method, the scientific attitude and view of the world, scientific techniques and machines, and the fruits of science such as big machine-industry, great accumulation of wealth, and a new kind of economic and political order arising out of these. The domination by science is what gives distinctive character to the modern age and makes it different from every other time. There is much in modern life which is a continuation of the past and has not been greatly modified by science. But that which causes us to demarcate the life of today from that of other ages is the domination and control imposed on our world by the scientific attitude and by all the machines and devices brought forth by science. These have produced kinds of problems and ways of thinking and feeling very different from those of the times in which religion developed its ancient forms. Therefore when

247

religious living was surrounded by the climate of modern science it had to learn anew how to survive and flourish.

I. LIBERALISM AND TRADITIONAL SUPERNATURALISM

When the main trunk of Christianity found itself encompassed by this atmosphere of science it withered at the top, and two new branches sprang forth to carry its life under the changed conditions. One of these was called liberalism, the other traditional supernaturalism. It should be recognized that the traditional supernaturalism we know today is not the same as that form of Christianity which flourished prior to the age of science. What is true of Christianity is true of the other great world religions. They all have encountered these new conditions and have been forced to develop new offshoots adapted to the new times. Generally one sees in all of them the same bifurcation into two branches, one liberal, the other a striving to perpetuate the ancient ways under new conditions.

Liberalism was that form of religion which strove above all things to fit itself to the new age. It endeavored to take over those ways of thinking, those problems and attitudes, which characterize the modern world. It sought to adapt Christianity to the climate and atmosphere of science. It endeavored to connect modern life and religion in a vital way, which means a way that modified both. This was a good and necessary work, and liberalism accomplished a needed task. But it failed to bring its work to high fulfillment. The task of bringing these two basic interests of life into the right relation to each other was too much for it. It did not retain the essential truth of the ancient faith and neither was it true to that spirit of science which ruled and shaped the modern mind. It tried to introduce the empirical method into religion by basing it upon religious experience but without making clear what was the nature of religious experience and how it was to be treated scientifically. It left out the heart of science, on the one hand, and the heart of religion on the other.

All that we have said does not mean that liberalism itself was a failure nor that it merits the scorn that one-time liberals now give it. On the contrary, its great leaders deserve honor for having seen a great need and started a great work, even though they became confused before the program was finished. That they did not complete their task does not mean that the undertaking was wrong nor that they were failures.

Nevertheless it must be said that liberalism modified the forms of religion in such a manner that the vital sap of life could not freely flow through them. The power and uniqueness of the religious way was compromised. That is what is meant by saying it was secularized. Under the liberal reinterpretations, so the critics say, the religious way became indistinguishable from a mixture of various interests. It became a conglomerate of moral idealism, social entertainment, aesthetic enjoyment of music and other arts, practical guidance in the conduct of personal life, discussion of economic and political problems, the magnetic appeal of dominant personalities, all interfused with certain standard ceremonies and symbols, including the use of the Bible, but with nothing distinctively religious as over against the secular. All it offered could be got in other areas of life outside of the religious. Hence arose the question in the minds of many people confronted with this kind of Christianity: What is the use of being religious? What does it offer that you cannot get elsewhere? If the religious person does not show anything unique, distinctive, and important that cannot be got anywhere else save in religion, then I do not see the use of religion. This became increasingly the attitude of many toward the liberal form of religion. So liberalism suffered a withering at the top.

When we speak here of liberalism we do not mean that general attitude of mind which is indispensable to the high development of any culture and without which civilization cannot be maintained — namely, the tolerance of diverse views and the use of persuasion rather than force. We mean only a certain specific development which one branch of religion underwent during a certain period and still continues to undergo. Also it should be noted that many individuals and groups which took on the liberal form of religion did still retain in their own private lives the uniqueness and the power of religion in its most distinctive quality. When we speak of liberalism we do not mean the *actual* living of the deeply religious person, but we mean a certain theory *about* it. Some of the liberals, as religious persons, had that might and peace and triumph over time and fortune which is the peculiar gift of religion and the manifestation of the sap of life which flows at the heart of the great tree of religious growth. When we say that liberalism missed the heart of religion, we are speaking of certain intellectual interpretations of religion and not of individual religious lives. Generally speaking, that interpretation of religion called liberalism is dying down.

We said that the central trunk of religious development divided when it entered the modern world. One branch was called liberalism, the other traditional supernaturalism. This latter branch also has been withering, but for a reason exactly the opposite of that applying to liberalism. As liberalism strove above all things to establish living connections between religion and modern culture, and thereby lost the heart of religion in great part, traditional supernaturalism strove above all things to preserve the ancient faith, and thereby lost connections with modern life. It could not deal intimately and religiously with modern problems. If the liberal interpretation tended to cut men off from the throbbing heart of religion, the interpretation of traditional supernaturalism tended to cut men off from the heart of modern life. The church made for this traditional form of religion a sort of hothouse, in which the warm moist air which it needed could be retained. But a religion cannot flourish indefinitely when it is shut away from vital connection with the life of its time. So traditional supernaturalism has also suffered. Today these two branches, liberalism and traditional supernaturalism, are both sending forth new shoots from lower down on the trunk, and these must carry on the new growth.

II. HUMANISM

The new branch that has shot up from the stalk of liberalism is social idealism, sometimes assuming the form of religious humanism. The heart of religion lies in transforming society, say these devotees. Liberalism has spent itself on the rather academic labor of explaining religion and modern culture to each other. That is well enough as far as it goes. But there is no vital power in that. The power and the life of religion is social passion. So the social gospel arose in various forms. More recently it has become in some groups the struggle to stop war and fascism, or to change society into a socialistic or communistic order, or to support the cause of labor in some other way against the dominant powers. Religion has become merged with social idealism. In its more extreme forms it has gone by the name of atheistic humanism.

But does the idealism of humanism give us that deepest and most characteristic quality of religion which enables it to pour into human life something of great value which cannot be got in morality or art or politics or industry or home life or anywhere else? Social idealism has given to its devotees a drive and a social passion. In some cases it has become dogmatic and fanatical about some special program for social change. But social idealism and passionate devotion to a cause are not peculiar to religion. Devotion to an idealistic social cause can be found in many quarters. It is good and important. But is it that peculiar thing which religion in its most distinctive nature has given to men? Does it transform personality in that special way which is found only in certain forms of high religion? It does not. Furthermore, a creeping disillusionment has begun to spread among some of its leaders. Hence this branch, so recently sprouted, has already begun to die. After a lush growth it has begun to show that the innermost sap of life which is the essence of religion was not flowing freely to its top.

III. THE NEW SUPERNATURALISM

A new growth is springing forth from the stalk of traditional supernaturalism. It is called neo-supernaturalism. Its representatives come chiefly from the ranks of the liberals, but it is really an offshoot from the main trunk of the ancient faith. It is sometimes called dialectical theology and is led by Emil Brunner, Karl Barth, and others.

This contemporary development of religion has met one great need. Therefore it has spread with amazing rapidity and power. The endeavor of these leaders has been to recover and hold fast to that unique quality of religious living which makes it different from everything else. They have uncovered the wellspring from which flows a vitality which is to be found distinctively and solely in the religious way. In this respect the movement is a great present corrective of liberalism and therefore criticizes liberalism most severely.

Liberalism, as we have noted, undertook an urgent and inescapable task. It sought to interpret the ancient faith to modern thought and modern thought to that faith. But when liberalism had done, religion no longer seemed to be very important. Traditional supernaturalism, on the other hand, preserved the importance of religion by holding fast to that unique and mighty and saving fact which nothing else save a true religion can give. But it did so by setting up barricades against modern scholarship in the field of historical criticism and scientific findings. The new supernaturalism has tried to cut free of all this clutter from a bygone age and yet at the same time hold high and clear the unique and distinctive factor " which religion can offer." (Brunner would call it Christianity, not religion.)

In order to keep free from entangling alliances with all these outmoded rational structures of traditional supernaturalism, and also to keep free of the compromising rationality of liberalism, this new supernaturalism continues to cut away from all rationality in its view of God. God is the " Absolute Other," about which human thought can say nothing. Only revelation can speak. Thus the religious man is freed from any encumbrance which might interfere with his response to the modern world in the way of meeting the challenge of social reconstruction or social reaction or anything else. By his attachment to God, who is above all reason, he hangs suspended over the world, free to move in any direction. He does not need even to be rational. So independent is God of all these structures of thought and life which make up our world that he is not even good in any humanly conceivable sense of the word. Such is the explicit teaching of Paul Tillich, who is the chief representative of this group in America.

It is true that Brunner develops an elaborate system of ethics in his *Divine Imperative*. But this system must not be identified with God. It is merely a set of suggestions to indicate what seems in general to be the very best that a Christian can do in this evil world, taking things as they are. As Brunner himself would say, God's will cannot be prescribed by *any* set of principles laid down prior to the concrete and unique situation in which you act. God will guide you in face of the concrete situation if you act in the obedience of faith, seeking with all your heart for the very best you can find there. But such action can never be duplicated. It is unique, special, the will of God for that time and place. For that very reason it cannot be put into a system and carried over into another time and place by another person.

Therefore this ethic of Brunner has nothing divine about it. The divine enters in only when the Christian has direct dealings with God in the existential situation where he must act. No one can know what should be done until he stands face to face with the fullness of unprecedented actualities. He must then act in faith and learn what to do in the process of doing it under the direct guidance of God.

It is true that Brunner seems to set up his ethic as " Christian," and so superior to the " secular ethics " which he repudiates. But when he describes secular ethics in order to reject them, it is obvious that he is simply casting off the outmoded philosophies of yesterday which almost any modern mind would likewise abandon. What he calls "Christian ethics " is the insights derived from the teachings of modern psychology, the social sciences, current philosophical ethics, and other works of the " secular " mind of today, together with selected insights from the past. Indeed there is a remarkable similarity between Brunner's ethical teaching and that of John Dewey. We should also remember that in his student days Brunner studied in Union Theological Seminary, which adjoins Columbia University where John Dewey was teaching. What gives the ethics of Brunner the flavor of Christianity is that he tries to translate his findings into Christian verbiage as much as possible.

We must remember, then, in considering Brunner's *Divine Imperative,* that he himself says that no ethical system and no counsel of guidance can tell you what you should do in the exigencies of real action. In such moments of action you must deal with demands that are full to overflowing with factors which no preconceived system could foresee and which were never found and never will be found in any other situation. It is in confrontation of such a situation of action that God speaks, and not in Brunner's or any other man's system of principles or suggestions, called an ethic, even a Christian ethic. Brunner himself would subscribe to this statement.

So we see that the new supernaturalism, in order to avoid the two opposite errors of traditional supernaturalism and of liberalism respectively, has insisted that God must be left undefined but starkly real and free of all attempts of the human reason to state his nature, his will, his demands. Only when a man in the obedience of faith acts upon this overflowing richness of concrete situations does God speak. He speaks then in the action itself and not in rational systems.

We believe there is something profoundly true in what Brunner strives to establish. He and the others who support the new supernaturalism have learned from the mistakes of traditional supernaturalism that they must not allow the inner life of religion and the life of its action to be hampered and encased in rational structures of thought which are alien to our age. They have also learned from the mistakes of liberalism that they must not lose the uniqueness and the high, holy difference which religion makes in human living, by merging the idea of God and the ways to God with structures of modern thought which were not developed to solve these religious problems and do not squarely meet the issues of Christian living under God. They have learned from the mistakes of social idealism that they must not allow the religious man to set up any program of social reconstruction or idealism as the sovereign interest of life, however important such program may be for the social ethics of mundane living. If a man makes a religion of social idealism he will soon become either fanatical or disillusioned. Veering violently from these outcomes, the new supernaturalism announces that God alone, left undefined and outside this world, can be sovereign in the living of the religious man. Through such teaching it would recover the uniqueness and distinctive difference of the religious way.

It has become apparent now that the great teaching and mission of neo-supernaturalism is to make plain that religion must keep true to its own uniqueness. It must steadfastly present to man something which he cannot find in any other way, that something, moreover, which lets him triumph over the rise and fall of fortune, and lifts him into a realm where he can deal with changing circumstances with a detachment and independence which release all his powers of appreciation and intelligent inquiry from the cramping constraints which ordinarily distort and limit them.

Since neo-supernaturalism has corrected the worst mistake of traditional supernaturalism, of liberalism, and of social idealism, the vitality which once poured into these earlier branches is now pouring into it. It now shows the rapid, lush growth which was once displayed by these others.

But has it solved the problem on the essential level? Is it now and henceforth to be the valid carrier of the sap of life which feeds the growth of religion through history? Will it become the main trunk through which the unique power of Christianity grows into the future? Or will it also in time die at the top, forcing some other branch to grow up to become the main carrier of this faith into the ages that are to come?

We believe that the main carrier will not be neo-supernaturalism. It has removed the suckers which were sapping the life out of the other branches of the faith. But it has done so at fearful cost. It has done so by nothing less than cutting off rationality from the religious endeavor to know and live for God. God and the way to God, it asserts, are matters of super-rational revelation. Reason can and should undertake the task of interpretation, to be sure. But reason does its work effectively only when it falls into self-contradiction in trying to reach God and thereby demonstrates that paradox and myth alone are adequate to illumine the way to deity and the high destiny of man.

If our science-informed civilization survives, no religion which repudiates reason, as the new supernaturalism is doing, can survive along with it. Either the new supernaturalism will become dominant and its repudiation of reason will destroy civilization, or the civilization informed by science will prevail and will destroy it. The two cannot live together. Some of the neo-supernaturalists openly admit that their attitude cannot be harmonized with reason. They fail to see, apparently, that when reason is cast out, a hand begins to write upon the wall, and what it writes spells doom for all that lifts man above the savage.

Because neo-supernaturalism has discarded the rational approach of traditional supernaturalism and has refused to develop any other it is now in a state of acute instability. It bears all the marks of a transitional and swiftly passing form of religion. Its advocates hold fast to their gain — the unique quality of religious living — but without support from scientific procedures or any rational justification. At the same time they live and strive in a time that, above all other times in history, is dominated and shaped by scientific method, attitude, control, and construction. They can justify their religion only by self-contradictions which they try to render nonirritating by calling them paradoxes and dialectic. They try to bar out reason and scientific inquiry in every approach to the supreme realities of religious concern by endeavoring to show that all who make such efforts fall into confusion and contradiction.

An important symptom of the instability of this religious development needs to be noted. Neo-supernaturalists all show an inner tension, a kind of groping in desperation, which they uphold as a virtue because, they claim, it is the only way by which man in sin and in a sinful world can face the holiness of God. But there is some reason to think that this anxiety and this tension are at least in part due to the fundamental divisiveness of their position. They are trying to live in a world that is shaped and controlled by science, without any rational support for their religious claim. The resulting instability and uncertainty make an impossible situation. It cannot endure indefinitely.

But there is a much more deadly criticism of neo-supernaturalism than the ones we have mentioned. When the new supernaturalists repudiate in the field of religion every rational method by which to distinguish between truth and error, between reality and illusion, between good and bad, they open the gates to every form of bigotry, cruelty, and violence. In the last analysis there are only two ways by which an organized interest can support any claim against the assaults of those who do not accept it. One way is that of persuasion, reason, and the data of experience; the other way is that of dogmatic unreasoning enthusiasm, violence, and cruelty. The modern world in many quarters is being tempted to abandon the way of persuasion and revert to violence. Neo-supernaturalism, in repudiating the way of reason, is following the drift of the times and is augmenting the forces of evil in that direction. It is no accident that the chief home and source of the new supernaturalism today is also the land where rules the worst form of political violence and cruelty. We do not mean that the Barthians are responsible for the evils that appear in Germany. We only mean that they are the products in religion of the same influences which have brought about the repudiation of the methods of reason and persuasion in politics. They represent in religion that same unreasoned dogmatism which, when it turns to political action, becomes cruelty and violence. In time it will become cruelty and violence in religion if the new supernaturalism succeeds in upholding the claim that the ultimate reference of the religious man is rationally irresponsible.

The rejection of reason, of which neo-supernaturalism is one symptom, is an admission of cultural failure. If persisted in it will destroy either this age of scientific understanding and control or else be destroyed by it. We are faced with several possibilities. European civilization may disintegrate: if it does, neo-supernaturalism will continue there. America may escape the danger that threatens the life of western culture: if it does, neo-supernaturalism and other denials of the scientific approach to the problems of life will disappear, after the ground swell from Europe has had time to subside. The certainty before us is this: neo-supernaturalism cannot endure if our scientific civilization does.

IV. THEISTIC NATURALISM

We have said there is another of these recently appearing branches from the trunk of religion. It is the new theistic naturalism. These two philosophies of religion are developing vigorously and simultaneously, although neo-supernaturalism has manifested a much more rapid growth than has neo-naturalism. Since these two are still in their youth, while the other three branches have begun to die at the top, it would seem that the future rests with one or the other of them. Which will it be? We do not know; but since one or the other is likely in time to be the main trunk of future religious growth, it is important that we compare them.

Theistic naturalism is the exact opposite of the new supernaturalism in respect to the use of reason and the empirical method. It asserts that all we claim to know is mere guesswork unless it meets the tests of rationality and observation. Whenever we know anything at all there must be a series of material impacts upon the organism, giving rise to a series of actions and perceptions whereby our behavior becomes intelligently organized according to some pattern which directs it to predictable outcomes. We know only by acting, but action gives us knowledge only when we are able to predict in some measure what the outcome of the action will be. First we act under physiological propulsion. In time we learn, by observation, to know what the outcomes of action will be when it is carried out according to certain patterns under certain conditions. When we reach that stage we have knowledge; and knowledge gained in this way is the only knowledge there is. This applies to knowledge of God and to all matters of religious concern as well as to every other kind of knowledge. We learn by acting. Whosoever willeth, shall know, and in no other way.

But action does not give us knowledge merely because of the subjective states of feeling that may result. Action does not give us knowledge about anything outside ourselves unless we can predict something of what the environmental situation will be as an outcome of our behavior. In this way — namely, through action which is obedient to God — we must attain whatever knowledge we can ever have of God and of the way to God. But all knowledge gained in this way is knowledge of nature, because the distinction between nature and supernature would seem to be just this: nature is what we know through interaction between the physiological organism and its environment, while supernature is what we know (or allegedly know), and can only know, by revelation which is independent of this natural process of interaction between organism and environment.

Theistic naturalism is the philosophy which upholds devotion to God as found in nature by way of action as just described.

V. THE NEW NATURALISM AND THE NEW SUPERNATURALISM COMPARED

It will be interesting and enlightening to put a number of penetrating questions to each of these philosophies and note wherein they agree and disagree in their replies. We have prepared a dozen questions and will ask them in order.

(1). How does the religious man differ from all others? The two philosophies give the same answer to this question: The religious man differs from all others in his utter willingness to be controlled by a reality which transcends "this world" and is very different from this world. But though they agree about the fact they begin at once to disagree in their theories about the fact.

When the naturalist says that God transcends this world he means that God is the uncomprehended totality of all that is best. This totality is not of this world in the sense only that it exceeds, and in many cases diverges from and antagonizes, the goods and goals which are cherished in the minds of men. This is different from what the supernaturalist means by the super-worldly reality of religious interest.

(2). Is God hidden and does he transcend every culture? Both philosophies answer, Yes, to this question; but they interpret this hiddenness and transcendence of God in very different ways.

The naturalist says God is hidden because our conscious awareness is only a peephole compared to all the riches and all the horrors that are in this world. Also, what we most highly prize in specific form is by no means actually the best. (We never know the specific nature of the best that any concrete situation may yield until we actually are in that situation and act in a way to elicit the goods that are there.) Even then we have not the scope of consciousness, the diversity of perspective, the sensitivity and powers of discrimination, to sense the whole of the goods that differently endowed sensitivities would apprehend. Furthermore — and perhaps this is most important of all — the desires of the human heart are misdirected, so that we cannot apprehend the riches and height of beauty and love.

We know that abundant values are hidden because of the implication of certain discoveries; namely, the great scope and diversity of values brought to light by differently endowed personalities and different cultures; the great range of different values which reach our own consciousness in its changing states of existence; the great flood of value that streams into our experience in those rare situations when social relations are transformed in ways which are ordinarily impossible because of the established social order. We know there is great fullness of hidden value because we know there are innumerable "waves" of energy which are never caught by our sensitive organisms to be translated into color and sound and feeling.

We stand, therefore, always in the presence of riches that would be experienced if all the potentialities of sensitivity and fellowship could be realized. But human personalities would have to be radically transformed, both individually and in respect to the social order, to become aware of the total specific content of this reality which transcends our culture and is hidden to us. Perhaps we never shall be so transformed completely. But the uniquely religious man lives always in the presence of this light which is so great that it is to us a darkness. He is always oriented toward it. In every concrete situation he makes it the supreme and only object of all his living. Furthermore, he commits himself to the transforming power of this greater abundance of value. For it is not simply a set of passive possibilities to be achieved by men. It is an actual, operative reality which carries possibilities, but is not itself a mere possibility. It is an energy which works to transform men so that they can be appreciative of it. It works upon us and in us in the form of *growth* and unpredictable emergence of insight.

Let us summarize the answer of new naturalism to the question before us: God is hidden and transcends "our world" because the full riches of God's goodness in each concrete situation of the natural world are largely inaccessible to the human heart by reason of habits, attachments, pride, envy, greed, grouches, and other predispositions, in considerable part unavoidable by reason of the social order in which we live. These prevent us from responding to all the goodness that is there.

Now let us listen to the supernaturalist on this question. God is hidden and transcendent, he says, because God is outside nature and beyond the reach of all intelligent human inquiry. God is hidden because he is not in the world that is open to empirical search. God is hidden because man can do nothing to reach God. God is hidden until he breaks into the world from outside, by a supernatural act.

(3). Is faith a prerequisite to the knowledge of God? Both philosophies answer, Yes. But after both admit the fact, each gives a different interpretation of it.

When the naturalist says that faith in God is necessary before one can have knowledge of God he means that no one can know any reality of great value, in its character of value, until he is appreciative of it. Faith is appreciative interest sufficient to induce action. The reality of God has value so great that it ought to exercise absolute sovereignty over human life. Therefore to know God in his character of value a man must have interest so great as to induce the kind of action called absolute self-commitment. It must induce utter willingness of the total self to seek with all powers and all appreciative capacity in each natural situation for the best that can be found there however different it may be from one's pre-established desires and ideals. This is what the naturalist means by faith.

Now it has already been stated that according to naturalism one can get knowledge of anything only by action. He can know it in its character of supreme value only by appreciative action of the total self in response to it in the way just indicated. Therefore one must first have faith before he can have knowledge. That is simply another way of saying that one must first act before he can have knowledge, since faith is here identical with action.

The supernaturalist, like the naturalist, says we must first have faith before we can have knowledge of God. But when he speaks of faith, does he mean something different from what the naturalist means? Let him speak for himself:

Real faith always means obedience to God; it means a living obedience, offered here and now, at this actual moment of time, to his loving will, which has an absolute and special significance at this particular moment. If faith does not issue in such obedience it loses its meaning, and is perverted . . . it becomes a mere theory; obedience, too, becomes mere ethical legalism if it is not based on faith of this kind.[1]

Does the supernaturalist here mean to set forth the same idea of faith as that upheld by the naturalist? The context of this quotation from Brunner makes plain that by obedience he does not mean obedience to some formula or abstract principle. He seems to mean obedience to the best that can be found in each concrete situation. If so, the two philosophies agree on this point. But if Brunner means to repudiate the empirical method of discovering the best in each situation, the two philosophies are radically opposed. Brunner says obedience means to obey the loving will of God. But how is one to know what this will may be in the concrete situation? Is it by a kind of revelation which excludes the use of experimental action controlled by observation and reason? If so, it is here that the two philosophies diverge.

(4). Is faith in God and hence knowledge of him given to man by the grace of God and in no other way? Both philosophies answer, Yes, but they differ in what they mean by grace.

We have already seen what the naturalist means by faith. It is impossible to know anything in its character of value without appreciative interest sufficient to induce action in response to it, and this is faith. But one cannot acquire an interest by his own volition unless he already has the beginnings of it. If one has some interest in any matter he can work to increase that interest. But if he has no interest he cannot acquire an interest by his own efforts, because he must first have an interest before he can work to increase it. Therefore the interest must be given to him. In that sense it must be given by the grace of God.

But what is God's grace? The naturalist says it is growth. The grace of God whereby faith and knowledge of God come to a man is that transformation of personality and consciousness which come to a man through growth of culture and personality. Growth is never the direct work of man. The unconscious and unintended emergence and ripening of the supreme interests and appreciations are instances of growth. Such growth, says the naturalist, is the grace of God.

What we have just stated is a purely naturalistic interpretation of God's grace. It is not what the supernaturalist means. Yet the fact stands regardless of interpretations. The fact is that man's goodness, insight, faith, and fulfillment are not primarily his own work but the work of a superhuman power. This fact the naturalist and the supernaturalist both recognize, but each gives to the fact an interpretation widely different from that of the other. The supernaturalist means, by grace, the intervention of God from outside nature into the natural processes.

(5). Is the religious man primarily an idealist? Both philosophies answer, No.

In this reply they are united in opposition to the moral idealist, the liberal, and the humanist. These latter all say that ideals should command our highest devotion. It is true that they often teach that no specifically formulated set of ideals can be held as absolute because any envisaged ideal must always lead on to still higher ideals. But the naturalist and supernaturalist mean something far more than this when they say that ideals are only means to something else. The idealist and his philosophic brethren mean that we must ever reach out after a still higher ideal. The two philosophies we are now considering mean that we must reach out after something that is not an ideal at all. What we seek and serve must be the living God.

But at this point the unanimity between naturalist and supernaturalist ceases. For the naturalist, God is the totality of all that is best in each concrete situation, including, however, all that is unappreciated by the consciousness of the individual as well as what he is able or willing to appreciate by active response to it. For the supernaturalist God is something outside the natural world entirely.

In the naturalistic concept of God there is a significant implication. Ideals are not even tools, they are nuisances if they are not developed out of the concrete situation and made to fit it, not superimposed upon it. When the religious man makes reflective choice between alternatives of value, he is controlled by a reality which transcends all those ideal possibilities of value which circumscribe the scope and height of the prevailing culture in which he lives his life. It transcends every ideal whatsoever because it is not an ideal at all. It is the existing God. Therefore the religious man is not primarily an idealist, either for the naturalist or the supernaturalist.

(6). How is the religious man motivated?

The naturalist says that the religious man is motivated not by any lofty ideal, but by the richness of value that is already here and now, however hidden it may be prior to those responses which elicit it into appreciative awareness. The supernaturalist says that the religious man is motivated by obedience to God, God being entirely outside natural situations and independent of all human values.

(7). Do our rational powers fall short of a full understanding of God? Both philosophies answer, Yes. The naturalist agrees with the supernaturalist in saying that God is still very imperfectly portrayed by our rational powers in respect to his specific nature. Both would say, furthermore, that God in all probability never will be very fully nor very well understood. This is the fact on which the two philosophies agree, but in their interpretation of this fact they diverge very widely.

The naturalist says that this is true about God because it is true of all our knowledge of the more important aspects of nature, God being in nature and nowhere else, although not to be identified with the whole of nature by any means. Our very imperfect knowledge of God is due, first of all, to the limitations arising out of the way all knowledge is got. All knowledge about existent reality comes from first beginning to act in the concrete situation, and then taking note of the conditions, the consequences, and the pattern of such behavior. When we know the conditions, the consequences, and the pattern of our action, we have all the knowledge we can ever have of nature, and that means all the knowledge we can ever have of any existing reality, including God.

Some of the supernaturalists, if not all, would agree that this is the way we get all the knowledge we can ever have of natural existence. Emil Brunner, and perhaps others, would go further and say that this knowledge of nature gives us *some* knowledge of God.

Therefore of ourselves we cannot know the good or the will of God. It is, of course, true that God manifests himself as the incomprehensible one, mighty and wise in the works of creation, with an impressiveness which, even in the most unseeing, awakens awe in the presence of the mystery of the universe, and fills with wonder everyone who has not entirely lost the child-spirit. But being what we are, with our limited vision, this manifestation is not enough to reveal to us the will of the mysterious power which rules in nature.[2]

But the supernaturalist does not stop with this. He says there is another way by which we get knowledge of God and this other way gives us the more important knowledge. This other way is called revelation. This most important knowledge given by revelation cannot be expressed in rational terms but only in myth and paradox.

There is still another fact about the use of our rational powers in knowing God on which the naturalist and the supernaturalist agree, although for different reasons. It is the fact that God cannot be comprehended within any one single rational system and that therefore our knowledge cannot go on from more to more continuously, but rather we must discard one rational system after using it for a time, and develop another.

The naturalist holds this to be true because it applies to our knowledge of natural existence and is due to the following characteristics of our knowing of nature: the richness of the concrete world; the emergent unpredictable changes which are always occurring there; the essentially ineffable nature of immediate experience; the limitation of the applicability of every rational system to some one perspective and basis of reference; the new and different kind of knowledge that emerges when some new technique of inquiry is used; the extreme and fundamental changes which are likely to come over nature throughout aeons of time. All these conditions not only make all rational understanding of God and the rest of nature very imperfect, but make it necessary to discard one rational system and develop another when we come into some new perspective or deal with a newly emergent aspect of reality.

The supernaturalist interprets all these limitations of reason to mean that our reason cannot reach as far as the ultimate reality of God, but that there is a short cut to that reality called revelation.

(8). Are human values relevant to God? No, says the supernaturalist. Yes, says the naturalist.

We have already noted that God is not even good in any human sense of that word, according to the teaching of the new supernaturalists. God is absolutely other, so far as human values are concerned. God destroys and God creates and this destruction and creation have nothing to do with human values.

The naturalist, on the other hand, holds that God and highest human value are identical. However, he fully recognizes that men may be mistaken in what they hold to be highest and best. What they strive to achieve or obtain is often not good. What they endeavor to destroy or avoid is not bad in many cases. Certainly it is a common thing for men to discover that they err in their evaluations. But for the naturalist humanly cherished values are not irrelevant to God. Our values are different from the goodness of God when (*a*) we mistakenly or perversely cherish what is not good and (*b*) when we fail to comprehend the totality of all that is good. Since the desires of every man, and the values which inform every culture, are always infected with error, perversity, and limitation, God is always in great part other than "this world" — meaning the specific objects of human desire and aversion. Indeed the diversity and opposition between that actuality of value which is God and those systems of value which we cherish must be very great indeed. We know this must be so because of what we so well know about the error and perversity of men. But true values and all highest values are in God and God is in nature.

(9). Is God creator of all, including evil?

Yes, says the supernaturalist. God is "the creator of nature and of the spirit, of all that exists, and of ideas; his will is the source of that which is and the basis of that which ought to be." [3] "In him alone the existence of the world and the manner in which it exists, is based. . . . God controls everything that exists." On the other hand "as Redeemer he is the end, the goal, toward which all existence tends." [4] Thus God, in this teaching, is the foundation and the roof of the world, the source and the culmination. However, this mid-region where we now live is corrupted by sin and evil. Yet this empirical world with all its evil is the work of God, for God is "the creator of nature and the spirit, of all that exists, and of ideas." [5] Since God is the source of everything, including even our ideas and spirit, he is the source of all sin and evil. But he is not in these. These are his works, but he himself is outside it all.

The naturalist, on the other hand, says that God is not the creator, meaning the mysterious source of everything; he is only the source of the good, or rather is himself the good. The source of all good is simply the cosmic growing roots of all good, and these roots are themselves good. The naturalist accuses the supernaturalist of rationalistic and metaphysical speculation when he identifies God with the ultimate source, "Creator," and the ultimate end, "Redeemer." The supernaturalist is indulging in utmost flights of rationalistic speculation even though he calls it revelation. It is speculation because no one knows with any assurance anything about the ultimate source of this empirical world or its ultimate outcome.

(10). Is man a sinner? Yes, say both philosophies. But here again, while they agree on the fact they interpret it very differently.

The naturalist says man is a sinner because some things other than God count in his esteem. He allows other things to lay claim on him. He fears some things other than alienation from God. He prizes some things on other grounds than their relevance to God. He does not live solely for the hidden riches of God. He cannot freely give up his dearest desire even when assured that by so doing he would enter more fully into the experience of the uncomprehended totality of God's goodness. He is in that state of existence called sin because conscious and subconscious interests corrupt the singlehearted devotion to God. He is a sinner because he must be radically transformed before he can experience the fullness of the specific content of God's goodness.

The supernaturalist says that man as created by God was perfect and sinless, but in some primal state, symbolized by the story of Adam and the apple, he sinned, and ever after has been in this state. The naturalist knows nothing of a primal state in which man came perfect from the hand of God. He considers all such talk to be cosmological speculation about which we can gather no evidence.

(11). Does God forgive man in sin through Jesus Christ? Both philosophies say, Yes, to the fact, and furthermore both mean thereby to say that God gives himself to man even while man is a sinner. But after agreeing on the fact they disagree in their interpretation of the fact.

The supernaturalist says that God forgives man through Jesus Christ and that the incarnation of Jesus Christ was a supernatural act of God in which God gave, and gives, himself to man.

The naturalist says that Jesus Christ and his disciples formed a fellowship (or such a fellowship was formed by the disciples in consequence of their having experienced the life and death of Jesus). This fellowship has transmitted itself from individual to individual, group to group, and generation to generation. This is the living church.

But " church " here does not mean merely the individuals who have their name on the church roll. Neither does it mean the social structure of a great institution. It means rather a kind of communion which actually occurs between some individuals whether their names stand recorded on an official document or not. It is a communion wherein the individuals share a common devotion to the God of love, wherein they inform one another of the difficulties which stand in the way of that devotion in their individual personalities, in the local community, and in the basic social structure, and wherein they cooperatively strive to overcome these difficulties. It is a communion wherein each resolves with the utmost degree of sincerity to strive with all his powers of appreciation, of construction and reconstruction, to bring forth all the good that can be found in each situation.

This communion is not made by the getting together of individuals to form it. Instead of being made by individuals, the communion makes the individual. That is to say, an individual is caught into it and transformed by it. Being caught into this life-transforming communion which has issued from the life of Jesus Christ as a social-psychological, historical process, wherein the individual experiences a more profound community with his fellows and with God than anywhere else — this is what the naturalist means by God's forgiveness.

The supernaturalist and the naturalist agree that God forgives man in the sense that God gives himself to man on condition that man gives himself to God. But they interpret this in two very different ways, as we have seen. Says the naturalist: Wherever the growth of community with fellow men and with nature takes hold on a man with life-transforming power, God's forgiveness is accomplished. Says the supernaturalist: When God intervenes from outside of nature to accomplish this result, God's forgiveness is fulfilled.

(12). Does God reveal himself to man? Yes, say both philosophies, but they disagree in their interpretation of this fact.

The naturalist says that man can know God only because God takes the initiative in developing and transforming the consciousness of man so that the human mind can appreciate precious reality in its character of value. Furthermore, this growth and transformation do not occur to man in general, but only to men under certain required conditions. One very important condition is the life-transforming communion described in a previous paragraph as the church.

The supernaturalist says that revelation is a super-rational and supernatural act of God and therefore cannot be the natural outcome of certain specifiable conditions such as we have indicated are the natural conditions of natural growth.

We have put twelve questions to the two contrasting philosophies of religion and have received from each of them an answer to these questions. The remarkable thing we discover, as we look back over these answers, is that the two philosophies, while diametrically opposed in their theory *about* the facts, do in general agree on the facts concerning the religious life.

We can sum up the differences and likenesses between the several different philosophies of religion by saying that the new naturalism is closer to the new supernaturalism in respect to agreement about the *facts* that enter into religious living, while it is much closer to liberalism, traditional supernaturalism, and social idealism in its *theory about* these facts. It has much more agreement with these latter than with the new supernaturalism on the question of how we shall interpret facts, but it is much more in agreement with the new supernaturalism than with these others on the question of what facts shall be recognized as the proper material for religious interpretation.

Underneath all other issues that divide the new naturalism and the new supernaturalism is this basic question: What is the method by which religious devotion and religious knowledge are attained? It is super-rational and supernatural, says the new super-naturalist. It is rational and it is natural, says the naturalist.

This question of method is fundamental. Only as we settle this question can we hope to settle any other, for it underlies every other. Without agreement on method other agreements are accidental and will always be transitory and insecure. On the other hand, when we do agree on method our disagreements become creative, our errors fruitful, our findings cooperative and cumulative. Philosophies and theologies may disagree radically and their disagreements be all to the good, if they agree on method. We cannot have any large and creative and enduring union of the faiths of Christendom until we agree on what shall be the tests of validity for any faith.

VI. THE TREE OF RELIGIOUS GROWTH

We began by examining the great tree of the growth of Christianity through history. We saw the main trunk of this growth dividing, under the atmospheric conditions of modern life, into five branches: traditional supernaturalism, liberalism, social idealism, the new supernaturalism, and the new naturalism. Let us take a last look at this tree. We see that all of the branches have begun to die at the top except two, the new supernaturalism and the new naturalism. Therefore we have been examining these two with great care, for it would seem that here the growth of the future must lie, in one or in both. We see that the new supernaturalism is much the larger and is growing much more rapidly. But there is a reason for that. It springs out of the oldest and largest branch of all, which is traditional supernaturalism. The new naturalism, on the other hand, does not spring from any of the other branches, but rises up from the central crotch whence all the other branches diverge. Therefore it does not have a great feeder, as the new supernaturalism does.

After examining the two branches we have reached the conclusion that the new supernaturalism will be the growth of the future if and when and where our scientific civilization is destroyed and we revert to some more primitive form of culture. If, on the other hand, our scientific civilization should survive in some part of the world, and grow from more to more, the new naturalism will be the religion of the future in that culture.

NOTES

[1] Emil Brunner, *The Divine Imperative*, p. 118.

[2] *Ibid.*, p. 114.

[3] *Ibid.*

[4] *Ibid.*, p. 122.

[5] If Brunner means by " Creator " merely to designate a mystery, he is not true to his intention, for he does not leave it in the vagueness of mystery. He makes specifications and dogmatic statements. He says that everything in existence, the evil as well as the good, has just one ultimate source. He claims, furthermore, to know that everything will come out all right in the end by reason of the " Redeemer." These are far flights of cosmological and rationalistic speculation, even though Brunner himself is always denouncing rationalism and metaphysical speculation.

BIBLIOGRAPHY

Divergent developments in religion today are vividly exemplified in *The Nature of Religious Experience*, edited by Bixler and Calhoun, wherein eleven of the younger thinkers set forth their different religious viewpoints. A thoroughly documented survey of these tendencies is found in E. E. Aubrey, *Present Theological Tendencies*. A study of these developments limited to the American scene is *American Philosophies of Religion*, by Wieman and Meland. Liberalism, humanism and naturalism are presented by three different men, each representing one of these positions, in a conversation called *Is There a God?* by Otto, Macintosh and Wieman. *Contemporary Christian Thought*, by C. S. Macfarland, contains book reviews of most of the important books that appeared in the years 1934–35 and thereby reveals new growths in religion. *Contemporary English Theology*, by Walter M. Horton, is an illuminating survey.

9.

THE FACT OF RELIGIOUS LIVING

ACTUAL concrete religious living runs deeper into the nature of existence than does any theory about it. All philosophies, theologies, and interpretations of religion are concerned with this fact. None tells us the whole truth about this aspect of human living with its tremendous upthrust and downthrust of outreach and loyalty. Always there is something left out not yet explained by the best philosophy about it, as is true of any system of human ideas about any concrete event.

We have been studying what men of the past have thought about this quality of human living. We are about to undertake some further constructive theory about it for the present time and place. At this mid-point, therefore, it would seem to be important that we get before us as clearly as possible the concrete actuality which all these philosophies and teachings attempt to interpret.

There is one difficulty which we face at once. Any attempt to state this fact of religious living in its stark actuality will be shaped and toned by the theory about it held by the individual who tries to present it. Is it possible, then, to get at the essential fact, which underlies all the theories? Or is the mental apprehension of each of us so shaped by theory that it is no longer possible to see the fact except in the forms and interpretations which our pre-established theory must give to it? If there is to be any validity at all in our thinking, we must be able to get at the fact which our theory is about. Otherwise there is no possible way of testing our theories and one of these is just as good as another. If theory bars the way every time we try to get at fact, then indeed are we in a hopeless state.

It is true that we cannot know any fact except in terms of some theory. But it is possible to put aside the special theory we are trying to test, and use some more general theory which is closer to the raw materials of experience. That is what we shall try to do. We shall endeavor to state the fact in terms of a theory of life which is broader than any theory about religious living and so inclusive of all the different religious theories. In this way we may be able to distinguish that fact which underlies many different philosophies of religion and which they diversely interpret. With such an approach we hope that what we shall set forth as the fact of religious living will be just as acceptable to the extreme supernaturalist as to the extreme naturalist. We do not mean that they will agree in their theories *about* the fact. They may be just as far apart as ever in their patterns of interpretation of religious living. But we want to make sure that the fact itself is the same for all, namely, religious living in its essential and distinctive nature. If the rival theories do not deal with the same fact, then they do not even have ground for dispute. If each is treating a different fact, then each may be expounding full truth about whatever it is discussing and there is no argument. But to be rival theories they must be concerned with the same fact. It is the identity of the fact underlying the agreements and disagreements of all these various current philosophies of religion which we want to get before us.

There are some who feel that this difficulty of getting at the fact of religious living can be circumvented if they actually live this way. Genuinely religious people have first-hand experience of this kind of life, they aver, and so they do not need to be troubled with all this talk about the right theory. Spectators of the phenomenon are barricaded by theory and so may have difficulty in getting behind it to the actuality, but not so the people who are themselves experients of religious living.

This view is a mistake. We can see the error if we compare apprehension of religion with getting an understanding of something else, say personality. I am a personality. I experience personality from the inside, as it were, and so does everyone else. But despite universal experiencing of personality for centuries on end, there has been much dispute about the nature of it and many different theories concerning it, of which some must be nearer to the truth than others but probably none have the whole truth. So with apprehension of biological living: I experience it and so does every other animal. And who of all the living can answer truly the question: What is life? There are many theories and none can know what life is except by means of some theory. So also it is with this matter which is our present prime interest, religious living. Even those who have had first-hand experience of it cannot know it except by some theory. Many who live this way no doubt are unaware of their own theories or of the falseness of them. They live it without knowing what it is that they are living.

In the light of all this we conclude that there is no access to knowledge of anything, not even to knowledge of oneself, except by way of a theory. One may have access to some *reality* without theory, but not access to *knowledge* of it. Access to a reality, and access to knowledge of that reality, are two very different things. Because this is true, a good theory is of great importance. It is indispensable in an age when tradition no longer serves to guide one in his choices and in his methods. When one must use his intelligence theory becomes a basic requirement. Religious living today requires as never before that one use his intelligence in making choices and devising methods. Hence the truest theory (the truest philosophy) that one can discover is more important for religious living today than in the past.

I. THE PROBLEM OF OUR SEARCH

Many cases of avowed religious living do not have anything peculiarly distinctive about them. They are a mixture of moral idealism, aesthetic appreciation, sentimental attachment, loyalty to a group with which one shares a rich body of experience, and a set of habits which leads one to live in a certain uniform way. Added to all this, in some instances there may be a dominant devotion to some specific cause or objective. But in all this mixture there need be nothing which is uniquely due to religion in such wise that it could not be found outside religion. This mixture, neither in part nor in whole, is uniquely and distinctively religious. Every one of the constituents which go to make it up can be found entirely outside the bounds of religious living. Even the mixture taken in its totality is not necessarily distinctive. It is called religious living because it is sustained and directed by the institution which carries the title of being religious.

In face of this situation workers in the church, and religious people generally, often grope, sometimes rather desperately, to find what it is that religion can do for life that cannot be done in other ways. Are religious objectives merely unspecialized and rather weakened duplicates of the highest objectives which concern the rest of life? Or is there a way of living which is peculiar, distinctive, markedly different and incomparably precious, which can be found through religion and in no other way?

Our answer to this question is, Yes. There is a peculiar quality of living, incommensurate with anything else, which religion alone can give. Morality cannot give it. The practical arts cannot give it — industry, business, education, politics, agriculture, housekeeping. The fine arts and aesthetic appreciation cannot give it. Science, philosophy, intelligence, and all the powers of the mind cannot give it. Not even devotion to the loftiest ideals can give it. It is the rare and peculiar gift of religion and nowhere else can it be got.

By no means do we find it in all lives that are called religious. But in some we do. There is *a* religious way which invariably has it. But this distinctively *religious* way is only one manifestation amid all that medley which goes by the name of religion. Furthermore it is a trait which is ordinarily ignored, because the world today has no pattern of thought by which to distinguish it. It is difficult to make words set forth clearly its characteristic features.

Even the religious people who actually live in this distinctive and peculiar way are unable ofttimes to conceptualize it aright. They have no forms of thought by which to lift it up into the clear light of cognition, just as most people would find it difficult to tell how they breathe. The old forms by which people in time past were able to portray it, no longer carry the proper meanings; and new intellectual formulations of it have not yet been brought into common currency, even among the followers of this way. Therefore they who have found this rare and excellent path do often identify it in a fashion which blurs its outline.

In many cases, genuinely religious persons mistakenly identify the religious quality as moral idealism. Nevertheless, if you search their sayings, you will find something very different from moral idealism. To be sure, such people frequently are nobly moral, guided by ideals more lofty than those of others. But that is not always true. In this peculiarly religious way there may be all degrees of moral excellence and he who stands low in moral attainment may rank very high in the qualities of this distinctively religious manner of living. One may be deeply religious in this sense and have very low and mean ideals, providing he holds himself ready to learn better as soon as he gets more light.

Also it is not a matter of intellectual ability or intelligence. The most stupid might live in this deeply religious way, as well as the most highly endowed. It is true that the greatest intellectual powers cannot find the path that leads indefinitely to values ever higher unless they go in this unique way, because it is this religious commitment which can alone release fully the powers of intelligence from those prejudices, fears, hopes, insensitivities, and other conditions which blind or distort the judgment concerning what is most worthful. An individual using his intellect alone cannot search for — much less find — the highest values nor all the diverse forms of value which make the maximum richness of abundant living, unless he is interested in such values and so is sensitive, zestful, alert, and receptive to them. Intellect alone without trained appreciation, without openness, without readiness to cast away the highest known for something higher, cannot seek and cannot attain that way which opens into life's supreme fulfillment. The peculiarly religious way, as we shall find, provides this outreach and openness and thus releases the intelligence to search every concrete problematical situation for the highest and richest it may have to offer. Even though he who goes this religious way may not have much intelligence, what he has will be released to seek and find. The fact that he may not have very much intelligence to release, however, makes no difference so far as exemplifying the uniqueness of the quality of religious living is concerned. The most limited intellect, as well as the greatest, can go this way, and the most limited may be as completely committed to it and as fully released and awakened by it as the greatest. Those with less endowment cannot include so great a diversity of interests in this way of living, of course, nor perhaps build up so penetrating a concept of it, but they can live it as genuinely and appreciatively.

Nor is it the nature of the concept of God which identifies the religious way of living. People who live this way may have very diverse ideas of God, and some seem to have scarcely an *idea* of God at all. But a remarkable unanimity is found among them on one point: they all express a certain unique quality of life. It is the peculiar and distinctive trait which religion sometimes brings forth and which nothing else in life can engender.

Whenever we find this kind of living we must try to get some intelligent understanding of it. Only as we achieve such a grasp of it can we seek experimentally to attain it, or deepen and strengthen it, or foster and protect it. We cannot intelligently propagate it unless we can apprehend it in the form of concepts. Therefore, to the end of living it more effectively, we must try to get it into valid and usable forms of thought. Merely to think it is by no means necessarily to live it. But we must think it if we are going to seek it, protect it, deepen it, and spread it among others.

II. WHAT IS THE CHRISTIAN WAY OF LIFE?

To see how confused on this matter are many intelligent and devoted Christian men, let us glance at an actual situation that occurred very recently. A friend of mine, Professor Edwin Walker, and myself have just returned from a conference with Christian workers who represent in many cases some of the best we have known in the Christian faith. The following analysis of what occurred there I owe to Professor Walker.

The group were inquiring what it is that distinguishes a Christian movement from any other. They assumed that there were four distinctive characteristics: A Christian movement should be educational rather than propagandistic or doctrinaire; it should be democratic rather than manipulated by leaders; it should meet the particular tests of social idealism newly accepted by the leadership of the group; it should contribute to the development of the wholesome personality centered in accepted moral ideals. Here then, according to these people, are the criteria for discerning the heart of Christianity, the identifying marks which distinguish it from other manifestations in human life. They direct us to look for whatever is educational, democratic, and idealistic, and that promotes development of wholesome personality.

When these implicit assumptions about the nature of Christianity are thus set up clearly in the light of known truth, it is apparent that there is nothing distinctively Christian about them. Other movements not Christian, and not even religious, may carry all these qualifications. In much of today's struggle to specify the distinguishing features of the Christian way of life by which it can be set over against all the rest of the world, implicitly or explicitly we find one or another of the following criteria:

(1). True Christianity is that way of life preached and represented in the authoritative church. We are familiar with one large branch of Christendom which subscribes to this view.

(2). True Christianity is an authoritative body of beliefs. In its older forms it appears in the historic creedal formulations. There are several contemporary interpreters of Christianity who are attempting to distinguish it by identifying certain changeless beliefs in the Christian tradition. Such attempts have always failed and always will fail.

(3). True Christianity is to be found in the "way of life" of Jesus Christ. In essence this turns out to be nothing else than the highest socially accepted ideals of the group then and there claiming to be Christian.

(4). True Christianity is found in the "spirit of Christ." This definition escapes the disciplines of criticism only by its vagueness.

(5). True Christianity is found in some certain authoritative pattern of experience.[1]

If one accepts any one of these or any other similar statement of the essential nature of Christianity he is laid under a peculiar necessity in all his thinking and sharing of experiences. He must become an apologist. If he is committed to any of these as the

norm of Christianity, it follows that he cannot be free in his search
for truth and reality.

Each of the above definitions of the nature of Christianity has
arisen as an attempt to interpret it in terms of the current patterns
of thought and in harmony with the body of knowledge then contemporary. Therefore, instead of revealing the essence of Christianity, each simply shows how some earnest-minded Christians of
a certain time and place think about their faith.

What, then, is Christianity? Christianity is a continuing social
movement shaped by a certain historic past in which Jesus Christ
is the central figure. This past shapes the present social movement in two ways. First and most potently, it works unconsciously to shape the life of each individual born into the Christian
tradition. Second, it works consciously on those who willingly
seek all the guidance they can get from this tradition.

Everyone who is a Christian in the broadest sense of the term
is born into a living tradition which transmits to the present that
historic past which distinguishes Christianity. The thoughts, sensitivities, attitudes, and ideals of such an individual are shaped by
the Christian past from the day he is born. This is Christianity in
the most inclusive sense, as that way of life which distinguishes
Christendom from other cultures.

There is also Christianity in the more limited and distinctive
sense. To be a Christian of this sort means to draw consciously
upon the past just mentioned as the chief source of guidance in
history for the conduct of life. This means, ordinarily, to join a
fellowship of those who do likewise. But it does not mean to try
to hold, fixed and changeless as the authority over life, any one
cross section of the historic development of Christianity. There
is no one period in this historic movement called Christianity
which can be set up as sovereign over all the others. There is no
such cross section, and no fragment of such a cross section, which
can remain changeless through the changing processes of historic
movement.

Hence to be a Christian does not mean to hold fast to any one
thing in this great tradition as though it were final, but it does

mean to live at the growing edge of this historic continuum. It means to absorb all the insight, all the truth, all the inspiration, which this living tradition can provide from the early Christian church and from the relevant continuities of history stretching before and after. But it means also *to live in the present.* It means to search all the realms of being now accessible to human inquiry in order to find every intimation concerning the nature of God and the way of life for man. Such a Christian will not avert his eyes from anything which evidence indicates to be true, no matter how alien it may seem to be to all the beliefs in the Christian tradition. It is truth he wants, and the access which such truth may give to the most precious reality. He does not cherish the Christian tradition as an end in itself. It is the living God he wants, who works and lives in the present situation. The Christian past is of value only as it guides him into the fuller enfoldment of the living God who operates in the here and now.

This we believe is the only way to be a true Christian. Such a one will accept nothing as true save on grounds of good evidence, no matter how sacred it may have been to Christians of the past (for example, belief in a flat earth or damnation of infants). But besides this which he can accept as true, he will conserve a great mass of lore which he cannot now accept as truth but much of which will be the source of future insight. All growth of truth and richness in the living of man depends on conserving such a heritage of lore. Much of it may be false, much of it may be true, and much else neither true nor false but the lyric expression of human experience which deepens and ennobles. No individual and no age can appreciate all the values of such a lore. That is the reason why it is so important that each age do not cut it down to the meager proportions of what this man or this time can appreciate and use, but pass it on for those further uses and appreciations of a later time and of other individuals who have different insights and interests.

To summarize, then, a true Christian is distinguished by three marks. First, he is unconsciously shaped in his living by that historic past which centers in the figure of Jesus Christ. Second, he consciously turns to that past for all the insight and guidance he can find there, ordinarily requiring fellowship in a group who do likewise.   Third, he carries the lore of this past — not only that part of it which he can appreciate in all the fullness of its significance, but the total body of it so far as the generations have sifted and conserved it.

These are the marks that distinguish the Christian from other religious people.   But whether we approach religious living through a study of the Christian or of any other particular religious person, we must locate the deeper root that underlies the differentia of the several religions.   What is profoundly and uniquely religious is deeper than Christianity or any other one religion taken as a class term.   The Christian can, and ought to, live the way that is most peculiarly religious.   If he does, he draws upon the resources of the Christian past to inspire and guide him, and that is a very precious heritage indeed.   But, on the other hand, a man might be shaped by the Christian past both unconsciously and by reason of his own volition; he might commit himself to Jesus Christ — that is, to the ideals and principles which he understands Jesus to have upheld; he might accept any set of Christian doctrines one may want to list; he might join a Christian fellowship and he might cherish all the Christian lore; and still he might not be a religious man in the deepest and most important sense of that term. Still he would not have that which is most precious in the religious way.   If he does live in the deeply religious way which we are about to describe, the Christian heritage should be a great help to him and make his religious living markedly different from what it would otherwise be.   But if he does not follow the religious way, all this Christian past will not make him religious in the most important sense of that term.   To be uniquely and distinctively religious is more important than to be Christian, however precious the Christian heritage may be.

The deeply religious man loves the reality of God more than any belief, more than any tradition, more than any set of religious practices.   All the beliefs, all the traditions, all the sacred lore, all the religious practices, are only means to an end that is far greater than any of them. The religious man will seize on anything, no matter how foreign it may be to the Christian past or any other past, if it helps him to his chief end: that unmeasured fullness of value in each situation which is the offering of the living God. The strength of his love for the reality of whatever is truly good, as over against self-love for his own beliefs, will be measured by the rigor of the tests he imposes upon any belief which he holds to be true or any procedure that he follows.

III. THE DISTINCTIVELY RELIGIOUS WAY

In face of all the difficulties noted we are going to essay to point out what in the uniquely religious way is different from everything else in life.

To live in this religious way is to live only " for the will of God." The will of God is the creative synthesis of each unique situation. Every unique situation carries goods and ills that one can never know before he gets into it. Therefore he who enters such a situation looking only for what will satisfy the desires and ideals which he brings into it, will miss most of this unpredictable, unforeseen, emergent fullness of value. He will miss it because his established desires and ideals will make him unresponsive to it. But he who lives for the will of God, and that only, will always be looking for something else that is vastly more than his specific desires and purposes. Always he says, Not my will but thine be done. My ideals, my purposes, my plans, my program are merely instrumental. They are no more than tools which I use to guide my action until I can find the uniqueness and richness of God's will which is always immeasurably more than, and sometimes very different from, what I desire. Thus he who lives in the transformed way is ready and responsive to the unpredictable fullness of good which may be experienced in the uniqueness of each concrete situation. He commits himself, his whole self, to the whole of goodness that is in God's way.

We must let one of these transformed personalities express in his own words this way of life as he lives it. The following quotation was given to us and we do not know who wrote it. But it is obviously written by one who lives what he is describing.

The next moment, one simply turns and does what God would have one do. And one repeats that the next moment and the next and the next. One lives from moment to moment doing just that. And all the while one is willing as hard as one can to keep God as the directing norm of all that one does. This willing is not the physical tightening or buckling up. One is completely relaxed physically and spiritually. But one is alert, *listening* for the voice of God, that one may hear and respond instantly and oh, so gladly, to everything that he says. It is indeed a "being alive to the good spontaneously." But that is a result of willing that the Good shall control during every moment of one's conscious life.

It does mean more prayer. But remember that is not just a rededication — there must be an effort to clear up what is being withheld in that area. For instance, if I find myself ill at ease whenever a certain person is about and promptly rededicate myself when it happens, although I am taking care of the immediate situation, I am not taking steps to eliminate that reaction. That involves thinking over in the presence of God, all of my relations with that person; of seeing him as he really is, his characteristics which cause this reaction in me, and of asking myself what it is that I am trying to protect in myself in this reaction to this person. In this way one comes to get behind the specific "badness" and to make possible another area in which there may be nothing but spontaneous action. All this is to be done in the presence of God. Nothing can be found about oneself if one tries to do it without first getting oneself absolutely *right* with God. "Whoever willeth to do the will of God shall know . . ." not only whether Jesus' teaching was of God or of himself, but all else that concerns one who would *live*. To be willing to do the will — that is the prior condition of all knowing in the realm of the human spirit.

There must be no strain; for strain means holding on whereas in this striving hard to meet the condition, one is not holding on to anything but letting go of everything. We can let go all concern but one concern — to hold God in our consciousness. We need be tied up to nothing but to God. We need never work hard again except in one thing — to will nothing but what God wills. We need be anxious about nothing evermore except one thing — that when God turns his searchlight upon us, we shall be transparent to its light.

When one prays, one has just to realize what it is that one is trying to accomplish by means of it and then improvise prayer to achieve that end. And what one is trying to do is to annihilate self — to hand over the control to God — not part of the control, part of the time, but all of the control all of the time. And so one just searches oneself to clear up areas which conduct reveals are really concealing some recalcitrant factors. Every " bad break " is therefore made use of to discover more about oneself. Instead of being discouraged about such things, one should welcome them, thank God for learning so much about the way of life.

In the way described above one lives for the transcendental best. The transcendental best is what is better than anything which you can know in its specific nature until you actually experience it in the creative synthesis of concrete situations. Even then you know only so much of it as you have actually experienced, which is only a small part, for each situation leads on to the next. Also each situation always contains a vast amount of hidden good which we are too undiscriminating and unresponsive to detect.

This living under the control of a culture-transcending devotion should be contrasted with the ordinary way. The ordinary way of living is controlled either by physiological propulsion or by idealistic prescription. These ideals may be the best in the culture there prevailing. In this transformed way one does of course have physiological propulsions and ideals. But these do not exercise supreme control. They are subordinate and instrumental to something else. This something else is infinitely more precious than they. It is the uncomprehended will of God.

Living in this transformed way is not necessarily highly moral, although it may be so. One may not be so kind and winning nor have other socially prized endowments to so great a degree as others who do not live this way. What the person in this way does have is freedom from other controls so that he can respond to the unpredictable emergent good as it may arise in the concrete situation in forms that flout the pre-established desires and ideals of men. He does not always do even this, for he may lack the physiological or mental or social or other endowments that are required for such appreciative and creative response to the unanticipated good. But the point is that he is not prevented from response to it by the domination over him of his own desires and ideals. He is ready and willing to follow the uncomprehended will of God just as soon as he can find what it is, no matter how different it may be from his own wishes and anticipations prior to the moment when the new form of value arises in the fullness of the concrete situation. This is the identifying mark of the transformed life. It is not moral excellence, nor social graciousness, nor intellectual ability, nor power of achievement, nor zeal for social reform, although the person may have any or all of these. It is simply freedom from inner constraints to do the best that each situation provides to the limit of one's capacity because of absolute commitment to that best made in advance to cover the whole of the future. The result is that all future choices are predetermined to be in the direction of maximum value.

The uniquely religious man may or may not think about God according to some set of doctrines. He may not think *about* God at all. He may repudiate the term "God" because of unfortunate cultural associations with the word. But he lives for an uncomprehended totality of good which breaks into the world of human appreciation and purposive action unpredictably, in the thronging fullness of concrete situations creatively emergent. The religious man may say that he is "living by faith." Or he may call it "living eschatologically."

This utter willingness and expectancy to be transformed and ever again redirected in one's living by an uncomprehended goodness far greater and better than the specific content of any human purpose that man can ever have, is what gives the distinctive quality to the religious way when and if and in so far as a man is uniquely religious. But it is important to note that it is a matter of degree, and many avowedly "religious" people do not have it at all. Perhaps only a very limited number have it and they have it fluctuatingly. Many people not distinguished by the kind of living we here describe can be called religious quite properly according to well authenticated sociological criteria. We have no quarrel with such criteria. We only wish to point out that they do not distinguish the kind of people we are here discussing.

IV. THE RELIGIOUS WAY DISTINGUISHED
FROM MORALITY

It has now become possible to state why the distinctive religious quality is not at all to be identified with moral idealism. The religious man might be dominated by his devotion to the unforeseen fullness of value emergent in concrete situations (devotion to the will of God " now known only in part ") and at the same time ignore the call of moral idealism. Then he has the peculiarly religious quality without morality. Of course this is not usually necessary. He may be moral; typically he should be. But moral idealism and this distinctive quality of religious living are by no means identical. The difference between the two can be stated very briefly. Moral idealism is devotion to the highest *ideals* discoverable in the culture of one's time. The peculiar religious way breaks past these limits: it is devotion to the richest values discoverable in *existing* reality. An ideal is some possibility assumed to be so within your own powers of achievement that you strive to bring it into existence. Therefore an ideal is the exact opposite to an existing reality. In moral idealism life is shaped by devotion to the ideal. In peculiarly religious living life is shaped by devotion to the existing fullness of value which carries possibilities, to be sure, but is not itself *a* possibility.

Of course the moral idealist may have this peculiar kind of religion also, just as a politician may also be a father. There is nothing in the diversity of these two to make them exclusive of one another. They need not be separated, but they should be distinguished. It will mean more now to state that a great deal of religious living is nothing but moral idealism. Even when the ideal is held to be an impossibly high ideal of love, it is still moral idealism and not this distinctive and qualitatively different thing found in the uniquely religious.

This difference between moral idealism and the uniquely religious may be made still clearer if we take something more simple than religion and note an analogous distinction there. The devotion of a parent to a child has many aspects similar to religious devotion. A parent may be devoted to the ideal possibilities of his child as he sees them projected in the future of the child, but not to the actual living child except as the latter is raw material out of which to shape his ideals. Such devotion is analogous to moral idealism. On the other hand, it may be the actual child which the parent loves, the ideal possibilities being valued only because they are the tentatively discerned possibilities of this child. It makes a great difference whether one considers the child merely as so much raw material out of which to construct an ideal possibility, or whether he considers the ideal possibilities merely as so many devices by which to elicit the undiscovered best that is in this actual child. In the one case the commitment is to certain parentally conceived ideal possibilities, the actual child being a means to achieve these possibilities. In the second case, the commitment is to the actual growing child, the ideal possibility being a means to serve that child. Two totally different kinds of parenthood, and two totally different kinds of education, issue, according as one makes the first or the second commitment.

Now it is precisely this contrast that holds between peculiar religion and moral idealism. In religion that is distinctively genuine one does not commit himself to all that is in existence. He does not necessarily commit himself to ultimate reality nor to any other kind of existing reality save that one kind which is most worthful. He knows that the fullness of God's goodness far exceeds his specifications of its nature. It is to that fullness and not to his specifications that he commits himself.

Those great prophets who share in this peculiarly religious way have gone so far as to pronounce doom upon human life when it turns too exclusively to moral ideals in disregard of this uncomprehended totality of all that is essential to life, and more particularly to the best life. The prophets, in language very different from ours in this discussion, are always reminding us that every human ideal is abstract. It is abstract because it leaves out an infinite fullness of reality which is necessary to existence, doubly necessary to improved existence. Always there is some undiscovered functioning of an endocrine gland, some chemical reaction, some electric tension, some need of personality, some essential social relation, which the ideal does not take into consideration. This must be so for several reasons. For one thing, the human mind is too limited in its scope and penetration to comprehend all these elements. Second, every ideal is formed from some specific perspective, shaped by the social status and personal peculiarities of the individuals holding the ideal; it is not culturally comprehensive. Third, there is always an unconscious bias shaping the ideal to fit the interests of certain persons and groups and activities to the exclusion of others. For these and other reasons no possible human ideal can take into consideration all the essentials of the good life, not even of that part of it involved in biological survival. This is not to say, we repeat, that the constructing of ideals is worthless or evil. It is only the holding of the ideal as the supreme arbiter of one's course in life which is misleading, destructive, and unreligious.

Now as long as men are weak the insufficiency of their ideals is not serious on any large scale, because they have not the power to shape the world and life according to their ideal and hence in disregard of the ignored essentials of life. But when civilization develops and man's power becomes great, moral idealism without genuine, distinctive religion becomes increasingly deadly. Then men can develop the instrumentalities by which they really make the world fit their ideals to such a degree that the lack in the ideal of the essentials will increasingly bring life to ruin. Even in such elementary matters as diet, this possible denouement can be seen. However, modern science may master the intricacies of diet eventually because it is relatively simple. But the higher men climb into the complexities of human interests as they attempt to shape the world according to their limited and limiting ideals, the further they go from that great fullness of reality which encompasses them as a mothering matrix of life and sustains them in every moment of their lives, but which no human mind can comprehend in all the richness of its being.

Therefore, whenever men attain great power by way of civilization, they begin to destroy themselves. They destroy themselves because of a moral idealism which is not likewise peculiarly religious. It is being said that man's increasing power in civilization makes his conscious dependence on God less needful. Just the opposite is the case. The more civilized and powerful man becomes, the more masterful become his techniques and machines, then the more disastrous are the consequences of moral idealism that does not hold itself constantly subject to the hidden fullness of that encompassing reality which the peculiarly religious person senses. Hence the truth of what the prophets have always cried, in one way or another: Alas, alas, that great city Babylon! That mighty city!

V. THE MARKS OF THE DISTINCTIVELY RELIGIOUS WAY

The folk of the religious way here presented are distinguished by four marks. One is a peculiar kind of decision or self-commitment that is held to be foolish or eccentric by all who do not go this way. The second is the fact that they give supreme devotion to a reality that is unspecific, and hold it to be incomparably more important than all the specific goods and ideals that man cherishes and seeks. Third is their sense of alienation or sin. While they know the intimate presence of this uncomprehended totality of all that is good, they also know that a barrier intervenes between the human consciousness and the riches that are there. Finally, they are dominated by a world-transforming interest, which may take the form of eschatology, or of social reconstruction, or of waiting on God, or of waiting for death, or of seeking mystic experiences which seem to pierce the veil that hides the most precious reality, or some other sort of practice. Perhaps the most sane and wholesome expression of this interest is the striving to transform one's personality on the one hand, and the social order on the other, to the end of making life appreciatively responsive to ever more of that abundance of God which is now inaccessible to human consciousness in specific form because of the distorted predispositions of men. We shall consider in order these four characteristics of the peculiar religious way.

1. The Great Decision. The first feature we have noted about this peculiar way is that it requires a great decision. One cannot enter it until he makes the most fateful and life-transforming commitment. One will make it again and again, but the making of it for the first time, when made in all sincerity with the whole of the self, initiates the peculiar way of living.

This decision is different from all other decisions in one important respect. All secular decisions are choices of the better as over against the worse among specific goods and goals. The religious decision is choice of a total good largely unspecified in content as over against all the values and objectives which are specifically known and cherished. The religious man gives his absolute allegiance to this unspecific good which transcends this world — if by "this world" one means, as one generally does, all the specific satisfactions and ideals known to a man or ever to be known. The great decision is absolute commitment to a reality which is partially veiled by the established order of specific human desire and so transcendent to that order.

2. *The Unspecific Objective.* The peculiar religious way is distinguished, in the second place, by an unspecific objective. Ordinarily human living is dominated by desires for specific things, actual or ideal, and aversions from specific things. But these people of the distinctively religious way are not so dominated. They do experience and appreciate all the specific matters of ordinary life, but none of these are of *primary* concern to them. They are not *dominated* by specific desires and aversions.

Most noble lives are noble because they are dedicated to some highest specific cause of great worth, such as economic justice for the many, or political freedom, or scientific discovery, or the care and improvement of a certain home, and the like. They make all their choices and expend all their energies to the definite end of serving this which they have chosen as the highest good for them to serve. Some social workers, some patriots, some revolutionaries, some great humanitarians have lived like this.

The peculiarly religious way, however, is very different from all this. It is self-commitment to the service and enjoyment of something that is better, greater, richer than any definite thing or objective which can be brought very fully within the scope of our understanding. It is that supreme and total good of God which no man can put inside the boundaries of any particular thing, institution, social program, ideal, or definite objective. It is essentially indefinite so far as our understanding can reach.

The idea of God presented in traditional religion may seem to be very specific. The Deity is heaped with laudatory titles such as "omnipresent," "omnipotent," "perfect in justice, goodness, and truth." But these tell us nothing in terms of the practical and specifiable objectives of human living. When one gives his absolute devotion to God, thus lauded but undefined in terms of practical objectives, he has committed himself to something that is undefined with respect to the specific programs of human endeavor. Therefore, when God is so presented, he represents a goodness that transcends all the specific goods sought and achieved in the natural life of man.

We do not mean to suggest that all people who subscribe to the traditional idea of God, or to any other, necessarily live in the way we here portray. We only mean to say that there is nothing in their idea of God which prevents them from so doing. Even a false idea, if it represents the unspecified total Good may be a great help. Of course we hold that a true idea of God (when and if attainable) is much better than a false one. But whether or not the *idea* of God is used, the peculiarly religious way is self-commitment to the best that can be found in each concrete situation, but with deliberate and insistent refusal to identify this best with any one definite thing or program subject to human control. It is true past gainsaying that one can never know the richness of what is good until he finds it in the concrete, and in the concrete it always overflows the abstract specifications of human thought and active control. There is always more there than one could have calculated. When the idea of God properly guides the peculiarly religious way it always stands for the undefined and unexplored totality of what is best as it emerges sequentially in concrete situations where choices must be made and where, if the choices are to find the greater good, they must be guided by the fullness of the concrete situation and not by human preconceptions and prescriptions of what it ought to be. Thus God (called by another name or denied if you prefer) must always overrule and redirect human purpose and desire if the riches of life are to enter the appreciative awareness of men.

3. Sense of Sin. There is a third characteristic of this religious way which is equally important with the ones we have mentioned. Not only are the riches of life left indefinite prior to their discovery in specific form, while one holds himself always in readiness to respond to them no matter how alien they may be to one's pre-established specific desires and ideals; but one recognizes beforehand that the greater abundance of life is inaccessible as long as the prevailing order of human desire is upheld without change. Thus the religious man has a sense of alienation between the order of life's abundance and the established order of human existence. This must be so if he faces the fact that human desires require constant and progressive redirection in order to find fulfillment in the greater goods to be had. This must be so if he faces the fact that human desires as shaped by a competitive social order are now so directed that they work against one another; hence any attempt to bring them all to fulfillment would produce a chaos of mutual destruction between each and all; therefore they must be reshaped before we even attempt to fulfill them. However, even in a perfect social order there is the further fact that innovations and the creative synthesis of concrete situations which we see going on all the time would require this continuous and radical reordering of human desire. Thus we never escape the fact that God must always be sovereign and man's way must be constantly reshaped to fit God's way.

There are some religious people who quite sincerely feel themselves to be exempt from this demand that their lives be constantly remade to fit the way of God because they think that their specific desires are not alien and hostile to the order of supreme value which fills the world (along with all the evil). They will readily admit that the desires found in hearts of the nonreligious are thus opposed to the ways of greatest good. When they hold this opinion about

their own way of life it is because they overlook the facts we have
just noted. They fail to see that, no matter how devoted one may
be in the peculiarly religious way just described, his specific desires
are inevitably shaped to a greater or less extent by the society in
which he lives. We have no way of learning to want anything in
specific form save in terms of what our society enables us to want,
and this applies to everyone, the peculiarly religious people included. Also the unpredictable richness of every concrete situation
demonstrates the inevitable discrepancy, sometimes even opposition, between what we specifically want as we enter the situation, and the actual fullness of value in that situation over and
above our pre-established wants.

In the peculiarly religious way men realize that specific human
desires are thus maladjusted to the total goodness of God. Hence
they have a sense of sin. That means that they live for the order
of richest value which they know is far more than, different from,
and in many respects opposed to, the prevailing order of human
desire, their own included. This is not merely a state of feeling;
it is a way of acting. It means acting in such a way as to bring
about a transformation of human desire in response to whatever
hint or clue of richer value can be found in concrete situations.
Above all it means to strive to provide the conditions which favor,
and remove the obstructions which hinder, that kind of transformation of human desires and ideals called growth. It means that
one will hold all his desires and ideals subject to discarding or
transformation as soon as he can apprehend more fully the way
of that greater good which is the true master of his living. This
is the true meaning of the fact of sin and the sense of sin. One mistakes the true meaning of this fact and this sense of sin when he
apprehends it in terms of jurisprudence and thinks of it primarily
as that for which we are condemned and punished or associates it
with hell fire. On the contrary, there is a sense in which the fact of
sin is mark of man's glory. The acknowledgment of one's sin in
the sense we have indicated gives a great release. It delivers from
bondage to established interest. It makes one free and able to follow the good wherever it may lead and however alien and hostile

it may be to the specific desires which have dominated one's living up to the point where the greater good was discovered.

It must have become clear now that there is nothing morbid nor self-debasing in the sense of sin. Quite the contrary is the case. The sense of sin arises from the realization that the good which rightfully pertains to man is infinitely greater than, and qualitatively different from, the comparatively mean and little goods which we can get when we satisfy the specific desires which now actuate us. The fact of sin is the obverse side of the fact that man continuously and radically remade is capable of heights and riches which he cannot now even dream of or imagine in specific form. He can know there are such heights and riches, but he cannot form any adequate or comprehensive mental imagery of them. More than that, man can give his highest devotion to God, even while in some degree he is cut off from God by desires and social structures which are hostile and alien to rich values not yet apparent and accessible to human appreciation.

In the peculiarly religious way one struggles with each problematical situation not merely to achieve that kind of success which consists in fulfilling his specific objectives, but he struggles with creative interest also. By creative interest we mean that he will make the practical solution of problems a means by which to try to reconstruct life in such a way that the greater good can break into our experience in the form of the creative synthesis, the emergent order, the unforeseen richness that comes in consequence of growth.

The values to be found in each concrete situation are always in great part unpredictable. They can be known only after the self-conscious organism has responded most freely to all the fullness of it. This, of course, is a matter of degree. No personality can do it to a high degree as long as it is dominated by fears, inhibitions, pride, self-display, rigid habits, specific objectives, fixed attachments, and the interests which dominate the established social order. Every personality must of course have habits, specific objectives and attachments. Indeed these are constituents of personality. But to live for God with the sense that much of God's goodness is inaccessible by reason of sin, means to hold all these habits, specific objectives and attachments, constantly subject to radical and growing reconstruction in order to meet that hidden fullness of good and evil which enters into each concrete situation. It is hidden because it cannot be anticipated in any completeness by any fixed program. It is hidden because it cannot be appreciatively experienced except by radical and continuous transformation of life in response to the newly emergent riches of novel situations. This radical and continuous transformation of life, by which the personality or the group becomes progressively appreciative of the riches found in concrete situations, is growth.

Hence the religious man will work not merely for the fulfillment of specific objectives, but also, and chiefly, he will deliberately yield himself to the process of growth, sometimes called creative synthesis. He will be ready, plastic, sensitive, and responsive to the unforeseen good and the uncomprehended riches, emerging but largely hidden.

It is in this way that one can live for a transcendent totality of good amid the reality of human life. Devotion to the hidden riches of God's goodness, which one knows are shut out from experience by misdirected desire, causes one to struggle against the cramping confinements present in the established psychological and social order. He is therefore more quick than others to catch the gleam which leads on to a way of reconstruction of that order whereby more of the hidden goodness can become apparent, realized in appreciable forms as concrete situations develop, each with its unduplicated and overflowing fullness of better and worse.

To live for God in full realization of the fact that much of God's goodness is inaccessible, is to live with the greatest truth and vitality. One cannot live for God unless he realizes this fact, for otherwise he will identify God with the relatively mean and limited and mutually frustrative desires which characterize the established form of personality and social order.

4. *World Transforming Interest.* The distinctively religious way consists in taking seriously instrumentalism such as that which Dewey upholds but does not carry through to all its logical

implications. This radical instrumentalism demands the use of all the specifics of human experience as instruments to be used in seeking the transformation of them all into something better. It means to treat nothing which we are able to experience in specific form as the end, but to make all things means to an end that cannot as yet assume definite form in our experience because we have not attained it. It requires that we take the totality of all the specific formulations to be found in human living and offer them in devotion to something better. The something better is not a higher ideal; it is the uncomprehended totality of all that is best in the immediate concrete situation where one is now.

Man will never reach the final formulation of this something better. It will always be beyond what his limited experience can attain in specific form. But he can approach it more or less. He can find the path which leads into this unexplored abundance of value and can enter a little way along that path. He can give his heart's devotion to it. He can live for it and die for it, and experience it as a largely hidden glory that blesses and sanctifies. He can face toward it in all situations so that in his living and in his dying the light of it is on his face as a dim dawning, even when the form of it is still beneath the horizon.

We have tried to set forth that underlying fact which all the different philosophies of religion endeavor to interpret. We have tried to get beneath the theories to that actuality of living which the theories are about. If we have succeeded we have before us a way of living which the extreme supernaturalist can fit into his theory and also the extreme naturalist, and all the other philosophies which range between these extremes. Also, if we have succeeded, the task before us is plain. It is to search out the roots and the fruits of this way of living and all its important valid implications. We have traced this way of life from its early beginnings down through history and have seen it take on one set of beliefs and practices and then another. When rightly directed it can be immensely fruitful and beneficent. We shall try to find that direction for it wherein it can be most rewarding to all who follow it.

NOTES

1 This analysis is taken over bodily from Professor Edwin Walker, to whom I am deeply indebted for it.

BIBLIOGRAPHY

The Religious Way, by Gregory Vlastos, is a clear, vivid and compelling statement with special reference to social action. *Religious Living*, by Georgia Harkness, portrays this fact in simple language. Hornell Hart's *Living Religion* sets forth both the method and the character of the religious way of life. *The Structure of Religious Experience* and *Creative Society*, by John Macmurray, describe it in terms of naturalism and modern social movements. *The Social Substance of Religion*, by Gerald Heard, is another naturalistic interpretation of the religious way; so also is B. E. Meland's *Modern Man's Worship*. John Dewey's *A Common Faith* expresses the religious devotion of a great man who has not given much attention to religious thinking. *Living Creatively*, by Kirby Page, combines the author's interpretation with many quotations expressive of this way. *The Issues of Life*, by H. N. Wieman, considers a number of the common problems met in religious living.

10.

THE METHOD OF RELIGIOUS LIVING

THE way of living which we have described is not easily mastered. It requires a rigorous and constant discipline. The method of this discipline has been described in various ways by different people who have lived after this manner. Perhaps no two of these people would describe it in exactly the same way nor practice it alike. The form and practice of it will vary from person to person, and from one stage of man's development to another. But the general principles can be set forth.

Any attempt to analyze a vital procedure into distinct steps makes it appear artificial. In the actual practice of a vital process we do not divide it into separate stages. All parts run together. The activities in breathing or walking or talking can be analyzed and described and in the description must be set forth as so many different units of behavior. That is the only way the understanding can grasp them. But in the actual practice these units flow into a complicated continuity.

These warnings are necessary to forestall a misunderstanding of the following attempt to describe the discipline and method which are used by the people who live in the peculiarly religious way. The author has tried to clarify the method by labeling the different steps, but has not changed the description essentially from that given him by several different people. For purposes of exposition the method can be analyzed into five steps, which may be called propulsion, crisis, decision, release, and specification.

It must be emphasized that the method we are now presenting is not something peculiar to the author. What he says here is based upon the testimony of people who have lived in this way, have practiced this method, and have found thereby a great deliverance and fulfillment. The author himself tries to live this way and use this method. But he is describing something that belongs to a tradition, a fellowship, and a way of life that have come down through history. Also, it is necessary to realize that people often carry on some vital function and yet are not able to recognize it when it is presented to them in the verbal descriptions of another. People may be living in the way we shall describe and may be practicing the method we are about to present, and yet repudiate what we say because our words do not suggest to them the thing they are doing. In many cases people have no words to describe what they are doing and therefore no verbal statement of another would sound like a description of what they are experiencing. This is true not only of the way of living we have before us but of any vital function such as friendship and love, or the biological functions of eating, breathing, and the like. When people practice these things in unverbalized behavior, *any* verbalization of the matter will seem strange and unnatural to them. But that is a common problem we have to face, not only in stating the method of religious living but in describing any manifestation of life.

Nevertheless, difficult and unnatural though it be, verbalization is necessary if intelligence is to intervene. So we undertake the difficult task of describing the method.

I. STEPS IN RELIGIOUS LIVING

1. Propulsion. Admit that you want more abundant life and want it more deeply than anything else in the world. Allow this hidden and shackled propulsion of your nature to rise to consciousness. This deepest desire is in every man but it is choked and obscured by the clamant insistence of special fears and desires for specific goods. Beneath all these strivings to avoid this and achieve that is the ultimate desire for a satisfying life which is always more than any additive sum of these particular desires and aversions. All men need to give heed to this basic hunger in human nature. The first step in moving toward the peculiar religious way of living is to hearken to this demand that arises from deep within. One must let it speak forth in consciousness until it becomes a shaping imperative and a coercive propulsion.

This striving for the total best that life can yield before we know specifically what it may be, is a propulsion that is native to human nature. After early childhood is past it is suppressed or perverted in great numbers of people, perhaps in the great majority, so that it is not a common thing for men to be dominated by this desire. Each person grows up in a socially established order of life which prescribes certain things to seek and certain other things to avoid. We early take on these specifications and live according to them. Thus the hunger for a satisfying life is lost in the midst of these many preoccupations. A richly satisfying life is always more than simply seeking this and avoiding that because the established order so decrees. But to rebel against these specifications of the social order is worse still in most cases. The great hunger is satisfied neither by rebellion nor by conformity nor by fluctuating between the two, but by seeking and finding something more beyond.

This hunger is native to man, however hidden and distorted in the majority, because the human physiological organism is unspecialized with respect to its functional activities. Man is not predetermined by physiological structure to seek and find satisfaction in any particular kind of goods and goals. He is not required by his nature to eat any one kind of food, to live in any one kind of shelter, to associate with his kind in any single specific way, to travel one way rather than another, to find enjoyment in one sort of experience to the exclusion of many others. Thus his physiological organism, plus his free imagination and multiform sensitivity, have destined him for an unconfined totality of goods. All these, since they cannot be known in their specific nature prior to their discovery, merge into a total objective undefined in respect to its detailed content. The striving after this total good, to be found in specific forms of value in concrete situations one after another, but not known in respect to its content until these experiences are attained one after another, is the great hunger of which we speak. It is the libido of life. Freud calls it sexuality, Adler the will to power, Bergson the *élan* of life, and many others reduce it to the basic appetites of the organism. But obviously these are merely attempts to give some specific characterization to a propulsion which cannot be confined to any single sort of satisfaction, but reaches out after this sort of good or that, according to social conditioning, and therefore is not inevitably predestined to any one specific kind of good. So far as native endowment of man is concerned, this propulsion might be released to seek all the innumerable and unexplored satisfactions that can be harmonized with one another in meaningful and mutually supporting ways.

This then is the propulsion, the basic drive, the great hunger that should be acknowledged by the individual, confessed, and delivered from hidden suppression and allowed to take possession of his living.

2. *Crisis.* Recognize your own deficiency and your incompleteness. With the voice sounding in your ears of this deep demand for a richer and better life, keep probing into the facts of your past and present living until you see that you have failed to meet the requirements of this better way. Your life has been a series of defeats relative to this greatest need of human living. You have spent your time and energy seeking to satisfy certain ambitions, rivalries, appetites, angers, fears, which blinded you to the greater good that was to be had there in the commonplace and everyday situations of life in dealing with people and things. Your energies have been diverted into strivings that were not worth-while when so much of unexplored value lay waiting to be appropriated and responsively apprehended. So this second step consists in confessing that your life has been unsatisfactory, not consciously felt to be so by yourself perhaps, but unsatisfactory in the light of your deepest need. Look at yourself until you see that you are confused, at cross-purposes, cheating yourself, disappointed, frustrated. Tear away all the masks, all the rationalizations, all the sentimental make-believes.

The sense of defeat, disappointment, frustration, conflict, and misery within your life as it has been lived, may not come with full realization until some disaster serves to force it upon consciousness. Pride, self-deceit, the desire to think well of one's self and one's attainments, will keep it hidden often, until suffering brings it into the light of recognition. But with enough fearless honesty with oneself one may reach the crisis without so much external pressure of suffering.

This crisis is like a great divide from which one is able to look down to the right and to the left upon the two alternative ways of living. From the top of this ridge that divides the continent of life into two watersheds that reach to the horizon, one is in a position to make a choice between the two possible ways of living. On the one side is the life that is lived for particular goods and definable objectives. It is the life which our civilization compels us to live unless we wrench ourselves free from it. On the other side is the life that is lived for goods and objectives which reach beyond the scope of the known and definable values. It is life that is freed from the coercive control of bias and from fixated desire, and become plastic material for the growing of unlimited connections of value. It is life become an adventurous outreach after the unattained, the unfulfilled, the uncomprehended, the on beyond, but in which all the riches of the present are deeply appreciated.

When one has reached the point where he can see clearly this supreme choice, these ultimate alternatives, this final most fateful decision which life affords, he has reached what is called the crisis.

3. *Decision.* Having reached the crisis, one must decide one way or the other and the decision must be absolute, complete, and final. It must be sincere with an absolute sincerity. One must decide to commit his whole self to the whole of what is good, the greater part of which is unknown in its specific nature. One predetermines that in every situation throughout all the future one shall always seek the best, knowing that the best in every situation inevitably overflows the narrow prescriptions of abstract ideals and specific desires with which one enters the situation. He decides to live thereafter unto the death not for his own chosen goods but for that greater good that is to be discovered in actual situations and so cannot be foreknown and forechosen.

Once the new way of living has been started by this decision, there must be constant renewal and reaffirmation of the dedication, daily if not oftener, to keep the attitude sufficiently whole and pure to permit its functional expression. This decision does not necessarily involve an intense emotional experience. It is not necessarily aesthetic nor delightful in any way, although it may be so. But the essential thing is not the emotional or other quality of conscious experience. The essential thing is the redirection of the movement of the total self *from the pursuit of specifically chosen goods and goals to the pursuit of those goods which are unknown until they are brought to light in the creative richness of concrete situations.* In religious phraseology, this means to be seeking always God's will and not one's own. One gives up specific self-direction as at present established and commits himself to the direction of the best that is unpredictably brought forth in the ceaseless innovations and creative syntheses of actual living.

He will have ideals, he will have objectives and guiding principles, but they will be developed as tools, feelers, outreachings, tentative projects to facilitate the way to the greater good. They will not be the ultimate guides and goals of life. The controlling rulership over one's life will be the whole of what is best as it may be brought to light piece by piece, presenting one character in one situation and another character in the next, but never fully realized in any situation because the present always leads on to the next. This is the decision which one must make with his whole self and constantly reaffirm in order to live in the peculiarly religious way. For many people this reaffirmed commitment to the " will of God " takes the form of prayer. It is necessary to state, however, that much that is called prayer is not genuinely such.

4. Release. In order to fulfill this decision one must be released from the control of all other interests and loyalties save that highest one to which he has dedicated his living. He will continue to have many specific interests and desires, and the more complete his decision has become the more rich and numerous these will be. But he will not be bound down by any fixed set or order of them. He will be free to give up any of them or all of them, in order to take new and better ones at the command of the best that appears in the new situation.

But this release is not an easy matter. To attain it progressively (although perhaps never perfectly) one must search out the hiding places in the underbrush of his self-organization where lurk those interests that turn him away from, or hold him down from, the dictates of his highest loyalty. These recalcitrant desires and habits are hidden deep in his personality. They operate in him both consciously and unconsciously. He must bring them to light, one by one, just as far as is possible, and resolve in case of each one that it shall not direct his choices or shape his striving. In respect to each one, and in respect to all of them, he will resolve that the sole determining interest in making any choice will be the unlimited growth of connections of value. His guiding concern in every concrete situation will be not any specific desire, fear, or objective, but only the unexplored and undefined fullness of good.

After he has searched as deeply into his own personality as he can, and cut every bond that holds him, he will recognize that he still has many interests, prejudices, desires that are hidden because they are so deeply imbedded in the subconscious organization of his personality. The power that these may exercise over his mind he will counteract so far as possible by being forever on the alert to catch the first sign of their defecting bias upon his decisions and strivings.

This fourth step in the discipline of the religious way may be summarized by saying that it consists in letting go of all fixated specific interests as sources of control in order to be guided solely by the unknown higher good the moment any part of it becomes known. In case of every particular value — be it the esteem of his associates, success in his chosen kind of work, money to meet the needs of his family or himself, be it his own biological existence or that of any other, be it friendship, social standing, or any other good — he will be free to take it and equally free to leave it, according as the unlimited growth of value in this world may require. Thus will he seek release from the control of all specific interests so that exploratory imagination, experimental endeavor, and observation of all data may be shaped entirely by the one supreme interest in discovering progressively the emerging order of the unlimited good.

5. Specification. Finally we come to the step in this total method of religious living which is most practically effective. Here is where all that has gone before becomes implemented for constructive action. We have called it specification; it might be called the emergence of new ideals.

This fifth step consists in working out new procedures which are fitted to this new way of living so that one gets firm hold on actual situations in such a way as to transform them in the direction of the undefined totality of good which one is now serving. What specifically should I do, get, learn, remove, in order that my relations with this person with whom I have continued association may be progressively enriching? What new habits should I form, what materials should I secure, what new skills acquire, in order that my daily work with this group or in this office with these duties may bring to light all the fullness of value that is potentially there?

Here is where we find the real test of the sincerity of the four previous steps. Without this fifth step the previous ones may be actually dangerous and harmful because they may give a pleasant inner feeling of comfort, peace, and joy by reason of enhanced self-satisfaction, but leave the world practically the same as it was before. One may actually enjoy the pain of ferreting out the evils in his life, and the deeper the pain the greater the enjoyment, when the pain is unconsciously taken to be an expiation for all his evil-doing, or as evidence of his righteousness displayed in committing himself so nobly to so great a good.

When one comes to this fifth step one must do very practical and definite things. He must change certain arrangements of his living which may have become very comfortable and satisfying. However, he must change them not because it is difficult to do so and he can thus demonstrate to himself how grandly his life has been transformed. He must change them only when, and in the manner, required for bringing to conscious appreciation and devoted service more of the precious goods to be found in the world with which he daily deals. He must discover and put into practice whatever new specific objectives, habits of feeling and acting, norms, codes, rituals, organization of materials, and programs are required to elicit the fullest responsiveness of value between himself and the persons and things around him. Up to this point the method has consisted of a very generalized reshaping within himself, but now he begins to organize his will into specific forms which have as their end the developing of attitudes and the carrying out of undertakings which diverge or are quite antithetic to the established organization of interests of the-self-before-decision.

We have already made it abundantly plain that none of these new formulations, arrangements, and undertakings can be absolute or final. They must all be tentative, subject to the greatest worths as progressively discovered. The self must be wrenched out of its old grooves, but one cannot live with any effective power of action without patterns of some sort — that is, specific plans, purposes, habits, attitudes, adapted to specific situations. The difference is that these new " patterns " are not grooves at all, but paths which are followed experimentally just so long as they seem to lead in the direction of the maximum richness of life unpredictably unfolding.

The old self may have been well integrated and hence very satisfying so long as the great hunger could be kept latent and ineffective. The difference between the old self and the new is that the latter is progressively integrated on ever higher levels toward the unfolding apprehension of the fullness of all that is good. This is the highest practical discipline. It is the enlistment of the self and all that it commands in specific forms of service and appreciation of the *whole* of the best just as fast and as fully as this emerges into the situations wherein one is living. This should be so marked that the individual is aware of digression from previously established goods. Through this final step of progressive specification for the conduct of life the self-commitment achieved in the first four steps is validated and completed.

II. THE FUNCTION OF FELLOWSHIP

No man can live this religious life alone. He must have the fellowship of others who are trying to live in this way. This is so because the human personality above all things is a social entity.

It is created by association and shaped by association. Interchange of thought and feeling with other persons is the very breath of life of personality. As the organism must breathe to live, so the human personality must communicate to live.

The most potent group in which to foster the distinctively religious way of living is small in number. It should range from two or three or four up to twelve or fifteen, although the last number is too large except in rare cases. Jesus Christ chose twelve and that seems to have been too many by one. The number must be few enough to permit personalities to interact freely and know one another deeply, at least in respect to the nature of their ruling loyalty. One of the purposes of such a fellowship is to make inhibitions to dissolve away, the dark areas of personality to be illuminated, and the individuals to become translucent to one another.

Small groups of individuals who interact in this way and who live under the domination of a culture-transcending devotion such as we have been describing, constitute the church as a source of life and a saving power. The church in this sense, however, must be distinguished from the local congregation on the one hand, and on the other from the basic social institution which spans the continents and the centuries. What almost everyone thinks of when he speaks of the church is either the local congregation or the social institution. These two meanings are certainly legitimate and are the common ones. We only wish to say that neither the congregation nor the institution constitutes the source of life or the saving power of the church. Both the former involve many activities, persons, officials, real estate and other property, which have nothing directly to do with the sort of fellowship we here have in mind. On the other hand, however, we do not discount for a moment the importance of the local congregation and the great institution. The small groups of saving and life-giving fellowship are too unformed and structureless to survive with any regularity and stability without the protecting and nourishing social structure of the local congregation and the social institution. These latter, when fulfilling their rightful function, sustain and carry the life-giving fellowships. They are places where individuals who try to live in the distinctively religious way may find one another, where conditions and materials are provided which such fellowships may require in order to grow up and flourish. They are places, or should be places, where experiments are being constantly conducted to devise symbols, practices, arrangements suited to the ever changing conditions of life and thought, so that what was suited to the life-giving fellowship in one age will not be outmoded in another.

But after we have seen the service and the importance of the local congregation and the basic social institution, we must sharply distinguish between them and the life-giving fellowship. At best they are the structures, the shells, the mechanisms, which carry the fellowships. The fellowships may be found within them but are not identical with them. Also, it must be noted that many of the deepest and most vital of these fellowships which constitute the true church as a life-giving power may exist without any recognized or official connection with either the local congregation or the social institution. Many a home, many a school, many a business partnership, which would never think of calling itself a church, may have in it certain groups who live together in this way and are truly the church of Christ in the sense that they would not be living together in that way if they had not inherited the traditions that have come down from Jesus and his disciples. This is so even when the individuals concerned have no consciousness of being heirs of this tradition or of owing to the tradition the fact that they have the kind of fellowship they do have.

Our civilization is one in which people, as a usual thing, do not know one another beyond superficial levels. Consequently we are constrained, concealed, unconfessed, at best suave and smooth and efficient, with an oily ease in getting about and dealing with people. But the depths of personality are never exposed. Human personality cannot grow and flower in such dark crypts of social concealment. It must have the sunshine and rain of understanding and sympathy. Psychic madness, social revolution, and international conflict rise higher and higher as long as this personal isolation continues with its competitive attitude toward all comers.

In forming a fellowship to save personality from these evils the individuals should be selected with great care. A single wrong choice will ruin it. If it is found that there is some one who cannot interact fittingly, the group should disband and another be formed at some later time. Individuals selected should be ready to practice the method we have described. This exclusiveness is not selfish, for the main purpose of such a group is to release power to transform personalities and change the social order in the interests of greater community among all.

It is important to note that such groups often arise spontaneously. Many people are already members of such a group without knowing it. Such fellowships grow up like wild native plants. All we need do is to learn the disciplines required for fostering their growth that they may be more luxuriant and productive. However, we may be reaching a stage in our civilization where they must be consciously fostered, else they will not grow.

Members of the group should strive for most complete openness toward one another in relation to what is most important in their lives and in relation to the difficulties in their respective personalities which interfere with their ruling devotions. They should work out together a body of convictions they can share concerning what is most worthful. Deep communion and most complete openness between the members will make for spontaneity and freedom in dealing with all personalities and situations and provide for richer growth of all the connections of value.

Occasionally each member of a group should seek out among the members some friend whose love and ruthless honesty and insight he can trust. He should expose himself to the criticism of that other, for only the penetrating gaze of such a friend who shares devotion in this peculiar way of life can reveal to one the defects and obstacles which interfere with growth. However, not all persons are equipped to pass judgment upon another in this way, even when they are most sincere and loving. They do not know enough about life and personality. Hence there should be some criteria by which to determine who is able to render this service and who is not. On the other hand, it should be noted that even a mistaken judgment about oneself made in all sincerity by another may be very illuminating if one can take it objectively and discover the error in it. The discovering of the error in the judgment about oneself made by another, will often reveal truth about oneself that could not otherwise be detected.

The group should worship together, although the practice may not go by that name and should assume the form best fitted to their needs. It may be Quaker silence, or singing together, or reading together great prose or poetry or biography. Such practice helps to illumine the direction and meaning of their lives, unite them in their controlling loyalty, purge them of inhibitions, fixations, conflicts, and disturbing attachments. It widens their horizons, purifies their motives, quickens their devotion.

Such a group as we have described is a source of spiritual power. It is out of such power-groups that all the great world-transforming religious movements have arisen. The early Christian groups, the Franciscan and Jesuit groups, the early Quaker and Methodist groups, are examples.

Mass revivals are possible only when great numbers of people share in common the convictions and sentiments of an old and well established religion. But when these convictions and sentiments are in transition and many people contiguous to one another do not share them in common, such revivals as means of genuine spiritual transformation are impossible. Something like a revival may be forced by high-pressure salesmanship and skillful propaganda on the part of professional revivalists. But they are superficial and do not really transform either the personalities involved or the social order.

In a time like ours the only way that a new and transforming religious movement can be started is through creative fellowships such as we have tried to describe. He who lives in the peculiarly religious way must have the support of such a group. The devitalizing, competitive, atomistic social order is all around him.

It will suffocate or crush or desiccate the devoted life within him unless he has the support and nourishment of such a cell of spiritual renewal and power.

III. RESULTS OF RELIGIOUS LIVING

If one fulfills the conditions for abundant life, then such life will come — or else the method stated is not true. One will have to be very careful, however, not to call the method untrue in order to protect himself from admitting his own insincerity. He alone can know whether or not he was sincere. If one has reserved from the experimental commitment any known area, he has fallen short of complete sincerity. This sincerity is the most important requirement for getting results in any religious experiment. This method must deal with the totality of a person or not deal with him at all.

It must also be said that the descriptions of the specific results or outcomes of this process are never exactly the same for two persons, and so it would be futile for one who is experimenting with this way to seek to repeat in his experience some specific reactions which another had described. One of the things one must let go in his commitment is the desire for any particular kind of result, save that it shall be life-giving.

But some of the results are here noted: There develops more freedom from inner conflicts, tensions and inhibitions. This is a matter of degree and must be correlated with other things, such as the likelihood of more sensitivity which tends to make for conflict and tension, and past conditionings which may cause one person to have far more inhibitions and conflicts to overcome than another. Generally there result far greater sensitivity to the values in concrete situations, far more readiness and spontaneity of response, and increased insight into the problems of personality and of social relations. Further, one is better able to find his way through difficulties or to overcome them. Affections grow more deep and rich at the same time that power is increased. There is increase in creativity, both as to quality and quantity, which is more likely to be constructive in the social life of the time.

IV. SUPERNATURALISTIC AND HUMANISTIC INTERPRETATION

The fact of religious living which we have been describing is what most of the philosophies of religion are trying to interpret. They differ very widely in what they say about it. Their chief point of difference is in their views of that "something on beyond" which actuates the religious man. Some say this reality is entirely outside all existing things, being the creator of all that exists. They who say this are of two kinds, the traditional supernaturalists and the new supernaturalists. The former say that the human reason can know something about this creator. The latter say that human reason cannot reach that far or that deep because it falls into self-contradiction whenever it tries. We believe the latter view is more tenable if one is going to take the supernaturalist position at all, for it is obviously a self-contradiction to speak of a creator of all that exists, since it would seem that a creator would himself have to exist before he could create. But that means he could not create all that exists since he could not create his own existence.

Perhaps the humanists may find our statement of the religious way most difficult to accept, for they deny that there is something beyond. And yet we believe an examination of their propositions will reveal that they are by implication talking about this very thing, whether they admit it or not. One of their main propositions discloses the fact that they refuse to accept any ideal as absolute or final: all ideals are instruments, they say. But instrumental to what? To the good life. This sounds familiar, and so does this next proposition: they refuse to specify in any final and complete form what the good life is; they are constantly insisting that any attempt to do such a thing is a gross error. All of which proves that they are serving a supreme good which they cannot specify nor put into any final program. We do not agree with many major points in their philosophy. But we believe the fact of religious living now under consideration is the very fact which they are trying to interpret, even as are the supernaturalistic philosophies of religion.

V. NATURALISM AND THE TRANSCENDENT GOOD

Many will ask how the new naturalism can uphold the transcendental reference of unique religious living. How can a naturalist say there is anything in nature of supreme worth which is inaccessible to conscious experience except in fragmentary and imperfect bits? He can say it if he knows a general principle which demonstrates such a reality to have being. Such a principle comes to light when we study the way in which the mind knows its world.

The human mind is able to experience consciously only that which commands the attentive consciousness. What commands the attentive consciousness is determined by interests which are physiologically and socially shaped. Not only does the mind select the data of experience according to these interests from all the infinite wealth of stimuli which pour over the psycho-physical organism, but it also interprets and organizes these data under the control of these interests. Therefore the world we know is a human construct, made out of the few data and limited meaning which are the only data and meanings permitted to us by the interests which happen to dominate the minds of men at the present time.

This fact about " our world " is demonstrated by the " sociology of knowledge " developed by Karl Mannheim.[1] He shows that every mind sees the world in that perspective which is given it by the social group that creates the individual's mentality and shapes it through the years. The Prussian conservative is blind to rich areas of experience which a proletarian communist most vividly apprehends. Also the reverse is true. That does not mean that what is experienced and interpreted in one perspective is always true. Rather it means that the kinds of truth, the kinds of error, the kinds of problems, and the findings which emerge out of the solution of problems, are very different for the members of the different groups.

The conclusion is obvious. If we live in a society with customs, institutions, regulations shaped by the interests of fear, greed, resentment, competition, our minds will have the perspective of such a society. We shall be able to detect only those data and achieve only those interpretations of the data which our interests will permit. Our interests will be largely those of fear, greed, resentment, and competition with others. Hence the world we know will be the kind of world which such interests permit us to experience. These interests shape the mentality of everyone, even of "the saints," if such a distinction is possible. This is not due to any essential evil in the individual saint but to the fact that his mind is inevitably shaped by the society in which he lives. They who live in the peculiarly religious way have this mentality as truly as any other and live in the sort of world that results. The only marked difference between them and others is that they know there is the other kind of reality which is here all about us, waiting to be perceived and interpreted when the social and psychological order of our minds is appropriately transformed. Not only do they know it; mere knowledge does not make so much difference; others may have the knowledge. But the distinctive feature about the uniquely religious is that they give their supreme devotion to this other reality even when it is hidden from them by the order of life which holds them in its grip.

There are other ways of demonstrating that we are folded in the encompassing presence of great beauty and love which cannot enter the experience of immediate consciousness in the specific character of its nature. For one thing there is the artist of one sort or another who is especially gifted to discern certain forms of entrancing beauty in quarters where we are unable to experience it. We do not mean that any artist experiences all the beauty, nor even an intimation of other kinds of beauty besides those for which he is especially gifted; but what he is able to appreciate, what many do not even see, is enough to give us the evidence we require.

Then there are those people who are especially gifted in the ways of love. They find a great love wherever they go. Love and devotion follow after them. They elicit that kind of response. It is true that they may elicit hate also. But we are not denying that the existence of evil may be as much greater than what we immediately discern, as is the magnitude of good in excess of our comprehension. The point is that there are persons like St. Francis and Gandhi and others who leave behind them trailing clouds of loving devotion as they move about the world, revealing the fact, ordinarily hidden, that this world does constantly contain the raw materials for a love that surpasses the bounds of our imagination.

Still again, we all perhaps have moments when our sensitivities and interests are so awakened and directed that we live in a transfigured world, revealing what is here to be experienced if our minds were rightly ordered.

Finally, physics tells us that the world is not made of little lumps of " matter," but of radiant energy or waves. Of all these waves which the mind might catch and experience in the form of beauty and love, we catch only an infinitesimal bit, and even these we do not discern in such *Gestalten* as to reveal the infinite riches that might flood human life if it were socially and psychologically ordered in a way fitted to such experience. If we were biologically developed and disciplined to meet the requirements of such experience, if physical conditions were shaped as modern science might shape them, and if all our powers were directed by the vision of God which haunts the distinctively religious way, the scales would fall from our eyes and the sheath from our hearts, and the goodness of God would stand forth. Such is the naturalistic interpretation of the transcendental religious reference.

This point of view which sees God in nature and yet as indiscernible until man has earned the right to discover him progressively, is what we mean by theistic naturalism. But the " other," now unappreciated, world is just as natural as the present world, says this philosophy. It is just as natural in the sense that it is a world arising out of interaction between the organism and its environment. It may be known by the same cognitive powers by which we know this familiar world, experienced by the same organs of sense and by the total reactions of the organism. But while we must explore this other world with the same organic reactions used to explore our familiar world, the patterns of physiological reaction must be different; the forms of conscious experience must be different; the order in which data are apprehended, and the kind of data selected by consciousness, must be different; the interpretative formulas of the mind must be different. Because of all this we ourselves would be progressively transformed. We would develop different sensitivities and predispositions. This means that we would transform "our world." So it would be a world radically different from the world we now experience.

Thus the theistic naturalist, along with other interpreters of religion, says that the first distinguishing characteristic of distinctively religious living is decision, or self-commitment to a reality which is quite outside this world, even though man must live in this world, use its instrumentalities, seek its goods, and avoid its ills. This he must do, but in the religious way the controlling loyalty of his life must be to the transcendental Good. Consequently the religious decision or commitment is different from every other. All other decisions concern matters in this world. The religious decision is one which refuses to accept anything in this as worthy of supreme devotion, and chooses instead a reality which transcends this world. The other world for which the religious person lives as over against this world, and to which he gives his absolute allegiance, is a world which he cannot experience except in fragments and intimations, life being organized as it is. But it is a world which man could experience if his life were transformed. For that world of the transformed life, the religious man lives. Since men's desires and the objects of their attentive consciousness have not been transformed, their eyes are holden. They must love as not seeing, and commit themselves without any clarity or fullness of vision. But with the right attitude they can catch glimpses and portions of the richness of this better world in concrete situations with which they deal.

The deepest hunger of human nature, and its greatest need, is for that most abundant living which is found in God. But the specific goods on which men seize to satisfy this hunger and this need are alien to God. Also the methods they use are not akin to the ways of God. Hence they are blind and alien to God until they have made the absolute commitment of faith.

Let us summarize the interpretation of theistic naturalism. "This world" is what we are able to experience. What we are able to experience is limited to what our attentive consciousness can discern and interpret. What attentive consciousness can discern and interpret is determined by the ruling interests of the psycho-physical organism. Any "other world" would be those forms and qualities, meanings and possibilities, which man would be able to experience if his psycho-physical organism were dominated by radically different interests, say the interests of love. The interest of love would need to reach far deeper than consciousness. It would need to be a propulsion which shaped the selections and interpretations of the mind and caused men to strive after maximum community of the most diversified goods. Such a change in the controlling interests of human personality could not occur without a concomitant transformation of the social order. The method which must be practiced by the individual in taking the first steps into that gloriously better world of God's goodness we have tried to describe under the heads of propulsion, crisis, decision, release, and specification.

VI. TRANSFORMING DEATH INTO LIFE

Distinctively religious living faces all the facts. It does not avert its gaze from any nor try to slip by with hand before the eyes. Therefore all the great religions have faced the fact of death and held some interpretative view of it.

The problem of death for religious living belongs to the field of theory rather than fact, because it is not the occurrence of death to the individual which distinguishes the religious way of living but rather the view of death which the individual holds. Therefore no philosophy of life or religion is complete until it sets forth some view of death. All the important facts have not been taken into consideration until it has dealt with this fact which tends to overshadow life.

It is worth while to glance for a moment at the positions of various current philosophies of religion in regard to the fact of death. It is a weakness of liberalism to cling rather desperately but weakly to a belief in immortality, meaning the unending existence of the individual after death. It is a strength of traditional supernaturalism to hold clear and definite convictions upon the subject, and not to hurry over the problem as the liberals do because it is difficult.

Theistic naturalism limits its position to findings that can be verified. It finds no empirical evidence concerning what happens after death save what is known concerning the decomposition of the body. If there is some kind of immaterial entity which continues to exist after the body passes away, we have no observational data to that effect. Indeed observational data concerning an immaterial entity would be a contradiction in terms, since all observation requires some material impact upon the organism. Since naturalism requires observational evidence of some kind for all its beliefs, it cannot claim to know there is any continued existence of the soul after death. On the other hand, it is very sure there is much it does not know and it is very sure that God exists. More it cannot say. How, then, can it seek valiantly the abundant life, not reassured that there is any continuance beyond this earthly existence?

Naturalism, and certain other philosophies also, hold that one can make even his death and his failure promote the cause which he serves. He who succeeds by completing an achievement before his death can give to others his achievement and the inspiration of it. Equally he who dies and gives his life in devotion to a cause which is not complete at his death, gives to men a project which his devotion may lead them to carry on as they would not otherwise do. Socrates did not succeed in clarifying the concepts which he sought to define by discussion, and died in devotion to his cause. But this devotion and this death of Socrates were one influence which caused Plato and many a later philosopher to carry on the work which Socrates started. The same can be said of Jesus, and also of many an obscure man in relation to the people who knew him. Thus death, by acquiring creative potency for the cause one serves, is itself made a servant of that cause and so is transformed from a foe to a helper. This is one way of achieving some conquest over death. This thought is expressed in lines written by an unknown author and preserved for us in the Greek Anthology.

> A shipwrecked sailor, on this bleak coast,
>   Bids you set sail.
> Full many a gallant ship, when we went down,
>   Weathered the gale.

The growth of culture, then, is one great way by which the values achieved and enjoyed by individuals are conserved and accumulated. Not all the values are conserved. Not all that are worth conserving are preserved. But some are. And succeeding generations and individuals may add to the riches of this accumulating body of shared experience and precious value whereby the living, the dead, and the unborn are united in one community of interacting and mutually enhancing individuals and generations. Thus death is conquered in some measure. Each individual lives, enters into the great community, shares deeply in the accumulated wealth of value, makes his contribution, and passes out, while the great community goes on.

It is true that no such community, no such culture, goes on forever. But the great community may thus conquer the futility and fear and the limitation of the death of the individual. Its own death it cannot conquer. But here the community of communities may conquer the death of the one community, even as the latter conquers the death of the individual. After a people and a culture have perished and left no heirs, and all their works have faded from the memory of mankind, they may still be recovered and made to live again. Old cultures may be revived and become an enrichment and a quickening of life to others, and thus live on. This is what historians, anthropologists, and archaeologists are causing to happen all the time. How much of the dead past may be thus recovered and made to live in the ongoing present by the increasing technique of research, by the increasing amount of leisure from economic production, by the developing powers of appreciation and sensitive insight, and by catholicity of understanding, we do not know. But we shall doubtless go far along this line.

At the end stands the " heat death " of the universe when all life shall disappear. That at any rate cannot be conquered, so some say. Whether it will ever come no one knows with certainty. Whether it can be conquered if it threatens no one knows. But suppose it does come. Still the great historic planetary community of men will have conquered death with God up to that point. If then the end must come, so it must. But still the eternal order of value in God will have been actualized on this planet to whatever maximum degree may be. It will be a fact that on this planet God took on existence to this degree. It will still be a fact that the episode on this tiny granule in the universe was an actualization of precious value. It was superbly worth all it cost, tender and beautiful and tragic as it was. Furthermore, it was the actualization of eternal value in the sense that the order of value then actualized, forever waits in the form of possibility to be actualized again or to be more fully actualized. Also, it must be remembered, the actualization does not depend upon men. It depends upon God, men being only one small part of the great undertaking.

There are other ways to eternal life and the conquest of death than that of immortality. *Immortality* means unending existence of the individual after death; it is quantitative. *Eternal life* is qualitative. Eternal life is a certain kind of life which may be lived here. Eternal life is life that participates in what is eternal. It is life that is centered in, devoted to, lived for the eternal. It is life that experiences and appreciates the eternal. Whosoever experiences, appreciates, and loves supremely the eternal, partakes of eternal life.

But what is the eternal? The eternal is that order of value which is God. Its status in existence is always changing. As a form of existence in this world it may grow. But as order, structure, principle, whether in existence or not, it is eternal and changeless. When out of existence it is the possibility of existence. When in existence it is possibility actualized. It is never entirely out of existence, so far as we know, and it is never completely actualized.

But it is more or less actualized, more or less a possibility. When viewed in disregard of its status in existence it is eternal.

Eternal life, furthermore, is life devoted to actualizing this eternal order of value. One may have moments when he is conscious of having united with God in actualizing some bit of this eternal order of value. For a moment one is aware of the eternal incarnate in existence. The eternal essence and structure of God's own value dipped into existence with causal potency.

But perhaps the simplest way to conquer death is to take it as a completion and ending. This is possible only if one has attained ripe maturity. Hence a part of conquering death in this way is the task of providing such hygienic conditions and such prevention of accident that more and more people can attain the fullness of age. When one has reached such fulfillment he should be able to say: I have had my fill of life. I have drunk deeply of the bitter and the sweet. I have lived with zest, but now I have had enough. I wish to bring it to an end.

> I warmed both hands before the fire of life;
> It sinks, and I am ready to depart.

Again it has been said:

> Glad did I live and gladly die,
> And I lay me down with a will.

Not a few old people can say this with sincerity.

We have shown several ways in which death is mastered by life and made to serve life. But the greatest transformation of death into life is achieved in the distinctively religious way. With the vision of God as growth, and absolute commitment to God so discerned as the religious way, one can welcome death as the only means of rearing an order of life that is cumulatively enriched by the contribution of successive generations and an almost infinite variety of personalities. Without death this could not be. If every man lived on forever, the number that could inhabit this planet would be very few compared to all those who can come upon the scene and pass off in sequence. In this latter way alone can the riches of diverse contributions mount up toward infinity.

Also without death the progressive reconstruction of the order of life would be hindered so greatly that stagnation would almost certainly settle down over the whole planet for ages on end. Only by breaking the continuity with deaths, enabling each generation to start afresh and anew, does it seem possible to throw off the cramping, deadening routine of habit, custom, status, prestige, and established order.

Thus one might welcome death as the doorway into freedom and hope and progressive enrichment of life for the individual as well as for the race. It is so for the individual because he has been thereby dowered by a rich heritage from the past he would not otherwise have had. Also he has a future before him to which he can contribute, a future where can occur unlimited growth by creative synthesis, which could not be if each individual on this planet continued to live here forever and thus imposed the stagnation of the unbroken continuity of a single generation. Certainly there is nothing sure about the future. Growth might not ensue, but the gates of possibility are open as they could not be if death did not occur. Death breaks the iron bonds that would otherwise hold the race in a prison of routine and fixation. That danger constantly threatens all life as it is. Without death it would clamp down inevitably.

Since God (or the work of God) is unlimited growth of meaning and value, and since such growth could not occur without the death of the individual and a sequence of generations, we must say that death is one of the doorways by which God enters into human life and history. The infinite goodness of God can break into human life more and more through the opening made by death. This breach in the walls of stereotyped habit and convention makes way for progressive creative synthesis of the works of successive generations.

If what we have said is true, it shows how death opens the way to the unlimited enrichment of life. Death becomes the great deliverer. Through it God meets man and man is caught up into that growth which is God. This is so because the unlimited growth of connections of value could not go on without death. Death tears away the encrusted fixation which shuts God out from man and man from God. Without death the forms of life established by one generation would go on forever. So we can say in all truth: "Oh grave, where is thy victory! Oh death, where is thy sting!"

Why do we live? We live for the growth of meaning and value. Whether we live or whether we die it is for the enrichment of life unto him who has made the absolute commitment of faith. Life and death conspire together to bring the reality of greatest worth more vividly and richly to the consciousness of men when they practice the method of the distinctively religious way.

All this is so if the reality of greatest worth, commanding our utmost devotion, be growth of meaning and value. Whether we call it God or not, there is a growth that is greater than any individual. It is superhuman in the cosmic reach of its roots, in the unpredictable emergent richness of its creative syntheses, and in the uncomprehended possibilities of its possible outcomes. We live for this growth when we live rightly, and we die for it when we die rightly. Death is transfigured by it and sunset turns to dawn when dying is dedicated to it. But this brings us face to face with the problem of what God is.

NOTES

1 In *Ideology and Utopia.*

BIBLIOGRAPHY

One of the most elaborate and yet practical statements of the method of religious living is *Living Religion*, by Hornell Hart. *Reason and Emotion*, by John Macmurray, is concerned with education of our emotions to keep them true to our religious and other interests. *The Third Morality*, by Gerald Heard, correlates practical methods with a cosmology, holding that both are needed for religious living. *The Modern Family and the Church*, by R. W. Wieman, tells of methods for religious living in the family; *Methods of Private Living*, by H. N. Wieman, does the same for the individual. *Normative Psychology of Religion*, by H. N. and R. W. Wieman, considers the question of method in many different areas of life — individual, small groups, large social movements, counseling.

11.

APPROACH TO GOD

CLASHING planets and cosmic cataclysms may display power far greater than man can wield or control. But such power is not worth living for; it is not superhuman. It is subhuman because it is not directed in such a way as to achieve consistently any product or objective having a definable character. Explosions and crashing masses and vast inertia might produce chaos, but chaos has no definable character. So when we look for the superhuman we are not merely looking for magnitude of power. Anything superhuman must not only have power greater than man's, but it must be directed power. It must be so directed as to produce something regularly of a consistent character.

Now there is something going on round about us all the time which is superhuman in this sense. It is open to our observation and we see it all the while. It is so common that we scarcely think about it, and yet it is a great mystery. This to which we refer is the fact of growth. We have been suggesting that in growth may be manifest that reality which commands the supreme devotion of the most intelligent religious living. With this proposition in mind we wish to inquire into its nature and value. It may be that our most direct access to God in practical everyday living is by way of growth. Let us at any rate explore this fact of growth with the thought that such may be the case. Perhaps we shall find the intimate reality of God in so doing.

I. WHAT GROWTH IS

Growth is creative synthesis. It is the union of diverse elements in such a way that the new relation transforms them into a whole that is very different from the mere sum of the original factors. Chemical elements unite in this way and it may be that all growth is a chemical process. A flower grows by absorbing such elements as sunshine, air, water, and minerals, but these are transformed in the new synthesis so that the original elements are no longer recognizable. The mind of a human being grows by absorbing ideas, sentiments, attitudes from the social environment, but these are transformed in the new synthesis. The culture of a community grows by absorbing the ideas, techniques, skills, sentiments of the past and adding to these the newer developments of the present. But the gifts from the past and the present act on one another in a way analogous to that of chemical reagents. They do not merely lie side by side; they transform one another into a new kind of whole. When one culture makes contact with another, there is that same creative synthesis. This is what we mean by growth.

Growth is the formation of bonds of mutual support and mutual control and mutual facilitation between diverse activities. Mutual control means that the activities in this new union are so related that each operates to sustain the new unity or system. We say the same thing when we say that the whole new system operates to conserve the union and all its parts. Growth is the progressive formation of " internal relations " between diverse elements.

Growth extends from the lowest to the highest cosmic levels. We do not know that growth began with electrons, but for purposes of exposition we can so represent it. Electrons formed connections of mutual support and mutual control and thus gave rise to a new kind of unity called an atom. Atoms did the same and formed molecules. Molecules grew by creative synthesis, forming ever more complex molecules, until we had the colloid and at last the cell. Cells grew by creative synthesis giving rise to the multicellular organism. Similarly, we can trace the process up through growth of culture and the interpenetration of cultures. However diverse this growth may be at different levels (and it does show great differences) the one principle which concerns us at this point remains the same throughout, and that is the formation of connections of mutual support, mutual control, and mutual fulfillment between diverse activities of electrons, molecules, cells, organisms, minds, cultures.

What we have described is not evolution as science uses that term. Growth is only one form of evolution. A great deal of decomposition, conflict, and mutual destruction is going on throughout nature. Much of this would be called evolution by science. But through it all we also find the formation of connections of mutual support, mutual control, and mutual fulfillment between diverse activities forming new systems in which each part supports the whole and the whole operates to conserve the parts. The living cell is one of the most striking examples of this, as are also the multi-cellular organism and any one cultural group.

II. GROWTH IS SUPERHUMAN

We are exploring growth with the thought that we may find in it a superhuman reality which should command the religious devotion of all human living. When the Christian looks for something round about him which exemplifies the reality to which he commits his whole life and that of all his fellows, he asks, Is there love in it? Whatever the highest may be, it must not be alien to love.

Growth is the work of love if we mean by love the formation of bonds between diverse individuals whereby each works to conserve the system as a whole, and the whole works to conserve the parts in that relation to one another which constitutes the system. We have no assurance that there is any consciousness at the lower levels of growth, although some do hold this belief.[1] Many will say that we cannot speak of love until we have consciousness. We would not dispute with them, only we would point out that all the rich values of conscious love can be sustained and grow only within a vast matrix of such connections as we have shown to be the work of growth. Also the conscious love we know among men can arise only at the growing edge of such a cosmic system of growth. Love among men is the outcome of such growth and can occur in no other way. Growth that prepares the way for human love is the working of superhuman love. Also human love is mere contemptible sentimentality unless it operates to promote and sustain a system of mutually sustaining and meaningful activities.

Growth which is creative synthesis is superhuman. The outcome of creative synthesis can never be foreseen by the human mind until after instances of the same kind of synthesis have been observed. It is never the work of human mind. It occurs spontaneously when the required conditions are present. All growth is of this sort. It is superhuman although men can and often do provide the conditions which are required for the miracle to occur.

Men find wild plants growing. These they cultivate until they produce grain and fruit and flowers in rich abundance. Men find "wild" friendships growing in their midst as spontaneously as the flowers in May. These also they have sometimes cultivated, although we do not know the specific conditions required for growth of friendship nearly so well as we know those for the growth of wheat, figs, fish, and forests. Men find in their midst the wild growth of home life and love which has arisen without any more plan and purpose on their part than the growth of the physiological organism. This also they have cultivated to some degree, although their knowledge and skill here are still very limited. They have found and are finding the wild growth of community in the form of tribes and feudal systems and national states and international relations and economic exchange. All this is really saying that men find the wild growths of God, cultivate them by providing more richly the needed conditions of growth, and thus reap more abundant values. All these are examples of the formation of connections of mutual support, mutual control, and mutual facilitation. It is the growth of community which, when it becomes humanly conscious, we call love.

The human record, however, is not by any means an account of man's steady fostering of the growth of connections of mutual support and mutual control. On the contrary, men often fight against these bonds, tear them down ofttimes as fast as they develop, or else use the power of them to exploit their fellows and spread horror over the earth. But the gentle growth continues despite all the wreckage and destruction and other evil that man does with it and through it and upon it. The closer become these bonds of mutual support and mutual control between men, the more damage men can do to one another. They may succeed in rending or exploiting these bonds to such a degree that the human race will rot in its own carnage and filth. But still the superhuman growth goes on and in some measure men yield to its gentle power. When they do, they receive a larger portion of the riches of value which it bestows upon every human heart that yields to the transformations of the creative synthesis.

III. THE GOOD OF GROWTH

If growth is the manifestation of that reality which commands the devotion of the distinctively religious life, it must be not only superhuman but it must be supremely good. So we come face to face with the problem of value. What is value? By what standard or criterion can we say that anything is better or worse? We must briefly sketch our concept of value and then apply it to growth to see if we do have here in our midst a well known reality which is most directly expressive of God.

Let anybody start with any concept of value that he wishes. Some say value is a feeling-state of consciousness; others that it is the satisfaction of any interested activity; others that it is an eternal essence; still others that it is the will of God; and so on through many different views. But what we want to find is that operative reality which makes the world better, or which will or can make it better to the highest degree when the required conditions are met. So, for the time being, let us not dispute over these ideas of value.

Let us start with a specific instance of something that can be called good according to any of these ideas of the nature of value. Suppose we take the case of drinking water when thirsty. If drinking water when thirsty (or any other example of value you may choose) is good, then life is better if all other activities which might help or hinder the drinking are so connected with it that they support rather than frustrate the drinking. If the drinking is to occur, not only must many activities in one's physiological organism be so connected as to facilitate the drinking, but many environmental activities must also be so connected. Not only must this be the case with many things going on at the moment, but many past occurrences must have been of a sort that makes possible, or positively promotes, the drinking. Furthermore, if much good is to be attained the drinking must be connected with future activities which also yield the experience of value or otherwise exemplify it.

All that we say of drinking would be true of an aesthetic experience or high moral achievement. Occurrences which must be rightly connected in order to sustain the activity of drinking reach very deep into the nature of existence, social, psychological, biolgical, chemical, and physical. They reach far into the past and, if the value is to be great, they must reach far into the future.

But suppose the drinking is bad. Well, then, why is it bad? If one takes any example of what he can call bad, he will find that its badness lies in the fact that it prevents or destroys or renders impossible something that he can call good. So we are back again at our first principle of value, which is that anything which can be called good makes the world better when it is connected with other occurrences going on in the world in such a way that it is supported and not destroyed or prevented.

So we reach the conclusion that, no matter what may be your idea of the nature of value, the actual procedure by which the world is made better is that of organizing the diverse occurrences in the world in such a way that they support what is good. Also, since the bad is always defined in terms of opposition to the good, the elimination of the bad is the elimination of these conflicting activities.

We cannot here take space to elaborate more fully a theory of value.[2] We must take a leap and say that the process by which the world is made better is the forming of connections of mutual support, mutual control, and mutual facilitation between appreciable activities.

Appreciable activities are not necessarily appreciated, but they are activities which would be appreciated if we were intelligent enough and sensitive enough to be aware of their contribution to what is enjoyable. When we speak of connections of value between activities, we mean that any activity which we might enjoy

is better if it is so connected with other appreciable activities that
they all support rather than frustrate one another. The situation
is better still if all of them are so connected that they enhance one
another in such a way that the appreciative consciousness can more
vividly apprehend their value. It is best of all if, along with supporting and enhancing, they come to mean one another. The eating of certain foods, for example, may be good. But when the
foods are combined in certain ways they enhance one another.
Still further, the eating may signify (symbolize, mean) that we
who eat together are members of a fellowship. Activities without known limit in number and diversity may be connected in
this threefold way of mutual support, enhancement, and meaning.

Connections of mutual support between appreciable activities
may themselves be appreciable. However, these connections may
lie so deep, or be so wide-reaching or complicated or intimate, that
men never will appreciate them. Hence they may not be appreciable. But they are values just the same, for values are not merely
appreciable activities; they are connections of mutual support
whereby activities are rendered appreciable.

Now let us apply this criterion of value to growth. Growth, we
have said, is the formation of connections of mutual support, mutual control, and mutual facilitation between diverse activities.
Thus growth fits precisely our criterion of value. The cosmic
growth of such connections provides the matrix in which all human appreciation of value and all increase in such value must
occur.

IV. IS GROWTH EVIL?

But many instances of growth are bad, some will assert. Outstanding illustrations are those of cancer and overpopulation,
where cells or trees or human individuals destroy one another by
reason of too rampant growth. Here we shall fall into confusion
unless we keep our meanings and our distinctions clear.

Chemical compounds grow complex until they are called living
cells. Cells grow more complex, both within each unit and between the units, until they are collectively called a living organ-

ism. These organisms may unite either physically to form still more complex bodies, or they may unite culturally by signaling and communication to form communities.

Now each of these units of growth, from chemical compound to human group of many persons and communities, is constantly exposed to destructive influences. These units and combinations of units must protect themselves. There are two ways to do it. One way is for each unit to organize itself ever more compactly and exclusively. Each individual or group may form a protective shell by which external influences are warded off. This shell may be physical, like the bark of a tree or a thick skin, or it may consist of a complex system of protective devices which resists any invasion and transformation from the outside, such as rigid social conventions and military organization. That is one way protection is sought. So far as this procedure is followed, there is no growth taking place between the individual and other individuals. No formation of connections of mutual support and mutual control occurs between the one unit of growth and others so far as the protective device of exclusion serves its intended purpose.

But there is another way in which protection of unique individuality is sought and found, exactly opposite to the one described. In this second way the individual yields his self-organization to progressive modification under the influence of other individuals in such ways as to form connections of mutual support and mutual control between each individual and all the others involved in this process. This is connective growth, as compared to the competitive growth described in the preceding paragraph. Furthermore, this connective growth between individuals is the chief source of unique development on the part of each individual member of the community. Also it provides the most effective protection.

Competitive growth, on the other hand, does not develop individuality but tends to force it into rigid forms and stereotypes. The evolution of species wherein specialized protective devices were developed makes this very plain. Man develops more individuality than any other living thing because he, more than any other, is physiologically free of protective devices and is most open to the transforming, growth-producing connections with his environment, both social and physical. There is much more growth within the individual when there is connective growth between individual units, than there is in the individual unit where it excludes external influences by protective devices.

Here, then, we have a distinction of major importance. It is that between connective growth and competitive growth. Competitive growth always produces a situation which fixates growth and brings it to an end. Connective growth can lead on without limit, increasing mutual support between individuals and at the same time making them increasingly unique and distinctive. Competitive growth does just the opposite. It prevents diversification and the increase of mutual support, mutual control, and mutual facilitation.

Competitive growth which soon becomes static may yield a great increment of certain products. But increment is not growth. The distinction between the two must be clear. Bricks may be added to a pile, a wall may be built higher and higher, houses may be multiplied, the number of dead bodies may be increased indefinitely as the slaughter proceeds. We may figuratively refer to these instances of increment as cases of growth. But there is a radical difference between the organic process of growth and the mechanistic addition of units to one another. When growth springs anew after winter snows, when the personality of a child blossoms forth as he shares the interest of his associates, when personalities become ever more profoundly participant in one another so that we have growth of community, then we see this growth of which we speak. When works of art and attitudes of aesthetic appreciation, verified propositions, ideals, perspectives, and cherished loyalties are shared by one individual with his associates, and by one generation with its predecessors, while individuals and generations contribute further enrichment as the heritage passes through them, we have growth of culture. But the multiplication of products and the addition of units which are sometimes called civilization are very different. The multiplication of individual fish which feed on one another is not connective growth. It is a very limited competitive growth which then goes on to yield great increment of individuals. If these individuals progressively formed connections of mutual support and mutual enrichment, developing a higher degree of individuality in each, together with more mutual control and mutual facilitation, we would have connective growth. But much of the spawning of life in nature is due to competitive growth which, after it is fulfilled, ceases to be growth between individuals and becomes more increment.

We now see that the instances of the " evil of growth " are really due to the lack of growth. When the individual unit of growth protects itself by excluding the life of others from its own, and thereby enters into competition, if not destructive interaction, with others, we have an evil. But it is not the evil of growth. It is the evil of lack of growth. Growth would be the formation of connections of mutual support and mutual control. When, on the contrary, the individuals crowd one another out, or otherwise impair the growth of one another, or exclude cooperation by protective devices against one another, we have evil. There is much of this in the life of man, as well as throughout the rest of nature. But such evil is the exact opposite of growth.

The organizations of existence are constantly falling into those forms which make it impossible for individuals, or individualized systems, to form connections of mutual support beyond certain limits. Species of plants and animals, organizations of human personality, and social orders, are constantly getting into this kind of impasse. The system which thus obstructs growth must then be broken, transformed, or eliminated. When such orders arise the only possible way for life to continue may be by the destruction of one by the other. For example, man must destroy the malarial mosquito or be destroyed by him. But here the evil is not that of growth. It is just the opposite. It is the inability to form connections of mutual support and mutual enrichment. It may be that many forms of life have lost the capacity to undergo the further transformations required for developing more intimate or more extensive connections of mutual support with other forms, together with the further enrichment and uniqueness of individuality which go with this. This may apply not only to lower species, but to certain orders of social organization among men. However, the domestication and breeding of plants and animals by men shows how the lower orders can be woven into the order of connective growth.

At this juncture it may begin to seem that all this evil of mutual destruction occurs because the several individuals grow. That is true, but here again we must clarify our distinctions. The evil may come as a by-product of the growth of individuals. But the evil itself is not intrinsically a part of growth. On the contrary the evil itself is the absence of connective growth between the individuals concerned. The growth of each individual may have been good as far as it went. But it remains too exclusive, too separative, and almost always becomes competitive. Only when the growth of the several individuals is controlled and regulated by connections of mutual support and facilitation between them do we have growth which is both connective and individualizing and can go on without limit. When such growth occurs, the evil we have described is prevented or removed. It is the only way by which it can be prevented or removed.

V. PROTECTIVE COMPETITIVE GROWTH VERSUS UNLIMITED CONNECTIVE GROWTH

Tusks, claws, and monstrous size at the anatomical level, or, at the psychological level, habits, conventions, and sentiments, do grow of themselves. When these are protective and competitive they cut off the growth of connections of mutual support, control, and facilitation between the individual or group and others. They grow of themselves in the sense that cells within the organism, or habits, conventions, and sentiments between organisms, form creative syntheses on such a limited scale that they function to protect or destroy, but do not achieve wider and closer bonds of co-operation between individuals and systems.

Here we must distinguish between the two kinds of growth. On the one hand is the growth of the individual, whether it be an individual cell or group of cells, an individual organism or group of organisms, an individual unit or individualized systems of units. On the other hand is that growth which is not limited to any one individual unit, but works through individuals to form ever larger and closer bonds of support between ever more diversified activities and systems. The growth of the individual or single system is strictly limited. It has a beginning and an end. It seeks to protect itself against transformations. It builds up resistance by protective and destructive devices, both biological and social.

Over against this protective growth of the individual or individualized system, which is limited, is the connective growth which is unlimited. Each individual shows this growth which is protective and limited and also to some degree the connective growth which works through it and beyond it to widen and deepen the bonds of internal connection between the individual and other individuals and between one system and other systems. These are, respectively, the contractive and the expansive impulses of growth. Self-preservation is essential to the individual, and it may be contractive, but is not necessarily so. Also inalienable to the individual, however, are impulses which work for the species, and sometimes for the sacrifice of the species in the interest of an ever larger or more meaningful and intimate community. We have seen how the religious personality may undergo death for this purpose and in this way.

There is conflict between the demands of competitive, self-protective growth, and the demands of connective growth which lead on without limit to growth of meaning and value. Every personality has experienced this conflict in himself. Every social group, every institution, every culture experiences it. But the way of competitive growth, which permits only the hardiest to survive, always leads to death. A very clear example of this is the case where cancer kills a man, but any other instance of "survival of the fittest" would serve. The cancerous cells compete with the total organism instead of forming connections of mutual support with it as the other cells do. The cancerous growth destroys the rest of the organism and so is fitted to survive. It is true that when cancer kills the man it ultimately kills itself. But that is always what occurs when any unit of growth achieves survival by competition and destruction. Only when and if and in so far as it achieves survival by forming connections of mutual support with other individuals can it participate in unlimited growth. In the final analysis survival is never achieved by competition and destruction but only by mutual support through growth.

The doctrine of the survival of the fittest as a form of progress is a very good example of human confusion and evil arising out of failure to make important distinctions. When survival is achieved by mutual transformation of the individuals involved, so that a greater number and diversity of appreciable activities enter into mutual support and control, we have increase of value or progress. When, on the other hand, survival is achieved by one individual's or group's treating others as mechanisms and tools, and so killing them or otherwise excluding them from the community of mutual support, we do not have increase of value. Also it is not growth of value. It is not the kind of growth which can command the supreme devotion of human personality.

Thus all genuine increase of value comes through growth. When it is claimed that growth is an evil, a careful examination will reveal that the evil is the limitation of growth. It is self-protective and competitive growth within the individual or within the individualized system, and not unlimited connective growth which goes on between individuals quite as much as within the individual. When growth within the individual or individualized system of individuals prevents or destroys growth between them, the evil is not in the growth per se, but in the prevention or destruction of growth between them.

In chapters 9 and 10 we tried to show that the constant requirement of the peculiarly religious way is that the individual shall seek out the riches of the concrete situation. A study of the kind of living there portrayed reveals that it requires absolute self-commitment of the individual to unlimited connective growth even when it threatens to destroy him. In the way of living there set forth all the individual does to conserve and promote his own individual existence is for the sake of being more fully participant in unlimited connective growth. We saw that death itself was made to serve this end.

VI. MAN'S PART IN GROWTH

Suppose it turned out that growth was found to be a kind of progressive chemical transformation. If so, man might discover the combination of chemicals which bring it about. He might put these chemicals together in a test tube in the right proportions and then observe growth taking place beneath his hands and eyes. But even then the actual process of growth would not be the doing of man. Man's power could extend only so far as the providing of the required conditions under which growth occurred. The actual process of chemical transformation is never the doing of human intelligence. Human intelligence can bring the required chemicals together into that proximity and in that proportion wherein the transformation occurs. But when the conditions are provided the chemical transformation goes on of itself. Man can merely observe it. Whether or not growth is merely a chemical transformation, at any rate it has this character of being superhuman. It is always more than the doing of man.

This does not gainsay the fact that it is very easy for men to stamp out any particular instance of growth by the use of destructive violence. The way of growth and the power of growth do not lie in violence. Rather, it is a mysterious power of marvelous gentleness. Men can destroy any one instance of it but they find it exceedingly difficult to prevent new forms of growth from springing up to take the place of that which was destroyed.

Remarkable also is the fact that men can provide conditions wherein new kinds of growth will occur. Thus new species of plants and animals are brought forth, and new sorts of social community. But in all this man's only part is to provide needed conditions or to remove obstructive ones. The actual process of growth and creativity by which new forms of life come into existence is always beyond the power of man.

Men can select and foster most important kinds of growth.

The kinds of growth which have most importance in shaping the destiny of man and lifting the universe to highest levels of value are these: growing personality; the growth of meaning in the world; the growth of those habits, impulses, mutual enrichment of minds and shared meanings which we can call the growth of culture; and the growth of those economic connections of inter-dependence which force men to choose between an unendurable mutual destructiveness or a fulfilling mutual support and enhance-ment. In all these instances of growth we find that the same prin-ciples hold which we have stated. Always the growth is super-human. Men can set up conditions under which the growth will assume any one of many forms. They can change the conditions in such a way that the growth will proceed in a very different way. Still other conditions over which they have power may halt the growth or hasten it. But always the growth itself is more than the work of man.

If men are to do their part they must not confuse growth with inevitable progress or inevitable increase of good. Good that grows is constantly being destroyed. Enormous destruction of the values brought forth by growth is going on all the time. The evil of destruction is increasing all the time, but that is only because there is more of good to be destroyed. Therefore the fact that evil in-creases in the form of more destruction of precious growth is no evidence at all that the world is getting worse in the sense of hav-ing less of value in it. Rather the contrary is the case. There may be more value all the time even while there is more destruction of value also. Growth of good may be even more wide and deep than increase of evil. However, there is little profit in trying to balance accounts concerning the relative amounts of good and evil in the world. If man is to play his part well, the important points for him are to know that both good and evil are here, to know what is the character of the supremely worthful, to know of what evil consists, to give himself wholly to the growth of good, to be progressively transformed by it and used by it, and to fight with all his power against evil. What the final outcome shall be we may not be able to say. But we do know that we have everything to gain and nothing to lose by giving ourselves absolutely to the good, living for it and in it and with it, and fighting the evil.

VII. DANGERS IN THINKING ABOUT GOD

We are examining the fact of growth to see if we can find in it the manifestation of God most accessible to man in the practical affairs of everyday living. We have found that there is competitive growth which is limited to the individual or to the individualized system. We have also found that there is connective growth which is unlimited. Unlimited does not mean that it goes on irresistibly. Growth is never irresistible; it may be suppressed, beaten down, destroyed. But it is unlimited in the sense that it springs up again and again, not merely to preserve a particular individual, but to form connections of mutual control between forms and activities which are diversified progressively, and which are woven into more inclusive bonds of mutual facilitation until we reach the level of human meanings which may grow from more to more in richness and scope by these connections.

Here we have something that begins to look like the manifestation of God. It seems to be worthy of the supreme devotion of all human living and it seems to be that upon which man is dependent for the best that ever can be. On the other hand it is more than man; it constantly transforms man; it demands his absolute commitment; the desires and strivings of men are often opposed to it; the social and personal structures of human life are frequently faced with the alternative of either being destroyed by it or undergoing such radical reconstruction as to involve the perishing of individuals, groups, social structures, and whole civilizations. This begins to look like the manifestation of God in our midst.

But when we begin to form any idea of God we must note at once a great danger that accompanies any such undertaking. Perhaps the greatest obstacles in the way of God's *reality* have been the *ideas* of God which have shaped the lives of men and directed their highest ruling loyalties. We must try to guard against this danger.

In the distinctively religious way we have seen that the religious person refuses to specify with any finality the character of that for which he supremely lives. He refuses because any specific formulation which is allowed to dominate and direct the appreciative consciousness and responsive awareness will blind one to the unpredictable riches of concrete situations. God demands the freest and fullest responsiveness of the psycho-physical organism to all the riches of value that pack the concrete situation, and against all the evil that is there.

Perhaps one of the greatest evils in the world is the insensitivity of men to the goodness of God, which infinitely overflows and often antagonizes the narrow, specific goods of human desire. This insensitivity is often caused by the dominating control of some loyalty that is too narrow and fixated. The appreciative responsiveness of the individual is then chained and imprisoned within the bounds of this specific formulation. It is then impossible for the individual to appreciate or react to the innovations and richness of emergent concrete situations. But these uncomprehended innovations and riches are precisely the living goodness of the actual God which transcends every human ideal, program, or theory.

If what we have said be true, it becomes apparent that any attempt to form an idea of God is accompanied by possible evils. Any specific formulation of the nature of the deity which commands that kind of devotion required in religion, is very likely to engender a narrow and fixated loyalty which renders men insensitive to the wholeness of God. Allegiance to any specific *idea* of God will almost surely become the chief obstacle in the way of devotion to the *reality* of God which inevitably overflows any such idea. Not only does it overflow, not only does it transcend, but it must in many ways be antagonistic to such an idea.

VIII. TWO LEGITIMATE WAYS OF THINKING ABOUT GOD

If this be true, it would seem that there are only two legitimate ways of thinking about God. One would be to treat whatever idea of God one may have developed as a symbol which refers to nothing specific. It could then be used to awaken an unspecific devotion such as we have seen is the outstanding characteristic of the peculiarly religious way. It would represent God as transcending every specific truth and every specific good. It would represent God as being always other than our formulations and objectives. It would be the symbolic representation of the utter transcendence of God. It would be the idea of God championed today by Karl Barth, although some of his followers, like Emil Brunner, are beginning to introduce traditional and speculative specifications which impair the purity of their procedure.

There are certain obvious dangers and inescapable evils in this way of thinking about God. We shall not pause to mention all of them. We have already emphasized a number. One evil pertinent to this present discussion is that a symbol which does not refer to any specific course of action will almost surely come to be cherished for the sake of the feeling it gives one, in disregard of any objective reality. Thus it will become soporific. It will be an anesthetic to all thinking, all problem solving, all constructive action. It will induce a religion of sentimentality. Nevertheless such a purely symbolic way of thinking about God, which repudiates reason because God is held to transcend all the specific formulations of human thought, *might* be used to engender and sustain the peculiarly religious way that we have been considering. It *might* release one to seek and appreciate and serve the unpredictable fullness of the best in each concrete situation.

There is, however, a second legitimate way of thinking about God. It has dangers also, as does any such idea. But we believe the dangers are not so great as those involved in an idea which is an emotional symbol with no specific reference, such as we have just been describing. Also it serves important functions which cannot be served by the purely transcendental reference of the first alternative. It consists in using the idea of God (but not the reality of God) as one uses any idea in practical scientific inquiry. It means to look upon your *idea* of God as a very poor, very unsatisfactory, extremely inadequate instrument, to be used only because you have nothing better for the time being, to be discarded just as soon as you can find a better. A better idea would be one a little more commensurate with the richness and greatness of the reality with which you are dealing.

In this second way of thinking about God, one shapes his idea not to refer to a reality *wholly* transcendent and hence entirely unspecific. Therefore it is not, like the first alternative way of thinking about God, totally worthless in giving any direction to human living. In this second way of thinking the idea is shaped to fit all the evidence, and nothing but the evidence that can be gathered concerning the order of value experienced in life.

We have already noted that any *idea* of God sufficiently specific to give direction and guidance to human conduct and appreciative awareness, is likely to turn the mind away from the *reality* of God which is always more than we can think. But there are ways to avoid this danger.

In the first place, this danger can be averted if the idea is always held experimentally, if it is always being criticized and transformed in the light of further evidence, and if it is *always kept down to the dimensions of an operational idea.*[3] An operational idea is one that is shaped to guide practical behavior. But it is an idea into which no speculation is allowed to enter beyond the implications just mentioned. Of course one may well have speculative and analogical hypotheses. That is to say, one may ask questions about God at the same time that he is using a formulated operational idea. But he will not admit these speculations which are mere questions into his idea of God, until observable evidence found in the consequences of experimental behavior indicates that they are true.

In the second place, this operational idea of God, in so far as possible, must be of such a sort that it will not confine the mind to anything less than its utmost range of diversified appreciation and responsiveness to the riches of each concrete situation. It must give direction, but at the same time it must release the mind to seek for all that is good and for the best of all that is good, no matter how divergent it may be from the cherished goods of the past.

Is it possible to have an idea of God that will meet these requirements? We believe that unlimited growth gives us the fact and the idea which do. Furthermore, this idea is not something newly foisted on the world. It can be translated into Christian verbiage about the kingdom of God, the growing mustard seed, the vine and the branches, and when so expressed will be seen to be consistent with and inclusive of the great Christian insights. At the same time it uses the insights of modern thought. But it is experimental, and it is submitted to be criticized and improved in the light of all that we know from the past and the present. It is operational and directive, but quickly subject to change in the light of further evidence.

We hold that any legitimate idea of God must be either experimental, operational, and directive, or else it must be purely symbolic without any specific reference except as it refers to a realm wholly transcendent, beyond the reach of philosophical speculation, rational construction, empirical inquiry, or operational guidance. It must be either the *operational* idea of the new theistic naturalism, or the purely *symbolic* idea of the new supernaturalism with its " Absolutely Other." Either idea is legitimate only when and if it can be used to release in the individual his total capacity for appreciative response to the riches of the concrete situation, so that all his powers of action, intelligence, imagination, nervous energy, and emotional discharges are liberated to seek and to find the very best that can be disclosed in each situation, unpredictable and creatively emergent though it be. For here alone we find the *living* God, always more than we can think.

We believe that the directive, operational idea of the new naturalism is superior to the purely symbolic " Absolutely Other " of the new supernaturalism. Reasons for this preference have not only been indicated in the discussion of the last few paragraphs, but are found throughout the constructive portion of this volume.

Both these approaches to God, however, are united in repudiating the great majority of the theological and philosophical treatments of the idea of God. These are repudiated because they are speculative and analogical. There are two legitimate approaches to God, but the ways that are not legitimate are the common theo-

logical and philosophical approaches. We must show why we
think the speculative and analogical ways of thinking about God
not only misleading, but religiously pernicious.

IX. REPUDIATION OF SPECULATIVE APPROACHES TO GOD

Only an operational idea, constantly shaped and reshaped by the
immediately observable consequences of behavior, can guide action
in such a way as to make it pliable and responsive to the fullness of
the concrete situation. Only such an idea can lead to progressive
enrichment and transformation by the findings of action. A speculative idea cannot do this, because speculation means to form ideas
about a reality which cannot be directly acted upon in such a way
that the observable consequences of action will reveal its nature.
To speculate means to hold beliefs about something that lies behind, or beyond the reach of, the observable consequences of action.
Therefore a speculative idea of God is bound to have all the evils
which we have noted as pertaining to ideas of God, but none of the
virtues or correctives found in the purely symbolic idea of new supernaturalism or in the operational idea of new naturalism. The
speculative idea inevitably blinds man to the reality of God, because the only reality of God that can be truly known is that which
is revealed in the consequences of action. The speculative idea, by
its very nature, cannot deal with God as immediately accessible to
action. It turns the minds of men away from the immediate to
the remote and blinds them to the divine significance of the immediate reality.

One might think that the purely symbolic idea of God upheld
by the new supernaturalism would do this because it represents
God as wholly transcendental. It is always likely to do so, but
since it divests the reference to God of all intellectual structure,
since it tears away all the rational formulations of metaphysics,
theology, and philosophy generally, and makes it purely symbolic, it *can* be used to open the heart and mind of man to the
fullness of the concrete through action. However, a *purely* symbolic " idea " which refuses all rational structure save myth and
paradox is almost impossible to maintain, and Brunner has been

unable to maintain it. Hence the purely symbolic idea is almost sure to become either a source of fatuous sentimentality or else a speculative rational structure.

There are a number of speculative approaches to God which should be noted. One can think of God as away back at the beginning of things, as the creator who started everything. One can think of him as away down at the bottom of things, as the creator who sustains everything continuously by his mighty power. One can think of him as away off at the end of things, as the redeemer and saviour who makes everything come out all right at the end. One can think of him as away up at the top of things, as the perfect pattern of what ought to be. The furthest back, the deepest down, the final end, the highest up! Obviously all these approaches are speculative and cannot be anything else.

How everything got started no one knows and no one can ever know, because a pure beginning out of nothing is unthinkable. It is utter guesswork to speculate about it. Furthermore, it is very doubtful that things ever had a pure beginning out of nothing. It is quite as probable as any other guess that existence of some sort has always been.

The same speculative guesswork characterizes all the other approaches just noted. The idea of a God who underlies everything, sustaining the universe by his creative power, is another bit of metaphysical speculation, and has no great religious importance in any case. Here again it is an open question whether there is any one ultimate reality upon which all else depends. There may be several kinds of reality, all equally indispensable and all equally ultimate in the sense that all else depends upon one no more than upon the others. But if there are several such realities this most common speculative idea about God is false.

When it comes to the idea of God as the final end where " everything comes out all right " we again have a speculative idea about which it is impossible to gather any evidence save what can be learned by observing events as they transpire in the known history of the universe.

Anyone who puts God out at the beginning or at the ending or

at the top or at the bottom of everything is dealing with God as a
philosophical speculation and not as a religious fact. God as a religious reality with whom we must deal in our daily living must be
something in the actualities of the here and now where you and
I are living and our destiny is being shaped. Hence it is God in
our midst rather than at the beginning, bottom, top, or end who
can alone be a matter of religious interest. Also it is only when
God is sought and found in the midst of the concrete situation
where we are that he can be known through action; and action is
the only way in which we come to know anything in truth, but
especially any reality in its character of commanding our supreme
devotion and absolute self-commitment. On these grounds we
repudiate all the speculative approaches to God as self-defeating
and religiously pernicious.

There is another great evil in the speculative approach that must
be noted. Since such an idea cannot be shaped by the observable
objective consequences of action upon the concrete situation, it
must almost inevitably be shaped by the self-indulgent cravings of
the heart. One must decide whether his idea of God will be developed primarily subject to the needs of the heart or primarily
subject to the demands of the truth. One cannot do both at the
same time. To be sure the idea which is true may in some degree
satisfy the heart. It should progressively do so as personality is
transformed by it. But one cannot find the true idea by following
the guidance of human craving in the beginning. Craving transformed by learning to appreciate the consequences of intelligent
action is the only craving which can find satisfaction in true ideas.
But this requires the operational, and not the speculative, approach
to God, as we have seen.

While we repudiate the speculative way of thinking about God
we must recognize that it has been by far the most common approach in all theologies and philosophies. Let us note how the
four different speculative approaches prevail among contemporary philosophies of religion.

Few religious thinkers today would represent God as the initiator
who started everything. Yet many common men think of God

primarily in such terms, and some theological writers discuss the point. But most leaders today who speak of God as creator mean not so much the first beginner as the underlying, sustaining power who upholds and keeps all that exists. Traditional supernaturalism is one philosophy which has represented God in this way, but it has, indeed, represented him in all four of the different ways noted. God is the beginner, the sustainer, the ideal, and the end.

The new supernaturalism in the teaching of Emil Brunner is coming to emphasize the idea of God at the bottom, sustaining all things by his power. It also represents God at the end, judging and redeeming and bringing all things to their culmination. This last is what is meant by the eschatological element in the new supernaturalism. God as beginner, as highest ideal, and as a present process in the world of here and now, are discounted if not actually repudiated by this philosophy. However in its purest form, in the teaching of Karl Barth, these cosmological speculations are at a minimum and the idea of God is almost purely symbolic, as we have seen.

Liberalism has thought of God in all five of the different ways but has chiefly emphasized the ideal being of God. The religion of liberalism has tended to be a religion of idealism, hence it has emphasized God as at the top of everything, as the supreme pattern of what ought to be.

Humanism has also emphasized the ideal above all else and has done so much more exclusively than liberalism. Here again humanism shows itself to be the rigorous and logical development of the main tendencies in liberalism. In many cases the humanists have been clear-headed enough to see that a God who is chiefly an ideal reality and not an actual, existing power, can scarcely be called God at all. Hence they have sometimes rejected the idea of God and concerned themselves solely with the highest ideals.

The new naturalists have taken the operational approach to God and have repudiated the speculative approach. God is not primarily an ideal for them. Rather he is first of all an actual, existing, operative reality in our midst bringing forth all that is highest and best in existence, far beyond the scope of our specific understanding. He is the creative synthesis at work in the immediate concrete situation where we are.

X. CRITERIA OF GOD

If naturalism repudiates so much traditional thought about God, what right has it to use the word "God" to refer to the reality which it holds to be the central concern in religious living? It must not be arbitrary in the use of words. It cannot at pleasure set up what it likes and say that this shall be called God because we choose to use words in this way. The word "God" is too important for such arbitrary usage. What, then, shall be our criteria in shaping our idea of God? We must be true to the deepest strivings of the most important and distinctive kind of religious living. That does not mean that we must perpetuate all the patterns of thought which have been used in such living. We could not do that, for these patterns have been most multiform and contradictory. But we must be true to the aim of sincere religious living, to the direction of its striving, and to the values sought. It is to these that we must look to get our criteria, and not to the forms of thought which are so diverse and irreconcilable in many cases.

In order that we might be true to this deepest aim of the most distinctive and important kind of religious living, we have taken pains first to trace the history of religion, and then to make an elaborate analytical study of the concrete way of religious living. It is from these that we must get our criteria for the idea of God.

After the historical survey found in the first half of this book, Professor Horton wrote: " The purpose and goal of high religion may be defined as *the progressive reorganization of the world into a system of mutually sustaining activities humanly appreciated, whereby the endless growth of meaning and value is fostered. Its God is the Being whereon the accomplishment of this aim ultimately depends.* Man worships rightly when he makes this Being the object of his supreme loyal devotion, and makes himself a channel through which its power pours forth toward the above defined goal." [4] Also the findings of the two chapters preceding this one all bear upon this problem.

In the light of these studies, what can we say are the criteria which must distinguish any reality that can be called God? In other words, what must be the nature of such a reality if it is to satisfy the most distinctive kind of striving which we find in religious living?

Our answer to this question must be stated. God in the religious sense (as distinguished from cosmological and philosophical speculations) must be, and can only be, what rightfully commands the supreme devotion of man. Otherwise God would not be a religious fact. Anything which can rightfully hold the absolute allegiance and self-commitment of men must be a reality which is characterized in three ways. It must be superhuman, it must be the best there is, and it must be the greatest power for good. Otherwise men would rightfully turn their devotion to that something else which was greater than they, which was more worthful or which had more power for good. We do not say that all religious devotion has been offered to a reality which men thought to be characterized in this threefold way. But we do say that the *only religious devotion worthy of respect* has been offered to what men thought was of this threefold character. As we have said again and again, we are not interested in religion in all its conglomerate variety of form and value, but only in that kind of religion which is important.

First, the divine reality must be superhuman. It must have power for good which is greater than the intelligently directed efforts of men. If there is nothing in the universe more potent for good than the consciously directed strivings of men at their best, there is no God. This is the first identifying mark of God.

Second, God must be the best reality there is in existence. If there is anything in all the realms of being which is more worthful than what we think is God, then what we think of as God is not God. We are mistaken. God is such other reality having greatest value. Whatever else God may be, he can be no other reality than what is supremely worthful and what is the sovereign good.

Third, God must not only be superhuman and the best there is, but he must exercise the greatest power for good. To be the most worthful reality, and to exercise the greatest power for good, might seem to be identical terms. Ordinarily the same reality would deserve both descriptions. However it is conceivable that something might exercise greatest power for good and yet at the same time in other aspects be the greatest evil. In that case it would not be the most worthful reality in its total nature, but only in that aspect or function wherein it promotes the greatest good. We have already noted an example. The total cosmos exercises greatest power for good but also does the greatest evil, and for that matter does everything which lies between the extremes of good and evil. Such being the case, we must say that the universe as a whole is characterless in respect to the features of good and evil. It is both of these and is every gradation in between. But this shows that the universe cannot be identified with God. It also shows that God cannot be identified with the creator of the universe, for then he would be creator of all the evil as well as the good, and hence would exercise greatest power for evil as well as for good, and for all the gradations. In other words, the creator of the universe is just as characterless as the universe itself in respect to the criteria of good and evil.

Since one essential criterion of God is "greatest power for good," and since clear thinking shows that such a power for good cannot be the total universe, nor the creator of everything, it becomes plain that God must be something *in* the universe, namely that Something which exercises greatest power for good. Furthermore, this Something must be limited to what does the good, and must not include other activities or realities which do evil, no matter how closely associated these may be with the doing of the good.

When it is said that God is "that Something which exercises greatest power for good" it may be objected that what does greatest good may be many and not one. We believe that inquiry will show that what does greatest good is essentially one and not many. But such a unitary nature of the power for good cannot be set up as a criterion of deity. Deity might be many and not one. It is quite conceivable that there are many gods instead of one single God. Whether God is one or many must wait on inquiry. Uni-

Baillie 984

tary nature cannot be established at the beginning as one of the criteria by which God must be identified when found.

If we are correct in saying that the three criteria mentioned must characterize any reality which can be called God, we are prepared to search to see if there is any God. As a matter of fact we have already done our searching. We find that we have a reality before us which meets all the requirements. It is unlimited connective growth.

Some may think that we have played a trick on them. We first presented something which we wanted to call God and then invented criteria to fit what we had. The only way to know if we are guilty of that accusation is to look at the facts. Is it true or is it not, that the aim of the most distinctive and important kind of religious living is to serve and adore and commit human life to what is supremely worthful in the senses mentioned? It may be that we are mistaken, but the mistake must be set forth in the light of inquiry into the real aim of the distinctively ʾigious way.

Furthermore, we believe the procedure we have followed in finding God is true to human experience. Men do not in vital religion first set up criteria of what God must be, and then search to find. Rather they first experience God not knowing it is God, and then later get the criteria to recognize deity in what has been with them all the time. Indeed, we should say it is a pernicious error to try to teach a child or anyone else about God until one can point to something in that person's experience and say, Behold, that is what I mean by God. Otherwise God becomes a speculative idea which is not directive in the action and devotion of the individual's living.

We have found in growth the character of being superhuman. Also, we have found in growth the second criterion of deity, which is supreme goodness. Likewise, we have found the third criterion, which is greatest power for good. Can we not then say that God is manifest in growth of meaning and value, together with all those underlying processes of growth which issue in meaning and value and are indispensable to it?

We might distinguish between God and the work of God.

Then we could say that unlimited connective growth is not God but the work of God. Perhaps there is no serious objection to that. God would then be an eternal and changeless order, while the work of God, called growth, would be the partial and sequential manifestation of this order in the process of existence. This is the distinction between structure and function and can be applied not only to God but to anything else, say a human person. But those who apply this distinction to God should see that all their practical dealing with God in actual living must be by way of this growth of connections of mutual support and mutual control between appreciable activities.

Some of these growing connections may be so wide or so deep or so intimate that they are not discoverable to man and so not appreciable. Hence God will always be more than what is consciously appreciable to men. Therefore we do not say that God is growth of appreciable activities. Rather what we have said is that God is the *growth of connections between* activities which are appreciable. Of course many such appreciable activities are themselves connections of mutual support, but not all the latter are yet open to human apprehension, and may never be. Therefore God is always more than we can *com*prehend. But we can always *ap*prehend God if we meet the required conditions of self-commitment to the best that can be discovered in each concrete situation.

XI. THE FALSE PROBLEM OF EVIL

After we have found the reality of God in the most vital activities of living, there remains a true problem about the nature and place of evil. But this true problem is often concealed or confused by a false problem. We must get this false problem of evil out of the way in order to get at the real problem.

The false problem is that of how to uphold a basic assumption when the observable facts of life contradict it. The assumption which generates the false problem of evil is this: A perfectly good God creates and sustains the universe and all that is in it. The observable fact which contradicts this assumption is this: The universe has in it many monstrous evils. The contradiction is between the goodness of God's unlimited power and the evil in the world of which he is creator and sustainer.

He who makes an assumption which does not fit the known truth has a false problem when he tries to make the facts fit the assumption. It becomes a true problem only when he reverses the procedure and tries to change the assumption to fit what is known to be true.

Traditional supernaturalism is in trouble here because it rests upon the assumption which conflicts with the evidence. The new supernaturalism and liberalism make the same assumption and so have increasing difficulty with the false problem of evil. Humanism and the new naturalism, on the other hand, do not make the assumption which generates the problem. Hence they are not dogged by this specter. They do not have to solve this problem because it does not arise in their way of dealing with the issues of religious thought. They are not forced to try to reconcile facts with an assumption that contradicts them.

There are two ways by which one can escape the contradiction and hence the problem. First, he may deny that there is any real evil in the world. One religious cult officially does so. Few, however, can successfully blind themselves to the flagrant facts to such a degree as that claim requires. On the other hand, one who denies that God is the creator and sustainer of the universe, simply does not have the contradiction on his hands. This second denial does not require blindness to any facts. On the contrary, all empirical evidence and logic seem to support it. There is a creator and sustainer of all that is good in the universe, namely the power of growth we have been describing. Such a creator and sustainer, however, is not of the universe as a whole, but only of the good that is in it. Indeed, as we have shown, any creator or sustainer would seem to be necessarily in the universe and a part of it, and hence not a creator of the universe, since universe is supposed to mean everything. The idea of a creator of everything is essentially contradictory in itself.

There is a third way by which many religious thinkers seek to deal with the contradiction between the goodness of God's unlimited power and the evil of the world, and that is to insist that the two contradictory statements are true even though one must repudiate rationality in speaking about God. They who make this claim say that God is of such a nature that human reason inevitably falls into self-contradiction when it undertakes to think about him. Therefore the above contradiction in the basic assumptions of religious thinking is to be expected, they state. It simply demonstrates the super-rational nature of God. Since reason inevitably falls into self-contradiction when it tries to think about God and his ways, the contradiction between the sovereign goodness of God and the evil of the world does not call for a solution.

The trouble with this desperate device for perpetuating self-contradictory religious assumptions is that it takes from us the only means we have for distinguishing between truth and error, good and bad, holy and demonic. The hell that men enter and ofttimes make for others, too, when they go this way, is all too plainly written in the records of history. This is the most dangerous evasion of all.

Traditional supernaturalism and liberalism have struggled with this problem with different emphases. Traditional supernaturalism has tended to emphasize the mystery of God's ways, while liberalism has depended more on discounting the apparent magnitude of evil and showing how much that appears to be evil is not so in the long run or in respect to ultimate reality. In other words they " interpret " evil. They say evil is necessary in order to have free will in man. But such a statement ignores the real problem. The worst evils are precisely those that destroy free will in man, or prevent it from ever developing in small children. The worst evil of all is that of being bereft of free will.

The same evasion appears in another form when it is said that evil serves to develop moral character. The worst evil is to have a devilish character and such character is found in our world. The really great evils do not develop moral character, but just the opposite. They turn men into fiends. Evil that served to develop moral character would not be real evil any more than a game involving conflict is the same as war. Most attempts to solve the problem by showing that evil is not so bad as it seems are evasions of the real issue. They consist in selecting "evils" that yield to this kind of treatment and slurring over the evils that constitute the real problem, namely, those that do not serve any good purpose but just the opposite. Also this procedure tends to make the liberal a supporter and justifier of evil in order to save the reputation of God. If he does not justify evil he tends at any rate to blur the distinction between good and evil.

All these philosophies that struggle with the problem of reconciling the goodness of God's controlling power with the patent facts of evil in the universe fall back on the mystery of God's ways, on the one hand, and the good uses of evil, on the other. Always the problem is left unsolved essentially. All they succeed in doing is to veil the raw and bloody face of it. God is somehow good and the ultimate source of all, they aver, and yet evil is here indubitably.

Somewhat akin to this resort to vagueness is another way of evasion. It is the attempt to solve the problem by changing the names of evil. Evil can be called error of mortal mind, or the work of the devil, or the inevitable consequences of man's free will, or the perversity of human nature, or the result of Adam's fall. But all this juggling with words does nothing to remove the contradiction between the assumption that God's ruling power is good, and the facts of evil, whatever name may be given to the latter.

Professor Brightman's theory that evil is in God's own nature [5] does not really solve the problem but only reformulates it. He unites under the one label of "deity" two diametrically opposed realities, namely, the perfect and holy will of God and the evil nature which opposes that will.

So it is that, in spite of differences in efforts at circumlocution, all prevalent philosophies of religion which include belief in God, excepting theistic naturalism, come to the same final position after they have discussed the issues of this problem concerning an all-powerful good God and the fact of evil in the world. None has better expressed this position than J. Gresham Machen. He himself says that this statement of his applies to all liberals as well as to the orthodox. He writes: "How could a holy God, if he is

all-powerful, have permitted the existence of sin? What shall we
do with the problem? I am afraid we shall have to do with it
something that is not very pleasing to our pride; I am afraid we
shall just have to say it is insoluble." [6]

Exactly. It is insoluble because it arises from two contradictory
assumptions which are laid down as the foundation for all these
philosophies of religion.

XII. NATURE OF EVIL

We have said there is a legitimate problem of evil. What is
its nature and place as over against the goodness of God? This
does not involve any assumption that God is creator of the universe or exercises any greater control over it than what the facts
reveal concerning the scope of his goodness on the one hand, and
the scope of evil on the other. The problem no longer consists
in desperate and futile attempts to remove the contradiction between two propositions, such as: God's goodness rules the world;
and, The world is full of evil. The problem is simply an inquiry
concerning what is the nature and scope of evil as over against
the nature and scope of what is good. This inquiry requires, for
its extensive prosecution, a fully developed theory of value. [7] We
do not have space for this. But we can give a brief treatment of it.

One of the first things to note about evil is that there is no single
definable character which is common to all forms of it. Specific
evils have a definite character. But there is no general principle
which characterizes all evils save the negative one that evil is
opposed to good. Goodness does have a definable character.
There is a universal principle which applies to all cases of positive value. But there is none for negative value save that of being
negative to positive value.

What is the universal nature of positive value or goodness we
have indicated in our study of the goodness of growth. If the
good had no distinctive character common to all cases, we could
not define evil as being opposed to the good. One can identify
the universal principle of evil as the negative of good, providing
good has a positive character. But one of the two must be posi-

tive. Goodness is. Evil is not in respect to any universal characteristic, although particular instances of evil are very positive and aggressive. We do not mean to say that evil is negative in the sense of being merely the absence of something. Particular evils are destructive and positive. But for all the diversification of their destructive operations, there is no one single principle which describes them all.

However, evils may be classified in various ways. For instance, we can speak of three types: the destruction of good, the fixation of good so that it cannot grow, and the absence of good. But it should be noted that these are merely negative descriptions. In general evil is anything which interferes with the unlimited growth of connections of mutual support, mutual control, and mutual facilitation between appreciable activities. This interference may appear as destroying what has grown, as fixating growth at a certain stage so that it cannot proceed, and as preventing any growth from ever getting started. On the other hand, however, destruction, fixation, and prevention of growth are not always evil. In some forms and circumstances they may be the best way of promoting the unlimited growth of meaning and value. All of which shows that we cannot specify evil except in terms of that which impairs the unlimited growth of connections of value.

A great deal of evil is nondeliberate and is due to the insensitivity of men. This insensitivity, in turn, may be due to self-righteousness. Or it may come from following prescribed programs without regard to innovating situations and the richness of value that overflows any fixed program. Again, it may be due to torpor, haste, specialization of interest, self-protective reactions, pride, passion, and many other conditions.

Much evil comes from physiological deficiencies. The tale of evil traced directly and indirectly to this source runs on without limit.

Much evil is due to the power of brutish masses that move without being organized and directed to meet the requirements of those more delicate organizations of high value that are dependent on them. Fire, flood, earthquake, avalanche, famine,

are examples; many "accidents" are of this sort. The higher
values always consist of an organization of activities more delicate and easily destroyed than the underlying masses upon which
the higher are dependent. Much evil is due to the fact that these
lower orders are very incompletely subject to the higher.

These examples of evil will suffice. Our purpose is not to set
forth any complete list of all the different kinds of evil, but only
to point out the diversity of kinds of evil and to show that evil
has no single source and no universal principle which applies to
all forms of it. Thus the idea of a devil responsible for evil is not
justified because evils have no common character nor source. On
the other hand, the idea of God as growth of value and meaning
in the world, is supported by the fact that goods do have a common
nature.

XIII. GOD AND PERSONALITY

Perhaps a question has been forming in the minds of many:
If God is growth of meaning, can we then think of God in terms
of personality? Thinking of him so would seem to promise
closer unity with God, for personality is very precious and very
familiar to us all. What have the current philosophies of religion
to answer to this question?

The liberal in religion is emphatic in asserting that God is a
personality. At times he seems to make this the supreme issue.

The traditional supernaturalist also teaches this in many cases,
but the issue is not so clear. His doctrine of the Trinity does not
mean that God is three persons, but it does somewhat cloud the
teaching that God is one single personality in the sense that we
understand personality among human beings. Some traditional
supernaturalists say that God is not a personality in the sense that
men are. When that claim is made one is in doubt concerning
what is meant by attributing personality to God. Again, some say
that God is a personality in the sense that a man is, but with certain
powers magnified to infinity. This claim raises certain perplexing and perhaps insoluble problems which we shall not discuss
at this point.

The new supernaturalists are very emphatic in applying certain personal pronouns to God. God must be a "Thou." But they refuse to discuss the problem of personality in God. Here again they resort to the claim that God is super-rational and it is impossible to give any rationally coherent statement about his nature. All statements about God that are rationally coherent are irrelevant, incompetent, and immaterial. The fact that supernaturalists assert God to be "the Absolutely Other," set over against man as radically different and opposed to human nature, would indicate that personality does not apply to God in their view. But this group feels that any attempt to make a rational statement of what is the nature of God is doomed to error and futility and is, furthermore, a piece of blasphemous arrogance.

The humanists also say that God must be a personality but he is not a real personality. He is a fiction, like Santa Claus. This fictitious personality called God has been very precious to religious souls and has served noble ends. This fiction has acted as a symbol which served to inspire heroic striving, give peace and comfort in time of trouble, and generally produce highly beneficial attitudes or "religious experience." But the important value through all this was the religious experience induced by the symbol, not the reality of any divine personality. Some humanists are emphatic in their denials of any such superhuman personality. Others are agnostic, others believe. But always the important thing to them is the effect upon men of holding the belief, not the objective reality of the divine personality. Here again we see the continuity of humanism with liberalism, for this emphasis on human good, with belief in God as a tool to improve human life, was and still is the burden of the teaching of religious liberalism.

The new naturalists are like the new supernaturalists in holding fast to the reality of God, but they seriously question the character of personality in God.

This problem of God as personality really reaches much deeper issues than those ordinarily discussed. The basic issue is this: Does God respond to the intimate needs and attitudes of the individual personality? Or it may be thus expressed: Do human personality and fellowship find in God the source of their origin, the continuous source of their enrichment, and the condition of their most abundant flowering? If these questions are answered in the affirmative, the religious man has all that he is demanding when he asserts that God must be a personality.

Now the religious naturalist says that God does respond to the intimate needs and attitudes of each individual personality. But a being that is ready to do that for every different individual personality cannot be a personality. God is source of human personality and fellowship. God does give to personalities all their enrichment and their fullest flowering. God does catch up the intimate and secret outreachings of the human heart. But to represent God as a personality would be to give him a character which would make such ministrations impossible by reason of the essential limitations of personality.

The modern sciences of personality, psychology, social psychology, and anthropology, are beginning to make clear the answer to certain important questions about personality. What yields response to the most deep and intimate needs and attitudes of personality? What generates personality, sustains and promotes its growth, and brings it to highest fulfillment? The reality which does all this is a very complex and delicate system of connections of mutual control which grows up between the individual psycho-physical organism and its physical and social environment. Put in other words, it is the growth of community between the individual and his environment. This community is a living matrix of connections which flower into meanings and which generate personality in the individual, which sustain it, which respond to its deepest outreachings, which enrich it and bring it to highest development. Community generates all these values of personality when the person maintains the right attitudes of responsiveness and is kept free of undue self-concern.

In light of these discovered truths about human personality, one can approach God in two ways in the interest of personality. On the one hand he may flout all this scientific knowledge, ignore the known facts, and say that God must be a personality in order to meet the needs of personality. On the other hand, he may recognize the known facts and see that God must be, not a divine personality, but something that is more rich and pervasive and precious than any personality could ever be. In the one case you have a figment constructed to satisfy the craving of the heart. In the other you have a reality which does truly sustain, enrich, and foster personality.

Some who see that God cannot be limited to personality as humanly conceived say that God must be more than a personality but at least include personality. If by that one means that God encompasses and fosters and dwells in the personalities of men, it is true enough. God does encompass the personalities of men and fold them deep in love, meaning by love that whole system of connections of mutual support which keeps all the cells and organs of the body working together in the interest of the organism as a whole, which brings innumerable sources of life into the organism from the surrounding world, which brings the riches of thought and feeling to the individual from his social environment and from the accumulated meanings of the past. Far deeper than at the level of our consciousness does God sustain and foster and encompass with tender care each individual personality. Each of us lives in a matrix made up of innumerably complicated connections of mutual support, ranging from atoms to great historic cultures. This matrix is made of living, dynamic, delicately responsive bonds which move and change and transform one another in deep and delicate response to the changing needs of each individual.

This matrix of which we speak is not the whole universe. The universe, we have reiterated, is full of brutish, destructive masses and forces that ofttimes tear in pieces these bonds of mutual support and bring evils of many kinds to each individual. But all these evils do not make the power of good any less important or any less real.

God, then, is not a personality, but God is more worthful than any personality could ever be. God is not nature and he is not the universe, but he is the growth of living connections of value in the universe. If one wishes he can say this is not God but it is the work of God. Practically it comes to the same thing.

Another question is often raised on this matter of words applied to God. Why do we use the personal pronoun "he" if God is not a personality? The answer should be very plain. We simply do not have a pronoun with which to refer to a reality which is superior to personality. The pronoun "it" is almost always understood to mean not the superpersonal, but the impersonal, and "impersonal" is universally accepted in much the same sense as "un-American" and other negative terms of that sort. It means something less worthy than the positive term from which it is distinguished. The pronoun "it" certainly does not convey the meaning of God so adequately as "he," because God is not impersonal, meaning subpersonal, but is superpersonal. We can scarcely have a widely accepted pronoun for God until we have a better idea of God's nature which is widely accepted.

There is still another stumbling block of words for some minds. When we say that God is "growth of connections of value" they think the statement cannot be true if it sounds ridiculous when substituted for the name of God. For example, one can scarcely begin a prayer with the invocation, "Oh, thou growth of connections." The blunder here is so obvious that it would scarcely seem to require comment, but the writer has found that some minds are troubled by it. One does not address a being by a statement about the nature of that being. For example, one does not address his friend, "Good morning, psycho-physical organism." But the fact that such an address is an absurdity is no evidence whatsoever that the individual in question is not a psycho-physical organism. So it is with God. The name of the deity is God, and that is the word to use, or else other titles of honor. Certainly one does not use the description of his nature when addressing the Divine Presence, any more than he would do it in addressing any other object of respect. One addresses God: he does not address the definition of God.

XIV. THE FATHERHOOD OF GOD

If God is not a personality, what, then, are we to do with the time-honored, long cherished concept of God as Father? Although we may forget it, we all use " Father " as a *figurative* term in speaking of God. Perhaps if we study this figure reasonably we shall find its important meanings.

" The fatherhood of God " is a term by which we express three facts about God: first, that he creates human personality; second, that he makes us all brothers; and third, that he bestows a great love upon each of us. Now these three meanings that are included in " God the Father " are precisely what we have been setting forth as the distinguishing characteristics of God, when God is identified with growth of connections of mutual support. It is this growth which brings forth human personality, that is, creates it. Human personality arises when the connections of mutual control between psycho-physical organisms develop into meanings that are communicated by symbols. These symbols are the instrumentalities by which connections of mutual support and mutual meaning can be vastly enriched. The biological and social processes by which growth of connections of mutual support and control bring into existence the intimate group, and then foster in their midst the use of significant symbols by which meanings are communicated and personalities are developed — all this is now being set forth by writers and investigators.[8]

The love which God bestows upon each individual is a dynamic, active love. It is the love of tender care and delicate responsiveness to human need. It is not an almighty love. But it is far more pervasive, potent, and tender than any love of any personality could ever be. We are far from suggesting here that God has those visceral contractions and glandular modifications which go along with certain states of consciousness which we human beings experience and call our " love." We have the tendency to think that our own private states of consciousness represent the highest reality in the universe and that any being which did not have such states of consciousness would be less than we. What God may have in the way of consciousness or super-consciousness or beyond consciousness, we do not know. We do know the mighty gentleness, we know the tender care which characterize his being. We fall asleep every night in almost complete unawareness of the rhythm of billions of living connections that sustain and refresh and enrich. Why do we think it important to lift our puny little speculations and insist that God must have the sort of viscerally controlled consciousness that we have or else be less than we? Certain facts about God's being and nature we know. Many other facts we do not know. Let us rest on what we know, strive always to know more, but never insist that God must conform to our wishes and our feeling-responses prior to the factual discovery that such is the case. God in the mystery of his being is probably much greater than any wish we could have for him. Surely we do not think greatly of God when we insist that he be like us.

XV. THE USE OF AN IDEA OF GOD

The use of an idea of God is not that of luring people into the religious way of life. It is true that many have prostituted the idea to this function. They have tried to dress it with attractive adornments. To do that is just as pernicious as it would be for one, in explaining how to raise carrots, to try to set the ideas forth in a manner that would lure people into eating carrots. Operational ideas required to direct activities in such a way as to raise good carrots must not be made ornamental, else their true function will be perverted. One eats carrots, one worships God; in both cases the attitude must be appreciative. But the appreciation should be directed not to the operational *idea* about carrots, but to the *reality* of the carrots. So also the *idea* of God should not be so adorned as to lure people to it; rather its function should be to show people how to enter into conscious appreciation of the *reality* of God.

What is this reality of God which we should appreciate? It is that infinite wealth of value to be discovered in concrete situations of actual living. How are we to enter into conscious appreciation and devotion to this living reality of God? We stated the method in chapter 10 — propulsion, crisis, decision, release, and specification. This method is the way we open ourselves to the work of God. It is the way we divest ourselves of the hard covering which encloses our personalities like a shell, the way we get rid of the protective devices, the fixations, the unconscious resistances, so that connections of appreciation, affection, dynamic interchange, and creative action can grow between our individual personalities and all the rich fullness of the world round about.

God is growth of meaning. Meanings grow when connections do. It is clear, then, how a person can make his way to God. He must seek out and foster mutually sustaining and enriching connections between the activities which make up his living and those of persons and groups and physical nature round about him. When he maintains the right attitude, these connections grow marvelously. He and his world are transformed by the working of the power of unlimited growth. If one maintains the attitude, practices the method, is guided by the operational idea, this power can work in his living and in his dying; it can work in the moments of his deepest abasement and in his highest triumph. The transfiguring power of God is intimately present but largely veiled to our appreciative awareness. The veil can be drawn away by the right attitude, method, and operational idea. The transfiguration of the world waits on men to meet these conditions.

NOTES

[1] See Charles Hartshorne, *Beyond Humanism* (Chicago, 1937).
[2] See "Values — Primary Data of Religious Inquiry," *Journal of Religion*, Oct., 1936.
[3] See Bridgeman, *The Logic of Modern Physics*.
[4] See p. 231.
[5] E. S. Brightman, *The Problem of God*.
[6] J. G. Machen, *The Christian View of Man*, p. 42.
[7] See "Values — Primary Data for Religious Inquiry," *Journal of Religion*, Oct., 1936; also Wieman and Wieman, *Normative Psychology of Religion*, Chap. III.
[8] See C. H. Cooley, *Human Nature and the Social Order;* George Mead, *The Mind, Self and Society;* Regina Westcott Wieman, *The Modern Family and the Church*.

BIBLIOGRAPHY

Growth in individual personality and in community between persons, occurring beyond the scope of conscious human purpose, which we have taken as our approach to God, is well presented by John Dewey (without religious reference) in *Human Nature and Conduct,* Part I; by C. H. Horton in *Human Nature and the Social Order,* chap. 2; by Ellsworth Faris in *The Nature of Human Nature,* chaps. 2, 3, 11, 12, 27; by L. T. Hobhouse in *Development and Purpose,* Part I, chaps. 3, 4, 5, and Part II, chaps. 3, 8, 9; by H. A. Overstreet in *The Enduring Quest;* by J. C. Smuts in *Holism and Evolution;* and by A. N. Whitehead in *Religion in the Making,* pp. 111–20. The criteria by which to identify God are discussed by Georgia Harkness in *The Recovery of Ideals;* by B. E. Meland in *Modern Man's Worship,* chap. 12; by A. N. Whitehead in *Religion in the Making,* pp. 149–50; and by H. N. Wieman in " Values — Primary Data for Religious Inquiry," *Journal of Religion,* Oct., 1936.

12.

RELIGIOUS CREATIVITY

THE universe which we experience transforms its nature according to the conditions of our bodies. The world reaches our consciousness through the nervous system, through the sense organs, through the way the glands and other organs function in the psycho-physical organism. Therefore when an individual changes the connections which hold between the psycho-physical organism and its operative environment, and between the several parts of the organism itself, it is obvious that he will change the world as he experiences it. Hence a change in the basic attitude of the personality will change his world. That is to say, the world we experience arises from interaction between the psycho-physical organism and its environment, and between its own several parts. So when we change the psycho-physical organism we change the experience.

Some of these transformations of the universe due to changes in the organism are so commonplace that we take them as a matter of course. Getting a little drunk, or taking opium, or falling in love, or suffering from anemia, are ways by which the experienced universe is transformed most radically. Changes of certain glandular processes will change the experienced world for the subject, also. Furthermore, worship is a way of changing the basic attitude of the psycho-physical organism so that the experienced world becomes different, more rich with qualities of value. Worship does this as truly as does falling in love. Indeed love is a kind of worship.

I. CREATIVE WORSHIP

How the organism will be changed by love or worship depends upon what is loved or worshiped and how profoundly. The world may take on vividness and depth, color and sound, form and feeling by reason of the changed sensitivity of the organism and the quickened powers of appreciative consciousness, as it did for the poet who wrote:

This day I have seen lovely things I never saw before:
Sunshine through a glass of marmalade,
An egg yolk in a blue bowl,
A rainbow in soapsuds on dishwater,
The underside of a white oak leaf,
White ruffled curtains sifting moonlight on a scrubbed kitchen floor.
The crinkled smile of a little girl who had new shoes with tassels.
Empurpled mud under the willows where white geese slept.
A blue gate.
Ruts in the road at sunset.
My lover kissed my eyes last night.[1]

The world has an infinite variety of aspects, each aspect being relative to some disposition of the psycho-physical organism that reacts to it. Furthermore any one of these aspects is just as real as any other. The world is the totality of all its aspects. Anyone who talks about an inner core of reality which is supposed to be noumenal while all these aspects are mere external phenomena, is really confused in his thinking. He is really talking about some further aspect which no one has yet experienced, but which is no more real than these others. Any reality of this world which any mind might know would have to be either some aspect of it, or some set of aspects, or the totality of all aspects. The so-called noumenal reality would simply be some further aspect, namely the noumenal.

Now worship is one way of achieving a different kind of world by changing our way of reacting so that we are sensitive to certain qualities which could not previously reach appreciative consciousness, so that we do things we would not otherwise do and thus elicit features of the world that were previously inaccessible to experience, so that our imagination functions differently thus bringing to consciousness meanings and fancies and feelings that we could not before undergo.

It is true that no person can lift himself completely out of that total system of influences which make him react and have the attitude that he does have. The culture he inherits and the ways of thinking and feeling that prevail among the people with whom he most intimately lives will make him see and think and feel in one way rather than another. But granted all this powerful control exercised over the individual by his physical and social milieu, it still remains true that individuals differ in respect to what they can think and perceive and feel. Furthermore, individuals by certain practices and by self-culture may develop this uniqueness to an extraordinary degree. Artistic and aesthetic practices are one way to do it. Practices of worship, including the disciplines of mysticism and asceticism, are other ways of doing it.

People who have achieved a more gorgeous world by developing or transforming the basic attitude of sensitivity and appreciation might be divided into four classes. First come the artists and aesthetes — not the artists nor the aesthetes, but persons who are a combination of the two. This kind of person might not have the technical skill to write poetry or compose music or dance great dances or paint pictures. Neither would he be the kind of sentimental person that sometimes comes to mind when one speaks of an aesthete. But there are an artistic-aesthetic sensitivity and appreciation which enable one to experience a world very much more entrancing than the one that most people know, a world of the kind so well described by Kipling in " The Last Rhyme of True Thomas."

The artist-aesthete standing by the milk-white thorn can see in the common cattle grazing beneath the knowes something that is wonderful, that thrills him with its beauty or with the fancies it stirs in his imagination or with connections of meaning between it and other matters. He can see in the thistledown that floats against the naked sky something that stirs his imagination with its symbolism or that has rich aesthetic appeal. The world he experiences is rich with fancy, with aesthetic qualities, with matters that stir deep ecstatic feelings.

The second kind of person whose sensitive responsiveness transforms his world is the lover — not only those experiencing sex love, although they are included, but also those who love their fellow men with a very great and unfailing love. There are a few rare people who seem to love almost everyone just because he is human. Such people live blessed lives. They glow, they are radiant. The world they experience seems to be full of all manner of precious value. A good example of this kind of person is Father Vaillant in Willa Cather's *Death Comes to the Archbishop*.

The third kind of person whose attitude allows him to discern a more splendid world is the mystic-saint, like St. Francis of Assisi. We have a number of his chants and songs which tell us something of the kind of world he experienced, and how it differed from the world of ordinary experience as a sunset sky differs from the drab, smoky, cloud-lined vault that hangs over Chicago on a winter's afternoon.

Finally there is the prophet, who discerns a world which differs from those of the other three as these differ from one another. There is no clear demarcation between the several kinds of attitude we have thus far mentioned. They merge with one another at their edges, and perhaps no man can have a deep experience of any one of them without experiencing the others also to some degree. But they do differ in respect to the point of emphasis and major form that they assume. This is particularly the case with the prophet, for he is one who is torn between two worlds. Perhaps he has had an extraordinary number of glimpses of the world experienced by the artist-aesthete-lover-mystic-saint. At any rate he is profoundly convinced that this world of theirs has being, although he may project it into the future or into heaven, or beyond some great abyss which can be crossed only at cost of great suffering. At any rate he feels a terrific tension between the world of ordinary life which he experiences in part, and that other kind of world which is so much better. Perhaps an elaborate psychological study of the prophet would reveal that he had been exposed to two or more divergent and conflicting ways of life and had not been able to work out a *modus vivendi* by which to participate integratively in both.

We might say that the prophet's experience is due to the fact that he has a tendency toward an attitude that would give him one kind of world, but at the same time he is caught in the network of antithetic associations with other people that drag him down from that attitude; yet he experiences enough of that better world to prevent him from being content with the mean world shared with ordinary men. The experience of the prophet is described in a poem by Pushkin, rendered into English by Maurice Baring:

> With fainting soul athirst for Grace
> I wandered in a desert place,
> And at the crossing of the ways
> I saw the sixfold Seraph blaze;
> He touched mine eyes with fingers light
> As sleep that cometh in the night;
> And like a frightened eagle's eyes
> They opened wide with prophecies.
> He touched mine ears and they were drowned
> With tumult and a roaring sound. . . .
>
> And with his sword my breast he cleft,
> My quaking heart thereout he reft,
> And in the yawning of my breast
> A coal of living fire he pressed.
> Then in the desert I lay dead
> And God called unto me and said
> "Arise, and let my voice be heard!
> Charged with my will go forth and span
> The land and sea, and let my Word
> Lay waste with fire the heart of man."

The prophet comes passionately denouncing the world that is, and proclaiming the imminence of another world. He generally says that this other world is to be attained by men's undergoing a change of heart. "Repent," he says, "for the kingdom of heaven is at hand."

This change of heart is precisely what we mean by change in the basic attitude of the psycho-physical organism. We put the matter into modern psychological language, but the meaning is very much the same as that of the prophet who proclaims that the kingdom of God will descend upon men when their hearts are pure or when they repent of their sins and are cleansed and changed in spirit. Or the obverse side is equally true: the world will suffer devastation if men persist in their evil ways.

Worship, which includes repentance and may involve conversion, is the chief religious way in which men seek that transformation of attitude (change of heart or way of life) which will usher in a transfigured world. All we have said about the kind of world we experience when we take one attitude or another will be seen to bear directly upon the subject of prayer or worship when we remember that prayer and worship are precisely the cultivation of an attitude which is so adjusted to the source of all highest values that this source can pour its riches most abundantly into the world which we experience.

II. SOCIAL NEGLECT OF PRAYER

Why then, if worship can be so potent and enriching, has one of its major forms, prayer, fallen so far from use and into abuse? Is prayer an outworn procedure in religion?

Prayer as an impulsive act in moments of crisis will probably always continue. There are good psychological reasons why it should do so. Again, many still pray because they have formed the habit. But it is very true that prayer as a deliberate and professed practice is not so highly esteemed as in the past. Its social prestige has greatly declined. The occasions on which it is considered proper to pray are far more rare today than fifty years ago. Some deeply religious people may say that this is all to the good since prayer practiced as a mere propriety is not prayer at all. But the matter goes much deeper than that. There is reason to think that the occasions on which people sincerely desire to pray, or are able to pray, are much fewer than they were fifty or even ten years ago. It would seem that prayer as an important practice in human living, or as necessary in man's dealing with God, is no longer prized as once it was.

Doubtless there are many reasons for this change in our view of prayer and its practice. Some of these may indicate marked improvement. Unquestionably the elimination of a great deal of "praying" is matter for rejoicing. On the other hand, the right practice of prayer is of great importance and there may be irreparable loss when it is omitted. There is one cause for the prevalent neglect of prayer which might be corrected — a cause for which the interpreters of religion are responsible. They have not interpreted prayer in such a way that the modern mind can see its rational basis and its true worth.

In times when tradition rules religious living it is not necessary to have an understanding of current practices such as prayer. These practices are carried on because they are customary. In such a case there are both gain and loss with respect to prayer — gain when the custom perpetuates a sincere and profound religious practice, loss when the practice becomes a matter of formal propriety and nothing more. But when the authority of tradition declines, as it has done today, the inertia of custom is not sufficient to keep anything going, whether it be prayer or something else. In such times the critical intelligence awakens to ask, What is the good of it? Why should we do it? What is the rational justification for it? If no intelligent basis can be shown for the continuance of the customary practice people will tend to turn away from it.

It is true that mere rational justification succeeds no better than mere custom in perpetuating any undertaking. The only things that can keep it going are some vital need that finds satisfaction in it and the experience of great values issuing in its practice. But should intelligent inquiry seem to show that these resultant values are illusory and indicate that the vital need can be better satisfied in other ways, the more critically minded will lose their interest in the undertaking. Such has been the fate of prayer in the modern world.

We have said that the expounders of religion are themselves to blame for this state of affairs. They have not satisfactorily set forth the intelligible nature of prayer. Some will say that prayer has no intelligible nature, a statement which supports our contention that its intelligible nature has not been made plain. This is one of the major reasons why prayer has fallen into disrepute among intelligent people.

The liberals were the first who tried to interpret prayer. But their attempts were lacking in rigor and cogency. They did not meet the need for an answer to the questions, What is the good of it? Why should we do it? An interpretation or rational defense which breaks down before the inquiring mind is worse than none at all. It advertises the irrational nature of the practice in question.

After the liberals came the humanists, who said that the value of prayer, when it had any value, lay in its subjective effects upon the one who prays. Prayer is a kind of autosuggestion. In prayer you are talking to yourself and nothing more. When and if that does any good, prayer has some value. But to think that by prayer you can " change God " is folly, first because there is no God, and second because if there were your prayers could make no difference to him.

At this stage in the development of modern interpretation of prayer came the new supernaturalists. Seeing what a sorry mess resulted from the attempts to put prayer, and religion generally, on a " scientific " or " rational " or " intelligible " basis, they rejected with scorn the whole effort of modern thought to show any grounds of intelligence in the practices of religion. Religion, so far as it has any justification at all, is super-rational, they declared. Trying to climb up to God by the ladder of reason or scientific inquiry or intelligence is like trying to climb up into the sky with a ladder. There is nothing to lean it against except the azure depths, and they will not support anything at all. So the supernaturalists pushed the ladder to one side and claimed to be able to reach the goal of religious endeavor by a faith and a revelation which went beyond reason.

We have seen how poorly the liberals, the humanists, and the new supernaturalists have " defended " prayer. No wonder this ancient form of outreach has fallen into neglect. An age that regularly asks such questions as, Why? What for? What is the good of it? has got such answers as we have sketched! These are no answers at all. Has the new naturalism any more tenable position concerning prayer?

III. PRAYER ACCORDING TO NATURALISM

In prayer we are dealing with something very mysterious. Ah, says the bystander, there you go, hiding behind a mystery in order to excuse yourself from making any intelligible statement about the matter. But wait, it is not so bad as that. In prayer we are dealing with something as mysterious as that with which a gardener deals when he raises flowers and shrubs; as mysterious as that with which the parent deals when he ministers to the growing personality of his child; as mysterious as that with which the teacher deals in developing a mind, or a doctor in helping a wound to heal, or a consulting psychologist when he tries to restore a diseased personality to wholesome living or to bring a deranged or broken home back to a normal state. All such mystery is commonplace enough but very wonderful nevertheless. We know something about it in terms of biochemistry, physiology, psychology, and the social sciences. But all these tell us chiefly of mechanisms by which the organic process of growth can be assisted. The growth itself remains the mystery. It is a process of progressive synthesis whereby elements previously segregated are brought into relations of mutual control. So much we are able to say about it.

What has all this talk of growth to do with prayer, some may ask. Our reply restates that prayer proper deals with something very mysterious, as mysterious as growth. In fact, prayer is directed to God; and the work of God is the natural process of growth of meaning and value. Prayer cannot be intelligently examined apart from consideration of God. How prayer works can be known only as we see what the God is to whom it is directed.

Amidst all the clashing destructive forces that rend and tear and maim, we have already discovered that there is a vast, intricate network of connections of mutual support and control between diverse activities. These connections are constantly being broken down, torn asunder, and left hanging with ragged edges. But they are also constantly growing anew. This great growing process is very tender and very gentle and very mighty. Its might lies in the fact that connections grow anew when broken down, and that it cannot be entirely destroyed by all the chaos and conflict that tear down its several parts, so deeply is it rooted in the nature of existence. In making this statement about its indestructibility we are not talking about the future destiny of the cosmos, for no one knows about that. We mean only that all the destructive forces we now see at work have so far been unable to root out this deep, wide development of organic connections, this formation of internal relations, this growth of community, this progressive integration.

This formation of connections of mutual support and control occurs at all levels, from electrons and atoms and molecules up through cells, vegetables and animals, minds, brotherhoods, cultures and history. Each individual personality is submerged, sustained, and pervaded by this infinitely intricate formation of connections of mutual support between diverse activities. Electrons and atoms innumerable within the body of each person and in his environment work together to sustain him and enrich him. We repeat that not every occurrence among electrons and in the more complex bodies is working to promote the fulfillment of life. Quite the contrary is often the case. We only say that amidst all the obstruction and destruction which work against the growth of values there is also the growth itself which is rooted deep in the cosmic process. The growth of these connections which culminate in highest values forms a sustaining matrix that surrounds each personality and works through it to upbuild and enrich. The sciences of biology, genetic psychology, and social psychology make this plain.

The life of the body and of the mind are submerged and sustained and developed by this larger growth which roots in the depths of existence and flowers loftily in the highest manifestations of personality and culture. This complex working of connections of support in the mind and body of the individual, and round about it, is infinitely wider and deeper than the scope of human consciousness. The consciousness of the individual is like a tiny periscope which rises above the vast ocean of sustaining reality. Millions of cells are constantly working together in the body of the individual to sustain and fulfill his life. Heart, lungs, glands, and other organs are working together with one another and with innumerable factors in the environment. Enormously complex interchanges between individuals, groups, and institutions are going on in the social world. Besides the physiological complexities that support the development of the personality, and besides the contemporaneously social, we know that millions of persons and thousands and thousands of generations of the past have made contributions which are at this moment ministering to the life of the individual although he is not conscious of them. Without these the life of each individual personality would fall to a lower level or be destroyed altogether. Again let us repeat, however, that the forces of destruction are also vast and always busy. We are not talking of the cosmic whole when we speak of this work of God that sustains and lifts life to higher levels. We are speaking of something which works very widely and deeply in the cosmos but is not the whole of it.

All we have said in the last three paragraphs was intended to show that the individual person who prays is one who lives and moves and has his being in a system of connections that are ever forming and re-forming, losing and regaining, and that all his life and its fulfillment are the work of these. Such   of all this as comes within the range of his conscious understanding and control is infinitesimal compared to the complexity and magnitude of the whole.

We cannot understand prayer and its power until we see, with the naturalists, that the personality is thus woven into an enormously vast system which works for the most part outside the scope of its own consciousness and machinations. The second thing we must see is that certain attitudes of the psycho-physical organism can greatly facilitate the formation of innumerable connections of value that work outside the scope of consciousness but support and enrich the personality. The third thing we must see is that prayer is the attempt to form just such facilitating attitudes. Then we can see the need and the power of prayer. This is what prayer and its power are according to the new naturalism.

IV. SOURCE OF POWER IN PRAYER

There is one negative statement about prayer that needs to be reiterated again and again. People sometimes accept the negation consciously but then proceed forthwith to deal with prayer as if the negation had not been made. The negation is that prayer does not consist of the words that are used. The total process of prayer may include words or may not, but to confound the prayer with the words is to fall into hopeless confusion. In prayer one is talking to himself. But he is not praying to himself because the prayer is not the words. To be sure in prayer the words are not ordinarily addressed to oneself. They are addressed to God, and rightly so. But when we say that in prayer one is talking to himself we mean the words have no power over God. The words have power only over oneself. But the prayer does have power with God. The words affect oneself only but the prayer affects God. This difference between the words and the prayer is of fundamental importance.

What, then, is this prayer which does not consist of the words, but which has power with God? Prayer is that voluntarily established attitude of the personality which is so responsive to God that God can work more potently in the world than would otherwise be possible. Prayer is that attitude of the psycho-physical organism (when voluntarily established) which is so plastic and responsive to the growth of connections of mutual support between the individual and his environment that many increases of value can come to pass in the world as a consequence. Therefore, we say, when a man truly prays, God answers by bringing forth good in the world which could not have occurred without the prayer. This increased good that comes in answer to prayer is the further growth of connections of value between many diverse activities.

But we must note that this attitude of responsiveness which favors the formation of connections of value is prayer only when it is voluntarily established. If it is not voluntarily established it may be equally effective but it is not prayer. By " not voluntarily established " we mean it might be a stereotyped attitude due to early home training. It might be due to the individual's participation in a group which developed this attitude in him. In such cases the attitude would not be prayer because it would not be voluntarily established. But when this attitude is voluntarily established by him, it is prayer.

Perhaps all this can now be gathered into a definition of prayer. Prayer is that voluntarily established attitude of the personality which enables connections of value to grow far beyond the scope of ordinary instrumentalities of consciousness. Fortunately for us the psycho-physical organism of each individual is so made that a vast system of sustaining connections can keep on forming within it as fast as they are torn down and, under favorable conditions, can rise to higher levels of value. But all this can go on much more abundantly when the psycho-physical organism has the right attitude. It is always possible to improve the adjustment of the personality so that these connections can grow more widely, deeply, and loftily. Prayer is the attempt of the individual to make this improvement.

Man prays. But the growth of these connections of value is the work of God. Prayer is that disposition of the personality, voluntarily established, which enables the work of God to go on more abundantly and blessedly. History may be transformed by prayer; that is, when personalities have a favorable attitude toward one another and toward the total system of growing connections, this growth proceeds more richly and powerfully than when they are otherwise disposed. When and if men voluntarily improve their attitudes to this wide and deep formation of connections of mutual support between innumerable and diverse activities, goods come to pass which would otherwise be impossible. This is the power of prayer.

The power of prayer is demonstrated when once it is seen that a psycho-physical organism delicately responsive to the needs of the formation of new connections of mutual support can develop an attitude which will enable these formations to occur more frequently and diversely. This does not mean that all adaptive responsiveness of the psycho-physical organism to the formation of such new connections is due to prayer. Such connections are forming all the while within each cell and between the cells of the individual's body. They are coming into existence constantly between the different organs of his body. They are developing in the ceaseless transformations of interaction between his body and its physical environment. More important still, for the higher development of personal values, these connections of mutual support are forming every minute between the thoughts, purposes, feelings, impulses of one person, and those of others. They form first of all between people who are associated in personal acquaintance with one another. But beyond the fellowships of primary associations are hundreds and thousands and millions of other people with whom you and I are forming connections of mutual support or mutual frustration in ways that far exceed the scope of our consciousness. All that one does, says, thinks, feels, will make for mutual support or mutual frustration between himself and all these other people now living. Also his doing and thinking have connections with millions now dead and will affect millions not yet born.

Obviously it is wholly beyond the scope of consciousness to exercise any supervision over all this growth in connectedness. Effective connectedness depends primarily not upon an individual's conscious purposes and management, but upon the deep subconscious disposition of his personality. Is his personality shaped and directed by, and is it sensitively responsive to, the system of mutual support? Do his habits and impulses spring from a total orientation of his whole personality to God — understanding God to be the power that works in the form of growth of connections of mutual control?

What is the difference between this orientation of the total personality which makes for growth of connections of mutual support between him and the rest of the world, and that other orientation which makes for mutual frustration between his activities and those of other persons and of subhuman natural processes? We can answer that question with a very simple and trite term. The orientation characterized by good will makes for growth of connections of mutual support. Ill will or indifference makes for the opposite. Good will here means not that one agrees with everybody else and accords with all that everyone else is doing. Plainly that would be impossible and destructive. But what is meant by good will is that the total personality, subconscious as well as conscious, including impulses, habits, feelings, glandular processes, is so directed that the individual always strives for that reorganization of interests and conditions whereby the good of each may contribute to the good of all others, and vice versa. This however cannot be restricted merely to conscious purpose. Consciousness is generally preoccupied with specific purposes which are much more definite and limited than is this orientation of good will which we have mentioned. Rather this orientation of the total personality consists in a reliable readiness to recognize and seize upon every course of action which makes for community of good whenever it emerges in practical concrete situations. This readiness is not merely a conscious purpose. It must be deeper than that. It must be a voluntarily developed set or attitude or disposition of the total personality. When the conscious and subconscious orientation of the total personality is of this sort, much is accomplished where no specific purposes were formed. Many subtle, delicate, and unconscious reactions are made to all manner of conditions which favor the development of connections of mutual support in ways that conscious purpose cannot compass. Compared with this developed subconscious attitude, conscious purpose is narrow, cumbersome, and semi-skilled.

We can put the matter in still another way. It is commonplace to say that people today are interdependent in a wide and complicated fashion, far beyond the scope of any conscious purpose which an individual human mind can compass. This interdependence calls for mutual support between all our several doings and interests and purposes. Such support cannot be brought about by our having in consciousness a purpose so wide and intricate as to include specifically the interests of all these other people with whom we are bound together. The human mind is not great enough for that. Therefore the best we can do is to have our total personalities attuned to the demands of this close network of interdependence, so that we shall impulsively and habitually and subconsciously react to situations in a way that is receptive and responsive to the interests of others. In this way we can be subconsciously and progressively transformed by this total life of interdependence so that we shall habitually think and feel, not as others do, but in ways that can supplement those of others and cooperate with them. Such sensitivity and responsiveness to the demands of a vast and intricate web of interdependence are required for living today — not only for abundant living but for mere existence. They are achieved, we repeat, not primarily by the comprehensiveness of our conscious purposes, but by the disposition of our total personalities.

V. ANSWER TO PRAYER

Now prayer, we say, is establishment of such a disposition of the total personality. How this occurs may be briefly sketched. Prayer is self-commitment to God. God, at the higher levels of Christianity, means our Father in heaven. The fatherhood of God means that work of God whereby we are brothers. It means that power of God which works to make the whole world one family. To be a family means to have all activities connected in mutual support so that the unique individuality of each is fostered by the unique individuality of others. It means also to have animals and the physical processes of nature connected with human activities in mutual support and mutual control. By now it should be obvious that sincere self-commitment to God so understood will induce in the personality that attitude of readiness and responsiveness to all the complex and subtle interplay between the individual and others, and between man and nature, which is most favorable to the growth of such connections. Prayer directed to our Father in heaven, even when he is pictured as a big man up in the sky, will have this effect if the full significance of fatherhood is grasped.

Through prayer wounds can be healed which otherwise could find no cure. That is to say, when the total psycho-physical organism of the individual yields implicitly and completely to the healing power of vital connections between the cells and between them and the sustaining environment, it will often recover; worry and fret, on the other hand, militate against recovery. We know that sleep is one of the best means of healing for the wounded or ill or exhausted. Why should this be true? Because in sleep one sinks so deeply into this tender sustaining system of connections of mutual support that consciousness is submerged. Sleep is the best attitude for the re-formation of certain broken connections.

But for the formation of others, the most strenuous conscious activity is required. Such purposive activity may be of two sorts. It may be of the sort which subordinates all things to a fixed plan and destroys everything that interferes; then it is obstructive to the formation of those connections of value which far exceed the scope of conscious direction but which are indispensable to life and its enrichment. On the other hand strenuous conscious activity may always be kept plastic, sensitive, and responsive to all the tender connective growths. It may be informed by that attitude which favors growth of promotive connections, realizing that there are many of them of which one cannot be directly conscious. The person in whom this attitude underlies conscious activity finds rewards far beyond the fulfillment of the specific purposes which he holds in consciousness.

Prayer is the way one establishes this kind of creative attitude, whether one is engaging in strenuous activity or sinking into sleep. It is an attitude in response to which rich values grow. As a result of it friendships are formed which one could not possibly have included in his original plans; and social interactions occur between individuals and groups which they could not possibly have foreseen and directed, but which greatly enhance the good of living for each individual and for many others.

When one has this voluntarily established attitude of responsiveness to the work of God — that is, when he prays — not only cells and organisms and personalities and groups and historic processes work together for good; even inanimate physical things do so. If one picks up a stick to dislodge a cap that has caught in a treetop, or throws a stone to bring down an apple, or works with any other physical thing, the attitude of his total psycho-physical organism makes a great difference. If all the impulses of mind and body are responsive to the total relevant situation, so that every little posture, movement, pressure, glance, and touch is readily woven into connections of mutual support with the currents of air, the rays of light, the contour of the ground, the movements of the tree, the weight of the object, and so on, far beyond the powers of our analysis — then the physical world responds to one (and he to it) in the sense that it contributes its powers and resources to him. Then many factors work together in mutual support, far beyond the consciously directed movements in the total process. But if one's movements are jerky and arbitrary, if his total organism and all his impulses do not yield readily, plastically, and responsively to the innumerable factors operative in the situation, then formations of mutual support cannot occur so abundantly. The values are not nearly so great. His efforts are relatively ineffective. Human life will be infinitely less than greatest abundance until men in great numbers learn to pray effectively and frequently. Prayer is one of the essential requirements for intelligent living.

This attitude of responsiveness to God which is prayer cannot be established once and for all. It is never perfectly established; it can always be improved. It is never permanently established; it is always breaking down and declining. Hence prayer must be recurrent, like eating and sleeping and all activities which are in sustaining relation to the vital needs of human existence.

Prayer can be directed to the attainment of specific things *providing* one really prays. But to pray truly, we have seen, requires something far more than is involved in merely asking God for some specific thing. It requires primarily and fundamentally a self-commitment to the growth of connections of mutual support between the interests and activities of the individual and all else in the world that can be connected therewith in ways of mutual control. When this disposition of the personality has been established, or rather to the degree that it has been established, one may seek confidently for specific things. As a consequence of his prayer he is likely to get these if they are of such a nature that they can be woven into connections of mutual support and made a part of that community of interests which is the ever growing good of God. He is more likely to get them with prayer than without, because in prayer the total personality is yielded to the power of this ever growing good of God and made sensitive and responsive to it, and the doing of that personality and the doing of the rest of the relevant world are made cooperative to the attainment of good ends.

VI. WHAT IS CREATED BY PRAYER?

Perhaps most people who understand the organic process by which experience of the world reaches consciousness will agree with us when we say that a profound change in the psycho-physical organism's way of reacting to the environment will change our experience of the world and make it more gorgeous or more terrible or more drab than it was before, or modify it in some other direction. But some may raise a question about the objective validity of these experiences. They may say that all this is only a change in our subjective states, not a change in the objective world at all.

Our reply is that any change in the form and quality of experience caused by a transformation of the organic reaction is just as truly a change in the objective world as is a change brought about in any other way. The "world" that we experience arises from the cooperation of two factors. One is the response of the organism, including all the constructive powers of the mind; the other is the play of influence upon the organism from the outside. Change either of these two factors and you change the "world."

Now it is true that we may experience an illusory world. But we must carefully distinguish between illusion and reality. The mark of reality is not that our experience be commonplace or drab or familiar. One's experience may be as gorgeously rich, as full of intense emotion and of drifting, flaring streamers of imaginative construction as that of the artist, lover, saint, or prophet, and still be just as real as the most dull, routine, somnolescent sequence of experience that consciousness ever underwent. Illusion is not due to the content of immediate experience. Illusion is due to the interpretation we put upon our immediate experience, to anticipations concerning what will happen next. It is not due to the richness or strangeness of our present experience apart from such interpretative anticipations.

One experience is just as real as another. No matter how queer an experience may be, it is just as truly an experience of the world as any other. A familiar experience is no more real than one that is unfamiliar. The fantastic appearance which things assume when we take a drug is just as real as the most accurate computation of a physicist.

However, there is good reason for saying that the physicist's experience of transforming the world is true when that of the imbiber of drugs is not. But the reason is not that the feelings and sense qualities in the consciousness of the physicist bring him any closer to the heart of reality than do the conscious states of the opium eater. The user of drugs, the dreamer, the poet, the lover, the mystic with his strange raptures, all of these have conscious states which are just as close to reality as the physicist's.

Our justification for saying that the physicist has truth while the opium eater, the dreamer, the mystic, the moon-mad lover may or may not have it, is that the physicist understands his experience while the others may not. To understand an experience means to know how it is related to other experiences. It means to know what will happen next when certain actions are performed. It means to know what sequence of experiences will ensue when certain conditions are present. So far as the content of the experience itself is concerned, the tortures and the ecstasies of fanatic, lover, drunkard, mystic, the qualities of sense and of emotion and of dream which the consciousness undergoes when certain strange conditions are imposed upon it, are just as real as the experiences undergone in a scientifically regulated laboratory. The only difference in respect to truth is that when the conditions are scientifically controlled we know how they are related to one another, and by observing what happens when they are changed in certain ways we can know what experiences will be had when we pass from one condition to another. But the experiences themselves are no less real when we are unable to foretell what will happen next than when we can anticipate correctly. Every experience is just as truly experience of the world as any other experience.

Truth, then, consists in being able to forecast what will happen next when we have a certain experience. When men seek truth they tend to simplify experience down to those items which best serve as clues to what will happen next, and ignore all the rest. It is not correct, however, to say that truth can be found only in a simplified and impoverished experience which has shut out all the gorgeous qualities, dreams and raptures, and has narrowed itself down to the few meager elements that we have learned to use as signs for getting ready to deal with the next thing. Of course it is quite obvious that it is easier to learn how a few simplified items of experience are related to one another, than it is to know how great bursts of vision, dream, emotion, and sense quality may be connected in orderly sequence. It is much more difficult to learn how a gorgeous mass of experience may lead on to some further gorgeous mass. In the fine arts, however, especially in music, we have found an order of connection which enables us to do just that. One rapturous moment of experience makes us ready for the next. There is an orderly sequence which guides anticipation. That is precisely what knowledge is. In music and other arts, experiences magnificently rich in qualities of sense and feeling enable us to anticipate correctly what will be the basic order of future experiences.

To a much lesser degree we have learned how to anticipate the order of sequence in rich experiences of loving communion, especially between the sexes. But generally speaking throughout the world as a whole and in ordinary affairs, we are satisfied to forecast the next event in terms of the more meager and impoverished elements of experience. The most meager and impoverished are the quantitative as distinguished from the qualitative. In fact " quantitative " means stripping away all the qualities and attending solely to the units involved which we have learned to count by their numbers. Now it is probable that ratios of quantity will always provide us with the most accurate means of forecasting and ordering a sequence of experiences where such ratios are possible. In music, for example, that is the way it is done in great part. In music we know that certain ratios are correlated with certain riches of experience and these ratios with their correlated riches can be made to follow an orderly sequence by using the control of these quantitative standards. But there is a great difference between focusing attention solely on the quantitative ratios on the one hand, and on the other using these quantitative connections to guide us through the orderly sequence of experiences that are gorgeously rich in quality.

We have said that the world changes its character according as we assume one attitude or another — understanding by attitude a disposition of the total conscious and subconscious psycho-physical organism, involving a change in the way it interacts with the environment and the way its different parts interact with one another. When such a change occurs the world changes relative to that psycho-physical organism. Furthermore this new world is just as truly the real world as that old world was, for both worlds are nothing else than experience when experience is understood. Experience is understood when we know how one experience leads on to another. Therefore a change in attitude changes the world if we can understand the order that connects these new kinds of experience. Some saints have through worship attained an attitude which has changed the world of their everyday life into a kind of music or song. That is to say, their experience of the world as they went about their daily tasks has become greatly enriched with the qualities of value. This enrichment however does not impair the practical efficiency of their anticipatory reactions as they deal with pots and pans, tools and machines, trees and houses. The new experiences induced by drugs and disease, on the other hand, give us an unreal world because they cause us to anticipate an order of experience which never can be realized. But the beauties and loves that fill the consciousness of the saint may facilitate practical action even while clothing it with qualitative richness of feeling and sense. Therefore the world which they experience is not illusory. They experience one of the aspects of the real world.

The mystics, the artists, the lovers, the prophets experience a real world, no matter how gorgeous or terrible it may be, if their experience meets the criterion of reality we have indicated. We here recapitulate our discussion of this criterion. Illusory experience is not illusory because of the gorgeous or horrible qualities that fill it. The difference between illusion and truth is not in the content of immediate experience. The immediate content of experience is always real, even in the ravings of a maniac. The illusion arises only when an experience leads an individual to anticipate something which does not and cannot ensue as anticipated. The illusion always lies in the irrational nature of the anticipation, not in the immediate data.

We can transform the world, then, if we can change the disposition of the psycho-physical organism in such a way as to permit us to have more gorgeous experiences and yet control the order of these experiences so that our anticipations in general will be correct.

Of course, in any one moment of experience we can never anticipate the next in all its fullness. There is always surprise providing we open our attention to the novel features. No experience is wholly repeatable, not even in the most exact sciences. Identical repetition of the immediate content is never needed nor desirable. All that is needed is that we find some basic order running through the ever changing qualities of experience which will enable us to anticipate this order in the next experience, no matter how different in other respects it may be from the first. Such a guiding order might run through marvelously rich experiences full of innovations just as truly as through experiences that were drab and meager.

VII. FACTORS INVOLVED IN ATTITUDE

Now it is obvious that such a transformation of the world as we have suggested is by no means solely the work of worship and of its most characteristic practice in prayer which establishes attitudes of responsiveness to the source of all value. It is also the work of medicine and of all the arts and sciences. It is the work of politics and economics and of physical engineers. Alexis Carrel in his *Man the Unknown* has made some valuable suggestions concerning the means by which all the resources of modern science might be rallied to this task. But amid all the other ways and means of achieving a better world, the part of prayer and worship is much more important than the modern man is as a rule able to see, because the true nature of these religious practices has not been made plain to him.

Attitudes cannot be totally changed at will. Therefore prayer, which is a voluntary transformation of attitude toward God (conceived as the growth of connections of value), is by no means almighty. Attitudes are shaped first of all by hereditary factors. Next they are shaped by the physical environment, the food we eat, chemicals in air and water, atmospheric conditions, and much else. Third, they are profoundly shaped by other persons with whom we associate and by the traditions we inherit. No man can escape the forming and transforming influences of the group or groups with whom he lives and the culture that makes him.

But over and above all these factors which give to the psychophysical organism the kind of responsiveness which it has (its attitude), the individual is free to cultivate certain kinds of attitude as over against others. Of all voluntary acts which shape the attitude of the psycho-physical organism none go so deep and none are so effective as worship. This is so because of the nature of worship. Worship means the turning of the appreciative responsiveness of the total personality toward what the individual holds to be supremely worthful for all human living.

This shaping of the attitude by worship may be for good or ill, according to the nature of that which is worshiped. One might mistakenly revere as supremely worthful what is basely and mightily evil. For example, one might worship his race as predestined to trample all others beneath the heel of empire. In such case his worship would be demonic and would vastly augment the evil in the world. On the other hand, however, one might worship our Father in heaven, meaning the Father of us all. This in turn, as an operational idea, means the power that works to make us all members of a single family and to organize the subhuman world in bonds of love about the human family. The world is by no means such a family. But there is a power which works in the direction of making it one. This power is the growth of connections of mutual support between all men and between them and nature. When such a God is revered our worship fosters an attitude which enables the growth of rich value to flourish in the world.

VIII. WORSHIP AND SOCIAL CONFLICT

How attitudes acquired in worship can change the world may be made more plain, perhaps, by the example of a specific problem that confronts us all in daily living. Perhaps the most pressing modern problem is that of conflict. Everyone is involved in conflicts of many kinds. It may be conflict between husband and wife; for every couple, no matter how loving, is engaged in some degree of conflict, conscious or subconscious, most of the time. It may be between parent and child, or between fellow members of the office staff or competitors in business. Then of course there are the devastating conflicts between employer and employee, between races, between nations, and between other groups of all sorts. The life of every man is full of conflict all the time, whether he is aware of it or not. Conflict is not necessarily evil. Much of it becomes of highest value if one engages in it with the right attitude.

In trying to understand conflict the better, we may distinguish five modes. First there is that in which one individual (or group) seeks to prevail over another by showing through experimentation and rational demonstration that his own idea or purpose is more worthful. Or, second, in his attempt at rational persuasion one may employ the arts of appeal such as personal charm, eloquence, propaganda which is not deceptive, dramatic behavior, and other such ways of making his cause acceptable. Third, one may resort to trickery. The arts of appeal just mentioned are not trickery in our classification if they do not involve deception. Trickery is any kind of deception used to win victory over the opponent. Fourth, there is use of physical force up to the point of killing, but carried on according to the requirements of law. When violent conflict is kept within this mode its scope and kind are defined and regulated by legal prescription. In general, the police and the militia are delegated to use these means in conflict. However, co-ercive violence is used also by parents over children and by teachers over pupils, and there is much legal use of it between individuals and groups, although in civilized communities none except dele-gated officials can kill and none can torture within the law. Fi-nally, there is use of illegal and uncontrolled violence. This is conflict at its worst because it has no boundaries in kind and scope. Any sort of torture may be used and any amount of indiscriminate killing, because no order defines either its magnitude or its method. However, there may be times when even this mode of unlimited violence is the lesser of alternative evils. The criminal, the rebel, and the revolutionist use force in this extra-legal way. Anyone, including the police, may be criminal or rebel or revolutionary.

Now of these modes of conflict the first two are constant, inescap-able and, when rightly conducted, of great value. Any of the other modes may also on occasion be better than avoidance of conflict. But none of these modes is ever justified unless one has the right attitude when he engages in it. Here, then, comes the importance of attitude.

Four different types of attitudes found in conflicting parties may be distinguished. One may fight for the sake of a specific objective which excludes all consideration of the welfare of his opponent and of his opponent's objectives. Or he may fight against another for an objective which he thinks is best for the opposing party as well as for himself. Third, one may fight for a cause which he feels is best not only for both sides in conflict but also for all parties who may be affected, including many who are not in the conflict at all. For example, in conflict between employees and employers each side may profess, and conceivably might truly seek, to prevail over the other for the sake of attaining a situation which he thinks would provide greatest value for employees, employers, and the public.

Finally, however, there is a type of attitude vastly superior to any of these. One may fight for an objective which he thinks would be best for all concerned and yet hold his objective subordinate to a greater good which he knows might be attained although the specific nature of it he cannot at the time fully discern. For example, a parent might oppose a child for the sake of a specific goal which he believes is best for the child, and he might hold this goal subordinate to the process of the child's further development, knowing that this development will bring on situations and values which his present foresight cannot discern in their specific content. So also employers and employees might fight in this spirit, as might political parties, or races, or any set of individuals or groups.

Now this attitude in conflict which we have just described can be cultivated and maintained only by worship when the worship is directed to God as one who works throughout the world by way of unlimited connective growth. This attitude in conflict presupposes that there is a wide network of growing connections which bind the conflicting parties into a community despite their opposition to one another, and which is developing in such a way that it will bring forth values and valuable situations which cannot be foreseen in their specific nature prior to their emergence. This attitude, then, requires that the worshiper recognize as sovereign over every specific objective in conflict, the growth of connections of value carrying possibilities that transcend the comprehension of any mind now engaged in the fight. The worship of God, when God is identified with the unlimited growth of connections of value, may develop an attitude in the worshiper whereby his specific objectives in conflict are always held subject to the transforming and enriching power of a process which includes all parties in the conflict and works for the good of all.

Conflict which is sincere and which is conducted in this attitude is always good. It is good even when the specific objective of the fighters is mistaken. It is good because it will teach the parties the better way. Those who fight in such a spirit are always teachable and their fighting will teach them more profoundly and effectively than most experiences which do not involve conflict.

Now of course it is true that some conflicts are of such a sort that it is impossible to conduct them in this spirit and attitude. Warfare between modern industrialized nations is of this sort. Conflicts which cannot be conducted in this attitude, and in which it is impossible for the opposing parties to seek an outcome that may be best for all concerned, are always evil.

IX. TRANSFORMING LIFE BY PRAYER

The creative attitude is that state of the psycho-physical organism which makes all its sensitivities, impulses, habits, ideas, and strivings subject to the transforming power of the growth of connections of value in all situations, including even those of conflict. Such an attitude can never be established once for all. It is never perfect. But it can be constantly re-established, more deeply established and improved, by the practice of worship when worship is directed to the true reality of God.

Prayer and worship are directed to what the individual holds to be supremely worthful. When his prayer and worship are directed to the real God they contribute enormously to the good of the world.

NOTES

[1] By May Thielgaard Watts

BIBLIOGRAPHY

Creative worship is set forth in *Religious Values*, chaps. 7–9, by E. S. Brightman. A vivid and beautiful portrayal of creativity through worship is *Modern Man's Worship*, chaps. 16–19, by B. E. Meland. A classic on this subject is chap. 28 in *Meaning of God in Human Experience*, by W. E. Hocking. Hocking's idea is put into more popular and colorful form by Richard Cabot in *What Men Live By*, Part IV. Power of the prayerful attitude to change the course of events is described in *Normative Psychology of Religion*, chap. 7, by H. N. and R. W. Wieman. See also *The Wrestle of Religion with Truth*, chap. 3, and *The Issues of Life*, pp. 18–28, by H. N. Wieman.

13.

GUIDANCE OF RELIGION BY REASON

CREATIVE worship gives religious living incalculable power. Access to power and its use put heavy responsibility upon persons and institutions who have them. Power in itself is neither good nor bad and can of itself work either to promote good or impair its growth. Power must have direction. Direction for release and application of power may be sought in a number of places. One may seek it in authority or revelation or tradition or subjective inclination or reason. There has never been a period in history in which every one of these guides did not operate to give direction to the release and use of power found in religious living. However, certain eras tend to rely more upon the guidance of one or more of these and to neglect or repudiate others.

There is today a widespread tendency to repudiate reason in religion and in politics. Inner certitude, emotional ecstasy, loyalty to the group or the leader or the cause, " faith," the call of the blood — these are held to be more reliable or otherwise more worthy to serve as guides to human conduct than is the empirical use of reason. Much is made of the errors of rational induction and the arrogance and other evils that issue from conclusions rationally attained. It is amazing that those individuals who denounce the works of rational search fail to see that the evils they list are characteristic of human living rather than of rational procedure and are quite as heinously displayed in the nonrational as in the rational conduct of men.

This present turning away from the guidance of reason is due to a number of causes. One is a misunderstanding of the place and use of reason, a misunderstanding very widely found in religious circles. It is true that false claims have been made for reason, its limitations have not been clearly defined, it has been used in ways for which it is not fitted. However, these misunderstandings, false claims, and misuses of reason may be corrected. Then reason could be restored to its rightful place and function in religion and elsewhere, were it not that other causes also, more difficult to handle, are working against it.

In many quarters today men's hearts are full of fear, hate, suspicion, despair, disillusionment. When these emotions are driving hard it is difficult to maintain that objectivity which is required for rational induction. One is likely to decide a question by faith, by the demand of some ruling loyalty which has little reason in it, by inner certitude unsupported by evidence. This morbid state of mind springs from conditions which we cannot here take space to discuss. Our undertaking will be limited to the effort to set forth the rightful place of reason in religion and to remove some of the false claims and misuses that have been so common in religious circles. One thing at least we shall try to demonstrate: that when our interests are not guided by reason we plunge toward disaster. This is particularly true in the realms of religion and politics.

I. WHAT IS REASON?

Reason is the name we give to our imaginative apprehension of the forms and orders of experience. These forms and orders are first of all derived from behavior. The physiological reaction of the organism gives to conscious experience those forms by which we recognize the various objects known to us in our world. Emotions, obscure feelings, sense data, take on one character rather than another because our bodies act as they do. Also, it is something in the environment which arouses a certain order of reaction in the body. This character and sequence of reaction give to the content of consciousness order, *Gestalt,* form, which can be imaginatively abstracted from the feelings and sense data which give them concrete content. Such abstract treatment gives us a process which is ordinarily called reason.

The work of reason is first of all to lift these forms and orders out of the matrix of physiological behavior, feeling, and sense by means of the imaginative use of symbols. Then it enables us to trace them imaginatively in their diverse patterns without undergoing all the massive experience which fills them out when we put them into concrete practice. This is the great achievement of the human intellect. Not only do we, in abstract reason, consider these forms and orders of experience apart from the feelings and gross physiological behavior that go with them, but we develop new forms and orders out of the old. We elaborate, recombine, and draw out further forms and orders indefinitely, far beyond any which can possibly be experienced in the actual process of bodily behavior.

To put the idea of these forms and orders into disembodied abstraction was a tremendous achievement in the history of man. The Greeks were the first to bring this accomplishment to high development, and among them Plato was the man who was most deeply stirred by the vision of abstract form — so deeply, in fact, that he came to think of the realm of abstractions or " Ideas " as a sort of heavenly world where beauty and goodness and truth were perfect and supreme. We hold, on the contrary, that these forms and orders are chiefly important because they are the patterns of possible experience. They are to be prized and explored not for the sake of themselves as abstractions, but because they point out the ways in which the rich, concrete fullness of physiological experience can be brought to consciousness in new and more noble ways.

Here, then, we have the nature and power of reason. It is that use of the imagination which focuses attention upon the forms and orders of experience as distinguished from the total content of experience which may bear these. These forms and orders are first experienced as imbedded in all the qualitative richness of consciousness that arises out of the physiological process. But imagination through the process of reason can consider them apart from the concrete content in which they originate. Reason is the power to deal with them without undergoing the physiological behavior which embodies them. Of course some physiological behavior is always required, even when the forms and orders are considered in abstraction. But this behavior can be limited to the trivial content involved in operating symbols. Symbols trivial in themselves may symbolize a vast system of abstract forms. Pure mathematics is the best example of this.

It is sometimes thought that we know all things by means of sense data. That is only part of the truth and not the most important part. The real basis of our recognition of anything is our awareness of the way our bodies are reacting to it. This awareness of reaction within the physiological process often is vague but very profound. Yet it is what gives us the sense of reality. It is much deeper than sense data. If by some drug or in some other way we anesthetize this sense of physiological reaction and leave only the superficial sense data floating in consciousness, the sense of reality departs. Our experiences do not seem real. It is by way of the deep physiological processes that we experience our grip on reality and its grip on us. These give tone and depth to consciousness.

The importance of sense data is that they can be analyzed into distinct elements, and recognized as this bit of color, that sound, that touch. By breaking up the content of sense experience into minute, distinguishable factors, we can make certain very discriminating tests. We can watch to see if some particular bit of sense experience appears or does not appear, and its appearance or nonappearance may help us to ascertain if some particular item is present or is not. As the final step in some long process of scientific investigation, a bit of sense experience, like a tiny flash of light or color in a telescope or prism, may help us decide between rival theories. The prominence of isolated sense data in these moments of crucial testing makes them seem to take on an importance of function far greater than they deserve.

II. RIGHT USES OF REASON

If we are correct in our statement of the nature of reason it is plain that it has invaluable and noble uses. For one thing this use of rational imagination makes it possible for us to plan and to foresee a far-flung pattern of experience before it occurs. We can plan a pattern which includes not only the future physiological reactions of our own organism, with all the rich experience which

goes with them, but the reactions and form of experience of many
other men who may be associated with us. We can explore the
patterns which will characterize the experience of future generations. We can consider those basic forms which apply to all experience whatsoever. We can even speculate about a world radically different from the one we know.

It is plain that this power of imaginative reason vastly augments
the ability of man to avoid ills and achieve goods. In so far as he
anticipates those patterns which portray the forms of possible experience, man can set up conditions which will bring desirable
consequences and avoid undesirable ones. Thus he may vastly
augment the material comfort and security of his existence. This
use of reason to avoid the material ills and achieve the material
goods of life has been marvelously developed in our times through
the physical and biological sciences and through the invention of
machines.

But reason has uses other than this of providing comfort and security. It may search out those patterns * which enable us to become aware of the greatest qualitative richness of experience.

Innumerable influences are working upon and through the
psycho-physical organism all the time. But these influences do
not reach consciousness save to an infinitesimal degree. For the
most part they neutralize or cancel one another. They are too
faint or obscure or confused to be consciously apprehended. But
many of them can be brought to consciousness by being introduced
into a pattern which prevents them from neutralizing or canceling
out one another. They may be coordinated in such form that they
enhance and vivify one another. Then we are consciously aware
of a rich qualitative content of experience. This is called aesthetic
experience sometimes, or experience of beauty or of love.

Here, then, we have a second great function of reason. It is to
search out those forms of experience which best serve to coordinate
the innumerable qualities accessible to consciousness so that they
can be apprehended more abundantly. The riches of existence
are infinite. Nature is full of realities which can sustain and

* The philosophical name for pattern or form of experience is "concept."

enrich, can be adored for their beauty and loved for the intimate community which they establish between the individual mind and its world. But these realities cannot come to consciousness, they cannot enter awareness, until they are apprehended according to the right forms or patterns. But we cannot have any conscious experience of all this great abundance of existing reality until we organize it in such patterns that the mind can apprehend it. It is the aesthetic and artistic function of reason to give us these forms in which to experience the world.

We are likely to be misunderstood, however, when we speak of the artistic and aesthetic function of reason, for these words so frequently connote the specialized function of certain interests such as the fine arts of music, painting, and the like. The functions of the arts certainly are included in this function of the reason, but the special works of art are only a very minor part of the aesthetic and artistic use of reason. The latter's major work is to organize the daily and hourly experience of man, or at any rate certain high points of man's experience, so that the world can be experienced in the richer fullness of its many qualities. This is to be distinguished from that special kind of experience in which enrichment is achieved by the techniques of fine art, through some artificially segregated bit of the world as set forth by musical instruments or on canvas or the like. We do not wish to discount the value of the works of fine art. We only wish to make plain that we are here considering a function of reason which, while it includes such works, goes much deeper and is inclusive of much more. It strives not merely to segregate and enhance certain special areas of experience, but seeks to apprehend the qualitative richness of the world wherever possible in the ordinary run of life.

There is still another high function of reason that must be emphasized. There are forms of behavior by which minds can enter into most profound community. There are ways of acting by which meanings can be shared in abundance and the qualitative richness of one individual can stimulate correlative richness in the experience of the other. This function of reason overlaps its aesthetic function. Those forms which yield aesthetic richness are generally the clearest instances also of those forms in which many minds enrich one another. " Art is universal " in the sense that the experience of one mind is poured out in shared experience with another.

But this community between minds brings out another aspect of the matter. Communication between minds can be very abstract or it can be concretely profound, emotional, and rich with all the abundant qualities of experience. It may be an open question whether we ever actually communicate the intimate qualities of experience from one mind to another, but that is a matter of theoretical academic interest only. There can be little doubt that minds may be so associated that each vastly enriches the emotional and other qualities experienced by the other. Now the forms by which this growing community, this sharing and mutual enrichment, are accomplished, are the forms which it is the business of reason to discover and apply to the conduct of human living. These forms by which community grows might be called those of love, although here again the common meaning of the word is too narrow. So we had better stick to the word community, providing we remember that it designates the greatest possible mutual enrichment of conscious experience on the part of the participants.

We have now the answer to the frequent cry that reason is abstract. First we must recognize the truth in this declaration. Then we must point out that it represents only part of the truth. Generally, too, it betokens a misunderstanding of the right use of reason. We have said that reason finds its peculiar task in separating or abstracting the forms of experience from their concrete content and considering them in pure imagination. But we have found a real and vast good in this use of reason. The highest purpose of it is to make experience more concrete. Carried through to the end, reason-dominated experience is concretized in the sense of being made more rich in the sensuous and emotional qualities. This is accomplished wherever the rational consideration of abstract forms is used as a means by which those certain forms of behavior are discovered, selected, and put into practice, which best serve to enrich experience by enhancing the aesthetic qualities and deepening the community between minds. Thus the right use of reason leads in the end to fuller concreteness of experience.

But reason has not always been used in this way. It has often been used to focus attention upon abstract forms and to keep it there in disregard of any attempt to direct the physiological process of human living into ways of behavior that would yield greater richness and community of experience. The abstract forms have been explored for their own sake, under the illusion that we were thereby getting closer to God, or invading a higher realm of being, or otherwise participating in something more noble than the directing of the organic process in ways that bring greater values into the scope of human experience. This self-righteous and genteel preoccupation with abstract forms has often led to the impoverishment of life. Consequently it becomes important to our undertaking to consider the misuses of reason.

III. THE MISUSES OF REASON

The life of reason is often contrasted with the life of sensuous experience and rich emotion in a spirit of strong partisanship. Reason is bare, cold, unemotional, lacking in color and glow and enthusiasm — so it is said. Religion, on the other hand, is passionate, emotional, addicted to ecstasy or fear or other stirring emotions. Reason remains static, judicial, contemplative, maintaining the attitude of the spectator. Religion moves into self-commitment, devotion, deep participation of the individual in whatever is held to be of primary religious concern. Thus these two are sometimes set over against one another.

At other times religion and the life of reason have been very closely identified. Reason, it has been claimed, leads us into that high and lofty realm where the spiritual realities are to be found, free from admixture with earthly things and bodily processes. Or again, reason has been the great supporter and defender of revelation. Thus religious individuals have vacillated between two extremes in their attitude toward reason.

This vacillation, we hold, has been due to identifying the work of reason with its misuses. Just now we are passing through a period when many religious people are deliberately repudiating reason as a way to the goodness of God. These radical swings back and forth between misfavor and disfavor of reason are disruptive to the growth of genuine high religion. They can be corrected and the attitude of religion toward reason can be stabilized only when reason is kept to its rightful functions and these functions are properly understood and utilized. To this end we must try to get clearly before us some of the misuses and misunderstandings of reason.

Perhaps that misuse of reason which has done more than anything else to bring it into disfavor with the modern mind has been the tendency to cherish rational clarity and consistency as ways to high reality or important truth without relating them to known reality through subjecting these forms of pure reason to the empirical tests of the physiological process. Such disembodied procedure may lead to logical consistency and rational speculation, but it gives no reliable truth about the existing world. It has led human life astray many, many times. It has misdirected the lofty aspirations of whole epochs of history.

Still again, instances of rational clarity and consistency may be subjected to empirical tests and so give us some truth about existence, but men may fail to see that this clarified and verified truth is only a tiny and meager segment of the enormous abundance of reality which throngs about us and encompasses us. These tested and verified propositions, qualitatively impoverished though they be, are sometimes prized so highly that men turn with scorn on all those vague, befuddled gropings, intimations and intuitions which cannot yet be called verified knowledge but which are the raw material out of which knowledge and detection of error must be developed. It is important to note in passing that the discovery of error is almost as important as the discovery of truth, for error constitutes a problem, and problem-solving is the way to truth. Because of all this, it is very important that human beings carry with them a great mass of intuition, as inherited from the past and as created today. These intuitions,

likely guesses, hunches, vague presentiments, feelings of reality
undefined, this sense of the deep, dark, unplumbed abyss of existence — all these are very precious. To scorn this nebulous content of human apprehension, to ridicule it, to ignore it or to try to
get rid of it out of devotion to clarified reason and verified knowledge which exclude the riches of experience, is a gross misuse of
reason.

All this surplusage of intuition which is as yet neither knowledge
nor error but the material from which knowledge and error will
come, is perhaps the most important resource of human life. It
represents the hidden potentiality and the possibility of creativity.
It is out of this surplusage that we progressively develop whatever
clarified and verified knowledge we now possess. What is more,
through right use of this mass of untested intuition we shall and
must find our way into that other better world which will arise
when we learn properly to interact with our environment. The
abundant riches that may enter human experience wherever our
interaction with other persons and with the rest of the environment is rightly ordered, must be sought and slowly found by way
of this mass of intuition. Therefore, no matter how vague and
confused it may seem to be, one of the misuses of reason is to wall
off into forgotten prison cells called " the unrespectable," the very
material out of which reason's own achieved truth has been and
must be developed. It is the arrogant young offspring denouncing and casting out the mothering matrix of his existence. Reason
originates in, and is clarified out of, this vague nebulous mass of
groping intuition and feeling-apprehension.

In still a further fashion has rational truth been misused — when
it has been cherished for its own sake and not used for the better
conduct of human living. Truth, in the form of an endless accumulation of true propositions, has been sought for itself and not
as a means of shaping the behavior of living men toward greater
values.

.Yet again, the forms of reason may be applied to existence, and
used to control the processes of nature, solely in the interest of
comfort and security or in the interest of keeping the process

under control, but to no end beyond the efficiency of control. Now comfort and security are certainly good. They are indispensable as foundations for building further values. Efficiency in controlling the processes of nature is important in itself. It is also an indispensable first step in moving on to further enrichment of life. But the misuse here consists in remaining static and not moving on. Life may be made comfortable and secure and all things kept subject to rational control, and yet be miserably impoverished. The very efficiency of this control, and the very perfectness of the superimposed order, may increase the barrenness of experience. It is conceivable that the lower animals might have more aesthetic richness and community of interest than men, at least in some forms of experience. The very efficiency with which men can and do now control the processes of existence may cut them off from the richer levels of human experience if reason is used entirely to promote comfort, security, and order, and is not used to promote aesthetic richness and fuller community of minds. It is not possible to have too much efficiency; but it is quite possible to use efficiency to impoverish rather than to enrich. The maximum increase of beauty and love requires high rational efficiency. But the mere fact that men have high rational efficiency does not insure that they will use it to promote these high ends of life. On the contrary they may use their rational powers to carry themselves and their civilization in the opposite direction. Here is a fourth misuse of reason.

The first three misuses of reason which we have mentioned are faults common to the highly intellectual. But this fourth misuse is common to the ordinary practical man. He so uses his rational powers and his practical efficiency as to make it unnecessary for him to give attention to the multiform values of aesthetic experience and deep interchange of thought and feeling between persons. He can get a very high degree of comfort and security, and a sense of power and of progress, without paying attention to these "luxuries" of life; so he ignores them. People or animals with lesser power of control are often forced to pay attention to the qualities of experience and to the thoughts and feelings of others by which living is rendered more abundant. But the man of rational power is not so forced. He can get along without this further enrichment. And so he misses it. This possibility is another cause for the discounting of reason in the interest of feeling and qualitative richness of experience. But here again it is not reason per se that is at fault, but the misuse of it.

A fifth misuse of reason consists in holding some rationally verified proposition as a final, absolute, and complete unit of truth. Even though the proposition has been verified well enough by proper empirical tests, yet human knowledge is never complete and final. The proposition may fit the data of experience perfectly up to the scope of its present application. But further items of experience and wider perspectives may be encountered which will require the modification of the proposition. This refusal to modify verified propositions when further experience demands it, is one of the great evils of human life. One may ask, If the proposition is verified why is it not absolutely true? It may be absolutely true with respect to the items of experience to which it has now been applied. But it may be impossible to keep human experience within the narrow boundaries in which it holds true. For example, it is quite correct to say that the earth is relatively flat, if one is referring only to a very limited portion of the earth's surface. But to insist that that is an absolute, final, and complete statement about the shape of the earth is folly; in respect to wider reaches of experience it is not true. Newton's theory of space, time, and gravitation was quite correct in the sense that it fitted very perfectly the items of experience then available. But it is not true of the world when we consider speeds beyond a certain maximum. So here again we have one of those misuses of reason which have brought it into disrepute. To claim that some verified rational proposition is a final and complete statement about the nature of reality is to use reason wrongly. But to condemn reason because some people have used it wrongly is like condemning breathing because some people have used it to breathe poison gas.

A sixth misuse of reason is called by psychologists, rationalization. Reason functions rightly when it searches out that order of existence and possibility which yields the greatest aesthetic richness, community of minds, and material security; when it is searching after such an order of qualitative abundance and material goods or is criticizing false claims about such an order. But rationalization means to use reason to defend the beliefs which one wants to hold on grounds other than valid evidence. This is a very common practice. No one is entirely free of it. The destructive consequences of this perversion of the reasoning process have led many to condemn reason as a whole. But here again the condemnation is based upon a misunderstanding.

Doubtless there are other misuses of reason that could be noted. Our purpose, however, is not to set forth all the good uses and all the misuses of reason, but only to trace the distinction between these far enough to show their general direction and to make plain that the condemnation and repudiation of reason in religious circles and elsewhere is not justified. This is not to deny that the evils which are being condemned are real enough and should be removed. Rather it is of paramount importance to note that these evils arise not from reason per se but from its misunderstanding and misuse.

IV. PHILOSOPHY AND SCIENCE

In considering the use of reason we have not heretofore distinguished between its use in philosophy and in science. As a matter of fact the distinction is not so very important and the difference between the two uses is not so great as some have thought. To be sure philosophy more frequently than science has been identified with certain misuses of reason, such as rational speculation without empirical tests, or devotion to and exploration of forms (concepts) without consideration of their application to the psycho-physical processes of living. When philosophy is committed to these misuses, while science holds itself always to be an empirical use of reason, there is obviously a marked difference between the two.

But philosophy is not necessarily any less empirical than science.

The reason that it may seem to be nonempirical in some cases is
that the data of experience with which it deals are infallibly present. Hence there is no need to search for them by laboratory
devices, telescope or prism, or by climbing mountains or going
to the bottom of the sea.

For example, the general form of time characterizes all experience. One does not need to search the heavens or use a micro-
scope to find time. Man can sit in an armchair and philosophize
but that does not mean he is unempirical. He can experience
time in an armchair as well as when handling test tubes. Hence
the study of the general form of time as applicable to all experience
is a philosophical study. On the other hand, when we seek to
know the time of some particular event, we are seeking to know
that particular form of time which applies only to certain experiences. Hence we must search for the data. In such a case we
are engaged in a scientific study.

Or again take causality. Causality is a form of experience
which never leaves us. We do not have to search for it. It
pursues us; we do not need to pursue it. Hence the study of
causality in general is a philosophical study. But the endeavor
to know the form of some particular kind of cause is a scientific
study.

As a further example, we may note the study of the general
structure of all truth. There are certain general forms that characterize all truth, so that whenever you have any truth at all it
must conform to these general principles. The study of this
order or form or structure which is common to all valid knowledge is a philosophical study. But when we seek to know the
distinctive form of some particular truth which is not infallibly
present in all truth we have a scientific study.

Thus philosophy and science are distinguished. Philosophy
is the study of the general forms that apply to all experience or to
very extensive areas of experience, while science is the study of
those forms that are more limited in scope. But there is no hard
and fast line of demarcation between the two. How general
must a form of existence be in order to permit us to say that its

study is the province of philosophy? How limited and particular must a form be in order that we may assign it to science? The extreme limits in these contrasts belong respectively to philosophy and science quite plainly, but it is often hard to say in the mid-region whether we are dealing with philosophy or science. There certainly are areas of experience which need both approaches equally. Sociology illustrates these.

The main point to make plain is the fact that philosophy and science are both the domain of reason, and all the requirements for the right use of reason apply to both equally. The misuses are also found in both. Reason rightly used should always be empirical, whether in philosophy or in science. To be sure in both philosophy and science there is need to explore widely and searchingly the infinite system of possible forms of experience prior to the actualization of these forms by way of physiological reactions to this material world. It is exceedingly important that we know as thoroughly as possible in the abstract all these possibilities of concrete, psycho-physical experience. But the reason such theoretical exploration is important is that we can thereby anticipate, plan, and direct our dealings with the existing world in such a way as to increase the material security and, above all, to grow in the aesthetic richness and the community between minds. It is for the sake of concrete living that science and philosophy need to explore the infinite realm of abstract forms. But when they become lost in these abstractions, or become so fascinated with the forms as to disregard the needs of concrete living, we have a misuse of reason, whether it be in science or philosophy.

V. THE EXTRA-RATIONAL FACTORS IN RELIGION

We have tried to show that religion needs reason and cannot dispense with it except at the price of becoming degraded and perverted and missing its own high function. Religion rightly repudiated reason in its misuses. But when it has confounded all reason with these misuses it has been in error. There is no way to distinguish between truth and error, or between the high and holy on the one hand and the mean and base on the other, except by the empirical and experimental use of reason. Reason has its indispensable place in all worthy religion.

On the other hand, however, it is a mistake to say that religion is simply the exercise of reason and nothing more. To say that would be to identify religion with science and philosophy. There is just as much of the extra-rational in religion as there is in any of the practical arts and interests of life other than science and philosophy. These last two are concerned with reason preeminently. But in eating, in friendly intercourse, in politics and industry, in singing, in caring for an infant, reason enters in as only one of the factors. So it is in religion. The function of reason is to give direction and provide guidance, but that is only one element in religion.

The extra-rational factors in religion might be described as subrational on the one hand, and super-rational on the other. Subrational here does not mean degraded or mean or of lesser value than the rational. Neither does the super-rational mean something of greater value than reason. But the significance of the terms will be revealed as we proceed.

By the subrational in religion we mean the physiological process which makes man religious. Some will immediately hold up their hands in horror and say we are making the old mistake of tracing religion back to an instinct. We are not. On the contrary, we are saying that man is necessarily religious for the very reason that he has no fixed system of instincts which serve to direct his behavior automatically. Lacking such a system of automatic control and adjustment he cannot survive and flourish unless he constantly seeks out with appreciative awareness and affection all that is friendly and helpful in his environment, and constantly reshapes his behavior so that he can enter into community and cooperation with these sustaining and enriching conditions or forces. It is this constant outreach, this sense of dependence, this striving to become organically united with something outside himself, that make him religious. It is this sense of being separated from something that he vitally needs, this striving to change himself or to change that other and to be reconciled with a reality that is in the world or beyond the world, that make him religious.

Man is the most helpless of all of the animals from the point of view of his native endowment of automatic reflexes. He must learn to share deeply in the thoughts and feelings and interests of his fellow men, else he cannot survive, much less attain any satisfaction in life. More than that, he must learn to share deeply in the sustaining processes of nature, and change himself and these processes to the end of attaining deep rapport with them. If there is anything else beyond nature, anything which controls the processes of nature, above all he must find some community of life with that.

Therefore that physiological process in man which makes him religious consists of all those impulses in him that seek community, cooperation, and reconciliation with all reality which is capable of being approached in this way. If he were natively endowed with a system of reflexes that automatically adjusted his behavior to a sustaining environment, so that he did not have to seek consciously for such community, and did not have to yearn and hunger and wistfully strive for rapport with a sustaining reality in great part undefined by specific preestablished forms of behavior, he would not be religious.

Therefore man's religion, like everything else in him, is rooted in his physiological nature. Man is religious because his nerves, muscles, viscera, and glands function as they do. He knows he is not self-sufficient. He seeks for that which will transform him or be transformed, and will make him an integral part of a larger whole. He seeks reconciliation with sustaining reality. Such seeking is religion. Deep in the physiological processes of his nature is a sense which indicates that he is in danger unless he redirects his living. It also indicates that there is blessedness for him if his living is so redirected as to unite him and make him an organic part of an uncomprehended totality of what is best.

So we say that religion, like hunger and love and language and industry, does not originate in reason. It is primarily subrational; that is to say, it springs from physiological processes which op-

erate before reason develops. Reason arises rather as a means
by which these basic interests can be better directed towards the
fulfillments which they crave. The possible forms of experience
must be explored and appraised in order that human life may be
guided in the direction of what it needs. Reason is the name we
give to this exploration and appraisal of the forms of possible experience. Religion, along with the other subrational interests
of human living, develops reason to help it find what it is seeking.
Woe then to him who in the name of religion casts out reason,
in the face of the fact that reason originally arises in part as an expression of religious outreach and craving. Reason is, in no mean
measure, the hand of religion reaching up after God. Man is
not religious because he is rational but he becomes rational because he is first religious.

Closely correlated with the subrational physiological process
which generates religion in man is the super-rational lure. In
fact the two are inseparable. We said that man's body is so made
that he must seek by way of progressive transformation of self and
of environment to enter into wider and deeper community and
cooperation with all that is helpful or can be made helpful through
reconciliation between himself and it. He is physiologically driven
to do this long before he knows specifically what there is in the
world or beyond it which may be helpful. Therefore he feels the
lure of an uncomprehended reality with which he may be reconciled. He responds to it before he knows what it is. In this sense
he responds to a super-rational lure. It is not necessarily super-
rational in the sense that it is superior to reason. But it is super-
rational in the sense that man does not at first have any rational
grounds on which to assert that there is anything of a definable
nature with which reconciliation may be consummated. Also,
even when he has rational grounds on which to base his outreach
for previous unexplored reality, this reality always exceeds the
scope of his rational grasp prior to his actual experience of it.

There is still another sense, however, in which this lure is super-
rational. We said that abstract reason treats only of the forms of
experience. It does not and cannot grasp all the concrete rich-

ness of experience which enters consciousness in concrete situations. Much of this qualitative richness is ineffable, which means that reason cannot grasp it. It is therefore super-rational in the sense that reason cannot define it. It must be immediately experienced. It must be delivered to consciousness by the physiological processes of reaction. It must come in the form of imagery, feeling, and sense. It constitutes the massive fullness of experience. Reason can deal only with the forms. But the chief lure of life is this ineffable richness found in aesthetic experience and fellowship of minds.

So we have in religion a subrational urge and a super-rational lure. No man could be religious by means of reason alone. Some religious leaders repudiate reason on the grounds that reason by itself alone is not religious and a man who is purely rational and nothing more would have no religion. That is quite true, but to reject reason on that ground is to misunderstand its function. One might as well cast out reason from the domain of eating, or from the field of politics or industry or art and aesthetic experience. All of these would disappear, as would human life itself, if we all could be transformed into pure disembodied rationalists. To reject reason simply because it is not the whole of life is folly. Some other leaders have made the false claim that life finds its fulfillment in pure reason. That claim is false but its falsity is no justification for plunging into the opposite error and claiming that human life in any department can safely dispense with reason.

VI. THE FUNCTION OF REASON IN RELIGION

We have seen that a great deal of religion is not rational, just as a large part of every interest is not, although pure science and philosophy come nearest to being wholly rational. It now remains for us to show just where reason does enter religion and what its indispensable part is. The function of reason in religion is to direct the subrational urge toward the super-rational lure. There is no other possible way in which man can use any intelligence whatsoever in directing the religious urge toward the supreme lure of all human living than this way of rational induction or empirical use of reason.

We can compare the subrational religious urge to an automobile and the super-rational lure to the road and the destination ahead which are concealed by the darkness of the night. Reason is then like the headlight which helps the automobile find its way toward its destination.

What happens to religion when the light of reason is dimmed or put out entirely? What happens to the automobile when the headlight goes out? That depends on how dark is the night, how rough and crooked the road, and on how much power the automobile has. There have been times in the historic past when the movement of life was very slow. It was like a low-powered automobile crawling along at a snail's pace. In such times one might get along fairly well without the light of reason. The road of ancient tradition was fairly straight, with deep ruts hard to diverge from; the religious urge was not creatively dynamic. There are some people today who look back to such times and tell us that human living in certain religious golden ages of the past got along quite magnificently without the light of reason. They advise us to conduct our religious living as people did at that time, with only such use of reason as is convenient and advantageous.

Such people forget that today the automobile is far more powerful and is moving at great speed. There is no familiar rut of ancient tradition to make the direction seem plain and sure. The road is crooked and unknown. To think that we can dispense with reason today to the degree that some have done so in the past is to mistake the difference between our times and the past. Never did man need the searchlight of reason so much as he does today. We have enormous power; we are going fast; the road is dark and unknown before us; without the light of reason disaster is sure. It is true that reason does not light us far. But woe to him who takes away what little light it does provide. They who today are trying to extinguish reason as the chief guide of religious striving are the enemies of mankind.

VII. REASON IN THE METHOD OF RELIGIOUS LIVING

Religion rises from deeper sources in human nature than does reason. When blizzards of misfortune strike humanity, beating down to destruction the distinctive developments of human life, reason succumbs far more readily than does religion. Science, industry, politics, high moral ideals, all these die out of human life before religion does. Religion under propitious circumstances develops reason far more than reason develops religion. Indeed we may say that the power and depth and sovereignty over human life of religious devotion is not augmented at all by reason. Reason does not generate religion or foster it. Reason can be the servant of religion; it cannot be the sustainer, originator, or promoter. In time of distress, when these high gifts of human nature are threatened, religion must take the role of sustainer, originator, and promoter of reason, not the reverse. Reason continues in human life at the mercy of religion and can be destroyed by it. Religion cannot be destroyed by reason. When religion opposes itself to reason it is always shown to be in error. But religion can survive any amount of error, while reason cannot.

It is important for us to see that reason is created by religion and survives only when upheld by religion's sustaining might. By this we do not mean that reason survives only when upheld by the church. We are speaking not of the church but of those roots of religion that go immeasurably deeper into human life than any social institution. The religious impulse in human nature must assume responsibility for fostering reason, else reason will be beaten very low in the days of passion and conflict that seem to be coming upon us. Without the mothering care of religion, reason is an orphan child easily destroyed in times of great emotional stress.

On the other hand we have seen that reason is of prime importance for significant and effective religious living. So is it also for art, industry, politics, friendship and love. Reason can be the servant of all of these interests, but it cannot be the master of any of them, for these all underlie reason and create reason rather than being created by it. In times of passion they may at any moment cast off reason.

With this understanding of the relative roles of reason and religion we must answer the question, How does the individual bring reason into the method of his religious living? We have seen that the method of religious living can be analyzed into the steps of propulsion, crisis, decision, release, and specification. Also we have seen the creative power of worship. What has reason to do with these essential religious practices?

The first four steps in the method of religious living dispose the individual so that he can use reason to seek out the best that is to be found in each concrete situation and in life as a whole. Without the practice of this method of religious living one cannot use reason to find the rich and lofty goods of life. He cannot for several reasons. For one thing no man can find anything good by the use of his reason, no matter how great may be his rational powers, unless he seeks it. But he cannot seek it unless he wants it. He cannot want and so cannot seek for what is greatly good unless he practices, whether consciously or unconsciously, some such method as we have described. A re-examination of the steps of that method will reveal this to be the case.

Furthermore, even when one sincerely wants what is best, he cannot find it by the use of reason if his judgment is constantly distorted and the focus of his interest is constantly diverted by subconscious attachments to mean and little things, and if subconscious desires drive him toward what is destructive of all that makes life worth living. The method of religious living delivers a man from this distortion of judgment and this diversion of desire. Thus it releases his powers of reason to seek and to find in each situation the best that can be found there.

On the other hand, however, this method of religious living cannot find what is best without the use of reason. It comes to nothing if reason, thus liberated, is not used. Right religious practices prepare the way for reason to operate. If reason is not used, the individual cannot find the riches of God nor establish those habits and procedures which are required for effective living and divine growth. The method prepares him for the use of reason, but if reason does not enter when all has been made ready the whole thing becomes a fiasco.

Reason implements the interests which a man may have. If he has mean or destructive interests, reason will enable him to find the ways and means of achieving them even though getting them will lead to his own impoverishment or torment, along with that of many others. Religious living needs this implementation by means of reason as much as does any other interest. Also there is no way by which the rational implementation of destructive interests can be counteracted save by the rational implementation of the creative. If the method of religious living which releases the noblest interests in human life does not make the utmost use of reason to find the ways and means of effective action, these most excellent outreaches of the human spirit will be nullified by the mean and destructive propulsions which do make greater use of reason.

We have seen that creative worship makes accessible to human experience a great qualitative richness. Here again reason is indispensable. The qualities, the affections, intuitions, problems, imaginative structures brought into experience by the attitude of creative worship do not bear on their face the labels which distinguish the true from the false, the fruitful from the sterile, the anticipations which are valid from those which are foolish and disastrous. There is no possible way of making these distinctions amidst all the raw materials of experience brought to light through creative worship, except by reason. Creative worship will provide the intuitions, affections, visions, living interests for a more noble way of life. But all these come to nothing without rational structure Reason must be brought in to sift and interpret, analyze and test all this abundance of experience in order to find in it those patterns (concepts) which will guide action and anticipation into the ways of growth and away from the horror of those monstrous errors into which religious living has so often fallen.

Thus reason has its indispensable part to play in the methods of religious living. Reason must be used with the steps of propulsion, crisis, decision, release, and specification to find the way of growing life, for without reason all these procedures will end in futility and error. Reason must be used with creative worship to distinguish within the qualitative riches thereby brought to consciousness those forms and orders which lead on to increasing goods as distinguished from those which are illusory.

BIBLIOGRAPHY

None has sought more earnestly to establish reason as the guide of religion than E. S. Brightman. We give one reference only among many that might be given: *Religious Values*, chap. 1. Emil Brunner denies that reason can be the guide; see his *Theology of Crisis*, chap. 2, and *Philosophy of Religion*, chap. 5. With beautiful lucidity and persuasive power A. N. Whitehead in *The Function of Reason*, and Morris Cohen in *Reason and Nature*, chap. 4, show the work of reason in guiding the whole of life, which includes religion. But reason always works under the limitations and directive control of the interests which actuate, and these are shaped by the group to which one belongs; so teaches Karl Mannheim in *Ideology and Utopia*, chap. 2. E. W. Lyman, in *The Meaning and Truth of Religion*, chap. 9, would make reason only one of the guides of religion, intuition and faith being others on a parity with it.

14.

FORMS OF RELIGIOUS APPREHENSION

THE empirical use of reason is the only way to guide action, direct appreciative awareness, and incline idealism toward the ways of greatest value. We have seen that every one of the basic interests which belong to human living must use reason to attain fulfillment. This is just as true of religion as it is of industry, art, politics, friendship and love. But each of these basic interests uses reason to somewhat different ends and finds the realities of its quest by way of different forms of appreciative apprehension. Sometimes these forms of apprehension are held in opposition to reason. That is a mistake. On the other hand, the attempt is sometimes made to use reason in the service of one of these interests but in disregard of the forms of apprehension which belong to this distinctive area of human concern. For example, art as painting or poetry or music has certain forms of apprehension which must not be violated. Each of these must make use of reason, but reason must always work in the interest of these forms of apprehension and not in disregard of them. The same is true of friendship and love, politics and religion.

Some of the forms of apprehension which belong to religion are called faith, revelation, myth, intuition, and paradox. Now, as we have said, these may be cherished and promoted in religion without regard to reason. On the other hand, reason may be cherished and promoted in religion without regard to these. One procedure is just as much of a blunder as the other. Therefore we must see how reason may be correlated with these forms of apprehension which are native to religion and are just as essential to it as are the forms of apprehension peculiar to physics or chemistry or agriculture or woodcraft.

All the different philosophies of religion found in the modern world are struggling with this problem of how to adjust the work of reason (sometimes called scientific method or just plain intelligence) with these distinctive forms of religious apprehension. Some do it by sacrificing the forms of religious apprehension to the demands of certain rational procedures. Others do it by sacrificing reason for the sake of preserving certain forms of apprehension. This problem is not always explicit and self-conscious, but it underlies most of the issues that are raised in the field of religion today. One may have the stark truth so far as reason can deliver it, and it may even be the truth about the kind of reality which is of prime concern to religion, and still the religious man cannot see it, cannot appropriate it, cannot live religiously by means of it, if he cannot apprehend it in those forms which his religious living requires. Therefore, after we have seen the indispensable part which reason must play in religious living, we have dealt with only half the problem. The other half is to see how reason may work in and with the forms of religious apprehension.

All the different philosophies of religion today are concerned with this problem. It underlies almost all the issues that divide them.

I. TENDENCIES IN MODERN RELIGIOUS GROWTH

We have seen the growing top of the tree of Christian faith reach into the atmosphere of modern culture which is distinguished from all other periods by the domination of science. There for a little while we saw the uppermost branches of the tree wither. Now we can understand why. It was because scientific procedures had not developed those forms of apprehension that are necessary to religious living; or, putting it the other way around, religious living had not developed forms of apprehension which could make use of scientific procedures.

After this first dying down of the topmost branches two sprouts sprang up from the trunk. One was called fundamentalism and the other liberalism. Fundamentalism resisted the influences of modern thought in order to preserve the forms of apprehension that religious living seemed to require. (Trees have forms of apprehension, if we want to press the figure that far.) Liberalism, on the other hand, did two different things, both of which were disastrous: it relinquished the religious forms of apprehension and took over the secular, when scientific findings seemed to demand it, but struggled to hold fast to the old forms just as long as it could. Before long both fundamentalism and liberalism showed signs of not doing well, for reasons already noted.

Then arose two new movements, each doing clearly and without compromise one of the two opposite and irreconcilable things which liberalism had been trying to do. Humanism took over the forms of apprehension which pertain to the social sciences and made no attempt to preserve those which were native to religion. The new supernaturalism, on the other hand, cut free of all compromise in the opposite direction and lifted the native forms of religious apprehension clear beyond the reach of all the demands of scientific method and reason.

Finally, different from all of these, and rather inconspicuous amid these other lusty growths, is a small shoot growing out of the crotch of the central trunk whence all these other branches have diverged. It is the new theistic naturalism. It has dealt with the problem in still a different way. It has tried to develop forms of apprehension which are peculiar and necessary to religious living but which are so adapted that reason can work for them and in them without hindrance or compromise.

We must now see how these different branches of the faith deal with the problem of meeting the demands of reason on the one hand, and, on the other, of conserving the native forms of religious apprehension called faith, intuition, revelation, myth, and paradox.

Two great questions agitate the minds of religious thinkers to-day: Where is God to be found? How is God to be found? These questions are acute not because God is far away or difficult to apprehend but because we do not have forms of apprehension which enable the religious man to live for God devotedly and which at the same time enable the rationality of the modern mind to work through them without hindrance or compromise.

II. THE LIBERALS

The liberals answer the question, Where is God to be found? by saying that he is the inner pervasive purpose of the cosmic whole. They have been deeply influenced by Schleiermacher and the great idealists. Some of them are idealists today. Others have rejected idealism as a theory of knowledge. But they all agree in saying that we must turn to the content of consciousness (experience) to get knowledge of God. If it is not our feeling of absolute dependence, then it is our sense of the holy, or the attitude of moral optimism, or some intuition or other data of immediate experience, that gives us the clue. God, the inner purpose of the universe, speaks to us by way of religious experience. Just what religious experience may be is a matter of dispute. But they all agree in answering the question, How is God to be found? by saying, Religious experience.

Perhaps D. C. Macintosh has given the most thorough and systematic answer in terms of liberalism to the two questions. In *The Pilgrimage of Faith* he writes that if moral optimism is valid, and if we adopt it as our attitude toward reality and destiny, then,

is there anything that in strict logic we can infer from it with reference to the nature of reality? The answer is simple and ought to be obvious. If moral optimism is valid, the cosmos, ultimately considered, must be on the side of the spiritual. In other words, the God we imperatively need exists. If we define God as a superhuman Cosmic Factor great enough and good enough to justify an attitude of moral optimism on our part, it is undeniable that the metaphysical proposition that God exists is logically implied in the value-judgment that moral optimism is valid.[1]

This statement may be boiled down to the following words: If moral optimism is justified, then there must be a power for good that is great enough to justify it. But that leaves wholly unconsidered the question of whether optimism *is* justified. It assumes that of course optimism is right and that therefore the power for good which justifies it does truly exist. This seems to be arguing in a circle. This shows the fallacy of basing religious truth on religious experience, in this case the experience of optimism.

Liberalism has created what has been called the theology of religious experience. It denies that sense perception can give us knowledge of God; but there is some kind of inner experience which does indicate the presence of God. Rufus Jones, one of the most popular of these liberals, has suggested that the soul or personality or mind of man reaches far down beyond the depths of this physical and sensuous world into some kind of extra-physical, extra-sensuous reality. There the soul is conjunct with deity. If we turn to this inner sense deep within us, we shall find God.

This "theology of religious experience" has dominated the religious thinking of Americans for decades. But it is now waning and failing. Modern psychology has searched deeply into these inner states of consciousness and found them to pertain to the same world that the rest of human nature inhabits. The deep probing of modern philosophy into the procedures by which knowledge is got, shows that knowledge is not got in the way the liberals claimed.

The *requiescat* of this theology of religious experience, and hence of liberalism in the form it has assumed to date, has been pronounced in a book written by his students in honor of that great leader of this kind of liberalism to whom we have just referred. This is what one of them writes:

Theology, supposedly, is a study or theory of God and related matters. It is just that: a theoretical system. Its relation to "religious experience" is the relation, if any, of intellect to feeling. Conceivably, it may have as little to do with the religious life as the study of the physiology of living forms has to do with living itself. One may live and have a theology without being religious. There remains a clear line between the two.

The theologian of religious experience in his quest for certainty has assumed the unique cognitive significance of "religious experience." To make his case appear more secure he has employed that dubious word "experience," which is taken to mean an alignment with sense-experience and knowledge. It is not only conspicuous but significant to notice that preference has been made for the term religious *experience* in place of religious *feeling*. One is on the ground of cognitive uncertainty when one employs the term "feeling." To emphasize feeling at the expense of experiences (with the implied connotations) is to jeopardize the cause of cognitive certainty.

The mistake of theologians of religious experience has been to overload religious feeling with intellectual constructions in the interest of the kind of certainty desired. The Catholic theologians have rightly protested against this confusion; their insistence upon rendering to feeling the things that belong to feeling and to intellect the things that belong to intellect should have not gone unheeded. Feelings, we have indicated, are in themselves non-rational though linked to man's rational nature. . . . There is no necessity in setting up an organ of knowledge different in kind from the usual ways of knowing. The lead taken by theologians of religious experience is thus a mistaken one prompted, it may be repeated, by an apologetic hope.

The theologian's base lies in the realm of intellect and not in the dynamic nonrational side of human nature. If the theologian desires, accordingly, to make his discipline " scientific " after the pattern of the natural sciences, and " empirical " after the pattern of the realism implied by a theory of sense-experience, he will have to do it — following the above definition — not by appealing to religious experience as ground, but by linking his discipline to the rational work of the natural sciences and by cutting loose with them from that intimately personal phase of mental life associated with the term " feeling." The truth of his system should be as coldly formal as the truth of any systematic information presented by the natural sciences; its ideal of objectivity compels the continued avoidance of appeal to the realm of feeling.

A rational theology and not a theology of religious experience contains the more promising and reasonable hope. A theology of religious experience represents a detour away from the main thoroughfare of historical theology. It reflects an age searching desperately for a newer and more satisfying type of apologetic. When viewed from the perspective of the age which produced it, an age unsettled by the tremendous transitions of thought, one sees in the attempt the highest motif on the part of such theologians; when viewed, however, from a contemporary time which, though it remains quite as unsettled, has the advantage of a longer perspective for an appraisal, that commendable motif is seen to have contained a hope which outran possibility and a movement which in its embryo contained the seeds of its own dissolution.[2]

The liberals were led astray by an evasive ambiguity in their use of words of which they were not conscious. When they said that they were testing religious faith or insight or way of life, by " experience," it sounded as though they were being empirical. The word seems to represent a ground of validation which, if not scientific, at least has the flavor of a scientific test. At any rate it seems to meet the requirements of the modern mind.

But " experience " is hopelessly ambiguous. The mental procedure by which error is perpetuated and magnified is just as truly experience as the practice of that method by which truth is attained. / A hallucination which comes to one with high fever is every whit as genuine a case of experience as the method by which Isaac Newton brought to light the order of the physical world. The propagation of error is experience as truly as is the spread of truth. Therefore when the liberal says that religious insight must meet the tests of experience he is not saying anything at all of significance unless he specifies whether he means irrational experience or the experience of rationality, or something else that is neither.

b) The second error of liberalism, which we may call that of psychological introversion, was the attempt to validate a belief by pointing to the moral utility of it. / If the belief produced in one who held it a state of consciousness which could be called religious experience, such as a numinous feeling, and if it induced in him the kind of behavior which conformed to the highest, socially accepted moral standards of the time, then the belief was true. Therefore one could say that he was dealing with the living God and his ideas about God were true: they had met the test. But it should be plain that the subjective effects of a belief are no evidence at all of its truth. He who believes a lie will be influenced to act as though it were true. Parents and others sometimes try to induce moral behavior by telling lies. The moral behavior thus induced, however, does not prove the lie to be true.

Sometimes these two errors of evasive ambiguity and psychological introversion have been merged into one. Such has been the case when liberals have appealed to religious experience, meaning a state of consciousness dominated by the feeling that the good must prevail, and expressed in behavior by conduct that is morally approved.

It is apparent from what we have been saying that the liberals cannot give a clear and decisive answer to the question, How can God be found? Some of them have said it must be by intellectual inquiry. Some of the great idealists have so answered. But generally the liberal theologians say it must be by intellect plus intuition, revelation, feeling, faith, mystical insight, sense of the holy, moral optimism, and other ways. Which of these receives the major emphasis in any one instance depends upon the individual speaking.

III. THE SUPERNATURALISTS

The supernaturalists answer the question, Where is God to be found? by saying that God is the creator of the cosmic whole, but outside of it and greater than it.

Some might think that the very concept of the cosmic whole makes it include everything. Therefore God cannot be outside of it nor creator of it. He must be a part of it from the very meaning of the term when properly understood. But the supernaturalists do not understand the term in that sense. If you want to speak of a cosmic whole, they might not object. But they would go on to say that within this totality of all that has being, you must draw a clear line of demarcation between God and the rest of what is. God is unique, different, not to be confused with his creation. He is the source, the origin, of all; and he fixes the goal to which all must ultimately issue. But God is not the world and the world is not God. God is not a part of the world and the world is not a part of God.

God is not to be identified with any inner, pervasive purpose of the world. God's purpose works upon the world and through it. But it is God's purpose, not the world's purpose. (The liberals confused this issue.) The world does not have any single purpose running through it. Any realistic view must see that it is too full of conflict, tragedy, frustration, to be called purposive. Only romantic and illusory optimism can talk about a world-purpose. God's purpose created the world and God's purpose will overrule the world and bring forth the divine will in the end. But the world itself is full of sin and evil. There is war, there is cruelty, there is stagnation, there is chaos, there is self-indulgence and tyranny. God is not to be identified with any inner purpose of the world, for there is no such inner purpose. You must look to some source outside the world to find any such sovereign purpose or meaning.

This has been the answer given by supernaturalism, both the traditional kind and the newer sort. Also the two have agreed in saying that this reality of the world-transcending God and his will can reach the human mind only through faith and revelation. The human mind belongs to this world. It is a part of this creation. Hence it is separated from God and different from God in the same sense that all creation is different from and separate from the creator.

But this distinction and separation between God, the creator, and this world including human minds, which is the creation, is magnified by the new supernaturalists. Traditional supernaturalists said that certain parts of this world, like the Bible and Jesus Christ and holy church, were put into this world by God to bear witness of him in a very special way. They are to be identified with God much more closely than is the rest of creation. They are, in some sense, supernatural. They do not belong to the same order as the rest of the world. Also, human reason, while it belongs to this world with its limitations, when aided by the revelation brought to us through Bible, Jesus Christ, and holy church, can discover a great deal about God. Indeed the intellectual powers of men when thus aided, and when sanctified by the ministrations of Bible, Jesus Christ, and church, are one of the chief ways by which we learn of God and his will.

The new supernaturalism denies that the historical book called the Bible, the historical man called Jesus, and the historical church, are supernatural in any sense. Historical research, psychological probing, the social sciences, have made it all too plain that these bits of creation are not markedly different from the rest of the world. Error, limitation, contradiction, and conflict are to be found in the historical church, in the statements of the Bible, and in all the records we have about the historical Jesus. Therefore these cannot be identified with God in any special way.

Also human reason has demonstrated its fallibility all too plainly, say the new supernaturalists. Despite all the efforts of the greatest intellects it has been impossible to show by way of any rational procedure that there is a supernatural God with the kind of creative and overruling purpose which has been taught by this branch of the faith. What the intellect of man can demonstrate, according to the new supernaturalists, is that this world is not self-sufficient. It cannot create itself nor sustain itself. It must therefore have a ground or creator or sustaining origin which holds it in existence moment by moment. Furthermore, the human reason can demonstrate its own inability to grasp this ultimate reality. It can strive to apprehend God by powers of reason, but in so striving it inevitably falls into self-contradictions. Therefore we know that the divine reality is super-rational. It is beyond the reach of reason.

How, then, can we know this supreme God? By revelation and faith, by intuition and myth. God reveals himself directly to the heart and mind of the individual. Since reason falls into self-contradiction when it seeks to find the way to God, and since it cannot portray the nature of God, the human mind must make use of myth. When God is revealed to us we can set forth his being by means of myths, and there is no other way of doing it, since the abstract categories of reason fail us. How this is done we do not know. But the individual who receives this revelation and accepts it in faith, knows. He knows God. He cannot, by rational procedure, tell you what God is nor how he knows. But the knowledge is his. God and he are in living relation to one another. There is vital connection.

When any individual or group makes use of myth for the sake of its emotional appeal, and repudiates reason, a serious question arises. How is anyone to know which myth is true and which is false? Is it the nazi myth of *Blut und Boden* that shows us the true nature and will of God? Or is it the myth of capitalism, declaring that private ownership and operation of instruments of production is the way into the kingdom of God? Or again is it the myth of the superpatriot which says that America is always right in all its wars? If we are to reject these myths as being something less than the divine truth about supreme reality, on what grounds do we reject them?

Perhaps we may say that history will answer. We shall accept the myth which is most deeply rooted in the history of the race

and has inspired the noblest souls. Well, if we follow that procedure we shall be quite justified in accepting the nazi myth, for
it is a revival of a very ancient kind of religion, more deeply rooted
in history than is Christianity. Whether or not it has inspired the
noblest lives will depend on what we think is noblest; and what
we think about nobility will be determined by the myth we accept.
So there we are.

The rational tests have been repudiated. Then how shall we
select our myth? Perhaps we may take the one that our fathers upheld or the one that our group follows. Then we might well be
justified in taking the myth of naziism or one hundred per cent
patriotism or capitalism or some other.

This becomes a very perplexing question when you reject the
tests of the rational mind and depend on something else that may
be super-rational or irrational or subrational, but you cannot tell
which until you know what it is. It may be just your " blood "
which determines what myth you will have, as the Germans so
frankly say.

The repudiation of rational tests in judging what shall inspire
our supreme devotion and what shall release the floodgates of passion, is a very serious matter in this hour when our whole world is
threatened by a reversion to tyranny and blood, clothed in myths.
If religious leaders uphold myths as the way to divine reality and
repudiate the rational tests by which to ascertain their validity,
what is to protect us from the dark night that is rolling back on
the west?

Myth is necessary in any area of life which engages the emotions
and loyalties, and hence in religion. But its work is not that of giving us knowledge of reality which transcends the categories of reason. Rather its part is to render vivid and rich with feeling those
realities which we know by the tests of intelligence to be of great
importance. Reason and observation alone can give us the truth.
Once this question is settled, however, we must vivify these realities by means of myths. What we mean by this use of myth may
be illustrated by an example taken from an area more simple than
that of religion.

Hendrik Van Loon begins *The Story of Mankind* with these words:

> High up in the north in the land called Svithjod, there stands a rock. It is a hundred miles high and a hundred miles wide. Once every thousand years a little bird comes to this rock to sharpen its beak.
>
> When the rock has been worn away, then a single day of eternity will have gone by.

Here we have a myth about endless time. Reason tells us that time stretches on and on forever. But how can we be made to feel the power and importance of this reality? A myth is needed to make it vivid and colorful and to quicken our imagination to rise to the height of our rational understanding. Van Loon provides such a myth. It is a true myth in the sense that all valid myths are true. It is true not because it transcends the categories of reason. It does not grasp a reality which reason cannot grasp. But it makes us feel the import of a reality which reason shows us to be there. It quickens our emotional imagination so that it can rise to the height of our rational reach.

To say that " her neck is like a swan " is a myth, but it may be a true myth. It is in this manner that religious myths must be cherished. Most of the Christian myths which supernaturalists uphold have this kind of validity. The mistake the supernaturalists make is to misconstrue the significance of these myths. They have thought that somehow the vivid color and emotional glow inspired by the myth constituted a new kind of super-rational truth. The error was very natural but also very obvious. They are right, however, in saying that myth is indispensable for the fine art of human living in all areas of life and not least in religion.

Another error of the new supernaturalists is their use of paradox. Many supernaturalists are using paradox as though it gave us truths which reason could not state without falling into self-contradiction. Since many religious truths are best expressed in the form of a paradox, they declare that this demonstrates the incompetence of reason to grasp these truths. The self-contradiction involved in paradox is the overthrow of reason. Reason consists in logical consistency and rational implication. If religious truth must be expressed in paradox, we know that it is super-rational.

This, also, is a naïve error. A true paradox is not a self-contradiction. It does not state something which transcends the scope of logical consistency and strict implication. It is simply a short-cut method of stating truth without taking the time to run through all the network of fine distinctions and logical connections which form the rational structure of the truth involved. For example, Jesus said, "Whosoever loses his life shall save it." That is a true paradox but it is not a self-contradictory statement. A little analysis of the different meanings of the words involved will reveal quite clearly that there is a thoroughly rational structure underlying this proposition. One who loses the life of his self-centered self will gain that other kind of life in which the good of the self is merged with the total good of the kingdom of God. Therefore this paradox turns out to be perfectly rational and consistent. Such is the case of all true paradox.

One of the favorite paradoxes of the new supernaturalists is the statement that the best in us is also the worst. Here again it only needs a little analysis of meanings to show that there is nothing irrational or super-rational or inconsistent in that statement. It might mean simply that those powers and aptitudes which yield the noblest human life when rightly used, do just the opposite when wrongly used. For example, moral idealistic endeavor is one of the noblest traits of human life when all highest ideals specifically apprehended by a man or a culture are made subject to the sovereignty of the uncomprehended goodness of God. But any set of ideals becomes a great evil when it is held as though it were final and absolute and when men claim that nothing greater has any being whatsoever.

Again the new supernaturalists think they are giving us a paradox when they point to the indispensability of rational idealism for reaching after high value, conjoined with its incompetence in dealing with precious values. But this is another instance of half-baked thinking. It is true that any concrete existing thing or fulfillment is always vastly richer in content than the abstract form of any rational ideal. Hence the abstract ideal must always be held subject to the concrete fullness of the good. But there is nothing self-contradictory or super-rational in that. Perfectly rational grounds can be set forth for this procedure of keeping the abstract ideal subject and instrumental to the concrete richness of value found in actual occasions and fulfillments.

Evasive ambiguity by which problems are concealed instead of solved, and by which reason is said to be confounded and surpassed, are among the most dangerous practices in the world today. In this way men feel themselves released to follow the dictates of the blood instead of the brain. Destruction waits on human life when it goes that way.

Paradox, like myth, is often indispensable for vivid, dramatic statement. It is sometimes very laborious (and for some minds that do not delight in the fine distinctions of rational analysis it may be impossible) to trace the web of rational connection which gives consistency to statements of truth that are apparently self-contradictory. Some persons are peculiarly gifted in setting forth to the popular mind in vivid and compulsive form the great realities of life. Such persons will rightly use myth and paradox. It would be the height of folly and pedantry to insist that they always express themselves in the forms of logical consistency. But when they repudiate the tests of reason and set up as a way to the absolute goodness of God myth and paradox which do not require anything but untested " experience " and untested " insight " to validate them, they have set their feet on that slippery descent that plunges at last into the abyss.

IV. THE HUMANISTS

The humanists say that God must be found not in the cosmic whole and not in that realm beyond, where a creator should dwell, but in the field of human imagination. God is a figment of the imagination. Whatever the primitive mind greatly fears and greatly desires it is likely to personalize in the form of a god or gods. God at the best stands for highest human hopes.

John Dewey has gone a bit beyond this and said that God is the working of human imagination when it reaches out after the highest possibilities. Thus for Dewey God is not a figment of the imagination. God is a very real power. God is the power which rises up from the universe in the form of striving, climbing, idealistic imagination of man. God is the intelligent imagination, not when it is daydreaming, but when it is struggling after the highest and best that may ever be attained. God is to be known, then, by scientific inquiry, namely the science of psychology. If God is a construction of human imagination, or if God is the imagination at work in its highest capacity — in either case God is to be known by the techniques of psychological investigation.

But the humanists would say there is another way in which God can be known. When man has transformed the world into the kind of place he would have it be, when he has shaped the cosmic process to fit his loftiest dreams, then this cosmic process may be called God. For then it will be pervaded by purpose. It will be shaped by a purpose that is akin to man, nay, a purpose that has been put into it by man. When that time comes, we may speak of God as the indwelling purpose of the cosmic whole, being mindful that the indwelling purpose will be man's purpose. The humanist's penchant for this idea of God is another indication that he is an offshoot of liberalism. The theology of religious experience was man-centered. Its chief concern was the hopes, feelings, desires, purposes, ideals of men. God entered chiefly to justify moral optimism. This tendency very naturally has issued in religious humanism. Thus humanism is the outgrowth of the theology of religious experience.

V. THEISTIC NATURALISTS

Theistic naturalists answer the question, Where is God to be found? by saying that God is within the cosmic whole. He is one part of it. He is the most precious reality there is. God is here in nature, present, potent, real, intimately and widely operative. They say further that God is not the pervading purpose of the cosmic whole. The whole universe is not dominated by any purpose so far as we can discover. God is not to be identified with the cosmic whole in any way. Neither is he the creator of the cosmic whole, as the supernaturalists say.

Furthermore, God must be known by the same cognitive procedure by which other realities in nature are known. This procedure consists in finding the concept or pattern which gives meaning to the immediate qualities of experience. Getting this concept or pattern is what we call insight or intuition. It is required in every kind of knowledge from that of the physical sciences to that of love and beauty. But in gaining knowledge of any kind of reality having great value, the required pattern must be one which gives richest and widest coherence to the qualities of experience, sensuous and emotional, relating them in such a way that the psycho-physical organism can move freely and easily, with all its parts functioning in such a manner as to contribute to the qualitative richness of the experience and leading on continuously into further riches. For example, this is true in experiences of great beauty and great love.

There are only two possible ways through which reality can reach the human mind. They are through the body and through social communication with others. In fact communication with others must also come through the nervous system with its complex and subtle play of muscles, tonus, and glandular reaction. But the difference between communication by symbolic reaction, and that other kind of reaction which carries the meaning of a sign but not a symbol, is so great that we distinguish between the two. Thus we say there are two avenues by which reality reaches the human mind, the one by way of the body, the other by way of social communication between bodies.

This being the case, it is plain that all we can ever know must come through the concrete functioning of the psycho-physical organism. God must be known, and is known, in this way. God is first of all a reality that plays upon the body in a myriad of subtle and complex ways. But God thus present cannot reach consciousness until men have the responsiveness, the appreciative awareness, the pattern of apprehension, and the disposition of the total personality, which will enable them to experience the riches of divine reality. Every reality we ever know requires such favorable disposition of the personality before man can be conscious of it.

This should make it plain that knowledge of existing reality by way of reason is not knowledge of an abstraction. Our ideas, our concepts, are abstract. That is to say, the pattern is abstract when considered by itself and apart from the rich qualities of experience which it is designed to present in some form that renders them appreciable to the human consciousness. But the realities known by means of the forms of reason are not abstract. The true function of so-called "abstract reason," when rightly used, is to provide us with a pattern by which to relate the concrete riches of experience in such a way that they can enter consciousness most fully and continuously and, above all, to guide us into that way of psycho-physical functioning wherein the complicated reactions of the body will continuously pour into consciousness an ever richer flow of values of reality. Needless to say, the concepts now at our disposal and the ways of living which we have thus far achieved do this very indifferently.

VI. THE HIDDEN NATURE OF GOD

When the naturalist says that God is here in nature all about us, and when he adds that God is known through the ordinary powers of cognition, many people are confused. They look around them with senses alert, with mind active, but cannot discern any reality of such great value as to be worthy of their supreme devotion. If God can be known by powers of observation and reason, where is he? I do not discern any such being. Neither do the scientists. Nor do other men of whom I inquire. Your talk does not make sense.

This is a common misunderstanding that must be cleared away. There are many precious realities about us all the time which we do not discern because we do not have the right attitude. Our attentive awareness is not rightly directed. Our desires do not move in such a way as to catch them. Our faces are averted, as it were; our hearts and minds are turned away. Yet this turning of attentive consciousness and responsiveness to the right quarter and in the right way, is precisely what is required to know anything, such as our dog or a lost handkerchief or the blended colors of the lake. Nothing can be known unless the attention is focused on it. Most things in the world that are all about us we do not know because our attention is not rightly focused, our interest is not aroused, we have not learned to respond in the required way.

For example, on a spring day there is far more beauty around us than we can take in. Often we walk down the street and do not discern any of the beauty that is there. It pours over us like a flood, and we are unaware of it. Even when we are most responsive we are most keenly aware that we miss a great deal. We see enough in moments of greatest appreciation to know there is far more that we do not see. Often little children whose sensitivities and appreciations have not been dulled and surfeited do catch a particular kind of beauty in rich fullness, and make us know that we are blind to much that is real and intimately present.

For another illustration, take the values resident in the personalities all about us. When we have the right attitude, when we are sufficiently responsive to them, when we have the outreaching love, the loss of self-concern, the insight and grace, we find great riches of value in association with others. These moments of deep experience tell us how great are the values we miss because we are wrongly disposed, are otherwise preoccupied, have our interests so misdirected that all this abundance of rich living flows past us unsensed. Here again the great artists in fellowship, whose sensitivities and interests have been finely and magnificently trained to catch the great good in human association, make us see that we are encompassed with a reality of marvelous beauty and love, which is to be known in the same way that all things in nature are to be known, but which we miss because we do not have the right attitude.

Therefore, when the naturalist says that God is here with us all the time in nature, and when he says that this deity is to be known in the way in which anything else in nature is known and appreciated, that does not mean that any man can lift his eyes and see

God standing before him. Our interests must be redirected. The forms of our attentive awareness must be transformed, our desires must be turned toward other objectives, our whole personalities must be changed, before the goodness of God can pour into human consciousness.

When we say this about God, we are not saying anything about knowing God that is not likewise true in any case of scientific knowledge. One cannot be a scientist and get the knowledge that science seeks until his whole psycho-physical personality is transformed and disciplined and the bent of his interests redirected, so that he can have that kind of attentive awareness which the scientist in any particular field of inquiry must have. His desires must be rightly molded. Above all, he must be subjected to the transforming power of the tradition of science. It is foolish for anyone to think that he can go out and pick up any savage out of a primitive culture, give him the equipment of a scientific laboratory, and expect him to make important scientific discoveries. Even the ordinary man of the street, living in the midst of this age of science and shaped by its culture, cannot do that. Such a savage, or such a man of the street, might have as good brain tissue as Isaac Newton, and his senses might be as keen as anyone's; yet he would not be able to see and feel what the scientist must see and feel in order to make scientific discoveries. He would not have the interests. He would not have the mental patterns. His desires would not be rightly directed. The savage might be so obsessed by the bright shine on the polished instruments that he could not attend to anything else. The real scientist might never notice this shine because his interest is otherwise directed.

Science was so late in developing in human history and the spirit and discipline of scientific research are even yet so rare among men precisely because the human personality must be so radically transformed before it can see and know what the scientist must be able to apprehend. What to the ordinary untrained mind might be an inconsequential flicker, so insignificant that the mind could not retain it in consciousness, might to the scientist carry a cosmic meaning, and fill him with enthusiasm.

All we have said about the requirements for getting first-hand knowledge of the facts of physics and chemistry, the facts of psychology and beauty and love, apply also to getting first-hand knowledge of God. God must be known by using the same basic principles of knowing that the physicist must use, the friend must use, the statesman must use, the master mechanic must use. Every one of these must have his total personality ordered in the right way and adjusted to the reality in question, before he can become aware of the data that lead to knowledge. No man can have first-hand knowledge of the kinds of reality with which the above named men intimately live, unless his whole conscious and sub-conscious mind is so transformed and disciplined as to give him the required sort of awareness.

Surely this should make it plain how God can be present in nature, as real as a mountain or the life-giving air, and yet quite inaccessible to the appreciative awareness of human consciousness as long as the interests of men are so organized and directed that they cannot discern the divine reality that is all about them.

So it is that the naturalist says that God must be known as anything else in nature is known. But so long as men are dominated by self-concern they cannot see God save in rare, meager, and fleeting intimations. Self-concern shuts men in. It makes them unresponsive to the riches of life. So long as we are ridden with the fears and anxieties that are due to the dictatorship of self-concern God will be hidden from us, even as first-hand knowledge of the facts of modern physics is hidden from the keen-eyed savage. As long as our desires and interests frustrate one another, one set destroying the values in another set, both within the single personality and between personalities, God can be known to us only vaguely and remotely and largely second-hand. We must learn to live with God in God's way before we can know God. That means to live in the ways of loving appreciation of men and the rest of nature; that requires that the cells, glands, nervous system, attentive consciousness, total psycho-physical organism must learn to react to the presence and play of God. Even the best of the human race is as yet far from having attained perfectly this way of

living. The individual personality cannot be changed in this way
without a similar change in the social order.

Under proper conditions, however, men can know the reality
of God without being able to experience the specific fullness of
good that is God or to know the specific nature of God. Under
proper conditions their attentive consciousness can be turned toward God even while God is veiled to their vision. They can make
absolute commitment of their lives to God and live constantly
under the lure of God. That is what is meant by living in the
peculiarly religious way, as described in chapter 9.

VII. GOD HIDDEN IS STILL KNOWN

If God is hidden from our direct conscious awareness, how can
we know there is such a reality? We can know in the same way
that we can know the reality of many other things that exist but
which cannot be directly experienced by us except in fleeting and
fragmentary and meager bits of data. It is quite possible to know
that there is reality when the specific nature and qualitative richness of that reality are inaccessible to us. For example, a few
samplings can assure us that a forest is full of unique and beautiful
leaves and flowers, although we may never have direct experience
of more than a few fragments of the riches that are hidden there.
Or again, a few samplings are enough to demonstrate that trillions
of throbbing moments of rich experience have been lived by billions of people since the world began, are being lived by billions
and will be lived by other billions, although just what the content
of those moments may be we do not know, nor when and where
they occur, nor under just what specific circumstances. So it is
with many other things. So it is with that beauty and love which
are in the keeping of God.

We can know there is a reality which carries an unimaginable
richness of precious value, even when we cannot know the specific
nature and content of these values. We can know this through
those rare moments when our personalities have been so attuned
to the total situation as to give us a hint of what more frequent
and perfect tuning would yield. We can know it also because dif-

ferent individuals with different kinds of personalities bring to human consciousness very different kinds of value. Thus we know the values are there. Our need prompts us to want to bring them all together into one great fullness of conscious appreciation. Lastly, we know it because different cultures bring to light such diversities of value. So we know the realm of precious value is enormously vast and diversified, if only we could have the appreciative awareness capable of apprehending it all.

There is still another way in which we can demonstrate the reality of this most precious being. We can do it by the logic of mutual support. We know that when any two appreciable bits of experience are so connected that they support one another and enhance one another, the value is greatly magnified. We know that, if many such items are so related, the result is not merely the sum, but is much greater than the sum in value. Furthermore, we know that when such appreciable activities are so related that each activity can mean to the person who undergoes it the whole great system of qualitative richness of which it is a part, then indeed the value is prodigiously increased. In this way we know the world has in it the makings of a value infinitely richer than the little goods we directly experience.

The explanation we have given should make it plain that the naturalist does not appeal to the content of human consciousness to find God, as the religious liberal has done. Rather he says that the consciousness of man must be transformed and redirected before he can experience God in any fullness, and this transformation has a long way to go even with the best of us.

VIII. THE PLACE OF REVELATION IN NATURALISM

We have tried to show how man can know God. But the mere knowledge that there is a God is not enough to make any man religious. To live religiously one must appreciate God. He must take God as the one and only sovereign good in his life. God, and God only, must count in his living. Nothing, absolutely nothing else, must be worthwhile except as it leads to God or in some way signifies God. Perhaps such perfect height of religious living is not frequently attained, but that at least is the norm for all religious living. One lives religiously only as he approaches that norm. But to live that way requires far more than merely knowing that there is a God. It requires absolute self-commitment to God.

Now this appreciation of God, this self-commitment to God, even while God is largely hidden, cannot be accomplished by mere willing. One cannot be appreciative of the hidden God unless his personality is so transformed that he can have that appreciation.

Here we have a second kind of transformation of personality. The kind we have been discussing heretofore is the ultimate transformation, required to open the appreciative awareness of man to the fullness of good that is in God so that God will be no longer hidden. But now we are talking of a prior transformation. It is the change required to turn man toward God, to make him live for God, even while God is yet hidden.

This transformation can come only through social interaction. One must live with people who appreciate God and are committed to God, before one can himself make that commitment. One must be shaped by a life-transforming tradition before he can live that way. One must belong to a fellowship that transforms individuals in this manner.

Christianity, not merely as a set of doctrines and symbols and practices and morals, but as a life-transforming fellowship and tradition, has its source in the fellowship of Jesus and his disciples and the early church. These no doubt inherited a life-transforming tradition that went back to the Hebrew prophets. But Jesus and his disciples and the early church heightened, purified, and magnified the power of it. From them it has been transmitted from individual to individual and from generation to generation. Today it may be found in small groups as a living and holy communion which touches men and enables them to make the absolute commitment to God who is hidden, and live for him even while he is hidden.

Now this transformation by "the holy spirit" is what (rightfully) can be called revelation. It is not the giving of knowledge, but it is the giving of an attitude or disposition of the personality which enables one to acquire knowledge of God's way. It redirects the interests and desires and attentive awareness so that one can learn of God by the ordinary methods of intelligent inquiry. It removes, not the total blindness of man to God, but the impenetrable blindness of man. It enables man to learn progressively of God, in problematical situations where life-transforming problems are solved.

This, then, is the real nature and place of revelation. It is not a miraculous giving of knowledge. But it is that change in personality which, in one way or another, is required before a man can get any knowledge of anything that lies outside the range of his established organization of interests. It is a reorganization of his interests which enables him to know a new kind of reality.

IX. THE PLACE OF INTUITION AND MYTH

We have already indicated the nature of intuition. It is not a special way of getting knowledge. It is an essential part of any case of getting new knowledge. One cannot get new knowledge unless he tests a new idea. But one cannot test a new idea unless he first has a new idea to test. The entry into the mind of a new idea is what we mean by intuition. The baby experiences an intuition when he first gets the idea that his toes belong to himself. But he must test the idea in practice and observation, else it is not a living truth for him. Intuition is a very common thing; that is to say, it is as common as the acquisition of new knowledge. It is just as needful in getting knowledge about God as it is in getting knowledge about toes, but not any more so.

Also we have indicated the nature and function of myth in religious living. It is not a way of getting knowledge or transmitting knowledge, it is a way of using knowledge. It belongs not to intellectual inquiry nor to the acquisition of knowledge, but it does belong to the acquisition of the practical arts of living. It is often a required form of apprehension. For example, a singer is taught to think of his voice as coming from between his eyebrows. That will enable him to relax his throat in the way that good singing requires. To live with required appreciation of the significance of time we need perhaps to think of a bird wearing away a great rock by cleaning his bill upon it once every thousand years. These are myths which do not show us what is true but which enable us to apprehend what reason shows to be true. They are forms of appreciative apprehension which guide our feeling and acting so that we can operate more effectively with the realities which we do know through empirical use of reason. We need to have such myths to enable us to live more skillfully in the way of God. But we must not think that they give us some kind of super-rational knowledge.

X. FAITH

Belief is holding any proposition to be true. Knowledge is accepting a proposition to be true on grounds of good evidence. Faith is accepting a belief in such a way that it transforms one's way of living. A belief becomes knowledge when it is supported by good evidence. It becomes a faith when it shapes the controlling loyalties of a life. Knowledge is not necessarily faith. A man might know many things which do not appreciably modify the directional thrust of his life. On the other hand, however, a belief which does do this, and hence is a faith, might have as much evidence to support it as any case of knowledge, and hence would be knowledge as well as being faith. It is the life-transforming power of the belief, and not the lack of good evidence, which makes it a faith. To be sure, beliefs which do determine a man's way of life, and hence are his faith, may lack evidence. But there are no beliefs which should be kept more strictly within the bounds of solid knowledge than those which give direction to the total movement of a man's life; for if they are false the evil is very great. On the other hand, beliefs which do not make or destroy a personality can be false without so much disaster. Therefore a faith, more than any other kind of belief, should be knowledge in the sense of being based on good evidence.

But every worthy faith is self-commitment to a reality which has far greater wealth of value in it than those values of it which we have been able to bring to the light of specific knowledge. In other words, the belief which is a faith should be about something which has such great richness of value that it is to date very incompletely explored. Nothing is worthy of a life's devotion except what is great enough to require the exploratory search of thousands of people throughout many ages. But such a faith does not mean that the belief is any less sure than knowledge. I can be sure that some reality has great abundance of value in it beyond those specific items of value which I have thus far brought to light. A prospector can be thus sure [3] of a vein of ore. Therefore my faith, meaning that belief about the reality in question which directs my life's devotion toward it, may be as sure as any knowledge can be and yet all my life be given to exploratory outreach into the uncomprehended mysteries of its content.

A worthy faith should be an inquiring faith. There should be in it not only those beliefs which have been tested to the point of assured knowledge, but there should also be a great system of exploratory propositions. These propositions which have not yet been tested should not be treated as life-transforming beliefs. That is to say, they should be not the faith itself, but rather the searchlights of faith. They should be the tools of inquiry. The commitment of faith should be to that uncomprehended, incompletely explored reality which is surely real. It should not be to these exploratory propositions. These should be only the means by which the faith searches out specific truths about the reality which is known to have being.

Every worthy faith, says the naturalist, should have a vast system of these exploratory propositions, built as high and wide and deep as a creative and disciplined imagination can build them. They should serve, as it were, as an enormous net by which the man of faith drags the vasty deep to bring to light the further precious truths about that reality in which he has faith. But the fact that every worthy faith should have a great system of exploratory propositions which are not yet assured knowledge — that is, are mere hypotheses — should not lead one to think that faith itself is a mere hypothesis. The belief which gives basic direction to the thrust of a man's total life should be a very sure belief. The substance of his faith should be a validated belief. These other untested propositions are only the prospecting tools of faith.

This distinction is very important and no faith is mature until it has clearly drawn the line between its two resources — the life-shaping beliefs which are tested knowledge, and the exploratory propositions which are the tools of inquiry. Let us change the figure of speech. Truth-supported faith is the shining sun. Exploratory hypotheses are the searchlights which probe the outer darkness lying beyond the illumination of that assured belief which is the faith.

XI.   TRUTH AND VITALITY IN RELIGION

Truth and vitality in religion are not altogether identical. A religion may have truth and not vitality; it may have vitality and not truth. However, neither is good without the other. Truth may be increased and yet the basic interests of life may decline because the forms of appreciative apprehension are lacking which enable a man to assimilate the truth into these interests. On the other hand, if one has forms of appreciative apprehension which are well fitted to his living, he may get great vitality from very meager bits of truth even though they be mixed with an enormous amount of roughage in the form of error.

We have tried to draw the line of distinction between religious truth which can be found only by way of rational induction, and those forms of appreciative religious apprehension which are required for religious vitality. Faith, revelation, myth, intuition, and paradox are forms by which the religious person apprehends truth in such a way that he can vitally appreciate it and live it. Through these forms dead propositions are transformed into living processes. But it is very important that the propositions be true.

When we rise above the divisions and subdivisions among religious thinkers we see one great distinction between them. It is with regard to the way they treat truth and the way to truth on the one hand, and those forms of appreciative religious apprehension by which truth is vitalized, on the other. For the most part these two, between which a clear line of distinction should be drawn, are hopelessly confused. We find some fighting to perpetuate forms of vital apprehension but without any regard to the method by which the truth apprehended shall be sought, found, and validated. We find others fighting for the way to truth but without regard to those forms of appreciative apprehension by which religious living can make any use of it. We find others fighting for both but without integrating them, so that the forms of appreciative apprehension cannot be applied to the truth that is held, and the truth makes the forms appear to be absurd. We find some fighting for forms of apprehension, thinking they are the ways to truth which stand over and above reason. We find others fighting for valid truths but thinking they are forms of appreciative apprehension when they are not.

All this wild confusion in which the method of getting truth and the forms of its appreciative apprehension are mixed together, so that people do not know which is which, must be cleared away. Much of the controversy going on and much of the energy being expended are wasted because of failure to see this distinction. But individuals and groups who study the matter can make the distinction and can find in the resources of the modern world all the materials needed for a magnificent upthrust of creative living. Truth for significant religious living and forms for appreciative apprehension can be had without trying to force the modern mind into forms of another age which are alien to it, and without abandoning the rational methods of testing truth.

NOTES

1 P. 200.

2 Vergilius Ferm in *The Nature of Religious Experience* (Harper and Bros.), pp. 41–43.

3 We are here using the word "sure" in the ordinary practical sense of high probability.

BIBLIOGRAPHY

God in Christ, by Horace Bushnell, contains a first chapter, "Dissertation on Language," which should be known and read far more widely than it is, for it reveals a fine sensitivity to the forms of religious apprehension. Hocking's entire book, *The Meaning of God in Human Experience,* is an elaborate study of the forms of religious apprehension, but special reference may be made to chaps. 7, 11, 16, 23. The same theme underlies Lyman's *Meaning and Truth of Religion.* Particular attention should be given to chap. 5, " Reason and Mysticism," and to chaps. 7–9. " The Sense of Wonder," chap. 15 in B. E. Meland's *Modern Man's Worship,* portrays the uniquely religious form of apprehension naturalistically interpreted. Devoted action is shown as a requirement in any form of apprehending God by Gregory Vlastos in *The Religious Way.* H. Richard Niebuhr, in chap. 5 of *The Nature of Religious Experience,* argues that the order of value which is God is starkly real in nature, but we cannot discern the divinity of it until our hearts and minds are transformed. Reinhold Niebuhr, in chap. 6 of the same book, upholds myth and paradox as forms of religious apprehension.

15.

NATURE AND DESTINY OF MAN

RELIGION rises out of human nature. It is inherent in human nature in such wise that if man lost his potentiality for religion he would cease to be human. No other manifestation of human culture is more deep-rooted in man's existence than is religion. From many directions testimony to this fact has been accumulating in this study. Human nature is potentially whatever religion is or can become. Furthermore, religion can never become anything save what man's nature can become, otherwise it could never be a part of human life. Every adequate philosophy of religion must show how religion rises out of human nature, what human nature can do with it, and, most important of all, what religion can do with human nature.

There are many standpoints from which to view the nature of man. These different perspectives present different aspects of his nature. When one approaches man from the standpoint of biology one asks questions very different from those engendered by a social perspective. Different questions bring forth different answers and so reveal man in different characters and roles. We here distinguish five among the several possible standpoints and perspectives in which human nature can be studied. One of these is the religious, another the biological, a third the anthropological, then the psychological, and last the social.

These five must be differentiated from one another and the distinctive problem of each set forth. In this way the religious approach to the nature of man can be seen in its unique character as over against the others. It will then be plain that our findings when we study man under the direction of the religious interest are as different from our findings when we approach him with the biological interest as those of the latter viewpoint are distinct from the findings of social inquiry. These different views of man, to be valid, should not contradict one another but should be supplementary in developing a total picture of his nature.

I. THE FIVE PERSPECTIVES OF MAN

The religious questions about man are: How is human nature related to the most worthful reality there is? Is human nature identical with this most worthful reality? Is man the highest and best there is in the universe? Does the cosmic whole reach its apex in man? Is the imagination of man the only power known to us which strives after ideal possibilities; and is this striving the most divine expression of the cosmic process? Must we sing with Swinburne, " Praise to Man in the Highest, for Man is the Master of things "?

Some philosophies of religion have answered these questions affirmatively. But other religious inquiries have yielded different replies. These latter have asked, Is man not the most evil and debased of all existing things? Is he not sunk in sin, with a great gulf intervening between him and God? Is he not by reason of his sinful nature diametrically opposed to what is best? Is not God in heaven and man on earth, with the two separate and basically opposed except as God breaks through the barriers of evil and rescues man from his evil estate?

Or still again a third group asks, Is man not divided in himself, with something divine in his nature which can be identified with God, but with much also that fights against God?

However answered, the prime religious question about man is, What relation holds between his nature and the supremely worthful? We have used the term " supremely worthful " instead of the name of God so as to accommodate those religions and philosophies which repudiate the idea of deity. On the other hand, however, whether they use the word God or not, if the question is a religious one it must be about this connection or lack of connection between man and the most worthful reality, whether the most worthful be conceived as ideal possibilities or be considered some form of actuality. Therefore the prime question stands: What identity or difference, separation or connection can be discovered between man and the best that is or ever can be? That is the question which religion asks about the nature of man.

The questions for which biology seeks an answer are very different: What is the bodily constitution of man? What are the physiological processes that make up his nature? It is the generation and the development, the sickness and the health, the inner workings and the outward reactions of the human body which are the subjects of inquiry for this approach. In the last two hundred and fifty years we have discovered more about this aspect of human nature than about any other. The answers which biology found to its basic questions told us most of what we know today of the cells, the organs, the glands, the nervous system, the musculature and the bones, the marvelous ways in which they resist disease and other destructive agencies, and the way they build themselves anew and meet the needs of the total organism.

The anthropological question about man is this: How did culture originate and develop and what does this growth of culture reveal concerning the nature of man? Culture is the peculiar product of the human being. Nothing else produces it. It is therefore something which sets apart the way of human living from everything else. Culture is the accumulation from generation to generation of a lore, of techniques, of ideals, of programs and systems, institutions and regulations. Above all it is the development of a system and order of ideal standards socially enforced which guide the conduct of life in all its many interests. How do such a system and order of life develop and what light do they throw on the nature of man? Bronislaw Malinowski, Gerald Heard, and Franz Boas are names taken at random from among the many who are making this inquiry.

The psychological question about man is: What are the mental processes which enter into human behavior? The thoughts, the feelings, the sentiments, the impulses and habits, the way the mind learns, its pathology, its health, its development, and its potentialities are under inquiry. Psychology in many quarters has been very specialized in its narrowly selected fields of search. This specialization doubtless has been necessary for purposes of scientific investigation. But it has resulted in putting to one side the problems that involve the personality as a whole — problems which are the important issues for human living. To meet this need the so-called newer psychology has been developed. It began with techniques for helping diseased minds to recover their balance. The problems of how to maintain the human personality in health of mind, and what may be the requirements for its higher development, are now under consideration by such workers as Piaget, Jung, Burnham, Kuenkel, Gesell, Sheldon, Dewey, and others. These studies should in the course of time tell us much about human nature.

The social question about man splits into several related ones: How does association between individuals and groups make human nature what it is? Are the human mind and personality, as over against the biological organism alone, created by communication between individuals? Do human minds come into association or does association create the human mind? Is the nature of man essentially and ineradicably social so that he becomes deranged and degenerates toward the subhuman when deprived of association? The forms of human association, such as those of the family and all intimate fellowship, together with the economic and the political, all throw light on his nature. From among the many who have been or are working on this problem may be mentioned C. H. Cooley, G. H. Mead, John Macmurray, F. Allport, and Kimball Young.

They who seek to answer the religious question about man must turn to all these others for help, even as they all turn to one another. For man is one organic whole and no one of these aspects can be understood apart from the others. Different questions are asked in these different approaches, but the answer to any one of these questions depends partly upon the answers to the others. However, the biological question can be answered with much more independence of the others than is the case the other way round.

The religious understanding of man cannot be achieved until the inquirer goes to the findings of biology and gets an answer to the question: What does the physiology of men reveal concerning the relation between human nature and the highest? We know that if man is separated from God, or has any peculiar connection with the most worthful reality, the indications of it will appear in his biological processes.

Also the religious inquirer will ask of the other perspectives: What do the origins and early development of culture reveal concerning the connection between most worthful reality and the essential nature of man? What do the psychological processes of the human mind reveal concerning the same matter? What does the social nature of man indicate concerning his highest vocation and destiny? Thus the religious study of man must draw upon all these other studies to get the knowledge it seeks. Yet the religious answer is no mere compilation from the others. It has a distinctive problem which cannot be solved under the guidance of any other interest save the religious.

II. ANSWERS OF THE DIFFERENT RELIGIOUS PHILOSOPHIES

The five outstanding divisions in current philosophies of religion set forth different answers to the religious question about man. Traditional supernaturalism, liberalism, humanism, the new supernaturalism, and the new naturalism, all make characteristic statements upon this issue.

What traditional supernaturalism says about man can be found in the writings of such persons as Augustine, Aquinas and Calvin, and of Professor Machen of our own time and country. These answer: Man is made in the image of God. Yet God and man are clearly distinct and separate and the image of God in man has been badly marred by sin. Man was created perfect by God but yielded to temptation and became a sinner deeply and helplessly sunk in wickedness. Man is powerless to find his way back to the goodness of God. A great gulf separates the two. But God in his great love and mercy chooses to save some. This redemption is made possible without impairment of the righteousness of God by the sacrifice of his Son, Jesus Christ, who died for the sins of men. By reason of this sacrifice it is possible for God to predestine a few to salvation, but the great majority are damned according to the dictates of the laws of righteousness.

Human nature was made for God and man can find no peace until he unites with God, they aver. But the barrier of his sin makes such union impossible until this obstruction is taken away by divine forgiveness. Jesus Christ has made it possible for God to forgive sins. Thus man can come to God when he accepts the divine forgiveness. But before he can be forgiven he must acknowledge his sins and his lost estate. Everyone can come to God if he will accept this forgiveness. But sinful arrogance, a self-assured sense of power and independence, makes it impossible for many to come to God by way of this forgiveness. Yet this way of forgiveness is the only way by which the nature of man can recover its lost connection with the most worthful reality.

Liberalism, riding on the crest of the wave of new knowledge and power won in modern times, turned in revulsion against the contumely heaped upon man by traditional supernaturalism. Liberalism has never been uniform in its teaching except in so far as it rectified the opposite emphasis of tradition by declaring the goodness of man. By implication, if not in explicit statement, it tended to reverse the relation between God and man. In traditional supernaturalism man existed to glorify God. In liberalism God existed to glorify man. The importance of God lay in the fact that he was needed by man. Man could not attain his highest ends without God. Therefore men should turn to God. The sin and the helplessness of man were not denied, but they fell into the background.

The greatness of man lay in his idealism. He was the aspiring animal. He could apprehend ideals and strive to achieve them and reconstruct the world to conform to them. He was dependent on God, to be sure, and he needed God's help to achieve his supreme goals. But God also fell somewhat into the background while man stood in the center of the picture, heroically striving after the highest possibilities of existence. The chief note of liberalism was optimism about man, about society, about history and the cosmos. The liberals were liable to disillusionment, but that was inevitable. One is most likely to be disillusioned when he has optimistic illusions which need to be corrected. Liberalism painted a glorious picture of man. The individual personality was set up as the most important thing in the universe.

The ranks of religious liberalism have been depleted of late and their optimism about man has been shaded. Some of its strength has gone into humanism, some into the new supernaturalism, and some into the new naturalism. Representative liberals are B. P. Bowne, W. A. Brown, D. C. Macintosh.[1]

Humanism is very optimistic about man, although subject at times to deep pessimism. It completes the tendency to push God into the background. According to humanism either God does not exist or his existence is doubtful, or he is quite subordinate to the great enterprise of human life. Man carries the ideals of the universe and there is no other carrier of them so far as we know. Human imagination is that outreach of the cosmic process after highest possibilities of value. In this idealizing imagination of man the universe takes on meaning and purpose. Here and here only, so far as we can discover, does material existence reach up after the better and the best with purpose and desire to attain it. Human nature, then, in the form of man's idealizing imagination, is identical with the supremely worthful reality. John Dewey, R. W. Sellars, A. E. Haydon, and Max Otto uphold this religious interpretation of man.

The new supernaturalism is a radical repudiation of liberalism and humanism with their optimism about man. It declares that man and God are separated even more completely than traditional supernaturalism taught. In human reason man and God unite, Thomas Aquinas held. The new supernaturalism not only denies this, but declares that human reason is one of the chief ways in which man expresses his arrogance and autonomy. Only when reason resolves itself into self-contradictions and thereby demonstrates its incapacity for dealing with the things of God can it illumine the way that connects the divine and the human. Traditional supernaturalism, as we have already noted, taught that the church or the Bible, both occurring in human history, were divine.

Thus through these historic events human nature found connection and kinship with God. But the new supernaturalism denies this divinity of historic book and institution. These are all too human and full of the weakness and evil of human life.

The ideals of men and human values generally are not to be identified with God, according to the new supernaturalism. Human goals are often diametrically opposed to the way of God and in any case do not throw light on the connection between human nature and the highest. All man's attempts by way of religious endeavor and moral striving to reach up to God are futile and often produce great evil, making human life much worse than it was before. They are demonic.

Nevertheless man is created by God, he belongs to God. He is doomed to disaster and destruction except as he is joined with God. But this deliverance can be accomplished only by God's act. Divine grace only can restore man to health and living connection with what is supremely worthful. Karl Barth, Emil Brunner, Paul Tillich, and the brothers Reinhold and H. Richard Niebuhr are representative of this viewpoint.

The new naturalism has also repudiated liberal and humanistic interpretations of man. Therefore it has certain similarities with the new supernaturalism. But it has gone a different way. Its view of man is represented by A. N. Whitehead, B. E. Meland, John Macmurray, Gregory Vlastos, Charles Hartshorne, and, as the reader must have guessed, by the present author. Perhaps its view of man can best be made clear by comparing and contrasting it with the teachings we have just been considering.

It is like liberalism in saying that God and man are united in certain processes of nature. But it is diametrically opposed to liberalism on one point: it holds that man exists for God, not God for man. Also it is opposed in that it gives far larger place to evil in human nature. It is not dominated by optimism in the sense that it must stand or fall with the view of a happy outcome for the world. In this respect, perhaps, it differs from all the other philosophies we have considered, for even the new supernaturalists insist on an eschatology, meaning that sometime, somehow, by miracle or otherwise, God will intervene in this world and make all things come right. The new naturalism, furthermore, is opposed to liberalism in saying that actual reality, and not ideals, should command our first consideration.

The new naturalism is like humanism in repudiating the supernatural, but it is opposed to humanism in holding that God is not only real but supremely important — much more important than man himself.

It is like the new supernaturalism in saying that man exists for God and not God for man; that man can find his vocation and destiny only in God and suffers destruction when he departs from God; that the higher man rises in his civilization, the more imperative becomes his need of God and the more destructive are the consequences of his refusal to make absolute self-commitment to God. It is like the new supernaturalism, furthermore, in saying that there is much in human nature that fights against God and consequently human life is involved in great evils and dangers; that the evil in nature, both human and subhuman, is so great that there is no assured outcome; but that man gains all the good there is, and escapes all the evil that can be escaped, when he gives himself absolutely to God. Then, at this point, the naturalist can add a comment which the supernaturalist would hold to be unthinkable, and thereby he strides beyond the supernaturalist in his devotion to God. He can add that man gains all in absolute devotion to God even though God at last should go down to defeat before the forces of evil.

Still again the new naturalism is like the new supernaturalism in saying that human reason is not what identifies God and man. Human reason deals with abstractions while God's work is that of concrete growth.

While these two philosophies have the points in common which we have summarized again, they are diametrically opposed on many issues. According to the new naturalism man must approach God by way of values. Values are the data by which God is sought and found. That does not mean, however, that God can be identified with whatever men may happen to cherish nor with the highest socially accepted ideals. It claims, furthermore, in opposition to the new supernaturalism, that human intelligence can know God. It rejects the supernatural entirely, while the new supernaturalism makes the supernatural all-important.

III. THE IMPORTANT QUESTIONS ABOUT MAN

We have noted the central question which religious inquiry asks about human nature. But the answer to this question concerning man's highest vocation and destiny can be sought intelligently only if certain prior questions are asked. The central religious question can be analyzed into components. Answers to these will enable us to get the knowledge we seek in the religious query. These subordinate questions are: What is it in man which distinguishes him from the rest of nature? What is it in man that makes him religious? What is it in man which connects him with God? What is it in man which makes him a sinner? What is man's highest destiny? How is that destiny achieved? An alternative wording of this last question is: What is the way of salvation? We shall not treat each of these questions separately and in order, but rather use them to prepare ourselves to think through the problem. Nor shall we go into subtleties and hidden matters, but keep to the rather obvious elements.

The features which distinguish man from the rest of nature are these: He laughs, he talks, he plays imaginatively, he uses tools and machines, he reasons, he worships, he rears a culture.

1. Man Laughs. Laughter is a rare and strange phenomenon in nature. Nowhere else do we see it in clear form save in man. Furthermore it is one of the most spontaneous and irrepressible expressions of the human being. Ordinarily man does not laugh because he plans to do so. He laughs because he cannot help it. Laughter gushes up from hidden levels. It throws off concealments. As a man laughs, so is he. The heart is exposed in laughter. Perhaps we can find through this expression of human nature the wellspring whence issue religion, saintliness, art, and culture generally.

What is the general nature of that which strikes us as funny?

Is it not the sense of incongruity when the incongruity is suddenly resolved into a higher synthesis? Peek-a-boo makes the baby laugh. In peek-a-boo, first you are there and then you are not. The sudden appearance and disappearance produce an incongruity of phenomena which vivify each other by contrast. But the incongruity is easily resolved into a higher synthesis wherein the contrasting and incongruous elements find their place in an intelligible whole of vivified experience. Is not this what occurs whenever we experience the funny? In every good joke two or more meanings are brought together in what at first seems to be an incongruous connection. But when you " see the point " and laugh, you see how the apparently incongruous factors do really fit together into a larger totality of meaning wherein the apparent incongruity serves to bring out more vividly the several factors by mutual contrast with one another. For example, the newcomer to America had difficulty learning to pronounce such words as " enough " and " through " and " bough," all requiring a different pronunciation for the same spelling. However he began at last to see light and was getting along fairly well when he noticed an advertisement for a movie which read, " Cavalcade pronounced success." He gave up. He could never learn to pronounce a language addicted to such caprices.

The funniness of this joke taken at random would seem to be typical of all that is funny. There must be first an apparent conflict of meanings or perplexing juxtaposition of parts which, however, yields to insight and becomes a richer harmony by reason of the contrast. Conflicting interests are brought into a higher unity. It is the experience of overcoming conflict by resolving it into a richer synthesis of mutually vivifying parts. It is the experience of growth or progressive integration.

Thus laughter reveals that man finds a peculiar kinship and spontaneity of delight in the experience of creative synthesis in which diverse elements are transformed by being caught up into a meaningful whole producing an unpredictable emergent richness of experience. Something deep in the nature of man spontaneously responds with joy to the process of resolving conflicting or incongruous factors into a unity of mutually enhancing parts creatively and unpredictably synthesized. In his laughter he reveals that his nature is made for God if it truly be that God is this ⟩ creative synthesis which we have called growth working throughout the world. If God works always to bring diverse and conflicting activities into relations of mutual support and mutual enhancement with unpredictable mergents, then we see in man's laughter that there is something in him deeper than conscious intent which rises up in joy when this quality in the work of God suddenly appears before him in swift and easily comprehensible form.

There is a further requirement for the experience of funniness and laughter which is just as important as the one noted, and equally significant. In order to experience the delight of laughter in seeing apparent conflict swiftly resolve into a richer synthesis, one must view it in disregard of his own personal loss or gain. Just as soon as he becomes concerned about some advantage or disadvantage for himself in the process, he loses the sense of humor to that degree. One may laugh at a situation in which his own gain or loss is involved, but when he does so he is appreciating it in spite of its effect upon his personal interests.

Contrariwise, the man who lacks a sense of humor, and who rarely laughs, is the man who is so absorbed in certain personal interests that he cannot view a situation objectively with delight in progressive synthesis per se, and in disregard of its utility for him. He takes himself too seriously or he regards his own specific goal as so important that he cannot appreciate the wider enrichment of life which overflows the bounds of his particular undertaking. He may cry, " Give me Scotland or I die," but he cannot say, " Not my will but thine be done." In the latter instance one yields himself, his goals and wants, to that progressive transformation accomplished by growth whereby the world is enriched in value more deeply and widely than any possible preconceived goal can comprehend.

Comedy is always like that. It brings in a concrete wealth of qualities which we did not anticipate, which our program did not cover, which requires us to turn our gaze for a moment away from our fixed objective and consider the riches of life that flower about us outside our own planting. A comedy of errors may require you to transform your program quite radically. If it goes deep enough it is called tragedy. But true tragedy is also a creative synthesis which wrenches us out of our fixed program and opens a fullness of experience we did not plan. It may be a fullness we cannot receive unless the whole order of our life yields itself very profoundly to that creative synthesis which is the work of God. It may require us to give up our whole lives in order to make way for this other kind of development which we did not plan. But Joan of Arc in the midst of her tragedy might say, "If I pass through the fire I shall pass into the hearts of the people forever and ever."

It should be apparent from what we have said that the experience of fun is a kind of dramatic, aesthetic experience. It differs from other drama in being so superficial and moving so swiftly, to its denouement.

Laughter also carries the germ of sainthood and of religion, for in laughter one forgets himself in his enjoyment of the growth of harmony between diverse and conflicting activities which may run counter to his own plans and self-esteem. Also, since laughter makes for mental and physical health and gives peace, joy, and fulfillment as far as it goes, it indicates that man is made not to seek satisfaction for himself but to find satisfaction in forgetting himself in devotion to the growth of unity between diverse and contrasting elements. St. Francis of Assisi and his followers show the continuity of development from laughter to sainthood. They called themselves the *jongleurs de Dieu* — the tumblers or jesters of God. They were God's little fools, quite worthless and insignificant in themselves but on that account able to glory in all the goodness of God. What gave them joy was the great community of brotherliness. There were Brother Wolf and brother beast of every sort; and all the birds and flowers, and the earth and the sun were brothers and sisters of God's little fools, all these made the great community in which the little *jongleurs* danced and played.

We say that laughter reveals in human nature that bent which issues in devotion to the growth of community throughout the world in disregard of what happens to self. Every individual, whether plant, beast, man, family, nation, culture, represents the formation of connections of mutual support and control within a limited scope. But every such " epochal occasion," to use Whitehead's phrase, must die. That is to say, the growth of connections of mutual support between activities, so far as they enter into the existence of any one such individual, is limited. Therefore each individual unit or system (which includes any historic culture or race) which has the reflective power to be aware of the issue, must decide whether it will live to bring its own individuality to completion or whether it will live for the unlimited growth of community throughout the world, without regard to its own individuality save as a contributor to this growth and an appreciator of it.

Now laughter shows that man is made by nature to find his greatest joy in serving and delighting in the unlimited growth of organic connections and not in making such development serve merely the fulfillment of his own individuality. His own individual self, his own group, nation, culture, must in time die in order that unlimited growth be not confined to such " epochal occasion." Each must make his contribution to the growing enrichment of creative synthesis. How is man to enjoy this unlimited growth if each contributor must perish in offering up his all to it? The answer is found in laughter. Man is so made that he finds his greatest delight in serving and appreciating such creative synthesis without regard to his self-centered or group-centered interests and unhindered by the fact that each must perish in order that unlimited growth may go on. Laughter shows that man is destined to find his greatest joy in the inevitability of his own destruction. With laughter man triumphs over fortune, good and ill.

In the light of laughter man's vocation, man's destiny, is not to achieve his specific goals of endeavor. He must have such goals and work for them. But if he is to find the kind of joy which is revealed in laughter he must be receptive to that glad surprise of unpredictable connections and denouements. He must not be so absorbed with his ideal or program that he is unappreciative of those creative syntheses which make his program seem funny and trivial compared to the richness of the outcome that he could not foresee.

When the greater issues are involved and the unpredictable creative synthesis is far more profound it is no longer the experience of the funny. It becomes experience of beauty, or of tragedy, or of love, or of the sublime, or of the holy. But the basic principle is the same: it is joy in the creative synthesis of interests previously diverse and conflicting, the synthesis occurring in disregard of the self-centered interests of individual or group, and often demanding that these be radically transformed or sacrificed in order that the wider and deeper community may be attained.

The blessedness of the saint is found in such joy. Laughter at either the superficial level or the profound level shows that such joy and such devotion are native to man. It shows that man at his center is made for God if God be the unlimited growth of community throughout the universe by way of creative synthesis.

2. *Man Talks*. Man not only laughs. He also talks. Talking is just as significant as laughter in revealing the primal vocation of man.

We must distinguish at once between human talk and the bay of the hound that calls other hounds to cooperate in pursuit of the prey, the cry of the trapped bird that brings other birds fluttering to the rescue, the cluck of the hen that causes the chicks to come scuttling to the food.

Communication by human talk does not require the communicator to participate actually in the undertaking which is communicated. When the dog signals that he wants me to go to a certain place he pulls me in that direction. He must actually undertake in some measure the things he wants to communicate to me. So likewise the hound's bay, the bird's cry, the hen's cluck, are always uttered in the midst of the actual situation which embodies the meaning. These signals are parts, tiny fragments, as it were, of the total physical movement or thing which is the subject matter of the communication. Human talk does not require any such participation in the event. Dogs, so far as we can discover, do not sit down and discuss the problem of catching the rabbit. To communicate to one another anything about the rabbit, they must actually be after a rabbit or act as though they were. This is an immense difference between talk and the signals of animals. In human talk the meanings are divested of all the massive weight and corporeality of the actual situation. Hence they can be developed indefinitely beyond any concrete situation. Thus meaning can be added to meaning in ways that would be impossible if the burden of actual situations had to be carried along. Thus " free meanings " are released, meanings that are free of the actual world. Thereby imagination is released and the human mind is enabled to construct fantastic illusions, perpetrate errors and perversions that none of the lower animals could ever achieve. Also it can attain a vision of reality that no other animal can reach.

There is another distinguishing characteristic of human talk as over against the signaling of animals. When the dogs, Jock and Rover, go abroad, a certain kind of yelp by Jock informs Rover that a rabbit's trail has been found. There is a great difference between knowing there *is* a rabbit's trail, and knowing that some one else has *found* a rabbit's trail. In the first place you are informed of an objective fact which you recognize from your viewpoint. In the second place you are not only informed of an objective fact, but also of a certain other individual's viewpoint of that objective fact. In the second case you are not only informed of a certain fact, but of that fact in a certain perspective which is different from your own.

Thus human talk not only informs us about objective fact, but makes possible the combining of different perspectives. The other can inform me of his perspective, I can inform him of mine. Thereby can occur a creative synthesis of perspectives or an organization of them. As we have already noted, this combination of diverse perspectives which are at first incongruous but are resolved into some kind of higher system, is what constitutes the funny when the interests involved are not very serious and are swiftly and easily combined. When the interests are serious, such combination and transformation yield the experience of drama, high tragedy, love, sublimity, and the heights of mysterious holiness. Through the creative synthesis of diverse perspectives man develops a growing vision of reality which can be achieved only through a combination of perspectives. Such a growing vision we call culture. It may assume many forms, of which these few are examples: mythology, art, an unlimited accumulation of techniques, science and philosophy.

In talking we share one another's minds. In signaling we induce cooperation, fellow feeling and sympathy, but we do not share the perspective of the other. In signaling we cannot develop an unlimited growth of meaning shared by each member of the group. In talk we can and we do. Talk generates a progressive accumulation of shared meanings that can grow from generation to generation. Talk generates the human mind as distinguished from any other kind of mind there is. In talk personalities participate in one another, and in the mutual creativity of one another, as no other creatures can do.

This growth of profound community is not what men intend when they talk. They simply find this growth going on as a consequence of their talk. Perhaps we should better say they do not even become conscious of this growth of community which ensues when they talk until they attain a rather high degree of self-consciousness.

Therefore it is in talk that we see a growth going on which creates and progressively transforms the human mind and personality without the knowledge and direction of men. It is another case of the " wild growth " of God, a superhuman growth, which men may learn to cultivate but which they do not originate, which they did not at first intend, which they cannot determine inasmuch as it transforms the very mind itself with all its purposes and plans.

When an individual discovers that talk is generating this kind of profound creative community between himself and others, he may take alarm at its revelatory nature and so fight against it. He may try to stop it or destroy it by lies and all manner of deceptions. He often builds up a barricade of words designed to conceal his deeper and truer meanings. He tries to hide his inner self, but does not ordinarily succeed very well. However, he can and does succeed in isolating his deepest self so fully that he suffers many kinds of mental ill and social aberration. Yet the growth of community goes on despite man's resistance. Man can block it and distort it to a considerable degree. It does not then bring forth the values in his life that it would if he yielded gladly and freely and fully to it. But it always stands there ready to fill his life with loving community whenever he will yield to it. Environmental factors often make it difficult for an individual to yield because of the social order that shackles him and makes him a secretive competitor more than a free and open communicator and sharer.

Here again we see that man is made for ways of God as nothing else can be. By virtue of his talk he can participate in the unlimited growth of meaning, the unlimited growth of community, the unlimited growth of connections of value. Other existing things can form connections of mutual support only from the standpoint of their own existence. Man as an existing thing must do this also, else he could not exist. But he can also use his own existence to contribute to the unlimited growth of such connections among persons, and find his joy in this growth, quite regardless of the fact that in the end his own individual existence must be cast off and perish in order to release this growth from the narrow bounds which his own continued existence would impose upon it.

So we see that human talk reveals about human nature and its supreme vocation the same fact which we found revealed in laughter — the fact that man's highest blessedness is attained in devotion to a growth that is not originated nor directed by him to preconceived ends; which does not center in his own existence, but to which his own existence can contribute; and which he can ecstatically experience even when perishing for the sake of its enrichment. Thus man is made for God and is the child of God in a very peculiar sense.

The nature of talk reveals another human characteristic of great import to religious persons. It shows that human nature demands community with an insatiable craving. The distinctively human personality demands the sharing of meanings with a demand as imperative as the physiological demand for air. The human mind cannot exist without this accumulation of shared meanings. When it is deprived of community it becomes deranged or degenerates and tends to resolve into the mentality of the lower animals. The human mind is created by the communication of meanings and develops only by such communication. It cannot exist without such community, and at last it must die in order that community may grow from more to more. This growth of community is God.

3. *Biologically Man Chooses Community.* Man is the most helpless of all the animals so far as concerns the physiological mechanisms. He has no great speed, no defensive coloration, no thick hide nor hair nor bony covering. He has neither the smallness that hides nor the mass that overwhelms. None of the specialized devices by which other living things protect themselves are his. He cannot rend and tear by tooth and claw, nor shut himself in a bony shell, nor spawn in millions, nor dart with lightning speed. He has no way to protect himself or sustain himself except by cooperation and by yielding himself to the transforming growth of connections of mutual support and control with his environment.

More than any other existing thing man must win the extensive and intensive cooperation of his environment in order to exist at all. We have already seen that his mind cannot come into existence nor continue to exist without sharing the meanings of his associates. Also he must cooperate with physical forces and win their beneficence by skillfully fitting his ways to theirs and theirs to his. At every point where the line of evolution has divided, the branch that led to man has sacrificed protection for sensitivity, independence for cooperative interdependence, fixated strength for the transformations of creative synthesis, closed exclusiveness of individual or group for wider and more intimate connections of mutual support with the manifold activities of the encompassing world. Man has always been the weak, timid, jabbering, sensitive, emotional, unspecialized animal whose existence depended entirely on weaving the web of mutual support and meaning ever wider and closer, weaving it again and again as it was torn down, and yielding himself to the required transformations of this growth.

The Neanderthal and other such primitive men are not in the direct line of human evolution. They represent side lines that became extinct. They could not issue in man as he is today because they developed specialized mechanisms for defense and attack which rendered them unable to multiply ceaselessly the bonds of mutual support, mutual control, and mutual meaning with that delicacy and scope which modern man must exercise. Their natures did not demand love as man must have it, understanding by love this mutual participation of each in each. Their natures did not demand the unlimited growth of connections of mutual control and meaning. They were not the children of God in that peculiar sense which applies to man.

Man's progenitor was a living, pulsing network of nerves and feelings. He was made up of innumerable feelers forever held out to connect with whatever there was that might be helpful. Only such a creature can weave the bonds of connection so wide and high and deep as to bind the remote ranges of the universe into one great growing system of meanings. The outermost stars, the innermost atoms, and all the innumerable activities of the universe that fall between these extremes, are being woven progressively into a system of interconnections by a growth that makes use of this rare, finely sensitive, laughing, talking material called man. Man does not do it, but he can yield himself to it willingly and ever more completely, and he can do a great deal to aid or hinder it. He may even block it and throw it back to levels of existence lower than man. But if he does he will destroy himself in doing it.

We have said that man does not possess biologically any structures of offense or defense which can seriously and permanently block the unlimited growth of connections of mutual support and mutual control. Every other form of existence does block its own way after the growth has reached a certain height. It sacrifices growth for the sake of stability. So far as we can see enormous masses of matter have stopped this growth after reaching a certain level of chemical composition. In vegetables and animals matter has attained much higher levels but stops at definite limits beyond which it cannot rise. Only in man has growth broken through protective resistances elsewhere met. Here it seems to have found a way that opens upward without limit. But man himself may fail.

Man need not fail because of the limitations of his physiological organism. The possible connections which the neurons of the forebrain of man might form are almost if not quite infinite. But the failure of man, if he fails, will lie in another direction. It will be due to his misuse of power.

Biologically man has no protective structure which prevents the unlimited growth of meaning and value. But with advancing civilization he fashions hard impervious social structures of defense and offense. Groups of men with those implements of civilization called science and machinery can shut themselves in against their fellows and against the rest of nature, so that the growth of connections of mutual meaning and creative synthesis cannot go on. Not biologically but with the works of civilization man can rear hard and mighty structures which resist the gentle transforming influences that make life meaningful and rich. He can construct a social order in which every man is turned into a competitor of every other; in which every group, especially every national group, becomes the armed aggressor or defender of rights which exclude the other and thus set up barriers which block the growth of connections between them which are meaningful, enriching, and sustaining. In such a society each individual can become barricaded against the growth of meaning by both material and psychological devices of offense and defense. When this occurs the growth of God begins to fail and die, rent asunder or suffocated by these aggressive or defensive devices.

We do not mean to say that there is anything inevitable about this. We do not mean that cultures follow any natural law which must issue in such decline. We are not preaching Spengler. We are only pointing to the fact that this sort of thing does very often occur and that it is the most threatening danger in the present hour for man.

As long as the growth of the connections of mutual support and creative synthesis is going on man lives dangerously, interdependently, sensitively, openly, communicatively, laughingly and lovingly. Whenever he begins to draw in for safety, for independence, with hardness, with secretiveness, into a hidden inner life characterized by hollow laughter and little love, the growth that is of God fails and dies. When man does this he is seeking safety or self-aggrandizement. But he never succeeds in getting there that way. On the contrary he moves straight toward his own destruction, because no person can live that way. Biologically, psychologically, and socially he is made for the unlimited growth of connections of mutual support and mutual control, and of meanings that unfold from more to more. When he departs from that way of life he cannot survive any more than a fish can survive out of water.

Whenever a wide and compact system of mutual support has been developed, the more intelligent and aggressive individuals and groups are always tempted to exploit this system and turn it to the service of their exclusive individual units. Always men are tempted to seek protection, pleasure, and power, each for himself or for his group, and thus to turn away from the one high devotion to unlimited growth. They turn away from that ecstatic joy found in appreciating the values of community, beauty, and love. They turn from the joy of living to serve the growth of these values and from the joy of dying at last to release this growth from bondage to the needs of any one individual or group.

Man's deepest sin consists in the great reversal of life. It consists in making connective growth serve individual existence rather than making human existence serve connective growth. From this sin man is never entirely free. Strong drives are always turning him back to seek protection or pleasure or power, turning him away from the ecstasy of uttermost devotion and dangerous openness to all the connections of community that can form between himself and the world round about. He is not always ready to die when death is his greatest service. Man is the battleground wherein contend the claim to subordinate all to man and the claim to subordinate man to unlimited growth. Yet man himself is not free to choose. His own biological evolution has chosen for him. He can hang back. He can refuse to go the way for which he was made and to which he is called. But when he does so he chooses not another way of life; he chooses death. Whenever he tries to make any achieved organization of interests an end in itself, whether that organization be an individual person or a nation or a culture, he goes down in the end to ruin. He must make every achievement serve that unlimited growth whereby the activities in the universe are progressively organized into richer aesthetic harmony, greater love, and more abundant meaning. The deepest reaches of his self have been taken hold of by this growth and so refined, sensitized and otherwise fitted to this destiny that he cannot turn back except by plunging to his own destruction. At this hour of history he stands gazing into the abyss, trying to decide whether to go on or whether to plunge more deeply into his own ruin.

4. Man Worships. There are many theories about how religion and worship originated. No one knows the historical facts. But we do know certain things about the physiological organism of man on the one hand and his mentality on the other that would seem to make worship an inevitable expression of his nature.

Physiologically man is not predestined to seek any specific ends. No other animal is so free of the control of the pre-established linkage of units of behavior as is man. He is not bound to crave just one kind of food, one kind of shelter, one form of sexual satisfaction, one procedure for procuring these several goods. His organs are not specialized. He has innumerable impulses that can be organized in innumerable different ways. The enormous complexity of his forebrain by which these impulses can be connected with one another into almost an infinity of different patterns, means that his strivings and wants will not be channeled down one set of grooves to fulfill themselves in the attainment of any delimited system of fulfillment. Rather, under favorable conditions, his strivings will always be reaching out beyond any achieved set of goods. Thus he will come to have a sense of unexplored goods on beyond. He will reach out after an undefined totality of good or a good which is better than anything thus far attained.

This craving for an unlimited good arising out of the nature of man's physiological organism is supplemented by a free rational imagination. Thus he can construct ideas about this unexplored totality of good, or supreme good, and of whatever conditions and agencies, as yet unknown in their specific nature, may be the keepers of this greatness beyond his present specific achievements. Since he is not sustained and directed by inner mechanisms he must seek out whatever is most helpful in all the world and whatever is supremely worthful, and his imagination will picture all this before he knows what it is.

It would seem that all this must, under favorable circumstances, induce in him a sense of mystery, of wonder, of being dependent on uncomprehended reality, and a seeking for what is unknown in its specific character save only that it is better than what has thus far been attained. This state leads to worship. Worship in its most primitive form is the moment when consciousness is dominated by the craving for unlimited enrichment. It is awareness turned fully toward the unexplored realm of better and worse. Worship is man become aware of a mysterious destiny. Worship so begun can take on all manner of forms and often become nothing but a form. But if our interpretation is correct it has a vital function.

If the original nature of worship be of the sort we have indicated, it shows that man is subject to progressive transformation and can yield himself to a creative process of growth which widens and multiplies without limit the bonds of connection which are of value. Looking for something beyond, he never finds it in any specific and limited good. This craving and outreach can be suppressed and killed in the individual. But when conditions are right it springs anew in that human propulsion which points to the supreme destiny of man.

5. *Man Makes Tools and Domesticates Animals.* The making of tools implies two things about man. It implies the ability to distinguish diverse units of change and see how they can be rearranged and connected with one another to make a system of mutually sustaining activities whereby products of value are achieved. It implies, also, that man is seeking to bring the world round about him into cooperative or brotherly relations with himself. A tool or machine is some part of the environment so modified that men can cooperate with it and it with human effort with unusual facility. A stone with a chipped edge is something with which men can cooperate more effectively than with one unchipped. But the use of the chipped stone changes man's behavior and way of living as much as, or more than, he changes the stone. The same principle applies to all tools and machines.

Thus the making of tools and machines brings about creative synthesis and the transforming growth of connections of interdependence. These transformations occur beyond the intent and control of men. So here again we see superhuman growth occurring when men yield themselves intelligently to it and extend to one another the cooperation and good will which the new system of interdependence requires. When they refuse to do this they bring on themselves greater evils than existed in the more primitive mode of life which preceded the making of the machines.

When men make and own their own tools and use them constantly, they come to love them like a part of their persons. They decorate them and care for them. Even when they do not own them but are permitted to have control of them for a considerable period of time, this attachment develops. It is said that a locomotive engineer sometimes addresses his locomotive with the endearing terms and pronouns which indicate loving attachment. The same is true of the relation between men and their domesticated animals. It is true that in all such cases men can be, and often are, brutal, cruel, and arrogant. They may exploit the whole system of mutually sustaining connections formed by means of tools and domestic animals. On the other hand, however, they often serve this growing system of value, including their fellow men, and find their greatest joy in appreciating and promoting this order of life, which is a community of men, tools, domestic animals, and natural conditions.

When men begin to buy and sell their tools and animals, the bonds of connection cease to be cherished to the same degree. Above all when the owners cease to work with the tools and animals and perhaps never see them but let them out to hirelings; and when the workers are not allowed to have exclusive use for any long period of the same tools, animals, and conditions; and when, worst of all, the workers sell their own labor and come at last to feel that the only good of their service is to get money and leisure for self-enjoyment outside of work hours — then indeed the bonds of affection are loosed and the joy of devotion to the growth of the system fades out. Nevertheless the making of tools and the domesticating of animals do show that man is the medium through which occurs the growth of connections of mutual control between diverse activities, transforming man as well as the animate and inanimate things about him in such a way that they can all work together in a single organic system of life.

The fatherhood of God means the power that makes us all brothers, cooperators, and members one of another. In other words, God or the work of God is this connective growth whereby the activities of men and animals and things are all so mutually modified as to work together as parts of a living whole. In making tools and domesticating animals man shows that he is child of such a God. By no means is he always a faithful child. As we have seen, he often perverts the whole process by trying to subject it to his own aggrandizement, comfort, or protection, rather than yielding himself to the progressive transformation required by the order of value embodied in it. But when he does pervert the order of life in this way he cannot long continue without coming to grief. His nature can be changed in the way required by this growth which is the work of God. But it cannot be changed in the sense of making him immune to the demand of creative synthesis involved in these growing bonds of interdependence.

6. *Man Reasons.* Pure abstract reason is that use of the imagination whereby patterns or forms, first experienced in behavior of interaction between the organism and its environment, are lifted out of that concrete world, refined, clarified, and developed into implicative systems. For example, one may break a stick in two and then get the pattern or relation of twoness. He may treat this abstract form of two, not as two pieces of stick, or two men, or two something else that is concrete, but simply as two anything. He may combine it with other twos, and thus develop the whole system of mathematics. In the same way he may imaginatively take the geometrical forms and treat them in the abstract, combining and rearranging at his fancy. So also the forms of causal connection may be developed into a vast order of abstract "law." So again with the forms of before and after, giving the abstraction of time that reaches interminably into the past and future; the abstract forms of greater and lesser; the abstract forms of organic connection of many kinds; and so on without end.

Thus the reason, which is imagination working according to the principles of logic, may rear an infinite system of abstract forms. These forms may be tested by experiment and observation, and by these tests reordered, selected, and transformed, until man has a rational system which is relatively true, meaning that it is descriptive in part of the existing world when one views the world within a certain perspective, using some specified basis of reference or system of coordinates. Such abstract forms, when properly tested and transformed to fit the actualities of existence, give to man those patterns of behavior by which he so interacts with his world as to achieve the goods of life. These goods at their maximum, and hence at the level which commands his highest devotion, must be a systematic ordering of appreciable activities whereby the many different goods support and enhance one another. The great service of reason in this devotion and quest is to discover a pattern, rather a sequence of patterns, which will guide human endeavor in promoting such an organization of the world. At its higher levels we call this work of reason by the names of science and philosophy. When it is less rigorously disciplined but more richly inclusive we call it lore, mythology, and the traditional way of life.

Through reason, combined with the tests of experimentation, human imagination is released to explore the heights and depths and breadth and fullness of nature. When the forms of behavior are emptied of their concrete fullness and experimentally elaborated without limit, the infinite outreach of the human spirit is released. We saw how the physiological nature of man was made for this. But this physiological nature must be further equipped through rational use of experimental imagination before it can exercise the potential powers that are resident in the peculiar organism of man.

This rational power, we must remind ourselves again, has its dangers and evils, just as has every other of the endowments we have noted. Men have turned away from the actualities of nature and its potentialities, and from that growth in nature which is God, and have given their adoration to these constructions of their own imagination as though *they* were very God. These forms have been thought to constitute a kind of higher reality, a sort of supernatural reality, over and above the existing world with all its hidden riches and potentialities.

Men have also assumed that a rational system established as true inside the bounds of certain limited experimental tests, can be true absolutely, finally, from every standpoint, and throughout an infinity of experimental operations under all conditions. No such rational structure of all comprehensive truth has ever been achieved by human reason and never will be, because of the creativity of new perspectives. A rational system truly applicable to the world from certain standpoints of the past must fail to cover all that is brought to light in the new perspective.

But here again we see the vocation of man. It is not to a rational system that man can commit himself, but to the increase of those relations with fellow men and the rest of nature which such a system can be made to serve. Human reason must yield truly to the service of the growth of community. Whenever it rears itself as an absolute and final authority to which all life must be subordinate, evil ensues. Doubtless there are guiding principles of life which are always true. But they must be so vitally, that is, plastically, expressed as to give room for the unlimited growth of connections of value. The arrogance of reason tends to stop this growth or make it serve the interests of some established system of thought or of living.

7. *Man Rears a Culture.* The development of a culture is the inevitable outcome of the nature of man as we have thus far described him. It is plain that any animal which has the powers we have described must rear a culture.

We may distinguish within culture two factors. On the one hand are all the instrumentalities, such as techniques and specific ideals, by which man gets what he wants. All this we may label civilization. Over against civilization, but inextricably conjoined with it, is the growth of connections of mutual control, increasing greatly and actively through becoming wider, more numerous, more closely woven, or qualitatively by creative synthesis bringing new emergent wholes of value. This growth of community and meaning is what always, in the course of time, makes any given set of instrumentalities or ideals incompetent, irrelevant and immaterial. It makes it necessary to transform any established political system, any economic order, any institutional structure of religion, any educational organization. Civilization consists of these instrumentalities, particularly these ideals, which must be ever transformed to fit the demands of the growing or changing community of activities. It consists of these political, economic, educational, and religious structures.

Now these two factors which go to make up culture, namely civilization and the growth of community, are often in conflict. Indeed one of the greatest evils and catastrophes of human life arises when civilization becomes so powerful that it can try to dominate, control, and regulate the growth of community. Men always tend to set up their own ideals as the chief controlling power of human life and the rightful objects of their supreme devotion. When civilization is weak there is no great danger of this. That concrete growth of community, which is infinitely rich in all the essentials for human living and for progressive transformation of life to higher levels, is not unduly suppressed by human devotion to ideals as long as the powers of men are slight. But when men become sufficiently powerful to begin actually to shape the world to fit their abstract ideals, they inevitably leave out innumerable factors which life requires but which the limited powers of man's intellectual grasp never can fully comprehend.

Therefore whenever the ideals of a powerful civilization are made to dominate the life of man and the world that he controls, the great evils of psychic madness and social disruption always ensue. Never must ideals be made the masters of life. They are necessary tools for living, but they are only tools. They are instrumental. Civilization is the work of man. Growth of community is the work of God. Man must always live for God. Whenever he tries to make God live for man disaster ensues. The living God alone can be master of human life and all its strivings.

The periods of high civilization are always times of danger. We are in such a crisis today. Ideals have been unduly glorified. They have been identified with God. Sometimes this identification has been concealed by claiming that God is a supernatural kind of existence and by subtly and unconsciously transforming human ideals into a kind of supernatural actuality. Then men try to shape the world to fit their ideals, mistakenly held to be an existing power.

There is an existing power. It is God. But it is not an ideal, meaning a possibility of value which does not yet exist but which we strive to bring into existence. Neither is it a kind of being which exists in some other world outside of nature. The living God is the infinitely rich and complex and yet unified growth which we have been describing. When men subject their ideals and all the powers of their civilization to this growth, they find the way of life for which man's nature is made.

8. *Man Suffers Conflict.* Human life is full of conflict. We have noted this fact all along, in our description of the various aspects of man's nature. Man is the battleground on which a great

fight is always being fought. It is conflict between the demands of unlimited growth on the one hand, and, on the other, the demands of some limited form of growth, whether it be the individual personality, or a home or small community, or a nation or a culture, or some planetary epoch. Always in man is the demand to defend, to stabilize, to fixate some such order of life, and to attack and destroy all that threatens it. On the other hand, there is also that deepest demand of his nature, that demand which is the urgency of God within him, the demand for unlimited growth. Always in man is the tendency to aggrandize himself or to subject himself to some individual, group, or system which seeks to glorify itself. This tendency runs counter to the demand of God which requires the total self-commitment of every individual, group, or system. The sacrifice demanded is not the deprivation of good; it is the yielding of all self-centered good in order to receive the greater good that is God-centered. God-centered good is the kind which makes men laugh, as we have already noted. It also makes them sing and it may make them gladly go to the flames. It is the good which is found in unlimited growth; and because it is unlimited, it is a growth which requires that every achieved system perish, whether the system be an individual personality, a group, or a culture.

IV. ACCUMULATION VERSUS GROWTH

Something magnificent is being done in cosmic existence by means of human nature. But great obstacles are in the way. These in general are of two kinds. On the one hand are the inertia of the material order and the difficulties of maintaining in existence the highly sensitive and plastic organization of human life. Against the brutishness of the world, the life of man has been beaten to death or to torpidity or to some other gnarled and distorted form. With the development of a technical civilization these obstructions can and may be overcome. But then the second difficulty appears, which is fully as bad: man comes under the domination of his own techniques, his own programs and ideals. These rule his life instead of that creative synthesis in concrete situations which is growth and which we have identified with God.

Perhaps we can summarize the tragedy of civilization thus: When the civilized man goes forth to seek his father's asses he does not find a kingdom as did Saul in the days of early Israel. He finds instead his father's asses and nothing more. This is so because the civilized man is able to master circumstance sufficiently to get what he wants and to put aside whatever would turn him to a good higher and richer than his own ideals and programs. This is the great reversal of life. This brings about the very opposite of religious living.

Man is being used to bring forth a greatness and richness of good that his own mind cannot compass. But when civilization sinks low he is beaten down by the brutishness of existence. When civilization rises high he is destroyed by the autonomy of his own power. There is however a way that he can go which runs between these two evils. It is the way of unlimited connective growth. In so far as he goes that way his destiny is achieved.

V. THE HEART OF RELIGION

Among all the ways of men what then is the distinctively religious way? And how does it manifest itself in the concerns of men today? The way is absolute commitment to the total will of God before this is fully known, and then the utmost use of sensitivity and intelligence to find it in each concrete situation. The will of God is for the religious man in action simply the best that he can possibly discover in each unique combination of circumstances, no matter how that best may diverge from his pre-established desires and ideals. The will of God is the unpredictable fullness of value to be found in the creative synthesis of decisive moments. The will of God so understood can be discovered only when faith and intelligent action are combined.

Faith is wholehearted and utter readiness for the fullest and freest spontaneity of responsiveness to the unforeseeable riches of each emergent situation. Without this commitment of the total personality through readiness for spontaneous responsiveness to emergent riches, the best in each situation can never be discovered even by the greatest intelligence in the world. Without this prior act of faith intelligence will simply find in each situation that which fits into the program and purpose of the person who is acting. Indispensable therefore to the religious way is this commitment of faith. It should lift the uttermost hidden depths of personality to the dynamic state of readiness for responsiveness to all appreciable activities. Faith of this sort is required to open the vision to the goodness of God in each time and place of action. Otherwise God is hidden and men can know nothing of him save by hearsay.

Faith is essential, we have said, but faith alone is not enough. After one has become responsive to the fullness of emergent and unpredictable riches, one must use his intelligence to the utmost of his ability to distinguish the better and the worse. The commitment of faith which we have described releases intelligence from the constraint and bias of fixed and narrow purpose, fear, envy, self-righteousness, and the many other blind spots which prevent us from receiving what God would give. Intelligence involves imaginative experimentation as well as physical manipulation. It includes consultation with others on some occasions, or again some access to the teachings of the past. We need not here list the resources of intelligence. Our responsibility is to point out that intelligence must be added to faith. The two must go together.

This religious way of living is different from every other found among men. It differs from that of the moral idealist. The idealist picks out of each situation whatever will promote his ideal. All the rest he ignores or fights or tolerates. He is blind to all the abundance that overflows or conflicts with his ideal. Over against the idealist stands the man of uninhibited desire. His way of living differs from that of the religious just as much as does that of the idealist, but at the opposite extreme. He picks out of the riches of each situation whatever will satisfy his specific desires, but all the rest flows over him unappreciated and unapprehended. The religious man on the other hand, in contradistinction from both of these, explores sensitively and reverently for the emerging new meanings in each situation, the while holding his desires and ideals in control as experimental instruments to be used in guiding him into the situation where they are bound to be transcended or submerged by the richness of value which he cannot possibly apprehend before he experiences it in the full concreteness of consummatory synthesis.

The steps by which one achieves this way of religious living — propulsion, crisis, decision, release, specification, and fellowship — cannot be taken once and for all. They constitute a practice that is repeated again and again. Especially is this true of those acts labeled decision, release, and specification. Specification could also be called the emergence of new ideals.

This life which we have described is the faith that saves the world. It serves both the needs of individual personality and of society in the only ways which can enable this age to escape destruction.

This spontaneity of free and full and plastic responsiveness down to the deepest level of the organization of the psycho-physical organism is the prime condition for all mental health. The psychological desperation of our time is shown in all the multiple forms of mental ill and derangement of personality which are increasing steadily and amounting to madness in many cases. The religious way which we have described does surely protect from these mental ills. A glance at some of the major sources of the derangements of personality will make this plain. Men suffer these psychic ills when they struggle to do what is impossible and cannot resign themselves to the inevitable; when they strive to maintain a certain view of themselves in the face of incoming evidence to the contrary; when they cannot relinquish some desire in the face of a conscience or society that condemns. But all these disorganizing conditions fade out and disappear when the total personality becomes plastic; when it becomes freely and fully responsive to the best possible in each situation; when it finds in the full flood of circumstance the riches of laughter, of tragedy, and of fulfillment, but does not cling to the impossible and does not demand that any fixed desire or fixed ideal be satisfied.

This way of living brings health not only to the personality, but also to society. Our social ills, for purposes of brief and simple classification, can be traced to idealism, to efficiency, and to interdependence. These in their present systematized and exalted form are products of a suddenly advanced civilization. It is imperative that we see the connection between them and the social disorder that prevails. We shall examine each briefly in turn.

The evil of ideals is not to have ideals but to put them in place of God as sovereign over human living. All the requirements for a good life, or even for bare existence, as we have already shown, cannot possibly be included in the program of any ideal or set of ideals, least of all when the life of a complex society is concerned. This fact, however, causes no great difficulty as long as men have not the power to control all conditions so rigorously as to exclude the ignored necessities. As long as the control over conditions is weak, men will get the needed vitamins or other required ingredients, even when these are not prescribed in the ideal diet by reason of human ignorance of them; nature provides them anyway. But when men have power to control natural and social processes with sufficient rigor, they can keep out, or change, the elements which are necessary to life when they do not understand or know these elements. The same is true of education. As long as the power of control is weak the conditions necessary to development of wholesome personality and normal social relations will often slip in unknown to men, even when the ideal program leaves them out by reason of ignorance or prejudice. So it is with all the other requirements for a wholesome life. The inadequacy of ideals is not fatal as long as men have not the power to subject the bounty of nature to the limitations of their own understanding and interest. When, however, the power of civilization is suddenly magnified, and the administrative devices, the instruments of propaganda, and the mechanisms of social control become sufficiently coercive to exclude almost everything save what the ideal prescribes, then a deadly impoverishment of life begins. Then men grow restive, discontented, missing something but not knowing what it is; then psychic madness and social revolution, suicide and war, begin to spread and mount; and at last the devouring monster of the totalitarian state begins to raise his head — all in the name of idealism.

Over against this governance by human idealism is the religious way wherein the uncomprehended good of the will of God is put in place of ideals as sovereign over life. Here all the powers of civilization, all the ideals and programs, all the mechanisms of social control are exercised only to the end of being transformed continuously to meet the needs of concrete situations. Our present political name for this procedure is democracy — when democracy is rightly understood.

The second danger we noted was that of efficiency. Efficiency can best be regarded under its two major aspects, techniques of action, and abstract clarity of thought in communication. When techniques are used to control each situation so that it will fit into a smoothly running program where nothing is admitted save that which is predictable and prearranged, efficiency becomes deadly. It destroys the richness of experienced value. Techniques find their rightful place when used to serve the unpredictable emergent fullness of concrete situations by being refashioned, cast aside, or otherwise manipulated to promote maximum appreciative awareness of the goods of life. This is what is meant by saying that techniques should be kept subject to the will of God. If they are not kept so subject, men will be cut off from the unforeseeable enrichments to be experienced in the emergent synthesis of creative moments.

Clarity of intellectual understanding, the second aspect of efficiency, is excellent in its proper place and function. But clarified concepts used in technically accurate discourse do not communicate sentiments, loyalties, appreciative and deeply emotional responses. Evocative, expressive words which convey emotional responses are generally very vague, ambiguous, confused so far as intellectual understanding is concerned. For example, " tootsie wootsie " does not express a precisely defined meaning. It may, however, express a deep sentiment and a wealth of shared appreciations. A college yell does not communicate a meaning that lends itself to mathematical definition. But it does induce a rich and deep community of sentiment and loyalty. Now the good of life can be increased only by that growth of community wherein a rich body of appreciations, sentiments, attachments, enthusiasms, and loyalties is accumulated. Clarity of understanding is not the prime factor here. In the religious way that we here describe, however, it is not slighted. It is sought to the highest degree possible. But its limitations are recognized and it is always kept subject to the function of serving the will of God, that is, the unlimited growth of community.

The third source of social ill we traced to interdependence. Interdependence, like idealism and efficiency, is required for any satisfactory living. But it also must be made subject to the will of God else it will destroy us. When groups are interdependent one of them will have vital wants which only the cooperation of some other group can supply. This second group will be in the same position relative to wants that only the cooperation of the first can bring to realization. As long as groups with incomplete and contrary purposes are bound together inextricably so that neither can get what it wants without exploitive subjection of the other, destructive conflict is inevitable unless there can be found a level and a process where the two or more can function profitably and with mutual consideration. This situation eventuates when the highest loyalty of these groups is not to their specific objectives but to the growth of community and creative synthesis. But this last means to make the uncomprehended will of God[2] supreme over all plans, programs, techniques, clarified concepts and directed social processes. Hence absolute commitment to the total good of God before we know what its specific nature may be, is the only way of social salvation. We have already seen that it is the only way of individual salvation.

It is clearly apparent that only in the religious way lies the path of deliverance from the warpings of personality and the ills of society which beset our age. Barren impoverishment and destructive conflict *can* be surmounted in personalities and in society and these both *can* find their fulfillment progressively and together in constructive struggle if they follow the religious way.

This way of salvation can be described as accepting Jesus Christ as our only Lord and Master. But this description requires interpretation. Jesus Christ must not be used, as he frequently is, as a pious device by which one conceals his own specific set of ideals and programs. One must not presume to specify what the ideals and principles of Jesus were beyond defining them as devotion to the uncomprehended will of God. Every man's ideals and programs are imperfect and partial. Worst of all they are infected with the hidden malice of the human heart. This holds true even when one uses Jesus Christ as a cloak behind which to conceal his own bigotry, intolerance, narrowness, and coldness of heart. Jesus Christ becomes the only way of salvation when one recognizes (1) that Christ stands for a total good that is infinitely richer, higher, deeper than any specifications we are able to set up; and (2) that Christ stands for that way of life in which the only sovereign control is the uncomprehended will of God, to be sought in each situation with utmost sensitivity and intelligence, but without prescribing it beforehand and with utter readiness to follow it at whatever price to one's own prior wishes.

One may accuse us of doing the very thing we condemn in others, namely, using Jesus Christ to enforce our own prescriptions for the good life. A moment's thought, however, should make it apparent that we are doing just the opposite. We are pointing to Jesus Christ as the way of deliverance from prescriptions, excepting the prescription that we shall be free.

In its basic character this saving and transfiguring commitment which we have described is the same as it always has been and always will be. The forms in which one apprehends the reality of God, and in which the needs of life are served, must change from age to age. But the way of the ancient faith remains unchanged and will be so forever. As long as human life shall endure the only way of deliverance and the only way of abundance for man will be this: Absolute commitment to the total goodness of God before one knows what it is, and then finding this good progressively by intelligent action and sensitivity of response in each concrete situation.

NOTES

[1] Whether E. S. Brightman should be classed with the liberals or with the naturalists to be considered later is uncertain. His independence and originality make it hard to classify him.

[2] You speak of " the will of God " and yet question the personality of God, some will exclaim. We confess to the difficulty of language when speaking about God. We could avoid the term by technical language, but feel more would be lost than gained in doing so.

BIBLIOGRAPHY

A book that seems to yield new insight into human nature no matter how many times it is read is John Dewey's *Human Nature and Conduct*. Part IV is most pertinent to our discussion. C. H. Cooley's *Human Nature and the Social Order*, George H. Mead's *Mind, Self and Society*, chap. 3, and M. P. Follett's *Creative Experience*, chaps. 11, 14, 15, demonstrate that human personality is created, fostered and enriched by social interaction. The newer psychology, based on therapeutic measures for helping disorganized personalities, is throwing a flood of light on the nature of man. The best summary of these findings to date is in L. F. Shaffer's *The Psychology of Adjustment*. One of the most illuminating anthropological studies of human nature is Gerald Heard's *Source of Civilization*. Nicolas Berdyaev, in his *The Destiny of Man*, combines great scholarship and profound insight with a transcendental metaphysics which few in America will be able to accept, but chaps. 3 and 4 are richly rewarding.

INDEX

INDEX

Abraham, 125
Absolute, the (Hegel's), 213
abstractions, 240–45 *passim;* ideals as, 288; and reason, 397 ff., 475
accumulation, vs. growth, 479–80
action, 254, 344; as approach to God, 347; and knowledge, 258–59, 261–62
Adam, 125, 161
Adler, Felix, 191, 301
Adventists, 141
aesthetics, viii
Agni, 10, 40
agnosticism, 180, 182
agnostic school: *See* naturalistic school
agricultural stage, 29
Ahimsā, 54
Ahmediyya movement, 199
Ahriman, 102, 104
Ahura Mazda, 101–2, 103, 104
alchemy, 83
Allah, 56, 126, 127, 128, 130
All-Father, 25
Allport, F., 452
Amaterasu, 89–90, 91, 92
Ames, Edward Scribner, 218; definition of religion, 216
Amida, Amitābha, 85, 87, 94
Amish, 163
Amon, 33
Amon-Ra, 34
Amos, 110–11, 130 n. 7
Anabaptists, 162, 163
Anan ben David, 119
Ānanda, 68, 71 n. 33
ancestor worship, 9 ff., 11, 75, 76–78, 80, 90, 91, 220, 226
ancestral spirits, 23, 77
Anglican Church, 148
animals: communication among, 463–64; community among, 406; domestication of, 473–74
animism, 11–12, 13, 14, 16, 19, 26, 98,

123, 168 n. 2, 205, 216, 218, 219, 220, 226
anthropology, 7 f., 11, 14, 449, 451, 453 ff.
Antiochus Epiphanes, 115
antireligious museums, 193
Anubis, 32, 33
Apis, 33
apocalyptic, 118, 136, 143, 175
Apostles' Creed, 147, 148, 160
apostles, message of, 140 ff.
apostolicity, 146
apostolic succession, 146
apprehension: forms of, 237; and intuition, 405; and reason, 420 ff.
apprehension, religious: *See* religious apprehension
Aquinas, Thomas, 154, 453, 455
Arabs, 125, 126
Āranyakas, 41
arhat, 74, 84, 150
Aristotle, 154, 175
Arjun, 57
Arjuna, 47–48
ark of Yahweh, 108
Arminians, 53
Arnold, Matthew, 109, 209, 232 n. 6
art, 240, 249, 315, 333, 388, 401, 402, 416, 420, 465
Aryans, 39, 41, 50, 51, 100; religion of, 37 ff.
Ārya Samāj, 58, 59–60, 71 n. 28
asceticism, 41, 42, 54, 55, 150, 157, 169 n. 23
Asherah, 106
āśram, 36, 70 n. 9
astrology, 175, 227
Athanasian Creed, 148, 160
Atharvaveda, 70 n. 4
atheists, 181
Ātman, 42, 45–46
Aton, 31, 33
atonement, 140

491

56; philosophic, 41 ff.; popular, 47 ff.;
reform movements in, 51–60
Hindus, 100, 101, 102, 106, 125, 132, 168
n. 2, 222, 223
Höffding, Harald, 209
holiness, 146, 149–51
holy, the, 20
holy orders, 151
Holy Spirit, 141, 142, 143, 144, 146, 147,
149, 163, 169 n. 22
homoöusios, 147
Hōnen Shōnin, 94
Hopkins, E. W., 55
Horus, 31
Hosea, 111
Hosso sect, 92
Hsüan-Tsang, 69, 99 n. 11
Hsün Tzǔ, 81
humanism, 223, 250–51, 263, 360, 422;
atheistic, 251; and evil, 354; and God,
348, 360; and knowledge of God, 433–
34; and nature of man, 453, 455, 457;
new, 182, 183, 187, 191, 192, 194, 222;
and prayer, 375; religious, 250–51; and
religious living, 313–14
"Humanist Manifesto," 191, 192
Hume, David, 181, 207, 208, 244
hunting stage, 27
Huss, John, 156
Huxley, Julian, 216
Huxley, Thomas, 190

Ibn Saud, 129
idealism, 180, 182, 188, 213, 230, 263–
64, 398, 423, 426, 454; Hegelian, viii
idealism, moral, 249, 263, 275, 277, 481;
vs. religious living, 287–90
idealism, social, 250–51, 254–55, 270, 271,
278–79. *See also* humanism
ideals, 451; evil of, 483 ff.; and religious
living, 287; as tools, 304, 313, 477
idolatry, 56, 59, 123, 126, 135, 162, 225–
26
Ignatius Loyola, 155
images, 68–69
image worship, 223
immanence of God, 184, 187, 190, 198
immortality, 103, 118, 182, 183, 186, 207,
319, 321. *See also* eternal life, future
life, resurrection
imperialism, 177

Inari, 90, 97
incarnation, 127
increment, vs. growth, 333–34
Independents, 163, 164
Indians, American, 27
Indra, 40
industrialism, 177, 178, 218
Industrial Revolution, 176, 245
infallibility, 60
initiation, 22–23, 49
inner light, 86, 163
instrumentalism, 296–97, 313
intellect, and value, 277–78
International Missionary Council, 166, 193
Intichiuma rites, 15
intuition, 420–22, 426, 429, 435, 443
inventions, 173, 179, 230, 400. *See also*
techniques
"inward ho," 245
Irenaeus, Bishop of Lyons, 147
Isaiah, 111, 130 n. 6
Isis, 31, 134
Islam: *See* Mohammedanism
Izanagi and Izanami, 89, 99 n. 12

"Jacobite" churches, 148
Jainism, 46, 54–56
James, brother of Jesus, 142–43
James, William, 11, 209, 218, 221, 232 n. 6
Jastrow, Morris, Jr., 220
Jefferson, Thomas, 203 n. 7
Jehangir, 57
jen principle, 80–81
Jeremiah, 112
Jesuits, 155, 311; in Japan, 93, 94, 96
Jesus, the Christ, 85, 107, 125, 132, 136 ff.,
141, 144, 151, 168 n. 6, 186, 188, 228,
268–69, 279, 280–82 *passim,* 308, 309,
319, 428, 432, 442, 453, 454, 486; cruci-
fixion of, 132, 139–40, 168 n. 13; and
Lao Tzǔ, 83; message of, 136 ff.; resur-
rection of, 140, 168 n. 16; teachings of,
168 n. 6
Jews, 105–6, 112, 114, 119, 121, 122, 123,
125, 126, 135, 142, 168 n. 2, 168 n. 5;
liberal, 191. *See also* Hebrews, Judaism
Jezebel, 110
Jimmu Tennō, 90
Jina: *See* Mahāvīra
Joan of Arc, 461
Jōdo sect, 94, 222